CW00764295

THE CAMBRIDGE COMPA:
FANTASY LITERATU

Fantasy is a creation of the Enlightenment, and the recognition that excitement and wonder can be found in imagining impossible things. From the ghost stories of the Gothic to the zombies and vampires of twenty-first-century popular literature, from Mrs Radcliffe to Ms Rowling, the fantastic has been popular with readers. Since Tolkien and his many imitators, however, it has become a major publishing phenomenon. In this volume, critics and authors of fantasy look at its history since the Enlightenment, introduce readers to some of the different codes for the reading and understanding of fantasy, and examine some of the many varieties and subgenres of fantasy; from magical realism at the more literary end of the genre, to paranormal romance at the more popular end. The book is edited by the same pair who produced *The Cambridge Companion to Science Fiction* (winner of a Hugo Award in 2005).

A complete list of books in the series is at the back of the book

THE CAMBRIDGE
COMPANION TO
FANTASY
LITERATURE

EDITED BY
EDWARD JAMES AND FARAH MENDLESOHN

CAMBRIDGE
UNIVERSITY PRESS

University Printing House, Cambridge CB2 8BS, United Kingdom

One Liberty Plaza, 20th Floor, New York, NY 10006, USA

477 Williamstown Road, Port Melbourne, VIC 3207, Australia

4843/24, 2nd Floor, Ansari Road, Daryaganj, Delhi - 110002, India

79 Anson Road, #06-04/06, Singapore 079906

Cambridge University Press is part of the University of Cambridge.

It furthers the University's mission by disseminating knowledge in the pursuit of education, learning and research at the highest international levels of excellence.

www.cambridge.org
Information on this title: www.cambridge.org/9780521728737

© Cambridge University Press 2012

First published 2012
Third printing 2012

A catalogue record for this publication is available from the British Library

Library of Congress Cataloging in Publication data
The Cambridge companion to fantasy literature / edited by Edward James, Farah Mendlesohn.
p. cm.
Includes bibliographical references and index.
ISBN 978-0-521-42959-7 – ISBN 978-0-521-72873-7 (pbk.)
1. Fantasy literature, English – History and criticism.   2. Fantasy literature, American – History and criticism.   3. Fantasy literature – History and criticism – Theory, etc.   4. Fantasy literature – Appreciation.
I. James, Edward, 1947– II. Mendlesohn, Farah.
PR149.F35C36   2012
823'.0876609 – dc23   2011035585

ISBN 978-0-521-42959-7 Hardback
ISBN 978-0-521-72873-7 Paperback

Dedicated to Diana Wynne Jones 1934–2011
for her critical fictions.

CONTENTS

CONTENTS

CONTENTS

NOTE ON THE CONTRIBUTORS

BRIAN ATTEBERY is author of a number of studies of science fiction and fantasy literature, including *Strategies of Fantasy* (1992) and *Decoding Gender in Science Fiction* (2002), and currently edits the *Journal of the Fantastic in the Arts*. He is a Professor of English at Idaho State University; he also teaches cello in the ISU music department and is a faculty member in the Graduate Program in Children's Literature at Hollins University.

MARK BOULD is a Reader in Film and Literature at the University of the West of England and a founding editor of *Science Fiction Film and Television*. He is the author of *Film Noir: From Berlin to Sin City* (2005), *The Cinema of John Sayles: Lone Star* (2009), and *Science Fiction: The Routledge Film Guidebook* (2012), co-author of *The Routledge Concise History of Science Fiction* and co-editor of *Parietal Games: Critical Writings By and On M. John Harrison* (2005), *Red Planets: Marxism and Science Fiction* (2009), *Neo-noir* (2009), *The Routledge Companion to Science Fiction* (2009) and *Fifty Key Figures in Science Fiction* (2009). He serves on the advisory editorial boards of *Extrapolation*, *Historical Materialism: Research in Critical Marxist Theory*, *Paradoxa: Studies in World Literary Genres* and *Science Fiction Studies*.

ANDREW M. BUTLER is the co-editor of books on Terry Pratchett, Ken MacLeod and Christopher Priest, and is the author of Pocket Essentials on *Philip K. Dick* (2000, 2007), *Cyberpunk* (2000), *Terry Pratchett* (2001), *Film Studies* (2002, 2005, 2008) and *Postmodernism* (2003). With Mark Bould, Adam Roberts and Sherryl Vint he is the co-editor of *The Routledge Companion to Science Fiction* (2009) and *Fifty Key Figures in Science Fiction* (2009). He is currently co-editing the journal *Extrapolation* and researching 1970s sf.

CATHERINE BUTLER is a Senior Lecturer in English at the University of the West of England, specializing in children's literature. She is the author of *Four British Fantasists* (2006) and editor of *Teaching Children's Fiction* (2006) and has written numerous articles on children's authors including Alan Garner, Diana Wynne Jones, Catherine Fisher, Penelope Lively, Gillian Cross and Catherine Storr. She is currently co-writing a book on the uses of history in children's books with Hallie O'Donovan. As an author of fiction she has so far produced six novels for children and teenagers, as well as some shorter works. The latest of these, *Hand of Blood*, was published in 2009.

JIM CASEY is an Assistant Professor at High Point University in North Carolina. He received his PhD from the Hudson Strode Program in Renaissance Studies at the University of Alabama. Although primarily a Shakespearean, he has published on such diverse topics as textual theory, performance theory, Shakespeare, Chaucer, *Battlestar Galactica* and the work of comics artist David Mack.

GREGORY FROST is the author of seven novels, the most recent being the acclaimed fantasy duology *Shadowbridge* (2008) and *Lord Tophet* (2008). Others include the World Fantasy Award Finalist *Fitcher's Brides* (2002), a recasting of the 'Bluebeard' fairy tale. He has worked with fairy and folk tales as well in short stories and in articles, including those covering the eighteenth-century French salons and the history of *The 1001 Nights* for *Realms of Fantasy* magazine. Many of his short stories of the fantastic are included in the collection *Attack of the Jazz Giants & Other Stories*. He is currently one of the fiction writing workshop directors at Swarthmore College, in Swarthmore, Pennsylvania; and he has taught at Michigan State, UC San Diego and Temple University.

GREER GILMAN writes fantasy. *Cloud & Ashes: Three Winter's Tales* (2009) and *Moonwise* (1991) are set in a Northern mythscape, linguistically intricate. Her Cloudish tales have won a Tiptree Award, a World Fantasy Award and a Crawford Award and have been nominated for the Nebula and Mythopoeic Fantasy awards. Besides her two books, she has published other short work, poetry and criticism. She has been a Guest of Honour at the International Conference for the Fantastic in the Arts and at Readercon. She holds a Master of Arts from Cambridge University and is a graduate of Wellesley College. For many years a librarian at Harvard University, she lives in Cambridge, Massachusetts.

ALEXANDER C. IRVINE is the author of fourteen books, including *Buyout* (2009), *The Narrows* (2005) and *A Scattering of Jades* (2002), which won the Crawford award in 2003. His most recent is *The Vertigo Encyclopedia* (2008). He has also written numerous comics, short stories and articles. He teaches creative writing and American literature at the University of Maine.

EDWARD JAMES is Professor of Medieval History at University College Dublin. He specializes in the history and archaeology of early medieval France and Britain; his most recent book is *Europe's Barbarians, AD 200–600* (2009). For fifteen years he was editor of *Foundation: The International Review of Science Fiction*. He has received the Pilgrim Award from the Science Fiction Research Association for his contribution to the study of science fiction and won the Eaton Award for his *Science Fiction in the Twentieth Century* (1994). He was co-editor of *The Cambridge Companion to Science Fiction*, which won a Hugo Award in 2005, and is the co-author of *A Short History of Fantasy* (2009).

ROZ KAVENEY is a freelance writer, critic and publisher's reader living in London. Among her books are *Reading the Vampire Slayer* (2003), *From Alien to the Matrix* (2005), *Teen Dreams* (2006) and *Superheroes!* (2007).

PAUL KINCAID is a past winner of the Thomas D. Clareson Award. He administered the Arthur C. Clarke Award for eleven years and co-edited *The Arthur C. Clarke Award: A Critical Anthology* (2006). His collection of essays and reviews, *What It Is We Do When We Read Science Fiction*, was published in 2008 and was nominated for both a BSFA Award and a Hugo Award.

KARI MAUND was trained in the Department of Anglo-Saxon, Norse and Celtic, University of Cambridge, and held research and teaching posts in early medieval British and Scandinavian history at the universities of Bangor, Cambridge, Leicester and Cardiff, and the Institute of Advanced Studies in Dublin. She is the author of six books and many articles on early Wales, England, Ireland and Denmark. As Kari Sperring, she was reviews editor of *Vector: The Critical Journal of the British Science Fiction Association* and is the author of a novel, *Living With Ghosts* (2009). She lives and works in Cambridge, UK.

FARAH MENDLESOHN is Reader in Science Fiction and Fantasy Literature at Middlesex University. Her publications include edited collections on Terry Pratchett and *Babylon 5*, as well as authored works: *Diana Wynne Jones: Children's Literature and the Fantastic Tradition* (2005), *Rhetorics of Fantasy* (2008) and *The Inter-Galactic Playground: A Critical Study of Children's and Teen's Science Fiction* (2009). She was co-editor of *The Cambridge Companion to Science Fiction*, which won a Hugo Award in 2005, and co-author of *A Short History of Fantasy* (2009).

MARIA NIKOLAJEVA is a Professor of Education at the University of Cambridge, UK. Prior to that, she was a Professor of Comparative Literature at Stockholm University, Sweden, where she taught children's literature and critical theory for twenty-five years. She is the recipient of the International Grimm Award for lifetime achievements in children's literature research. In 1993–7 she was the President of the International Research Society for Children's Literature. Her most recent publications include *How Picturebooks Work*, co-authored with Carole Scott (2001); *From Mythic to Linear: Time in Children's Literature* (2002); *The Rhetoric of Character in Children's Literature* (2002); *Aesthetic Approaches to Children's Literature* (2005), and, co-edited with Sandra Beckett, *Beyond Babar: European Children's Literature* (2006). She was one of the senior editors of *The Oxford Encyclopedia of Children's Literature*.

NNEDI OKORAFOR is a novelist of Nigerian descent known for weaving African culture into creative, evocative settings and memorable characters. In a profile of Nnedi's work titled 'Weapons of Mass Creation', *The New York Times* called Nnedi's imagination 'stunning'. Her YA novels include *Zahrah the Windseeker* (winner of the Wole Soyinka Prize for African Literature), *The Shadow Speaker* (winner of the CBS Parallax Award) and *Long Juju Man* (winner of the Macmillan Prize for Africa). Her much-acclaimed first adult novel, *Who Fears Death*, was released in 2010. Her YA novel *Akata Witch* and a chapter book, tentatively titled *Iridessa and the Fire-Bellied Dragon Frog*, are scheduled for publication in 2011. Okorafor is a Professor of Creative Writing at Chicago State University.

ADAM ROBERTS is Professor of Nineteenth-century Literature at Royal Holloway College, University of London. He is the author of the *Palgrave History of Science Fiction* (2006) and a number of critical works about Romantic and Victorian literature. He has also published a number of science fiction novels, the most recent of which are *Yellow Blue Tibia* (2009), *New Model Army* (2010) and *By Light Alone* (2011).

VERONICA SCHANOES is Assistant Professor of English at Queens College – CUNY. She has published articles on Harry Potter and on interstitial literature, and has published fiction in a variety of venues. One of her stories was included in *The Year's Best Fantasy and Horror* (2008, ed. Ellen Datlow, Kelly Link and Gavin Grant).

W. A. SENIOR holds a PhD in Medieval and Renaissance Literature from the University of Notre Dame. A past President of the International Association of the Fantastic in the Arts and the editor of *The Journal of the Fantastic in the Arts* from 1998 to 2007, he has also published scholarly articles on medieval literature, modern fantasy and science fiction, and *Stephen R. Donaldson's Chronicles of Thomas Covenant: Variations on the Fantasy Tradition* (1995).

SHARON SIEBER teaches all levels of Spanish and Latin American literature and language at Idaho State University. Her research interests include postmodernism, neo-baroque, feminist theory, magical realism and the study of time. She has published articles on such authors as Jorge Luis Borges, Rosario Castellanos, Carlos Fuentes, Elena Garro, Julio Cortázar, Juan Rulfo, Miguel Angel Asturias, José Lezama Lima, Rigoberta Menchú, Octavio Paz and Kurt Vonnegut. She is currently editor of *Rendezvous*, ISU's Journal of Arts and Letters, and she is the Campus Fulbright Program Adviser.

GRAHAM SLEIGHT lives in London, UK, and has been writing about sf and fantasy since 2000. His work has appeared in *The New York Review of Science Fiction*, *Foundation*, *Interzone* and *SF Studies*, and online at *Strange Horizons*, *SF Weekly* and *Infinity Plus*. His essays have appeared in *Snake's-Hands: The Fiction of John Crowley* (2003, ed. Alice K Turner and Michael Andre-Driussi), *Supernatural Fiction Writers* (2003, ed. Richard Bleiler), *Christopher Priest: The Interaction* (2005, ed. Andrew M. Butler), *Parietal Games: Non-Fiction by and about M. John Harrison* (2005, ed. Mark Bould and Michelle Reid), *Polder: A Festschrift for John Clute and Judith Clute* (2006, ed. Farah Mendlesohn), and *On Joanna Russ* (2009, ed. Farah Mendlesohn). In 2006, he began writing regular columns for *Locus* and *Vector*. He took over from Farah Mendlesohn as editor of *Foundation* from the end of 2007.

SHERRYL VINT is a Professor at Brock University, the author of *Bodies of Tomorrow* (2007) and *Animal Alterity* (2010), and co-author of *The Routledge Concise History of Science Fiction* (2011). She has co-edited the collections *Beyond Cyberpunk* (2010), *The Routledge Companion to Science Fiction* (2009) and *Fifty Key Figures in Science Fiction* (2009), and is an editor of the journals *Science Fiction Film and Television* and *Science Fiction Studies*.

GARY K. WOLFE, Professor of Humanities and English and former Dean and Associate Provost at Roosevelt University in Chicago, is the author of eight books and hundreds of essays and reviews. He is senior reviewer for *Locus* magazine and serves on the editorial boards of two academic journals. His *The Known and the Unknown: The Iconography of Science Fiction* received the Eaton Award in 1981, and he has since received the Pilgrim Award for criticism and scholarship from the Science Fiction Research Association (1987), the Distinguished Scholarship Award from the International Association for the Fantastic in the Arts (1998) and the World Fantasy Award (2007). His recent book *Soundings: Reviews 1992–1996* was a Hugo nominee and received the 2006 non-fiction award from the British Science Fiction Association. His latest book, *Evaporating Genres: Essays on Fantastic Literature*, was published in 2011.

CHRONOLOGY

Titles in brackets after the main title indicate the name of the trilogy or series of which this is the first volume.

800 AD?	Anon.	*Beowulf*
1100?	Anon.	*The Mabinogion*
1469	Sir Thomas Malory	*Le Morte d'Arthur*
1590	Edmund Spenser	*The Faerie Queen*
1678	John Bunyan	*The Pilgrim's Progress*
1695	Charles Perrault	*Tales of Mother Goose*
1697	Madame d'Aulnoy	*Tales of the Fairies* (transl. 1699)
1704	Antoine Galland (trans.)	*The Thousand and One Nights*
1726	Jonathan Swift	*Travels into Several Remote Nations of the World, by Lemuel Gulliver*
1764	Horace Walpole	*The Castle of Otranto*
1777	Clara Reeve	*The Champion of Virtue: A Gothic Story*
1794	Ann Radcliffe	*The Mysteries of Udolpho*
1796	Matthew Lewis	*The Monk: A Romance*
1798	Charles Brockden Brown	*Wieland, or The Transformation*
1811	Baron de la Motte Fouqué	*Undine*
1812	Ludwig Tieck	'The Elves'
1814	E. T. A. Hoffmann	'The Golden Pot'
1816	E. T. A. Hoffmann	'The Sandman' and 'The Nutcracker and the Mouse King'
1818	Mary Shelley	*Frankenstein, Or A Modern Prometheus*

1927	John Masefield	*The Midnight Folk*
1928	H. P. Lovecraft	'The Call of Cthulhu'
1929	Virginia Woolf	*Orlando: A Biography*
1930	Charles Williams	*War in Heaven*
1931	Thorne Smith	*The Night Life of the Gods*
1932	Abraham Merritt	*Dwellers in the Mirage*
1932–6	Robert E. Howard	Conan stories in *Weird Tales*
1934	P. L. Travers	*Mary Poppins*
1935	E. R. Eddison	*Mistress of Mistresses*
	Charles G. Finney	*The Circus of Dr. Lao*
	Dennis Wheatley	*The Devil Rides Out*
1936	Evangeline Walton	*The Virgin and the Swine* (aka *The Island of the Mighty*)
1937	H. P. Lovecraft	*The Shadow Over Innsmouth*
	J. R. R. Tolkien	*The Hobbit*
1938	C. S. Lewis	*Out of the Silent Planet*
	T. H. White	*The Sword in the Stone*
1939	Fritz Leiber	'Two Sought Adventure'
	James Thurber	'The Secret Life of Walter Mitty'
	Alison Uttley	*A Traveller in Time*
1940	Jorge Luis Borges	'Tlön, Uqbar, Orbis Tertius'
	Robert A. Heinlein	'The Devil Makes the Law!' (reprinted as *Magic, Inc.*)
	L. Ron Hubbard	'Typewriter in the Sky'
1941	L. Sprague de Camp and Fletcher Pratt	*The Incomplete Enchanter*
1942	Hannes Bok	'The Sorcerer's Ship'
	C. S. Lewis	*The Screwtape Letters*
1943	Mary Norton	*The Magic Bedknob*
1945	George Orwell	*Animal Farm: A Fairy Story*
1946	Tove Jansson	*Comet in Moominland* (trans. 1951)
	Mervyn Peake	*Titus Groan*
	T. H. White	*Mistress Masham's Repose*
1948	Fletcher Pratt	*The Well of the Unicorn*
1949	John Myers Myers	*Silverlock*
1950	C. S. Lewis	*The Lion, the Witch and the Wardrobe*
	Mervyn Peake	*Gormenghast*
	Jack Vance	*The Dying Earth* (collection)
1952	Mary Norton	*The Borrowers*
	E. B. White	*Charlotte's Web*

1973	William Goldman	*The Princess Bride*
	Diana Wynne Jones	*Wilkin's Tooth (US 1974: Witch's Business)*
	Astrid Lindgren	*The Brothers Lionheart*
	Gabriel García Márquez	*One Hundred Years of Solitude* (trans.)
1974	Stephen King	*Carrie*
	Octavio Paz	*Children of the Mire*
1975	Diana Wynne Jones	*Eight Days of Luke*
1976	Marion Zimmer Bradley	*The Shattered Chain*
	Gordon R. Dickson	*The Dragon and the George*
	Michael de Larrabeiti	*The Borribles*
	Patricia McKillip	*The Riddle Master of Hed*
	Anne Rice	*Interview With the Vampire* (Vampire Chronicles)
1977	Piers Anthony	*A Spell for Chameleon* (Xanth)
	Terry Brooks	*The Sword of Shannara* (Shannara)
	Italo Calvino	*The Castle of Crossed Destinies* (trans.)
	Stephen R. Donaldson	*Lord Foul's Bane* (Thomas Covenant)
	Peter Straub	*If You Could See Me Now*
	J. R. R. Tolkien	*The Silmarillion*
1978	Virginia Hamilton	*Justice and Her Brothers*
	Michael Moorcock	*Gloriana; Or, The Unfulfill'd Queen*
	Chelsea Quinn Yarbro	*Hotel Transylvania* (Saint-Germain)
1979	Octavia Butler	*Kindred*
	Angela Carter	*The Bloody Chamber and Other Stories* (collection)
1979	Samuel R. Delany	*Tales of Nevèrÿon* (Return to Nevèrÿon)
	Elizabeth Anne Lynn	*Watchtower* (Chronicles of Tornor)
	Tim Powers	*The Drawing of the Dark*
1980	Jonathan Carroll	*The Land of Laughs*
	Suzy McKee Charnas	*The Vampire Tapestry*
	David McKee	*Not Now, Bernard*
	Ruth Park	*Playing Beatie Bow*
	Gene Wolfe	*The Shadow of the Torturer* (The Book of the New Sun)
1981	John Crowley	*Little, Big*
	Christopher Priest	*The Affirmation*

1995	Sara Douglass	*BattleAxe* (Axis Trilogy)
	Robin Hobb	*Assassin's Apprentice* (Farseer Trilogy)
	Gregory Maguire	*Wicked: The Life and Times of the Wicked Witch of the West*
	Philip Pullman	*Northern Lights* (US: *The Golden Compass*) (His Dark Materials)
1996	Neil Gaiman	*Neverwhere*
	George R. R. Martin	*A Game of Thrones* (The Song of Fire and Ice)
1997	Kate Elliott	*King's Dragon* (Crown of Stars)
	J. K. Rowling	*Harry Potter and the Philosopher's Stone* (Harry Potter)
1998	Nalo Hopkinson	*Brown Girl in the Ring*
	Guy Gavriel Kay	*Sailing to Sarantium*
2000	Mary Gentle	*Ash: A Secret History*
	Nalo Hopkinson	*Midnight Robber*
	China Miéville	*Perdido Street Station*
	K. J. Parker	*Colours in the Steel* (Fencer Trilogy)
	Sean Stewart	*Galveston*
2001	Lois McMaster Bujold	*The Curse of Chalion*
	Ted Chiang	'Hell is the Absence of God'
	Cecilia Dart-Thornton	*The Ill-Made Mute* (Bitterbynde)
	Neil Gaiman	*American Gods*
	Hiromi Goto	*The Kappa Child*
	Charlaine Harris	*Dead Until Dark* (Sookie Stackhouse)
	Gwyneth Jones	*Bold As Love*
	Kelly Link	*Stranger Things Happen* (collection)
2002	Ted Chiang	*Stories of Your Life: And Others* (collection)
	Lisa Goldstein	*The Alchemist's Door*
2003	Nalo Hopkinson	*The Salt Roads*
	Dan Simmons	*Ilium*
2004	Charles Butler	*The Fetch of Mardy Watt*
	Susanna Clarke	*Jonathan Strange & Mr Norrell*
	Elizabeth Hand	*Mortal Love*
	Margo Lanagan	*Black Juice* (collection)
	China Miéville	*Iron Council*

EDWARD JAMES AND FARAH MENDLESOHN

Introduction

Fantasy is not so much a mansion as a row of terraced houses, such as the one that entranced us in C. S. Lewis's *The Magician's Nephew* with its connecting attics, each with a door that leads into another world. There are shared walls, and a certain level of consensus around the basic bricks, but the internal décor can differ wildly, and the lives lived in these terraced houses are discrete yet overheard.

Fantasy literature has proven tremendously difficult to pin down. The major theorists in the field – Tzvetan Todorov, Rosemary Jackson, Kathryn Hume, W. R. Irwin and Colin Manlove – all agree that fantasy is about the construction of the impossible whereas science fiction may be about the unlikely, but is grounded in the scientifically possible. But from there these critics quickly depart, each to generate definitions of fantasy which include the texts that they value and exclude most of what general readers think of as fantasy. Most of them consider primarily texts of the nineteenth and early twentieth century. If we turn to twentieth-century fantasy, and in particular the commercially successful fantasy of the second half of the twentieth century, then, after Tolkien's classic essay, 'On Fairy Stories', the most valuable theoretical text for taking a definition of fantasy beyond preference and intuition is Brian Attebery's *Strategies of Fantasy* (1992). Building on his earlier book, *The American Fantasy Tradition* (1980), Attebery proposed that we view fantasy as a group of texts that share, to a greater degree or other, a cluster of common tropes which may be objects but which may also be narrative techniques. At the centre are those stories which share tropes of the completely impossible and towards the edge, in subsets, are those stories which include only a small number of tropes, or which construct those tropes in such a way as to leave doubt in the reader's mind as to whether what they have read is fantastical or not. This group of texts resolves into a 'fuzzy set' (a mathematical term), and it is the 'fuzzy set' of fantasy, from the core to the edge – that sense of more and less fantastical texts operating in conversation with each other – which is the subject of this book.

Once we leave the project of defining fantasy, the most useful theoretical text is formed from the entries by John Clute in *The Encyclopedia of Fantasy* (edited by Clute with John Grant, 1997). When read together, these construct a grammar of fantasy which draws together notions of structural and thematic movement in the text, of moods, and of tropes and metaphors which have become part of the conversation. Clute's most significant contribution to the language of criticism has been his definition of the 'full fantasy' in the entry FANTASY. In the full fantasy, a text (which may be a multi-volume work) passes through WRONGNESS, THINNING, RECOGNITION and HEALING (using the *Encyclopedia*'s typographic style). What becomes clear from the *Encyclopedia* as a whole, and from wide-ranging reading in the genre, is the degree to which an awareness of the conversation between authors and texts is one of the defining characteristics of the form.

The most recent contribution to the theoretical debate (and one which is referenced by many of the contributors to this volume) is Farah Mendlesohn's *Rhetorics of Fantasy* (2008). Mendlesohn abandons the search for definition and accepts Attebery's fuzzy set and Clute's grammar, but argues that there are four distinct modes of fantasy, defined by the way in which the fantastic enters the text and the rhetorical voices which are required to construct the different types of worlds which emerge. The four categories are the portal-quest, the immersive, the intrusion and the liminal. In the portal-quest, the protagonist enters a new world; in the immersive, the protagonist is part of the fantastic world; in the intrusion, the fantastic breaks into the primary world (which might or might not be our own); and in the liminal, magic might or might not be happening. What the schema offers is a way of considering fantasy on its own terms rather than in the terms used by critics of mimetic fiction. It may even offer a way of evaluating the quality of a particular fantasy: as just one example, an immersive fantasy that uses the rhetorical (and over-explanatory) voice of a portal-quest fantasy is, Mendlesohn argues, unlikely to be effective.

Fantasy's companion genre, science fiction, has been segmented relatively easily into subgenres that most fans, critics and writers recognize, even if only to argue about (such as space opera, cyberpunk, hard sf: see *The Cambridge Companion to Science Fiction*). The study of fantasy, on the other hand, has only just moved on from attempting to define the form, and the subgenres that have emerged from the marketing of fantasy frequently feel transient and commercial ventures. This book endeavours to take the body of genre fantasy on a multiplicity of terms that recognizes academic, reader and commercial understandings of fantasy as equally valuable. This is reflected in the overall shape of the book.

Part I consists of five chapters which survey English-language, and to a lesser extent European, fantasy from the late seventeenth century through to the present day to build up a picture of the vibrant and diverse range of writing commonly grouped together under the rubric 'fantasy', or sometimes 'the fantastic'. It is in the seventeenth century that we can find the first critical awareness of the separate existence of a genre of 'fantasy'; this book therefore ignores those earlier fictions about the fantastical – *The Odyssey*, *Beowulf*, *Sir Gawain and the Green Knight*, *Orlando Furioso*, *The Midsummer Night's Dream* and very many other texts – even though writers within the modern genre of fantasy have been inspired by them and have frequently reused and referenced them.

Part II is entitled 'Ways of reading' and consists of, first, five chapters focusing on the most common academic readings of fantasy fiction (structuralism, psychoanalysis, political readings, modernism and postmodernism, and thematic criticism). In this section we want to demonstrate the degree to which fantasy opens up to a number of critical responses. However, this is not solely an academic concern, or one bounded by formal theoretical responses. One of the most exciting aspects of the field has been the degree to which working writers have wished to engage with modes of reading the fantastic. The next three chapters begin with fantasy author Greer Gilman's chapter on the languages of the fantastic, which gets right down to the bones of the genre, beyond story, beyond character, beyond theme, to examine the way in which the fantastic is actually written. Kari Maund, an historian and novelist (as Kari Sperring), continues with a discussion of the pleasures of reading series fantasy, in which worlds and narratives can be extended across many volumes, and Gregory Frost completes the section by considering the reading strategies used in the fuzzy margins of the set called 'fantasy'.

One of the difficulties of teaching fantasy in the classroom is that there is very little consensus around a canon. Two people's understanding of the fantastic can be sufficiently different as to generate a list of texts with little overlap apart from Tolkien (and sometimes not even him). This is enormously liberating. There are no texts that one feels one *must* include. However, it does make a book of this type rather problematic. Rather than end this book with a series of author studies, we have chosen instead to offer studies of author-clusters that are intended to serve as discussion-openers. We hesitate to call these clusters 'subgenres' (although some will). Rather, the clusters selected have been chosen because between them they allow for a very broad coverage of recent authors worthy of discussion and demonstrate at the same time the way an individual author's works can be reconfigured to answer different questions. Furthermore, the sections in Part III have been deliberately selected to be in tune with the current market labels, and to avoid any suggestion that some modes of writing the fantastic are more worthy than others.

Part III – 'Clusters' – begins with Sharon Sieber exploring the works of magical realism, placing them in their original context and explaining why they have become such a vital wellspring for commercial fantasy. Nnedi Okorafor examines the very particular approach to fantasy of writers of colour, influenced both by their own literary traditions and by the experience of Western dominance. W. A. Senior continues with a consideration of the form of fantasy that has dominated the bookshop shelves for over thirty years: quest fantasies are often derided but, as Senior demonstrates, they can be sophisticated and complex. The next two chapters look at two other 'clusters' currently enjoying great popularity. Alexander C. Irvine, himself a writer of gritty and unusual urban fantasies, considers the development of the form and its new subversions. Roz Kaveney concludes with a discussion of the highly unstable label 'dark fantasy' and its latest offshoot, the 'paranormal romance'.

Children's fantasy, which, for reasons explored by Gary K. Wolfe and Maria Nikolajeva in Part I, has always had a semi-autonomous existence, came into critical prominence at the end of the twentieth century with the unexpected success of J. K. Rowling and Philip Pullman. Catherine Butler, in her chapter, details the important innovations that can be found among writers of fantasy for children in the last few decades. Finally, in the last two chapters, we turn back to history, where we began, but this time history as viewed by fantasy writers. Veronica Schanoes considers the popularity and interpretations of different periods of history in works of fantasy and mulls on the role that ideologies of history and scholarship have played; Graham Sleight moves on to consider the ways in which fantasy has allowed iconoclastic thought-experiments in the area of history and religion.

PART I

Histories

1

GARY K. WOLFE

Fantasy from Dryden to Dunsany

On 1 July 1712, in his magazine *The Spectator* – which, widely available in coffeehouses, was probably the closest thing eighteenth-century England had to what we would now think of as a popular blog – Joseph Addison introduced a topic of discussion that might sound familiar to modern readers of fantasy:

> There is a kind of writing wherein the poet quite loses sight of Nature, and entertains his reader's imagination with the characters and actions of such persons as have many of them no existence but what he bestows on them; such are fairies, witches, magicians, demons, and departed spirits. This Mr. *Dryden* calls *the fairy way of writing*, which is, indeed, more difficult than any other that depends on the poet's fancy, because he has no pattern to follow in it, and must work altogether out of his own invention.[1]

Addison, of course, wasn't thinking of anything like the fantasy novel in the modern sense – his main purview was poetry and drama – but his observations were pertinent enough that a contemporary scholar, David Sandner, has argued that Addison could be regarded as 'the first critic of the fantastic'.[2] Addison does not quite use the terms 'fantastic' or 'fantasy', however, speaking instead of 'the reader's imagination' and 'the poet's fancy' – both terms which would increasingly, over the next century or so, move to the foreground in discussions of the fantastic imagination.

In fact, of all the various terms we now employ to talk about fantasy literature, probably the first to evolve was this distinction between imagination and fancy, widely familiar to modern readers from its most famous formulation in Samuel Taylor Coleridge's *Biographia Literaria* in 1817. But, as Addison demonstrates, the debate over these terms – and indeed over the whole notion of fantasy as a mode of poetic creation – had been going on for more than a century prior to Coleridge's essay. In another issue of *The Spectator*, Addison wrote, 'There are few words in the English language which are employed in a more loose and uncircumscribed sense than those of the fancy and the imagination.'[3] In setting out 'to fix and determine the notion of these two words', Addison proposed the notion that both originally derive from sight. In other words, what we call imagination or fancy has to do with our reactions to or memories of objects of nature or art. Addison's view partakes of what was already a long-standing view of imagination as a 'mirror' of the external world, to use a metaphor from Yeats borrowed by M. H. Abrams in his classic 1953 study *The Mirror and the Lamp*. But in the late eighteenth and early nineteenth centuries, this view of imagination, thanks largely to the Romantic movement, would come to be supplanted by a view of imagination as a 'lamp' illuminating unseen worlds beyond perceived reality – the 'fairy way of writing', to use the term from John Dryden that Addison borrowed.

This new view was already a topic of vigorous discussion by the mid eighteenth century. In 1741, the German critic, poet, and translator of Milton's *Paradise Lost*, Johann Jakob Bodmer wrote:

> The imagination is not merely the soul's treasury, where the senses store their pictures in safe-keeping for subsequent use; besides this it also has a region of its own which extends much further than the dimension of the senses... It not only places the real before our eyes in a vivid image and makes distant things present but also, with a power more potent than that of magic, it draws that which does not exist out of the state of potentiality, gives it a semblance of reality and makes us see, hear and feel these new creations.[4]

By 1762 a similar definition of imagination had entered the English language with Lord Henry Home Kames writing in his *Elements of Criticism*: 'this singular power of fabricating images without any foundation in reality is distinguished by the name of *imagination*'.[5]

This shift in the theory of imagination led, predictably enough, to a new attitude toward the fantastic (which the German poet and critic Friedrich Schlegel already claimed in 1800 as a defining characteristic of Romantic literature), and in turn to a number of debates about the proper uses of the fantastic, including the relative merits of figures and images drawn from nature, and those that sought to go beyond nature. The brothers A. W. and Friedrich Schlegel, for example, devoted much of their influential journal *Das Athenaeum* from 1798 to 1800 to debates about the rules of fairy tales or *Märchen* and other forms of Romantic literature. In his 1810 'A Vision of the Last Judgment', William Blake equated imagination with 'Visionary Fancy' and set this apart from fable or allegory, 'a totally distinct & inferior kind of Poetry... Fable or Allegory is Form'd by the daughters of Memory, Imagination is surrounded by the daughters of Inspiration'.[6] Blake's distinction not only anticipates Coleridge (albeit with a different set of terms), but also anticipates a critical battle that authors of fantasy from George Mac-Donald to C. S. Lewis would wage: namely, that fantastic narratives are not necessarily allegories or fables.

But it was Samuel Taylor Coleridge's 1817 distinction between fancy and imagination that set the stage for the critical debate that would occupy much of the nineteenth century and that arguably surrounded the birth of the modern fantasy narrative. Writing in the early chapters of *Biographia Literaria* about Wordsworth's poetry, Coleridge describes his growing conviction 'that fancy and imagination were two distinct and widely different faculties, instead of being, according to the general belief, either two names with one meaning, or, at furthest the lower and higher degree of one and the same power'.[7] Later he describes the imagination as 'the living Power and prime Agent of all human perception', the most godlike of human qualities, while the fancy 'has no other counters to play with, but fixities and definites. The Fancy is indeed no other than a mode of Memory emancipated from the order of time and space'.[8] In other words, the earlier concept of imagination – that it is essentially a mode of memory – Coleridge relegates to the secondary status of 'fancy', while the imagination represents something new and entirely different – what Coleridge was to call the 'esemplastic' power of the mind. More than seventy years later, the Scottish writer George Mac-Donald, nearing the end of his career as one of the Victorian era's leading fantasists, would return to this distinction between fancy and imagination, offering his own variation: speaking of literary forms, he wrote, 'When such forms are new embodiments of old truths, we call them products of the Imagination; when they are mere inventions, however lovely, I should call them the work of the Fancy.'[9]

In English literary discourse, Coleridge's famous distinction did much to establish the terms by which fantastic literature would be discussed for the rest of the century, and to give legitimacy to the notion of a vocabulary of the fantastic. Indeed, according to Stephen Prickett, 'by 1825 something very extraordinary had happened. From being terms of derision, or descriptions of daydreaming, words like "fantasy" and "imagination" suddenly began to take on new status as hurrah-words.'[10] But while Romantic poets and their critics could undertake debates about the nature of imagination as revealed through literary art, and while Romantic narrative artists such as Edgar Allan Poe and Sir Walter Scott could begin to construct theoretical examinations of the nature of their craft (a tradition continued by later fantastic authors from George MacDonald to J. R. R. Tolkien, C. S. Lewis, and Ursula K. Le Guin), critics in the major English journals remained sceptical of the uses of the fantastic in works of fiction, and within a few decades the currency of the fantastic had been devalued once again.[11] Fantasy elements were widely regarded as superstitious, to be tolerated only if supported by evidence of actual belief or if supported by didactic or moral purpose. This, at least was the argument addressed by 'Some Remarks on the Use of the Preternatural in Works of Fiction', an essay published anonymously in *Blackwood's Edinburgh Magazine* in September 1818 but widely attributed to the Scottish critic John Wilson. Fantastic or supernatural elements, the author argued, 'should be sparingly used, in order to avoid monotony, and prevent the disgust which is always sure to be felt, when they are no longer regarded with astonishment'.[12]

Even Sir Walter Scott himself, discussing both E. T. A. Hoffmann's work and Mary Shelley's *Frankenstein* (1818) in his essay 'On the Supernatural in Fictitious Composition' (1827), demanded that fantastic elements should be 'rare, brief, indistinct', yet characterized by 'philosophical reasoning and moral truth'.[13] Scott's essay is of interest not only because it represents one of the earliest critical discussions of a work now widely regarded as science fiction, but because it reveals an attitude that would become increasingly dominant in the later nineteenth century: that fantastic inventions, in an increasingly pragmatic and industrialized age, required some sort of extra-literary rationale for their legitimate employment in a work of literature. Scott's essay also proved influential in France: translated as 'Du merveilleux dans le roman' in the April 1829 issue of *La Revue de Paris*, it was later reprinted (in considerably truncated form, with references to Mary Shelley omitted) as the introduction to a French collection of Hoffmann's tales – though Scott's phrase 'the fantastic mode of writing' was translated by editor J.-B. Cefauconpret as 'genre fantastique'. Together with an earlier enthusiastic essay on Hoffmann by the philologist Jean-Jacques Ampère (son of the famous physicist and pioneer in electrical theory) in the magazine *Le Globe* in 1828, it helped give currency to *le fantastique* as a genre in French critical thought, a notion further advanced by Charles Nodier's 1830 manifesto in *La Revue de Paris*, 'Du fantastique en literature', which ranged from Homer and the Bible to Goethe and the German Romantics in a wide-ranging defence of the fantastic. Nodier himself was a pioneer of the *conte fantastique*, through such tales as 'Trilby, the Fairy of Argyll' (1822, written after a visit to Scotland during which he met Walter Scott) and the more Gothic-flavoured 'Smarra, or Demons of the Night' (1821).[14]

In England, though, fantasy clearly remained suspect. In an anonymous essay titled 'The Progress of Fiction as an Art', which appeared in the *Westminster Review* in 1853, the author (who may have been George Eliot, a subeditor of the magazine at that time) argued that art, like technology, progresses from more primitive to more sophisticated forms, and 'a scientific and somewhat sceptical age has no longer the power of believing in the marvels which delighted our ruder ancestors'.[15] The fantastic, in other words, was inappropriate for an age of science and morality, and the values of realism came to dominate literary discourse, despite the fact that the Victorian age itself was one of the great periods in the development of fantasy literature. 'Falsehood is so easy, truth so difficult,' wrote George Eliot in her 1859 novel *Adam Bede*. 'The pencil is conscious of a delightful facility in drawing a griffin – the longer the claws, and the larger the wings, the better; but that marvellous facility which we mistook for genius is apt to forsake us when we want to draw a real unexaggerated lion.'[16] The sort of domestic realism which Eliot champions here came increasingly to supplant the Romantic celebration of the imagination during the Victorian period and in many ways survives yet today in discussions of the novel as an art form. It is hardly surprising, then, that when something reasonably resembling modern fantasy began to emerge, it often did so in the disguise of children's literature (as with John Ruskin, Lewis Carroll, or Charles Kingsley), pseudo-historical fiction (as with Walter Scott), hermetic or occult fiction (as with Edward Bulwer Lytton), or pseudo-medievalia (as with William Morris).

In fact, the modern term 'fantasy novel', with its implication of a narrative which combines novelistic characterization and theme with the sort visionary imagination that Coleridge and Blake described, might well have seemed an oxymoron to literary readers in the late eighteenth and nineteenth centuries. Early novels often presented themselves as histories, as in Henry Fielding's *History of Tom Jones, A Foundling* (1749) or Daniel Defoe's *The Life and Strange Surprizing Adventures of Robinson Crusoe* (1719), which argued in its preface that it was an actual journal discovered by its editor, Defoe, who claimed it was a 'just History of Fact'. In contrast to these 'private histories' (as opposed to the more public histories that were seen as the purview of historians) were narratives that identified themselves as 'romances', including such classic early Gothic stories as Ann Radcliffe's *The Mysteries of Udolpho: A Romance* (1794) or Matthew Lewis's *The Monk: A Romance* (1796). The comparative virtues of the two forms were debated in numerous essays, sometimes by authors as important to the history of Gothic fiction as William Godwin ('Of History and Romance', 1797) and Charles Brockden Brown ('The Difference Between History and Romance', 1800).[17] The modern fantasy novel, and to an arguable extent the modern novel itself, is in part an outgrowth of this debate.

While we can reasonably argue that the fantastic in the broadest sense had been a dominant characteristic of most world literature for centuries prior to the rise of the novel, we can also begin to discern that the fantasy *genre* may well have had its origins in these eighteenth- and nineteenth-century discussions of fancy vs. imagination, history vs. romance, the mirror vs. the lamp.

More specifically, we can trace particular elements of this genre to three important literary traditions which evolved during this period: the imaginary 'private histories' mentioned above (in other words, the early novel), the popularity of the Gothic romance, and the renewal of interest in folk and fairy tales leading to the literary or 'art' fairy tale (or *Kunstmärchen* in Germany, where this form achieved a particular vitality during the Romantic era). Since the 'private histories' are a part of the history of the novel as a general form, and since the Gothic is the purview of another essay in this volume, we will focus here largely on the emerging role of the *Kunstmärchen* as a kind of cauldron of literary fantasy during the nineteenth century.

Literary fairy tales, both original and adapted from folk sources, had been both familiar and popular since the late seventeenth century through the work of Countess d'Aulnoy (*Les Contes des Fees* [Tales of fairies], 1697), Charles Perrault (*Les Contes de ma Mère l'Oie* [*Tales of Mother Goose*], 1697), and others. But with the Romantic movement, especially in Germany, such tales became the topic of a deliberate movement related to the debates between fancy and imagination discussed earlier. Some of Friedrich Schlegel's comments in the journal *Das Athanäum* virtually read like manifestos for a new narrative art form, and debates over the nature and meaning of *Kunstmärchen* continued in the frame story of Ludwig Tieck's *Phantasus* (1812–17), which collected many of his earlier stories and dramas dating back to 1797. While Tieck and others readily acknowledged the influence of Goethe in the development of this new kind of narrative (Goethe's seminal 'Das Märchen' had been published in 1795), it is in his work and that of his contemporaries E. T. A. Hoffmann, Novalis (Friedrich von Hardenburg), and Baron de la Motte Fouqué that we can begin to trace a more or less direct line of descent through Victorian and later fantasy. For example, Tieck's 1812 story 'The Elves' concerns a little girl who, while playing with her brother, crosses a footbridge which has been forbidden because it leads to what appears to be a poor settlement of gypsies. Instead, she finds herself in a verdant world of tall, beautiful elves and elemental spirits, where she visits their palace, meets the 'Metal-prince' and enjoys various adventures. When she returns home the next morning, she learns that seven years have passed. She spends the remainder of her life remembering this magical world, until years later her own daughter again gains access to it. In many ways this story anticipates the form which Farah Mendlesohn calls the 'portal fantasy',[18] even introducing the time-shift aspect which becomes a common feature in such later examples of the form as C. S. Lewis's Narnia.

'The Elves' was one of five tales by Tieck translated by Thomas Carlyle – along with others by Johann August Musäus (who had begun publishing collections of folk tales as early as 1782), E. T. A. Hoffmann, Friedrich de la Motte Fouqué and Jean-Paul Friedrich Richter – in his very popular two-volume *German Romance* in 1827, the same decade that saw Edgar Taylor's English translations of the Brothers Grimm and the first of several editions of Thomas Keightley's worldwide compendium *The Fairy Mythology; Illustrative of the Romance and Superstition of Various Countries*. The sole Hoffmann story included in Carlyle's collection was the novella 'The Golden Pot', originally published in 1814 and rightly regarded as a masterpiece of Romantic narrative literature. Subtitled 'A Fairy Tale for Our Times', the Hoffmann story prefigures modern fantasy in another way: it begins in the contemporary urban setting of Dresden, where the hapless student Anselmus finds himself drawn into an increasingly complex world of elemental spirits, alchemists and snake-ladies. Partly through the influence of Carlyle's and other translations from the German, partly because of the popularity of the Brothers Grimm stories and partly because of the wild popularity of Hoffmann throughout Europe (a ten-volume edition of his works appeared in Germany in 1827–8, and a twelve-volume edition of translations appeared in Paris in 1830), Germanic settings became almost a convention of literary fairy stories in early Victorian England. John Ruskin's bestselling *The King of the Golden River* (1841, published 1851), for example, is set in the Styria region of Austria, with the protagonists named Hans and Schwartz.

It may be significant that *German Romance* was originally published in Edinburgh, since the writer who most fully embraced the aesthetics and techniques of the German romantics was George MacDonald, sometimes credited as the author of two of the earliest modern fantasy novels, *Phantastes* (1858) and *Lilith* (1895). MacDonald, who was only three years old when *German Romance* appeared, may well have come to the Germans on his own (though he had a copy of Carlyle in his library); in one of the more intriguing mysteries in the development of Victorian fantasy, he (according to his son Greville) was hired to catalogue a vast library in a castle or mansion in the far north of Scotland when he was only eighteen, in 1842. No one knows where that library was, or what was in it, but after this experience he was clearly enamoured of writers such as Hoffmann and Novalis, even issuing his own privately printed translations of several of Novalis's 'spiritual songs' in 1851. MacDonald's first novel, *Phantastes*, concerning a young student named Anodos who is drawn into a dreamlike fairyland when the furnishings of his room gradually transform into an enchanted forest, is liberally sprinkled with quotations from Novalis, and the story as a whole owes a great deal to a long interpolated fairy tale in Novalis's unfinished 1802 novel *Heinrich von Ofterdingen*. More important, perhaps, is the manner in which it adds to Tieck's and Hoffmann's anticipation of modern fantasy narratives, most strikingly in a scene in which Anodos looks into a mysterious cupboard and realizes that, beyond the household cleaning supplies and brooms, a tunnel leads toward a night-time sky – a clear prefiguration of the opening of *The Lion, the Witch, and the Wardrobe* by C. S. Lewis, who once claimed that it was MacDonald's novel which 'baptized' his imagination.[19]

MacDonald was undoubtedly a key figure in Victorian fantasy, very nearly bookending its golden age with his two adult fantasy novels published thirty-seven years apart. He was a friend of both John Ruskin and Charles Dodgson (who photographed his children) and urged Dodgson to publish what would become the most famous of all Victorian fantasies, *Alice's Adventures in Wonderland* (1863), which appeared under the name Lewis Carroll. He met the major English poets and novelists of the age and even befriended American writers such as Longfellow and Mark Twain. And, far from abandoning fantasy during the decades between his two major adult works, he instead shifted towards those modes of fantasy that seemed to be more acceptable to a literary culture increasingly devoted (as we have seen) to domestic realism. He wrote a series of regional Scottish novels (some of which, such as *The Portent* [1864], included fantasy elements), but achieved his greatest success with a series of books and stories for children, including 'The Light Princess' (1864), 'The Golden Key' (1867), *At the Back of the North Wind* (1871), and *The Princess and the Goblin* (1872), sometimes regarded as his masterpiece. These, along with other classics by Carroll, Ruskin, Thackeray (*The Rose and the Ring*, 1855), and Charles Kingsley (another MacDonald friend, now known best for *The Water-Babies*, 1863), helped create the impression that the Victorian era was something of a golden age of children's fantasy, while remaining all but intolerant of fantasy for adults. Samuel Taylor Coleridge's own daughter Sara produced a fascinating German-influenced fairy tale titled *Phantasmion* in 1837, which, with its complex plot, fully realized secondary world and political machinations (six different countries of 'fairyland' are presented), anticipates a number of key features of a particular type of fantasy novel. When Hans Christian Andersen's tales were translated in five volumes in 1846, they were enormously successful, and Andersen himself toured England the following year as a major literary celebrity, meeting Dickens and other major figures.

Yet there remained a substantial tradition of adult fantasy, even if it operated very nearly in exile. The ghost story thrived, with some of its most famous examples coming from the major figures of the age, including Charles Dickens ('A Christmas Carol', 1843; 'The Haunted Man', 1848),

Edward Bulwer Lytton ('The Haunted and the Haunters', 1859), and even the champion of realism George Eliot ('The Lifted Veil', 1858). Edward Bulwer Lytton, who had gained fame in 1834 with his apocalyptic *The Last Days of Pompeii*, flirted with the mystical ideas of Rosicrucianism (a kind of nineteenth-century version of Scientology, in terms of its hold on its followers) in his novels *Zanoni* (1842) and *A Strange Story* (1862), the latter of which had the distinction of being the next novel serialized in the periodical *All the Year Round* following Dickens's *Great Expectations*. Wilkie Collins and Joseph Sheridan Le Fanu helped transform the materials of the Gothic novel into the 'novel of sensation', prefiguring many elements of the contemporary thriller, and Le Fanu produced a classic of vampire literature in *Carmilla* (1872). The vogue for Orientalism, which had begun in the eighteenth century following the early English versions of *The Arabian Nights* and which had entered the arena of the Gothic novel with the work of William Beckford and Clara Reeve, remained a consistently popular subgenre, giving rise to notable fantasy novels by authors otherwise known primarily for social realism, such as George Meredith (*The Shaving of Shagpat*, 1856) and F. Marion Crawford (*Khaled: A Tale of Arabia*, 1891). The *Arabian Nights* itself remained so popular that Robert Louis Stevenson (who also pioneered the psychological fantasy with *Dr. Jekyll and Mr. Hyde* in 1886) entitled his first story collection *The New Arabian Nights* (1882), while the *old* Arabian nights enjoyed renewed life following Sir Richard Francis Burton's unexpurgated ten-volume translation in 1885.

But while these and other subgenres (including the lost-race tales popularized by H. Rider Haggard and others) may have featured substantial fantastic elements, the next author to add substantially to the recipe for what eventually became modern fantasy was William Morris (1834–96). Today largely remembered for his association with the Pre-Raphaelite brotherhood and the arts and crafts movement, Morris had begun publishing fantastic stories and poems as early as 1856 in *The Oxford and Cambridge Magazine*, which he had co-founded. While some of these stories, like 'Lindenberg Pool' (1856), were notably Gothic-influenced (the narrator, visiting the pool of the title, finds himself transported back in time to the thirteenth century, where he encounters a vile and reclusive baron who turns out to be an enormous pig), others, such as 'The Hollow Land' (1856), helped develop the idea of a fully realized secondary world. Morris soon found other sources of inspiration as well. Between 1868 and 1870, he published translations of several of the Icelandic sagas which would later prove such a crucial influence on fantasy writers such as David Lindsay and J. R. R. Tolkien, incorporated retellings of some of these sagas in his massive (and very successful) poetry collection *The Earthly Paradise* (1868–70) and published *The Story of Sigurd the Volsung and the Fall of the Niblungs* in 1877. But perhaps his most significant contribution to fantasy history involved his efforts, late in his career, to revive the medieval romance through stories of his own invention, set entirely in imagined pseudo-medieval fantasy environments and written in such archly contrived antique diction as to make them a challenge for modern readers. Still, novels such as *The Story of the Glittering Plain* (1891), *The Wood Beyond the World* (1894), *The Well at the World's End* (1896) and *The Water of the Wondrous Isles* (1897) were among the first of what Mendlesohn calls 'immersive fantasies', set entirely in imaginary worlds that were not presented as dreamscapes or spiritual journeys (as they tended to be in MacDonald and others).

At the same time, fantasy imagery abounded in music and the visual arts throughout Europe, often in ways closely allied to literature, and several key writers were artists or composers as well. E. T. A. Hoffmann, as noted, was an active and popular composer (the 'A' stands for Amadeus, a name he chose for himself as a tribute to Mozart) whose only complete opera, *Undine* (1814), was adapted from de la Motte's fairy tale with a libretto by Fouqué himself. Ironically, though, Hoffmann's musical influence is today remembered far more for adaptations of his stories than for his own compositions. His fictional composer Kreisler, featured in three stories, provided the basis for Robert Schumann's eight-part piano suite *Kreisleriana* (1838). One of his most famous tales, 'The Sandman' (1816) inspired Delibes's ballet *Coppélia* (1870) and was one of three stories which formed the basis for a popular opera by Jacques Offenbach, *Tales of Hoffmann* (1881). Yet another tale provided the source for Pyotr Ilyich Tchaikovsky's ballet *The Nutcracker* (1892). Later in the century, Richard Wagner revived interest in German and Scandinavian myth and legend with a series of large-scale operas beginning with *The Flying Dutchman* (1843) and culminating in the massive four-opera cycle *The Ring of the Nibelungs* (1869–82), which remains among the most ambitious of all musical compositions. In Norway, Edvard Grieg's incidental music composed for Henrik Ibsen's fantastic play *Peer Gynt* (first performed 1876), with its trolls and goblins, is now better known than the play itself. The French composer Hector Berlioz's best-known work remains his *Symphonie Fantastique* (1830), a programmatic piece which begins by invoking an idealized love and ends with a fiery witches' sabbath. In addition to Tchaikovsky, Russian composer Nikolai Rimsky-Korsakov employed fantasy materials in such operas as *The Snow Maiden: A Spring Fairytale* (1881) and *The Legend of the Invisible City of Kitezh* (1905). Although Victorian England was perhaps less known for musical contributions, its most famous musical theatre collaborators,

W. S. Gilbert and Arthur Sullivan, also turned to fairy materials in *Iolanthe* (1882), after an earlier comic opera, *The Sorceror* (1877), had featured a village sorceror and a magical love potion.

As for the visual arts, Blake, of course, was a visionary artist as well as a poet, and the Pre-Raphaelite brotherhood – which included William Morris, Dante Gabriel Rossetti, Christina Rossetti and for a time John Everett Millais – is now more often remembered for its paintings than for its poetry. Along with the familiar Victorian representational genres of land-scapes, marine paintings, animal paintings, sports paintings and portraits, 'fairy painting' became popular in exhibitions as well as in book illustra-tions (such as George Cruikshank's widely praised illustrations for Taylor's 1823 translation of Grimm). Sometimes such paintings were inspired by literary sources such as Shakespeare (Sir John Millais's *Ferdinand Lured by Ariel*, 1849; J. Simmons's *A Midsummer Night's Dream*, 1867), sometimes by German tales (Daniel Maclise's *Undine*, 1855), sometimes by the artist's own earlier book illustrations (such as the work of one of the most prolific of all fairy painters, Richard Doyle, who had begun his career as a cartoonist for *Punch* and who, incidentally, was the uncle of Arthur Conan Doyle). Given the Victorian fondness for narrative painting (painting which seems to illustrate a scene from an actual or implied tale), those works which seem to suggest a fully realized but unarticulated fantasy world are of particu-lar interest, and of these the most remarkable may be Richard Dadd's *The Fairy Feller's Master Stroke* (1864), an astonishingly detailed and mysterious work which occupied the artist for some nine years while confined to Beth-lem mental hospital after murdering his father. On the continent, fantastic or grotesque imagery had frequently provided subject matter for artists as diverse as Francisco Goya in Spain, Caspar David Friedrich in Germany, Gustave Moreau and Odilon Redon in France, Edvard Munch in Norway, and many others.

Some of these artists, such as Moreau and Redon, were associated with yet another series of loosely related movements which would contribute to the emerging aesthetic of fantasy: Decadence, the Aesthetic Movement and Symbolism. Decadence (originally a term of derision later adopted with defiant pride by some artists and writers) was in part a reaction against both the mechanistic notions of progress of the earlier nineteenth century and the allegedly uncritical celebration of nature among the Romantics. Its most famous poet in France, Charles Baudelaire, was an enthusiastic promoter of the work of Edgar Allan Poe, and the movement also reflected a revival of interest in Gothic fiction. While its celebration of the fantastic is most immediately evident in the work of artists such as Moreau and Redon, Edvard Munch and Aubrey Beardsley, the movement also influenced a number of writers who found fantasy a liberating mode for exploring this new sensibility. Oscar Wilde's work included the comic ghost story *The Canterville Ghost* (1887), collections of literary fairy tales (*The Happy Prince and Other Stories*, 1888; *A House of Pomegranates*, 1891), and most famously his only novel, *The Picture of Dorian Gray* (1891), concerning a dissolute young man whose portrait ages in his stead. M. P. Shiel, who would later produce the classic last-man-on-earth novel *The Purple Cloud*, was notably influenced both by Poe and the Decadent movement in his first two story collections *Prince Zaleski* (1895) and *Shapes in the Fire* (1896). Arguably even more important in terms of influence on later fantasy and horror fiction was the Welsh Arthur Machen, whose classic 1890 story 'The Great God Pan', at the time regarded as scandalous for its implicit sexual content, can now be seen as prefiguring an entire tradition of fantasies involving the survival of older deities in the modern world. Machen followed this with a collection of linked tales, *The Three Impostors*, in 1895 – a notable influence on H. P. Lovecraft – and other works including the novel *The Hill of Dreams* in 1907 and the remarkable essay *Hieroglyphics: A Note upon Ecstasy in Literature* (1902), a critical work touching upon the uses of the fantastic in fiction.

If the nineteenth century began with a rediscovery of folk and fairy tale materials, largely influenced by German writers from Musäus to the Grimm brothers, it ended with a renewed interest in returning to these same materials. In 1888, the Irish poet W. B. Yeats, whose own poetry and drama made considerable use of fantastic and mythical sources, produced *Fairy and Folk Tales of the Irish Peasantry*, collected mostly from earlier publications. The following year the Scottish writer and anthropologist Andrew Lang published *The Blue Fairy Book*, inaugurating a series of twelve volumes of 'coloured fairy books' which would continue until *The Lilac Fairy Book* in 1910, selecting hundreds of stories from all over the world, most from previously published sources but some appearing for the first time in English. (Lang also collaborated with H. Rider Haggard on *The World's Desire*, 1890, a sequel to Homer's *Odyssey* cast as an epic fantasy novel.) 1890 saw Joseph Jacobs's *English Fairy Tales*, later followed by *More English Fairy Tales* (1894), *Celtic Fairy Tales* (1892), *Indian Fairy Tales* (1912) and *European Folk and Fairy Tales* (1916). Also in 1890, Sir James George Frazer's influential *The Golden Bough: A Study in Magic and Religion*, was published, a wide-ranging and highly speculative comparative study of myth and religion originally appearing in two volumes but expanding to twelve by its third edition (1906–15), which influenced generations of novelists and poets. Animal fantasies, once regarded as merely a subset of fables or fairy tales, took on a new and more sophisticated literary life with works such as

Rudyard Kipling's *Jungle Books* (1894, 1895) and Kenneth Grahame's *The Wind in the Willows* (1908).

At the same time, a younger generation of writers began developing reputations built largely around specific subgenres of fantasy: F. Anstey (Thomas Anstey Guthrie) with humorous or satirical fantasy (*Vice Versa*, 1882; *The Tinted Venus*, 1885; *The Brass Bottle*, 1900, all of which provided the basis of later stage or film adaptations); Edith Nesbit with a more contemporary style of children's fantasy (*The Story of the Treasure Seekers*, 1898; *Five Children and It*, 1902; *The Phoenix and the Carpet*, 1904); Lord Dunsany (Edward Plunkett) with story collections and novels that pioneered the immersive, invented environments that would later come to be associated with 'high' fantasy (*The Gods of Pegana*, 1905; *The Book of Wonder*, 1912; *The King of Elfland's Daughter*, 1924). Perhaps equally important was the generation of children for whom these and earlier authors, from MacDonald to Morris, were likely early literary experiences: the most famous of the later 'Inklings', J. R. R. Tolkien, C. S. Lewis and Charles Williams, were all born between 1886 and 1898; E. R. Eddison in 1882; Hope Mirrlees in 1887; H. P. Lovecraft in 1890. These were among the direct heirs of the traditions, conventions and ideas about fantasy that evolved during this most self-consciously rationalistic literary eras, and from these materials they arguably forged the lineaments of the contemporary genre.

NOTES

1 *The Spectator*, 419, www.mnstate.edu/gracyk/courses/web%20publishing/ addison419.htm.

2 David Sandner, 'Joseph Addison: The First Critic of the Fantastic', in David Sandner (ed.), *Fantastic Literature: A Critical Reader* (Westport, CT: Praeger, 2004), pp. 316–25.

3 Joseph Addison, *The Spectator*, 411 (21 June 1712).

4 Quoted in Lilian R. Furst, *Romanticism in Perspective* (New York: Humanities Press, 1970), p. 332.

5 Cited in 'Imagination', *Oxford English Dictionary*, 2nd edn (Oxford: Clarendon Press, 1989), vol. VII, p. 669.

6 William Blake, 'A Vision of the Last Judgment', in Geoffrey Keynes (ed.), *William Blake: Complete Writings* (London: Oxford University Press, 1967), p. 604.

7 Samuel Taylor Coleridge, *Biographia Literaria*, excerpted in *Selected Poetry and Prose*, ed. Donald R. Stauffer (New York: Modern Library, 1951), p. 156.

8 *Ibid.*, p. 263.

9 George MacDonald, 'The Fantastic Imagination' (1890), in Sandner (ed.), *Fantastic Literature*, p. 65.

10 Stephen Prickett, *Victorian Fantasy* (Bloomington IN: Indiana University Press, 1979), p. 2.

11 Ruth Amelia Berman, 'Suspending Disbelief: The Development of Fantasy as a Literary Genre in Nineteenth-Century British Fiction as Represented by Four Leading Periodicals: *Edinburgh Review*, *Blackwood's*, *Fraser's*, and *Cornhill*'. PhD dissertation, University of Minnesota, 1979.

12 *Blackwood's Edinburgh Magazine*, September 1818, p. 650. The essay is online at 'The Literary Gothic', www.litgothic.com/Texts/preter.html. Accessed 22 September 2008.

13 Quoted in Donald P. Haase, 'Romantic Theory of the Fantastic', in Frank N. Magill (ed.), *Survey of Modern Fantasy Literature* (Englewood Cliffs, NJ: Salem Press, 1983), vol. V, p. 2251. The essay is online at http://books.google.com/books?id=91TuWRyYEBgC&pg=PA284&lpg=PA270&ots=Up1OjJc2iN&dq=%22on+the+supernatural+in+fictitious+composition&ie=ISO-8859-1&output=html.

14 For much of the material regarding these French translations and theories I am indebted to Hans Kiesow's unpublished research, which he had generously shared through e-mail.

15 Quoted in Gary K. Wolfe, 'Contemporary Theories of the Fantastic', in Magill (ed.), *Survey*, vol. V, p. 2221.

16 George Eliot, *Adam Bede* (1859) (New York: Signet, 1961), p. 176.

17 Both essays are quoted in Jill Lepore, 'Just the Facts, Ma'am: Fake memoirs, factual fictions, and the history of history', *The New Yorker*, 24 March 2008. www.newyorker.com/arts/critics/atlarge/2008/03/24/080324crat_atlarge_lepore.

18 Farah Mendlesohn, *Rhetorics of Fantasy* (Middletown, CT: Wesleyan University Press, 2008).

19 C. S. Lewis, *Surprised by Joy: The Shape of My Early Life* (New York: Harcourt, Brace, 1955), p. 181.

2

ADAM ROBERTS

Gothic and horror fiction

The reputation of the Goths has followed a strange trajectory, such that the adjective formed from their name now means (variously): a people; their language; a medieval style of architecture; the modern revival of that architectural style; a late eighteenth- and early nineteenth-century mode of novelistic literature (the chief concern of this essay); a sanserif printing font; and a contemporary youth subculture centred on a particular sort of rock music and a penchant for black clothing and make-up. We might begin by asking: who were they?

Edward Thompson provides a textbook answer: the Goths were 'a Germanic people who left their original homes in southern Scandinavia about the beginning of the Christian era, and settled around the lower Vistula [in Poland] . . . in the period AD 150–200 they migrated to the lands north of the Black Sea and in 238 at latest they began to raid the Roman Empire'.[1] They divided into two groups: Visigoths and Ostrogoths. The Visigoths, who warred and settled along the Danube, moved into Greece, and thence to Italy, where (under the leadership of Alaric I) they sacked Rome in 410, finally settling in southern France. The Ostrogoths built a large empire in what is now the Ukraine, and after various military victories their king, Theodoric, ruled Italy from the beginning of the sixth century. By the end of the sixth century rule in Italy passed to another Scandinavian/Germanic people, the Lombards; but by this time the Goths had colonized much of Europe and, through interbreeding with other peoples, became simply European.

This little narrative may seem to have little to do with the writing of that mode of fantastic fiction characterized by David Punter:

> When thinking of the Gothic novel, a set of characteristics springs readily to mind: an emphasis on portraying the terrifying, a common insistence on archaic settings, a prominent use of the supernatural . . . Gothic fiction is the fiction of the haunted castle, of heroines preyed upon by unspeakable terrors, of the blackly lowering villain, of ghosts, vampires, monsters and werewolves.[2]

Indeed, for most commentators the connection between the Goths and the Gothic novel is arbitrary or simply non-existent. But bear with me. The word *Goth*, according to etymologists, is derived from a Proto-Germanic word, **geutan*, meaning 'to pour' or 'to flow':[3] and Gothic literature, like the Gothic people, has demonstrated a restless fluidity of situation, and signification that is as much a part of its meaning as its more familiar props, setting and metageneric conventions. This essay seeks, taking this as a starting point, to explore some of the currents of that Gothic flow as they relate to fantasy.

The conventional way to draw the connection between the Goths and the Gothic novel is through architecture: from the 1140s, with the rebuilding of the French Abbey of Saint-Denis by Abbot Suger, until the sixteenth century, a new architectural style of pointed-arches and elaborate ornamentation replaced the round arches and plainer look of the Romanesque that had previously dominated European architecture. Thereafter it fell from favour, and a more austere neoclassicism became the order of the day. Janetta Rebold Benton notes that 'in its own time' Gothic was known as 'the French style' but that 'sixteenth-century Italians thought the style barbaric, preferring instead the classical. Because the best known of the barbaric tribes were the Goths, the style was called Gothic, i.e. barbaric, the implication of the term definitely derogative.'[4] Neoclassicism, with its aesthetic emphasis upon clarity, precision and the subordination of contemporary art and literature to the examples of ancient Greece and Rome, connected with the European scientific and philosophical revolution we call the Enlightenment and was the dominant cultural logic of the later seventeenth and eighteenth centuries. The primary signification of 'Goth' at this time was that of barbarous anti-enlightenment. When George Berkeley, the English rationalist and philosopher, pondered 'whether every enemy to learning be not a Goth? And whether every such Goth among us be not an enemy to the country?', he was using the sackers of Rome as a shorthand for 'enemy of classicism'.[5] Bishop Berkeley attacked Newton and Leibnitz as 'infidels' because of their invention of mathematical calculus – the 'fluxion', as it was then called – considering its flow of infinitesimals corrosive of the solid foundations of Christianity. Poet William Cowper in 1782 praised John Milton in similar terms of enlightenment and order:

> Thus genius rose and set at order'd times . . .
> He sunk in Greece, in Italy he rose;
> And, tedious years of gothic darkness pass'd,
> Emerged all splendour in our isle at last.[6]

But even as he wrote this, Cowper's banishment of the barbaric violence and irrationalism of 'gothic darkness' was being contradicted by a revival of interest in Gothic aesthetics; and although this began, certainly, more out of romantic and slightly misty-eyed nostalgia for a medieval past than an outright hostility to the values of Enlightenment neoclassicism, it soon tapped a more barbaric cultural energy. In the words of Kenneth Clark, in 1750 the Middle Ages 'was still one dark welter from which the Goths alone emerged with a convenient name'.[7] The old-fashioned focus of Gothic fiction (something which in turn informed the self-conscious medievalism of the dominant branch of later fantasy) was more a matter of mood – of, indeed, emotional affect – than of strictly historical or archaeological interest. When Horace Walpole, in 1748, renovated his villa at Strawberry Hill in west London in a self-consciously old-fashioned 'Gothic' style, he was aiming not at restoring medieval architecture so much as augmenting modern building with a glamour and modish fulsomeness coded 'medieval'. The same impulse was behind his decision to write a short novel in the Gothic mode.

One thing that almost all scholars of the Gothic agree upon is that it was this short novel, *The Castle of Otranto* (1764), which initiated the late eighteenth-century vogue for Gothic fiction. The anonymous first edition opens with a preface that presents the book as an actual eleventh- or twelfth-century story translated into English for the first time and apologizes for the supernatural elements of the narrative: 'Some apology for it is necessary. Miracles, visions, necromancies, dreams, and other preternatural events, are exploded now even from romances. That was not the case when our author wrote.'[8] The immediate popularity of the book quickly prompted a second edition: Walpole added a second preface confessing to authorship and defending his tale against critics by explicitly siding with Shakespeare over neoclassical *philosophe* Voltaire. Overleaf is the third edition's title-page.

That the subtitle is printed in a slightly larger font than the title is not unusual for eighteenth-century novels; although of course it tends to draw out what would later become the generic quality, identifying the novel strongly with a signifier coded 'barbarous' and 'old-fashioned'. The Latin quoted does nothing to reassure the reader. It is from a portion of Horace's *Art of Poetry* in which bad writing is castigated: 'meaningless images are formulated in such a way that neither head nor foot can be rendered into a single shape'. Is this to be what the novel provides? A one-word answer might be: yes. In fact Walpole's epigraph can be read not as wry self-deprecation so much as self-knowing celebration of the anarchic imaginative possibilities his new sort of writing permits him – Walpole, after all, was also called Horace. *Otranto* is a book that literally disposes disembodied heads and

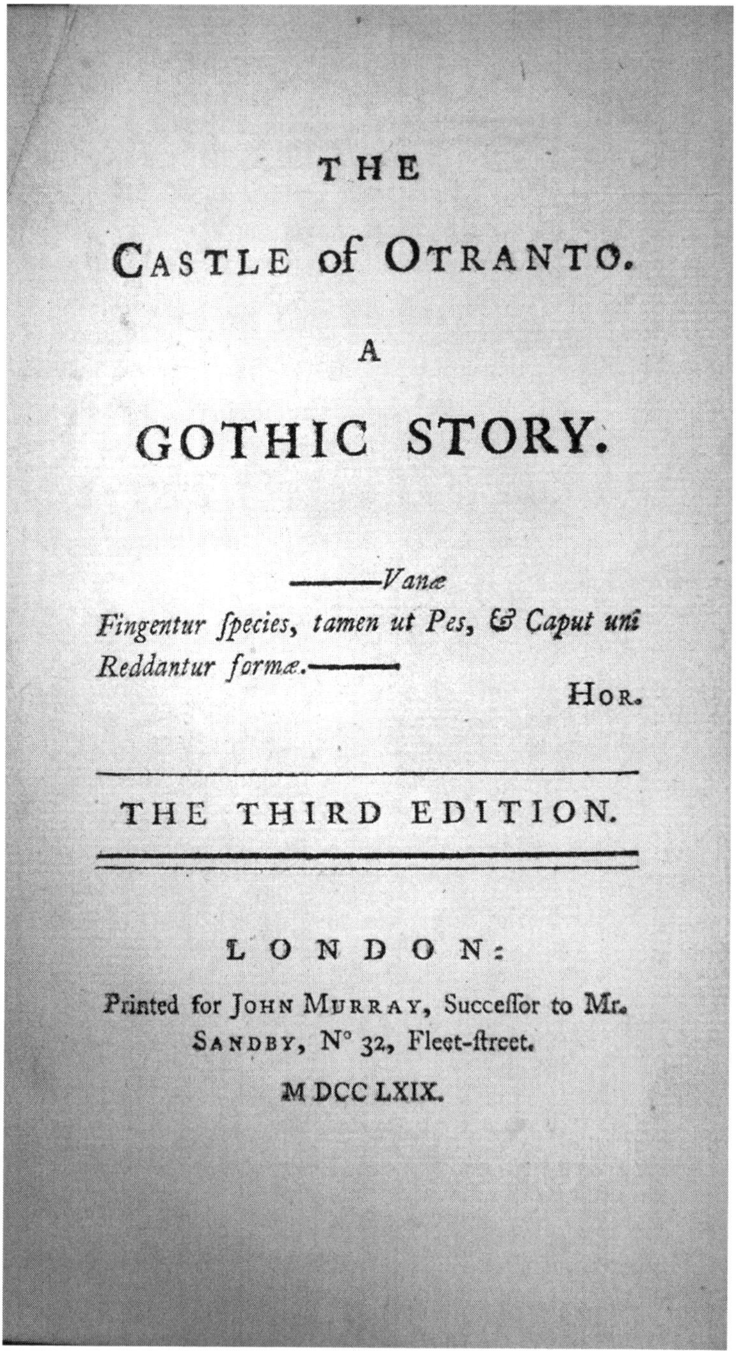

THE

CASTLE of OTRANTO.

A

GOTHIC STORY.

————*Vanæ*
Fingentur fpecies, tamen ut Pes, & Caput uni
Reddantur formæ.————

HOR.

THE THIRD EDITION.

L O N D O N:

Printed for JOHN MURRAY, Succeffor to Mr.
SANDBY, Nº 32, Fleet-ftreet.

MDCCLXIX.

Fig. 1 Title-page of the third edition of *The Castle of Otranto*.

limbs and disposes of its characters and plot to resist the amalgamation of either into a readily comprehensible whole.

Otranto is a rather hectic story, as often laughable as alarming; yet for all that packing considerable imaginative punch. Manfred is the tyrant of Otranto, in southern Italy. The marriage of his sickly son Conrad to the beautiful Isabella, taking place in his castle, is interrupted when a gigantic helmet appears from nowhere to crush Conrad to death: 'oh!' gasps a servant, somewhat bathetically. 'The helmet! The helmet!' (4). It has come, magically, from the titanic statue of the dead Old Prince Alonso; other elements from the statue also manifest themselves about the castle. When wicked Manfred (who poisoned Alonso to seize the throne) decides that he will divorce his wife and marry Isabella himself, the portrait of his grandfather comes alive and beckons him away. Terrified, Isabella flees through a pungently described subterranean vault, and meets our hero Theodore, the true heir. There's a good deal of toing and froing, mysterious friars, ghostly apparitions, fighting and the revelation of awful secrets before Manfred mistakenly stabs his own daughter to death, his castle collapses and the giant statue flies up in the air. Manfred confesses his crimes and dedicates himself to a religious life; Theodore marries Isabella and rules Otranto as rightful prince.

In *Otranto* we find, in nascent form, many of the props and conventions that were to reappear in the scores of novels published at the height of the Gothic vogue (from the late 1780s through, roughly, to the end of the century): moody atmospherics, picturesque and sublime scenery, darkness, buried crimes (especially murderous and incestuous crimes) revealed, and most of all a spectral supernatural focus. Many imitators tried to follow Walpole's commercial success by littering their novels with similar props, settings and conventions – the haunted castle, the night-time graveyard, the Byronic villain and so on – although such a mode of apprehending the success of the book is necessarily reductive. James Watt makes the point that 'the genre of Gothic' is 'itself a relatively modern construct' (he dates its creation to critics working in the early twentieth century) and notes that the novels typically gathered together as Gothic vary greatly and manifest 'often antagonistic relations' to one another.[9] More, *Otranto*'s success depended less upon the specificities of its spooky tricks and treats, all of which were standards of older romance (people have shared ghost stories since stories have been told, after all) and more upon a unique dynamic or quality the novel focused in itself: the same thing that Freud – whose theories have more often than any other been applied to interpreting the appeal of Gothic – labelled *uncanny*.

Fred Botting tries to put his finger on this quality when he writes that 'Gothic signifies the literature of excess'; but he doesn't specify the sort of excess he is talking about (excessive what? Alexander Pope's poetry might be called excessively poised and classical, but is hardly Gothic). He continues: 'it appears in the awful obscurity that haunted eighteenth-century rationality...[its] atmospheres – gloomy and mysterious',[10] which might give the unwary reader the notion that he means excessively vague. Vagueness isn't a good way of talking about Gothic. It would be better to say that the strength of Gothic literature was in smashing the portals of classical restraint and grabbing at the intensities and vigour of a form specifically understood to be new.

Obscurity, of course, was part of it; and certainly more than one contemporary attempted to dignify the popularity of this form of literature by connecting it with the philosophy of the sublime – a venerable philosophical theory of conceptual elevation and refined aesthetic apprehension given new impetus in the eighteenth century by the youthful Edmund Burke's *On the Sublime and the Beautiful* (1757). For Burke, art was sublime if it evoked a sort of refining terror, or horror; if it filled people with awe; if it gave our mortal brains a searing peek at infinity. It was for him, in other words, a fundamentally *religious* matter. The sublimity evoked by a book, painting or landscape was a particular blend of inspiration and fear that had to do with the scale of representation, and the transcendent possibilities. Obscurity and the fragmentary were important to it because by their nature they hinted at the unrepresentable – God – instead of purporting actually to apprehend it. There was for Burke a gender component too: beauty, that other category of the aesthetically worthwhile (though for Burke small-beer by comparison to the sublime) was not only smaller-scale but also effeminate. A well-tended garden might be beautiful; the Alps are sublime; a river or a lake might be beautiful; the ocean is sublime. Day is beautiful, the night is sublime. Woman is beautiful; man is sublime.

Burke was not writing about Gothic as such (his treatise antedates the vogue) but his ideas were, and have continued to be, taken by defenders of the mode precisely because they offer a way of dignifying an otherwise derided genre. The scares, shocks and thrills Gothic provides are precisely *not* cheap (the argument goes); they are, in an admittedly populist way, attempts to open the mind to the awe and terror of the genuine sublime. It is a case that has continued to be made, *mutatis mutandi*, with Gothic's generic descendents: science fiction's 'sense of wonder' is in effect a straight translation of the Burkean sublime into a cosmic, scientific and materialist idiom; fantasy's 'magic' is understood as more than merely a narrative device: readers picking up fantasy titles in search of a 'magical' or 'Faerie' mood are acting upon a desire to be aesthetically sublimated into a state of mind that does not admit of rational reduction.

It is not that this philosophical recuperation of Gothic as a mode is in itself wrongheaded. But it is for all that an attempt to bring respectability to a disreputable mode of writing; a desire to dress the barbarians in togas and assimilate them to classical dignity. To reread *Otranto* in the hope of encountering the sublime is, largely, to be disappointed. It is, in fact, a novel that does a weird violence to many of our expectations, barbarically violating classical poise, unity, harmony, propriety, plausibility and taste. By the end of the book the Italian location of Otranto (once ruled by the Italian-sounding Alonso) becomes the kingdom of Theodore, a man named after that king of the Ostrogoths who conquered classical Italy.

The desire to elevate Gothic with the philosophical seriousness of Burke's sublime is in part a desire to order and control the mode. When Clara Reeve published *The Champion of Virtue: a Gothic Story* in 1777 (it was reprinted the following year under the title *The Old English Baron*) she conceded in her preface that her novel was 'the literary offspring of *The Castle of Otranto*, written upon the same plan'. But she nevertheless attempted to distance her work from what she saw as the main flaw of Walpole's work: its *unfixity* of tone, the way it mixes the darkly thrilling with the merely risible:

> We can conceive, and allow of, the appearance of a ghost; we can even dispense with an enchanted sword and helmet: but then they must keep within certain limits of credibility. A sword so large as to require a hundred men to lift it; a helmet that by its own weight forces a passage through a courtyard, into an arched vault, big enough for a man to go through; a picture that walks out of its frame; a skeleton ghost in a hermit's cowl: – when your expectation is wound up to the highest pitch, these circumstances take it down with a witness, destroy the work of imagination and, instead of attention, excite laughter. I was both surprised and vexed to find the enchantment dissolved, which I wished might continue to the end of the book; and several of its readers have confessed the same disappointment to me.[11]

Reeve's novel, like many that followed during the great vogue for Gothic literature in the 1780s and 1790s, was simultaneously a work of creative imagination and a critical engagement with Walpole's originary text: a deliberate attempt to rectify the perceived faults in the original. In Reeve's case this resulted in a plodding historical fiction set in the England of Henry VI, a work that, whilst not purging itself of all supernatural elements, does limit them to one – haunting by ghosts – conventional and traditional enough not to upset her careful guarding of the borderline of tone and genre. Reeve seeks thereby to avoid the dangers identified with Walpole's proliferation of fantastical signifiers: that of bursting the limits of good taste. That Reeve's is a dull novel where Walpole's, though bizarre, embodies a palpable eldritch energy has little to do with the respective talents of these authors as writers, and everything to do with Walpole's implicit understanding that the strength of his fiction lies in its *transgressive* intensity.

Reeve sought, in other words, to inoculate Gothic literature against the virus of ludicrousness: but this was, in an important sense, to miss the point. Certainly the continued success of *Otranto* owed as much to its almost harlequin quality as it did to more serious-minded dilute preparations of the Burkean sublime, something its many adaptations to the stage tend to make plain.

Gothic is often genuinely horrific and full of terrors. Fans of the Gothic (as of fantasy) genuinely prize the uncanny tendrils it can drag across the tender membrane of their imagination. But at the same time – and in ways that are, strange to say, specifically linked to that effect – Gothic (as fantasy) *is* ludicrous. Most modes of literature have been mocked and pastiched, but crime, or love-romance, or the cowboy novel (for example) have not provided writers with whole careers simply writing parodies of the form. Fantasy has. This is, indeed, a rich tradition, tolerated within the genre perhaps as a demonstration that its fans 'can take a joke' but actually speaking to a much deeper cultural logic. Diana Wynne Jones' *The Tough Guide to Fantasyland* (1997) is a notable text in this regard; Terry Pratchett's important Discworld novels (1983–present) are even more significant. These marvellous novels began as parodies of the Fritz Leiber/Robert E. Howard school of heroic barbarian, and although they developed into something more than mere parodies they remain profoundly in touch with the unique combination of wonder and ludicrousness at the heart of fantasy as a genre. Less notable are the serial parodies of J. K. Rowling and J. R. R. Tolkien written by (respectively) Michael Gerber and the pseudonymous 'A. R. R. Roberts', although the fact of their existence, and many texts like them, is revealing. It is as if emphasizing the ludicrous aspects of the genre, rather than denigrating or diminishing the mode, actually *augments* it. Less robust cultural phenomena would be exterminated by such mockery; fantasy, on the contrary, thrives upon it.

This is in turn reflects in the ways in which Gothic developed. Most of the very many Gothic tales published in England alone between 1780 and 1820 are now wholly forgotten. The ones that have survived, and which informed the developing traditions of fantastical, science-fictional and horror writing through the nineteenth and twentieth centuries, are the ones that most fully inhabit the sack-of-Rome, sprawling, rhizomatic, trans-rational energies of Walpole's form.

In Ann Radcliffe's highly successful *The Mysteries of Udolpho* (1794) the orphaned heroine (Emily St Aubert) is separated from her true love (the handsome Valancourt) and sequestered by her wicked aunt in the titular castle, where her aunt's husband, the haughty and brooding Montoni, attempts to take control of her fortune. Emily is terrorized by a number of seemingly supernatural occurrences, but by the end of the novel all of these have been explained either as coincidences or as deliberate attempts by Montoni to intimidate Emily. The novel finishes, of course, with Montoni vanquished and Emily marrying Valancourt; and this narrative trajectory from irrational terrors to rational explanation, from the threat of transgression to the thumping reinscription of conventional values, marks the book's ambition as in effect *anti*-Gothic. (Radcliffe ends on an ethically utilitarian note: 'O! useful may it be to have shewn, that, though the vicious can sometimes pour affliction upon the good, their power is transient and their punishment certain.')[12] But the book's considerable commercial success was not a function of this didacticism. Rather readers loved the prolonged quasi-erotic suspense of the heroine's predicament, and more importantly Radcliffe's considerable if over-boiled descriptive powers, her ability to evoke landscape in particular. Radcliffe's own subtitle identifies the novel as 'A Romance, Interspersed with Some Pieces of Poetry'; and the poetic effort to render an exotic, other and sublime southern European locale leaves its trace in the reader's imagination when other features of the strained narrative have long gone. John Keats (in a letter to J. H. Reynolds, 14 March 1818) responds to Radcliffe's power of landscape even, as Gittings argues in his introduction to his letters, he precisely 'parodies' it: 'I am going among Scenery whence I intend to tip you the Damosel Radcliffe – I'll cavern you, and grotto you, and waterfall you, and wood you, and water you, and immense-rock you, and tremendous sound you, and solitude you. I'll make a lodgement on your glacis by a row of Pines, and storm your covered way with bramble Bushes.'[13] 'Damosel' nods to the insufficient authenticity of Radcliffe's historicizing (the faux-antiquity of her setting), but the running-on itinerizing of props from the repertoire of the Burkean sublime captures the feel of Radcliffe very well. More, this world-building – very much not limited to castles and subterranean passageways, as Keats's version makes plain – is one key way in which the Romantic Gothic opened imaginative spaces for fantasy in the broader sense.

Lewis's *The Monk* (1796), on the other hand, pours and flows through a number of quasi-pornographic intensities: Ambrosio, the hitherto virtuous titular cleric, is tempted by Matilda (herself disguised as a monk) into a sexual relationship. This debauchment leads to further lubriciously rendered sexually violent transgressions, including the rape and murder of the virtuous Antonia. Matilda is eventually revealed as being an agent of Satan, and the Devil himself makes an appearance late in the tale – Ambrosio signs away his soul in his own blood – in order to gloat in typically gnashing, over-strung style: 'Hark, Ambrosio, whilst I unveil your crimes! You have shed the blood of two innocents; Antonia and Elvira perished by your hand. That Antonia whom you violated was your Sister! That Elvira whom you murdered, gave you birth!'[14] This climactic litany of violations of taboo retains its capacity to shock, and the nature of that shock is perhaps trangressive of more than conventional morality. When Satan goes on, amongst a welter of Capitalized Words and Exclamation Marks – 'Inhuman Parricide! Incestuous Ravisher! Tremble at the extent of your offences!' (440) – we may wonder whether the excitement of the moment, and the nature of the trembling frisson to which it adverts, isn't precisely the point of the novel. It is true the book was widely condemned, and in places banned, on first publication; although by the same token it was enormously successful – not so much a paradox, this, as the typical dialectic reaction to the spectacle of the sack of respectable classical pieties. *The Monk* is not genuinely shocking (which is to say, it is not like Goya's *Los desastres de la guerra* etchings) because it retains, in its very exuberance, a sense of the way dark sublimity and ludicrousness so easily interpenetrate.

Certainly the early years of the nineteenth century, as the first flush of the Gothic vogue in fiction was starting to burn itself out, saw as many parodies as original novels. Gothic in its original form had become an overcrowded and derivative genre. New novels gave themselves elbow room either by embroidering more extreme and shocking detail upon Gothic tropes, or else by reverting back upon the form as parody. The most famous example of this latter is Jane Austen's *Northanger Abbey* (written 1798, published 1818), a work that is of a piece with all Austen's novels in being, at root, an exercise in the subordination of sensibility to sense. Gothic here functions solely as an index to the heroine's immaturity. Eaton Stannard Barrett's *The Heroine, or Adventures of Cherubina* (1813) played the mode straightforwardly for laughs.[15] More vigorous was Thomas Love Peacock's *Nightmare Abbey* (1818), a work at least awake to the rhizomatic possibilities of invention and imaginative frisson the mode it parodies enables. Another influential late Gothic text was Charles Maturin's version of the 'wandering Jew' myth, *Melmoth the Wanderer* (1820): a text whose over-arching narrative – the title character has made a pact with the Devil and, to his chagrin, is unable to die – pours and flows widely through myriad embedded tales, registers, modes and geographical locations. It would not be right to describe *Melmoth the Wanderer* as a parody, exactly; except in the rather specialized sense that Walpole's *Otranto* already reads like a parody of the form that went on to initiate it.

Of all the Gothic novels from this period the one that proved most influential was Mary Shelley's *Frankenstein*. Scientist Victor Frankenstein brings an eight-foot-tall artificial man to life; terrified by his own achievement, he abandons his creation and temporarily loses his memory. The creature (it is never named) blunders about the world, learning from its experiences, mostly the experience of the hostility of other people towards its hideous appearance, something it pays back to society in acts of murderous violence. Much of this tale, not only its fantastical premise, edges the absurd: for example, the creature learns not only to speak but also (ludicrously) to read and write by eavesdropping unnoticed on a peasant family. But nevertheless there is genuine pathos in the monster's loneliness, and a flavour of sublime grandeur in the trans-European trek it – and its maker, Frankenstein – undertake, ending up in the enormous wastes of the North Pole.

In a way more significant than the novel itself is the considerable influence *Frankenstein* exerted upon nineteenth- and twentieth-century culture; the monster flowing and pouring into a variety of other cultural forms, from stage adaptations and allusions via Carlyle, Dickens, Marx and into the twentieth century in cinematic, televisual cartoon and general cultural form.[16] These innumerable adaptations, which of course have rendered the story very well known, reflect both the continuing appeal of Shelley's core conceit and the ability of Gothic itself to flow into other modes of cultural representation.

More, Shelley's novel can be read equally as proto-science fiction (with the monster as the product of a strictly scientific endeavour) *or* horror (with the monster as an irrational eruption of the uncanny into ordinary life. Later Gothic novels spun variations out of their supernatural monsters, introducing different varieties of monster, as well as vampires – Polidori's *The Vampyre* (1819), or much more famously Bram Stoker's *Dracula* (1897) – and shape-shifting beast-men, such as George W. M. Reynolds's *Wagner the Wehr-Wolf* (1847) and Stevenson's *Strange Case of Dr. Jekyll and Mr. Hyde* (1886). What all these monsters have in common is their protean ability to transform, to move from unexceptional 'human' behaviour to barbaric, violent, transgressive and unfettered. In this respect they are emblematizations of the protean force of the Gothic novel itself; a form capable of being associated with supernatural excess, but one that proved easily capable of assuming the shape of mundane Victorian domestic fiction. Many of the most successful nineteenth-century novels contain, coiled within them, a beating Gothic heart. In Emily Brontë's *Wuthering Heights* family life and love receives a Byronic injection of Gothicized passion and terror in the form of Heathcliff; Dickens's novels try with varying degrees of success to contain grotesque, bizarre and eruptive urban forces within the narrative container of middle-class trajectories of life and love; Christina Rossetti wrote a great many controlled poems of Christian-devotional and confessional type, but is remembered today for the vibrantly realized children's-Gothic of her long poem *Goblin Market* (1862). Almost any mainstream Victorian writer can be characterized along these lines. By the time of John Ruskin's influential account of 'The Nature of Gothic' (1853) it is clear that 'Gothic' had become a synonym for 'Victorian', and indeed for 'northern European': Ruskin is explicit that his focus is 'this grey, shadowy, many-pinnacled image of the Gothic spirit within us', and his intention to '[discern] what fellowship there is between it and our Northern hearts'.[17]

This adaptive colonization of other modes also manifested itself on the Continent. Late eighteenth-century European equivalents lack the distinctive barbarism of English Gothic. For instance, the French 'roman noir' was epitomised by François d'Arnaud (1718–1805), who specialized in rather stately, 'sombre' novels that were (in Théophile Civrays' words) 'imités de l'anglais' whilst also being 'surchargés de déclamation et de sensibilité', in the words of Rousseau.[18] Germany was closer to the English situation with the 'Sturm und Drang' movement (the phrase means 'Storm and Drive' or 'Storm and Urge'); a movement particularly associated with Goethe, Schiller and Friedrich Maximilian Klinger, which was as fascinated with medieval culture, trangressive energies and passion as English writers of the period. But these works very often lack the specifically supernatural component that feeds into fantasy writing more generally conceived, and Sturm und Drang was much shorter-lived than Gothic ('After 1780,' Ernst Rose notes, it 'had practically passed').[19]

There are, of course, powerful examples of Continental European Gothic novels, but they all date from later in the nineteenth century and follow in the train of a specifically English vogue. E. T. A. Hoffmann's *Die Elixiere des Teufels* (1815) is in effect a rewriting of Lewis's *The Monk* (something the novel itself acknowledges). In France Balzac admired Maturin and wrote a necessarily derivative sequel to *Melmoth the Wanderer* (*Melmoth Réconcilié*, 1835); and Théophile Gautier picked up the idea of a supernatural Egyptian Mummy from Jane Loudon's slightly far-fetched *The Mummy! A Tale of the Twenty-Second Century* (1827) to write his own Gothic and historical versions of the trope ('Le Pied de momie', 1840; *Le Roman de la momie*, 1858). The Gothic elements of Polish author Jan Potocki's French-language *Manuscrit trouvé à Saragosse* (published after his death in 1815) are also parasitical upon earlier models. Guy de Maupassant's chilling 'La Horla' (1887), about an individual effectively driven mad by extra-terrestrial powers, combines Gothic with science-fictional logics. In Spain Benito Galdós's *La Sombra* (1870), 'a work that relies heavily on conventions of the Gothic tradition',[20] harks all the way back to Walpole, as the protagonist Anselmo terrorizes the wife he believes has been unfaithful to him with a portrait of Paris, from Greek myth, magically come alive.

What I am talking about, then, is a process of cultural colonization, and one that specifically maps out the territory in which modern fantasy was later to grow. The Gothic was one of the major vehicles by which Romanticism poured out to dominate literature – and, although it would be foolish to pretend to be able to define *that* cultural form in a single phrase, it is not out of place to stress the link between Gothic and Romantic aesthetic logics. Romanticism is, amongst other things, the barbaric energies of an imagined past pouring and flowing disruptively through previously established canons of classical taste: a replacement of the classical Mediterranean world with a northern medievalized one as the ideal in art. Heinrich Heine's 1849 definition of 'the Romantic school' is relevant here, not least as a way of characterizing the subsequent evolution of Fantasy: 'die Wiedererweckung der Poesie des Mittelalters, wie sie sich in dessen Liedern, Bild- und Bauwerken, in Kunst und Leben, manifestirt hatte'.[21] This, in their different ways, is what Bram Stoker and William Morris both were doing at the end of the nineteenth century. This, 'in Kunst *und* Leben', epitomizes Tolkien's ethico-aesthetic project, and the multiple interconnections between late twentieth-century fantasy and alternative and environmentalist lifestyles.

Which brings this essay back, finally, to Gothic, and the strange trajectory of its reputation. It began as a mode of fantastic writing confined to a small portion of land off the northern European coastline. But it poured; it flowed across the continent, overthrowing cultural logics predicated upon the ordered solidity of classical models and bringing a disruptive, sometimes violent and transgressive vigour. By the end of the century it had changed Greece and Rome from the rather frigid stasis of Winckelmann to the furious, sexually liberatory, sacred violence of Nietzsche, Swinburne, Wilde and E. R. Dodds's *The Greeks and the Irrational* (1959) – a reimagining of Western culture's classical heritage that is, in effect, a Gothicization of its cultural assumptions. But, having sacked Rome, it spread further, under two different names. Visigothically speaking, a materialist Gothic-fantastic proliferated and came to be called (in the twentieth century) science fiction: a great tribe of works that find quasi-sublime obscurity not in dark woods, subterranean caverns and middle-European night-times but in space – which rationalized Gothic monsters as aliens; and which sensed wonder in the terrors of the Gothic uncanny. Science fiction pretended to replace Gothic fiction's passion for antiquity with a passion for imagined futures, although these – Asimov's Roman-imperial Galactic Empire, Frank Herbert's medievalized *Dune* universe – were often the past passing itself off as the future. One of the consistent lessons of Gothic is that, though we may try, we cannot escape the past. Ostrogothically, though – and, eventually, to even greater commercial success – a different sort of Gothic spread (flowed, poured) over the cultural landscape: one that maintained Gothic's archaic focus and built its uncanny into a world-logic that defied scientific reduction. It turned its back, largely, on the possibilities of Greek and Roman myth and took up instead specifically northern European portfolio of stories and archetypes. Relishing the medievalism of the Gothic outlook as a specific and barbed critique of modernity, as in the fantastical writing of Morris, Lewis and Tolkien; inhabiting gloomy, ornate architectural castles like Mervyn Peake and T. H. White; or emphasizing the horror of the unspeakable and obscure as in Poe, Bram Stoker's *Dracula* and Lovecraft's Cthulhu Mythos. By this point Gothic fiction had interbred with so many other cultural modes and genres as to became, effectively, simply Literature.

NOTES

1 Edward Arthur Thompson, 'The Goths', in N. G. L. Hammond and H. H. Scullard (eds.), *The Oxford Classical Dictionary*, 2nd edn (Oxford University Press, 1970), p. 472. One of the editors wished to point out that this 'textbook answer' is probably quite wrong: see Edward James, *Europe's Barbarians, AD 200–600* (London: Longman, 2009).

2 David Punter, *The Literature of Terror: A History of Gothic Fiction from 1765 to the Present Day* (New York: Longman, 1980), p. 1.

3 See Julius Pokorny, *Indogermanisches etymologisches Wörterbuch*, 2 vols. (Bern/Munich: Francke, 1947–66).

4 Janetta Rebold Benton, *Art of the Middle Ages* (London: Thames and Hudson, 2002), p. 11.

5 George Berkeley, *The Querist: containing Several Queries Proposed to the Consideration of the Public* (Dublin, 1735), p. 42.

6 William Cowper, 'Table Talk' (1782), in *Table Talk, and Other Poems* (London, 1825), p. 20.

7 Kenneth Clark, *The Gothic Revival*, 3rd edn (Harmondsworth: Penguin, 1962), p. 24.

8 Horace Walpole, *The Castle of Otranto: A Gothic Story*, 3rd edn (London, 1769), p. vii.

9 James Watt, *Contesting the Gothic: Fiction, Genre, and Cultural Conflict, 1764–1832* (Cambridge University Press, 1999), p. 1.

10 Fred Botting, *Gothic* (London: Routledge, 1995), p. 1.

11 Clara Reeve, *The Champion of Virtue: a Gothic Story* (1777; reprinted 1778 as *The Old English Baron*), pp. iv–v.

12 Ann Radcliffe, *The Mysteries of Udolpho* (1794), ed. Bonamy Dobrée and Frederick Garber (Oxford University Press, 1980), p. 672.

13 Robert Gittings (ed.), *Letters of John Keats* (Oxford University Press, 1970), p. 75.

14 Matthew Lewis, *The Monk*, ed. Howard Anderson (Oxford University Press, 1973), p. 439.

15 See David A. Kent and D. R. Ewen, *Romantic Parodies: 1797–1831* (London and Toronto: Fairleigh Dickinson University Press, 1992), pp. 101–11.

16 See Chris Baldick, *In Frankenstein's Shadow: Myth, Monstrosity and Nineteenth-Century Writing* (Oxford: Clarendon Press, 1987).

17 John Ruskin, 'The Nature of Gothic', in *The Stones of Venice: Volume the Second, The Sea-Stories* (London, 1853), pp. 151–231, at p. 153.

18 Théophile Civrays, 'Arnaud', in François Mourreau (ed.), *Dictionnaire des lettres françaises: le XVIII siècle* (Paris: Fayard 1995), p. 87.

19 Ernst Rose, *A History of German Literature* (London: Peter Owen, 1961), p. 162.

20 Sylvia López, 'The Gothic Tradition in Galdós's *La Sombra*', *Hispania*, 81 (1998), pp. 509–18, at p. 509.

21 Jeffrey L. Sammons, *Heinrich Heine: Alternative Perspectives 1985–2002* (Munich: Königshausen and Neumann, 2006), p. 25.

3

PAUL KINCAID

American fantasy 1820–1950

To early European visitors, America was a land of the fantastic. Their reports were full of strange people, weird foodstuffs, incredible riches. Such travellers' tales inevitably became the basis of literature about America which, during the sixteenth and seventeenth centuries, was often written to advertise colonial ventures by people who had never been there. During the first 300 years of European settlement in America, settlers primarily saw themselves as British, French or Spanish rather than as American, and what literature there was, therefore, tended to continue such fanciful forms, or to follow European models, subject matter and sensibilities. By the time of American independence, however, journals featuring American poets, essayists and short story writers were being published in New York, Boston and Philadelphia.

Of the first generation of American novelists who used the Gothic mode around the time of the Revolution and in its immediate aftermath, the most significant was probably Charles Brockden Brown. Brown absorbed the Gothic sensibilities and radical perspectives of writers such as Mary Wollstonecraft and William Godwin. His reading informed a series of startling, often violent novels which appeared over a very short period at the end of the century. The first published was *Wieland; or, the Transformation* (1798), in which the title character is driven to madness and murder by a malevolent ventriloquist who makes Wieland believe he is hearing the voice of God. In *Edgar Huntly; or, Memoirs of a Sleep-Walker* (1799), Huntly sets out to find a murderer but, after a mysterious episode of sleep walking, discovers that the real villains are American Indians who committed the crime to foment a war against the settlers.

Although they contained nothing overtly supernatural, Brown's novels were rich with the menace and mystery of the Gothic, and his work would have a direct influence on later writers as varied as Mary Shelley and Edgar Allan Poe. Brown's manipulation of history and romance to produce dramatic tales set in a distinctive American landscape would also inspire James

Fenimore Cooper, whose Leatherstocking novels, beginning with *The Pioneers* (1823), would begin the mythologizing of the American frontier that has been a consistent feature of American literature to the present day, in both the fantastic and mainstream. As a leading literary figure in early nineteenth-century New York, Brown encouraged a number of younger writers, most notably Washington Irving, with whom the story of American fantasy really begins.

Irving is a significant but curious figure in the history of American fantasy, not least because of the way he would elide truth and fiction. He used numerous pseudonyms, and he prepared the way for his first book, *A History of New-York from the Beginning of the World to the End of the Dutch Dynasty, by Diedrich Knickerbocker* (1809), by anonymously placing missing person notices in New York newspapers for Knickerbocker, and another notice supposedly from a hotelier saying that if Knickerbocker failed to pay his bill he would publish the manuscript that Knickerbocker had left behind. The *History* was as much fancy as fact, but was an immediate success. In 1815, Irving moved to England and there produced his greatest literary success, *The Sketch Book of Geoffrey Crayon, Gent*. Published in numerous instalments and with different contents in Britain and America, this was primarily a compendium of essays on and vignettes of English life, including a number of pieces about Christmas that would provide a model for the version of Christmas presented by Dickens in *The Pickwick Papers* (1837). *The Sketch Book* also included a ghost story, 'The Spectre Bridegroom' (1819), and the two short stories for which Irving is now best remembered. 'Rip Van Winkle' (1819) tells of a lazy, henpecked farmer who falls in with a strange crew one day in the mountains and under their influence falls asleep for twenty years, waking to find his wife dead and his hometown transformed. 'The Legend of Sleepy Hollow' (1820) concerns a superstitious schoolteacher who one night encounters what he believes to be the legendary Headless Horseman. Both are based on German tales but relocated to settings, the Catskill Mountains and the little town of Sleepy Hollow near Tarrytown, that Irving had known in his youth. Irving showed his successors that America itself was a suitable and appropriate home for the fantastic; but Edgar Allan Poe, the most important figure in the history of American fantasy before the twentieth century, took up this challenge in only a few of his stories.

Right from his first published story, 'Metzengerstein' (1832), Edgar Allan Poe looked to European settings and themes, in this instance a parody of the Gothic that involved two feuding families in Hungary. In 'Metzengerstein' a horse becomes the embodiment of death, a figure who, in one guise or another, crops up frequently in Poe's more fevered and grotesque tales. Most famously, in 'The Masque of the Red Death', death is a blood-spattered, shrouded figure who silently intrudes on an aristocratic party while the revellers try to ignore the plague raging nearby.

Death hangs over nearly all of Poe's fiction, which takes to an extreme the tropes and devices of the Gothic novel. Often the stories proceed with no more logic than a fever dream. One of his best-known stories, 'The Pit and the Pendulum' (1842), is punctuated by regular blackouts which allow a series of horrors to be introduced and removed without the need for any scene-setting or scene-shifting. Thus our unnamed narrator is arraigned before an unknown court, blackout; the narrator is in a pitch-black cell, blackout; the narrator discovers a fathomless pit at the centre of his cell, blackout; the narrator is strapped to a table with a razor-sharp pendulum descending upon him but effects an escape, blackout; the narrator discovers the walls of his cell closing in, pushing him towards the pit, before at the last moment he is rescued.

At times Poe puts this morbid fascination with death at the services of stories that would be the precursor of the modern detective novel ('The Murders in the Rue Morgue', 1841); at other times he comes closer to science fiction (*The Narrative of Arthur Gordon Pym of Nantucket*, 1838, which leads through gruesome mass killings and cannibalism to end on the portal of a Hollow Earth story); most often, however, Poe's fantasies are driven by images of terror and despair. The same few motifs recur with horrible regularity. The death of a beautiful woman, for instance – which some critics have linked to the death of Poe's wife, Virginia, in 1847 at the age of twenty-five, though the theme was a consistent part of Poe's repertoire even before she began to show symptoms of tuberculosis in 1842 – crops up in 'Berenice' (1835), 'Ligeia' (1838) and 'The Fall of the House of Usher' (1839). This theme is overlaid with a dread of premature burial, the object of something approaching a mass panic in the early and middle years of the nineteenth century, when a corpse might go unburied for weeks or even months to ensure a comatose victim had not been wrongly diagnosed, and when devices by which revived people might communicate from the grave were regularly advertised in the newspapers. This dread would often crop up in the literature of the period, though no author explored it as obsessively as Poe, not only in 'Berenice' and 'The Fall of the House of Usher', but also in 'The Premature Burial' (1844), 'The Cask of Amontillado' (1846) and, obliquely, 'The Tell-Tale Heart' (1843). In 'Berenice' an obsessive young man falls in love with a beautiful woman, but as she slowly dies of some unspecified wasting disease he becomes fixated on the perfection of her teeth. After her death he is told that her grave has been disturbed; waking from a state of fugue he finds all of her teeth arranged before him. But when he took those teeth, he apparently did not notice that she was still alive in her coffin. 'The Tell-Tale Heart', which stands obliquely to these stories, features another unnamed but disturbed narrator who is driven to distraction by the 'vulture-like' eye of his landlord. Eventually he kills the landlord, cuts up the body and distributes the parts under the floorboards of the house. When the police arrive he is so confident that they will not find evidence of his crime that he is able to sit calmly and chat with them, until he begins to hear the beating of his landlord's heart, restless in its makeshift grave, and confesses. It is a clear precursor to much of the psychological horror that would emerge in the twentieth century.

Poe called the one collection of his stories that was published in his lifetime *Tales of the Grotesque and Arabesque* (published in two volumes, 1840). The title used terms more usually associated with Islamic art and architecture – terms that suggest elaborate decoration – which seems highly appropriate for Poe's often florid and always emphatic style. He wrote an elaboration of the Gothic, often parodying its excesses by being even more excessive. But the collection was not a success; the contemporary critical reaction was generally disdainful. In his lifetime, Poe was far better known as an acidic reviewer and as a poet. His most successful work was 'The Raven' (1845), a long, narrative poem that was itself freighted with Gothic imagery. It would be long after his mysterious and still unexplained death in 1849 before he was recognized as one of America's greatest short story writers: his work established a pattern for elaborate and grotesque tales that would be followed by later American writers from H. P. Lovecraft to Stephen King.

The other major writer of the fantastic in ante-bellum America could hardly have presented more of a contrast to Poe. Where Poe was extravagant, excessive, extreme, Nathaniel Hawthorne was cool, controlled and subtle. Even at his closest to the Gothic, in a story such as 'Rappaccini's Daughter' (1846), there is none of the exaggerated imagery and grim horror with which Poe's work is so redolent. Instead there is a tale set in a vague Renaissance past of a youth who falls in love with a girl he watches through his window as she walks in her father's garden. Heedless of all warnings, he goes to meet her, only to find that the girl has not only become immune to the poisons with which her father experiments, but has become poisonous in her turn. The atmosphere is bitter-sweet rather than grotesquely horrifying, but then Hawthorne's interest is not in the monstrousness of death but in man's capacity for evil, especially when disguised by good intentions or the norms of society.

Hawthorne had been appalled to discover that his great-great-grandfather, John Hathorne, had been a judge at the Salem witch trials. He added the

'W' to his surname to dissociate himself from his ancestor, but this sense of the legacy of America's puritan past haunts his best work. In 'Young Goodman Brown' (1835), which may or may not recount a dream, the protagonist witnesses his neighbours in seventeenth-century Salem drawn into a mysterious congregation in the woods by a figure who seems to be the Devil. In *The House of the Seven Gables* (1851), the home of the Pyncheon family, fallen on hard times in the mid-nineteenth century, is haunted by the sins of an earlier generation of Pyncheons at the time of the witchcraft trials.

Other ante-bellum writers, like Hawthorne, made the fantastic an unexceptional part of their work. Henry Wadsworth Longfellow referenced Norse mythology in his narrative poem 'The Skeleton Armor' (1841), and the legends of the Ojibway Indians in 'The Song of Hiawatha' (1855). An extended trance-like vision is at the core of Herman Melville's *Pierre: or, The Ambiguities* (1852); and there is something fantastical in the ambiguous figure at the heart of Melville's last novel, *The Confidence-Man; His Masquerade* (1857), though it has to be said that neither *The Marble Faun* nor any of Melville's later novels were popular or critical successes in their day. As the public mood darkened towards war, there seems to have been little patience for such dense, complex, philosophical (and non-realist) works.

Then came the war, and everything changed. The Civil War did not just effect a comprehensive political, social and economic transformation in the country, it also marked a significant psychological and philosophical change. Before the war the predominant philosophical mode in America was transcendentalism, best represented in the works of Ralph Waldo Emerson and Henry David Thoreau. Transcendentalism was utopian and nationalist (as in Emerson's 'The American Scholar') and propounded a strong relationship connecting man, nature and the divine. The influence of transcendentalism in the 1840s and 1850s was pervasive, and even if writers like Hawthorne and Poe were opposed to transcendentalism, they shared a sense of divine influence, of the connection between nature and the supernatural. After the war the predominant philosophical school in America was pragmatism, as propounded by Charles Sanders Peirce and William James. This was a practical, rationalist school of thought far better suited to the spread of industrialization, the rapid and unfettered growth of capitalism and the so-called 'taming' of the West. It was not a school of thought well suited to the fantastic.

It is notable, for instance, that despite the already thriving cult of death with its widespread fetishizing of grief (evident before the war in the sentimental account of Topsy's death in *Uncle Tom's Cabin*, 1851–2, by Harriet Beecher Stowe, and after the war in the death of Beth in *Little Women*,

1868, by Louisa May Alcott) that was the popular response to the horrendous casualty figures of the war, remarkably little of the literary response to the war that was published over the next half-century had any sense of the supernatural. 'The Angel of Mons', a representation of British reaction to the First World War inspired by a supernatural story by Arthur Machen, had no equivalent in the Civil War or its aftermath. 'An Occurrence at the Owl Creek Bridge' (1890) by Ambrose Bierce perhaps comes closest. It tells of a Confederate sympathizer about to be hanged as a spy by Union troops who, at the last minute, dives from the makeshift scaffold on the bridge to escape in the river below; only for this to be revealed as a fantasy experienced in the moment of his death. But unlike Machen, Bierce, who fought in the war and helped map the battlefield at Shiloh, where there is indeed an Owl Creek, was restrained and deliberately realist in its approach, and in the end his story offers no supernatural comfort, no sense of life after death.

The effect of the Civil War on American fantasy, therefore, is mostly oblique. It is there, for instance, in the Uncle Remus stories of Joel Chandler Harris, which began to appear in 1879. These tales of the trickster Br'er Rabbit combine elements of Cherokee myth with the oral storytelling tradition of the freed slaves. These stories enjoyed considerable popularity in the latter part of the century, mostly because of the rather benevolent view of race relations they presented at a time of heightened tensions caused by the ill-managed policy of Reconstruction and the early depredations of the Ku Klux Klan.

One literary influence of the war and of the culture of sentiment may be found in the growing popularity of the ghost story. Many authors wrote ghost stories, including Louisa May Alcott (under the pseudonym A. M. Barnard) and Julian Hawthorne, the journalist son of Nathaniel. However, most of these avoided specific reference to the war or its aftermath, preferring to follow the English model of Sheridan Le Fanu and, later, M. R. James. The best and most interesting of the American ghost stories from the late nineteenth century, for instance, was set primarily at a country house in Essex, and all the main characters are English. 'The Turn of the Screw' by Henry James (1898) is the story of a governess hired to look after two children by their absent uncle. She begins to see two characters, whom she identifies as the ghosts of her predecessor, Miss Jessop and Miss Jessop's lover, Quint. It seems that these ghosts are turning the children against her, but we may also be encountering the malevolence of the children or indeed it may all just be in the mind of the governess. It is this ambiguity, this enforced hesitation between our interpretations of events, as Todorov puts it, which has made this one of the most analysed ghost stories in literature. As one of the pioneers of literary modernism, James brought a new psychological sense to the genre that would become a significant part of the literary fantasies of the new century.

However, if the fantastic barely intruded on the Civil War literature, it certainly did play a part in the burgeoning literature of the West. The myth of the frontier first made popular by James Fenimore Cooper turned into the most abiding myth in American literature, the Wild West. Coincidentally, new cheaper paper and printing methods led to a number of publishers producing series of popular books collectively known as dime novels, the first of which appeared in 1860. Stories of the Wild West made for far and away the most popular of the dime novels, usually highly coloured if not outright fantastic adventures of genuine characters like Jesse James.

Such western dime novels became overtly fantastic in 1868 with the publication of *The Huge Hunter; or, The Steam Man of the Prairies* by Edward S. Ellis. Earlier in 1868 Zadock Deddrick of Newark had patented a 'steam man', a prototype robot, and this clearly fed into Ellis's novel, which in turn inspired *Frank Reade and His Steam Man of the Plains* by Harry Enton (1876), the first of a long series of dime novels featuring Frank Reade and later Frank Reade Jr. Combining the adventure of the still little-known frontier and a pragmatic, inventive hero of the type that many Americans, particularly from the industrialized north-east, liked to imagine themselves, these stories tended to follow a pattern in which the ingenuity of the (usually young) hero creates a mechanical device that saves the day. The long-running Tom Swift sequence, beginning in 1910, followed the same structure. Such tales of invention have been named 'Edisonades' by John Clute, after Thomas Alva Edison, though Ellis's dime novel preceded Edison's fame by a decade. Edison did actually feature in one such story, *Edison's Conquest of Mars* by Garrett P. Serviss (1898), a sequel of sorts to H. G. Wells's *The War of the Worlds* (1898). The Edisonades would transform themselves seamlessly into Hugo Gernsback's 'scientifiction' in the early years of the twentieth century, just as the dime novel gave way to another form of low-cost mass publishing, the pulp magazine.

If the dime novels presented the West as a place of opportunity and excitement, a very different view was presented by one of the most successful of all children's fantasies, *The Wonderful Wizard of Oz* (1900) by L. Frank Baum and W. W. Denslow. Here Kansas is an unwelcoming place of drought and hard toil. When Dorothy escapes to the magical land of Oz, she finds a place beset with problems of its own, but problems that she can solve as she could never solve the problems of Kansas. The book was an immediate success, prompting Baum to produce thirteen sequels over the next twenty years, as well as writing a musical version for the stage. By putting American landscapes, characters and experiences into his fantasies, Baum saw himself as creating a new type of fairy tale for American children (although it was the film version of 1939 that probably did most to cement its place in the American popular imagination). The end of the nineteenth century also saw a renewed interest in utopian ideas, surprisingly left-wing in orientation, compared to modern American attitudes. Some of these books were incredibly popular, most notably *Looking Backward: 2000–1887* (1888) by Edward Bellamy, in which a young man from 1887 wakes in 2000 to discover an ideal Marxist society of shared wealth, reduced working hours, early retirement, ready access to goods and, in the sequel *Equality* (1897), sexual equality. *Looking Backward* inspired utopian communities, political debate and a host of sequels by other hands. Jack London also presented a socialist vision in his dystopian novel *The Iron Heel* (1908), in which the United States is crushed under the extreme capitalist rule of the Oligarchy. The method by which London's new political order seizes power by crushing the workers and buying out smaller businesses is not dissimilar to the methods of the so-called robber barons active in American industry in the latter years of the nineteenth century. American literature at the time drew little distinction between realist and genre fiction, and London was able to move freely between the modes with equal acclaim. London also wrote a prehistoric fantasy, *Before Adam* (1906); *The Star Rover* (1915), a visionary account of reincarnation; and supernatural tales such as 'The Eternity of Forms' (1911). Mark Twain found it as easy as London to move between literary modes, producing one significant fantasy in *A Connecticut Yankee in King Arthur's Court* (1889), in which a contemporary practical American is knocked out and wakes in the Middle Ages, where he promptly begins to introduce American industry, an affectionate parody of the pragmatic, can-do attitude already noted in post-Civil War American literature. Though Twain wrote a number of works that are overtly fantasy, he imbued them with a hard-edged rationalism that means they can generally and as readily be considered science fiction.

The utopian socialist vision of Bellamy and London also led to *Herland* by Charlotte Perkins Gilman (serialized 1915, volume publication 1979), the first major feminist utopia in American literature. In the novel three men find themselves in a land ruled by women, a land in which poverty, war and disease have been eliminated, a land indeed in which asexual reproduction means that men have no role. A sequel, *With Her in Ourland* (1916), took one of the women from Herland into the land of men. Significant as *Herland* was, and a host of feminist utopias from later in the century have followed this initial model, Gilman's most important work has proved to be her earlier short story 'The Yellow Wallpaper' (1892), which, like 'The Turn of the Screw', hesitates between ghost story and psychological realism. A woman, confined to her room by her husband because of an earlier collapse, begins to sense other women behind the yellow wallpaper, figures which either drive her to insanity or provide a strange release. 'The Yellow Wallpaper' is one of the most powerful feminist statements in American literature, whether or not it is read as fantasy.

Bellamy and Gilman both combined serious literary sensibilities with strong political concerns, and even Baum's Oz novels can be read as political allegory (and it is perhaps worth noting that Baum was also strongly supportive of feminist ideals), but the most pervasive forms of fantasy to emerge during the early years of the new century, the colourful adventures of Edgar Rice Burroughs and the subgenres known as weird fiction and sword and sorcery, had little time for either literary sensibility or political allegory.

Burroughs was a not particularly successful businessman who took up writing to support his family and achieved success almost immediately. *Tarzan of the Apes* (serialized 1912) was particularly popular, and Burroughs went on to write some two dozen sequels over the next thirty years. These tales of an English aristocrat adopted by apes, who speaks the language of the animals and uses his knowledge of the jungle to foil the inordinate number of nefarious deeds that seem common in the African jungle, were quickly adapted for the cinema. The most successful of Burroughs's other pulp adventures were probably the stories of John Carter on Mars ('Barsoom'), beginning with *A Princess of Mars* (1912), and his hollow earth series, Pellucidar, beginning with *At the Earth's Core* (1914). Though these series might seem to have a science-fictional premise, they are really highly coloured fantasy adventures that pay little attention to the scientific assumptions of the day.

Weird fiction, a term popularized by one of its leading exponents, H. P. Lovecraft, in his critical study *Supernatural Horror in Fiction* (1927, revised 1934), was marked by an emphatic use of the strange and uncanny intruding upon contemporary reality. Weird fiction is a decidedly American form which owes an obvious debt to Poe's more outré mannerisms, though the ghost and horror stories of contemporary British writers such as M. R. James and Arthur Machen were significant influences. It would, however, be a mistake to imagine any sort of unity in the works variously categorized as weird fiction; indeed the work even of someone as closely associated with the genre as Lovecraft varied from outright horror to science fiction. After the launch of the pulp magazine *Weird Tales*, first published in March 1923, weird fiction might best be described as the work of authors associated with the magazine and those they most readily named as influences.

American weird fiction probably begins with Robert W. Chambers and his collection of linked stories, *The King in Yellow* (1895). Chambers was an artist who trained in Paris, where he had presumably come into contact with the fashionable decadence of the period, since that provides the aura surrounding these macabre stories. The first four stories in the collection are linked by a play, 'The King in Yellow', whose text can drive the reader insane, and this notion that greater knowledge is linked to madness became one of the abiding themes of weird fiction. Another early exponent is A. Merritt, whose florid fantasies of lost worlds tend to pit no-nonsense modern men against ancient forces such as the Dweller found in *The Moon Pool* (1919), or Nimir, the Lord of Evil, discovered during a quest for lost Inca treasure in *The Face in the Abyss* (1931).

Both these writers were a direct influence on H. P. Lovecraft, whose stories, time and again, suggested that forces incomprehensible to man steered a fundamentally alien universe, and that any contact between man and this cosmic horror could result only in madness. His best and certainly most influential works – 'The Call of Cthulhu' (1928), 'At the Mountains of Madness' (1936), 'The Case of Charles Dexter Ward' (1941) – combine into what has become known as the Cthulhu Mythos. Common features of these stories, often set in and around the New England town of Arkham, include a book of ancient and forbidden knowledge known as the *Necronomicon*, and strange ancient gods such as Yog-Sothoth. Lovecraft tended to evoke his dark and threatening horrors in an over-ripe language much given to terms such as 'eldritch', 'squamous' and 'ichor'. It is an idiosyncratic style that is parodied (often affectionately) even today, and tales of the Cthulhu Mythos are still being written, by authors as varied as Brian Lumley, Neil Gaiman and Charles Stross. But even during the brief period he was writing his Cthulhu stories (Lovecraft died of cancer when only forty-six) he inspired a close circle of friends and fellow writers who followed in the same path. The most notable of these were Clark Ashton Smith and August Derleth. Smith appropriated Lovecraft's Cthulhu Mythos, but tended to set his stories far away from Arkham in time and space, setting narrative cycles in Hyperborea, on Mars and, most commonly, in Zothique, the last inhabited continent when the earth is dying. Derleth, who invented the term 'Cthulhu Mythos', tended to work closer to Lovecraft's own model; indeed he seems to have seen himself as the keeper of Lovecraft's memory, founding the publishing venture Arkham House and completing a number of scraps of story ideas that Lovecraft left behind, which Derleth characterized as 'posthumous collaborations'. But where Lovecraft presented an amoral universe, Derleth's Christianity led him to recast the Mythos as an eternal struggle between the evil of the Elder Gods and the good of the Old Ones.

Though such supernatural horrors formed a large part of American weird fiction, the term also embraces a variety of other stories. The lost civilizations of Merritt's stories developed into the alternate universe tales of his friend, the artist Hannes Bok. In novels such as *The Sorcerer's Ship* (1942) and the posthumously published *Beyond the Golden Stair* (1970), Bok wrote of travellers from our own world who found themselves in colourful, magical lands that are far more attractive than our own. The sense that there was something magical and heroic in the distant past lay behind the stories of Robert E. Howard. Howard was a writer of swashbuckling adventure who combined this with an interest in weird fiction. The first significant result was 'The Shadow Kingdom' (1929), which introduced King Kull, a character who would appear in ten subsequent stories, only one of which was to be published before Howard's suicide in 1936. Kull was a warrior from Atlantis who repeatedly encountered magical threats as he travelled through a prehistoric landscape in what Howard called the Thurian Age; it is one of the early examples of the subgenre that Fritz Leiber would christen 'sword and sorcery'. Howard later rewrote one of the unpublished Kull stories as 'The Phoenix on the Sword' (1932), introducing an even more iconic figure, Conan the Barbarian. Set during the 'Hyborian Age', a period later than Kull's Thurian Age but still prehistoric, Conan encountered a thrilling if repetitive cast of outlaws, mercenaries, pirates, wizards and monsters in more than twenty tales, seventeen of which were published in the four years that separated Conan's first appearance and Howard's suicide.

Sword and sorcery continued to be a popular form into the 1950s, attracting such writers as Fritz Leiber who used it (while at the same time subtly poking fun at it) in the stories of Fafhrd and the Grey Mouser, a pair of rogues first introduced in 1939 in a story published in *Unknown*, revised as 'Two Sought Adventure'. Leiber was still writing about their adventures in the 1980s. Another writer who used sword and sorcery to open up new areas was C. L. Moore, the first woman writer of popular fantasy, whose series featuring the female adventurer Jirel of Joiry began in 1934.

The pulp adventures of Burroughs, Lovecraft, Howard and their fellows were like Busby Berkeley musicals for the page: big, colourful, often non-sensical spectacles that proved to be the perfect antidote to the stock market crash, the dust bowl, the Depression. The other popular movie response to the grim news of the day was the screwball comedy, and here, too, fantasy provided an equivalent in the novels of Thorne Smith. During the years of Prohibition, Smith wrote a stream of comedies, all of which involved copious consumption of alcohol and generally illicit sex. His biggest success was probably his first major novel, *Topper: An Improbable Adventure* (1926), the story of a straitlaced banker, Cosmo Topper, who finds himself haunted by a husband and wife team of hard-drinking, licentious ghosts. The novel spawned a sequel, *Topper Takes a Trip* (1932), three movies and a television series. Smith's other novels, which generally revolved around a hapless man, a sexually predatory woman, lots of drinking and an intrusion of the supernatural, include statues of Greek gods in New York's Metropolitan Museum brought to life in *The Night Life of the Gods* (1931); a bickering couple who find themselves transferred into each other's bodies in *Turnabout* (1931); a photographic experiment gone wrong, which results in the photographer and his dog periodically becoming invisible except for their skeletons in *Skin and Bones* (1933); and a witch condemned in the Salem witch trials brought back to life in the present in *The Passionate Witch* (completed by Norman Matson and published posthumously in 1941). This last was one of the inspirations for the long-running television comedy *Bewitched*.

Smith's *Topper*, with its joyful use of sexual innuendo and disregard for the censorious mores of the time, was part of a liberating fight-back within American fantasy against a new primness in American publishing. The Volstead Act of 1919, which brought in Prohibition, was part of a moral crusade which also prompted publishers to apply severe limits on what they would produce, but several writers, in very different modes of fantasy, were testing the limits of what could be written. The most famous example is James Branch Cabell, whose *Jurgen* (1919) became the cause of a notorious obscenity trial when it was banned in 1920 by the New York Society for the Suppression of Vice. When it came to trial the publishers were acquitted, though it emerged during the trial that the moralists objected to Cabell's satire on religion as much as to the dalliances and double-entendres with which the novel is littered. *Jurgen*, the tale of a year-long quest for the central character's missing wife which involves encounters with such mythic characters as Guinevere, the Lady of the Lake and Helen of Troy, is part of an extended and loosely connected sequence known as the 'Biography of the Life of Manuel', which tells of various incarnations of a redeemer character in a variety of fantasy lands centring on the realm of Poictesme. The sequence was so loosely connected that Cabell managed to shoehorn all his books before 1930 into it, even collections of non-fantasy stories such as *Gallantry* (1907). Together the eighteen-or-so volumes of the Biography were successful largely because of the notoriety of *Jurgen*, though later books such as the trilogy *Smirt: An Urban Nightmare* (1934), *Smith: A Sylvan Interlude* (1935) and *Smire: An Acceptance in the Third Person* (1937) did not sell well. Nevertheless, Cabell was one of the wittiest and most ironic of fantasy writers. Others who used fantasy as a way of undermining convention include John Erskine, who satirically revised traditional myths and fairy stories so that the characters betrayed contemporary American psychology and neuroses.

By the 1920s and 30s the freedom that had allowed Jack London to move readily between realism and the fantastic was becoming more restricted. A mode now most readily identified with the smutty comedies of Smith and Cabell or, more damningly, with the grotesque horrors of Lovecraft and the crude, highly coloured adventures of Howard, could not be employed for serious literary purposes. Literary figures such as Willa Cather and Edith Wharton occasionally produced ghost stories, while the cartoonist and short story writer James Thurber used fantasy effectively in works such as 'The Secret Life of Walter Mitty' (1939), in which fantasy provides an escape from the vicissitudes of everyday life. Nevertheless, by mid-century American fantasy was almost exclusively the preserve of genre writers; indeed it would not be until the English translations of Jorge Luis Borges's *ficciones* in the 1960s and the subsequent emergence of magic realism and postmodern fiction that the fantastic would receive serious critical attention in America.

Most of the genre writers, like L. Sprague de Camp and Fletcher Pratt, were long-standing contributors to the pulp magazines, writing fantasy and science fiction fairly indiscriminately. When the new editor of the science-fiction magazine *Astounding*, John W. Campbell, launched a companion magazine for fantasy, *Unknown*, in March 1939, he attracted many of the same authors who already wrote regularly for *Astounding*. The degree of cross-over between the genres is illustrated by de Camp and Pratt's *The Incomplete Enchanter* (1941), which has the structure of a time-travel story but in which the hero is transported into the world of Norse myth and into the world of Spenser's *Faerie Queene*.

There were, however, some writers who seemed to be part of neither the mainstream world nor the genre world. Typical of these was Charles Finney, who was never able to match the success of his first novel, *The Circus of Dr Lao* (1935), an absurdist tale of a Chinese circus that arrives in a small Arizona town to the discomfort of the inhabitants, although Finney's lengthy and patient explanation of the events in the novel suggest that he saw it less as a conveyance of wonder than as a pricking of contemporary small-town pretensions. The novel had an obvious influence on later tales of a mysterious and fantastic circus, notably Ray Bradbury's *Something Wicked This Way Comes* (1962). The other writer of the period who made a massive contribution to fantasy with one work but could not repeat it (and indeed wrote mostly outside the genre) was John Myers Myers. That work was *Silverlock* (1949), in which a traveller from our world makes a literal journey through literature, encountering along the way a bewildering number of characters from books and myths. It is a recursive novel that reminds us how much fantasy feeds on itself and, coming at the mid-point of the century, is an appropriate place at which to end this survey.

Any attempt to identify a distinctively American characteristic in the fantasy of this period is doomed to fail. Many used the American landscape; a typical hero would represent the pragmatic, can-do attitude in which the country prided itself; fantasy would equally often chaff against the puritanical restrictions that are just as much a part of the American character; but none of these traits are invariably to be found, even in the work of just one author. The most common venue for fantasy in America during the latter part of the period under discussion was cheap, low-paying popular magazines, the various dime novels and pulps of the era, where an extravagance of imagery and language that owes much to Poe was usual. If there is a characteristic of American fantasy in this period, it probably owes most to the fact that authors tended to read and associate with other American fantasists and hence to share influences and styles, as is shown by the way weird fiction flourished during the early years of the twentieth century. In the last third of the century, however, a new influence from England, J. R. R. Tolkien, would have an overwhelming effect on the character of American fantasy.

4

MARIA NIKOLAJEVA

The development of children's fantasy

Fantasy for children, similar to children's literature at large, could not emerge until childhood was acknowledged as a separate and especially formative period in human life. However, while the Enlightenment primarily resulted in instructive works for young readers, Romanticism, with its interest for, on the one hand, folklore, and on the other, the child as innocent and untouched by civilization, provided rich soil for the first fantasy stories explicitly published for children, naturally children of the upper and middle classes. In handbooks of children's literature, fantasy is frequently treated together with literary fairy tales, or under the misleading label 'modern fairy tales'.[1]

E. T. A. Hoffmann's 'The Nutcracker and the Mouse King' (1816) is internationally acknowledged as the first fantasy explicitly addressed to children, since the protagonist is a little girl, the point of departure is the nursery, and many characters are toys. The child is, however, instrumental in the story, which rather involves the animated toy, the Nutcracker, and his quest for the princess in the fairy land. The connection between the Nutcracker, an enchanted prince, and the enigmatic old man in the real world is hinted at. Yet play and playfulness, associated with childhood, make this story different from Hoffmann's other fantastic stories, even though it carries many philosophical and ethical aspects far beyond a child's comprehension. Similarly, Carlo Collodi's *The Adventures of Pinocchio* (1881), with its puppet as the central character, has always been considered a story for children, despite its narrative and moral complexity. Its main thrust lies fully along the lines of the primary purpose of early children's literature: to educate and socialize the child.

In the English-speaking world, priority in fantasy for children is given to Lewis Carroll's *Alice in Wonderland* (1865), accompanied by Charles Kingsley's *Water Babies* (1863) and George MacDonald's Princess books (*The Princess and the Goblin*, 1872, and *The Princess and Curdie*, 1883) and *At the Back of the North Wind* (1871). All these works have been questioned as books suitable for children, yet they cannot be omitted in this context. The three authors (ab)use the child, Kingsley and MacDonald mostly in adherence to the Romantic tradition, Carroll as an object for spiteful and intricate adult games. In Kingsley's novel, the poor orphan protagonist enters the underwater realm of death, and the plot rotates around the various moral lessons that are of little use for the protagonist, but instructive for the reader. Diamond, the angelic character in *At the Back of the North Wind*, explicitly labelled as 'too good to live', is a role model for young as well as adult readers. Killing off a child before he is old enough to sin is a common device in nineteenth-century children's literature. Carroll, on the other hand, humiliates his young heroine, making her lose her mental capacity and control of her body, and subjecting her to unlimited power from creatures that would normally be inferior to her. The issue of power thus becomes almost from start the engine for children's fantasy, as well as its tangible double address.

Education, entertainment and power

Edith Nesbit is frequently given credit as the creator of modern fantasy for children, as well as one of the first children's authors to use a modern narrative voice and adopt a child's perspective.[2] Inspired by the upside-down fairy tales included in Kenneth Grahame's childhood memoir *Dream Days* (1898), Nesbit started with fractured fairy tales, bringing into them tokens of modernity, such as lifts, diving bells and mathematical calculations. Nesbit's contribution to children's fantasy cannot be overestimated,[3] and she certainly brought enjoyment and comedy into the genre; yet her main purpose remains educational and power-related. Following the path of her predecessors, Nesbit introduced magic into the everyday rather than sending her child characters into magical realms. *Five Children and It* (1902), *The Phoenix and the Carpet* (1904), *The Story of the Amulet* (1906), *The Enchanted Castle* (1907), and *The House of Arden* (1908) feature magical agents (objects or creatures) that make mock of the children and demonstrate their inferiority as they prove incapable of controlling magic. Learning bitter lessons from their adventures, the children voluntarily give up their empowering implements. While this certainly provides a necessary closure of the plot, the message is a child's incompetence when encountering the limitations and consistency of magic. Paradoxically, the adults in Nesbit's novels generally do not notice the effect of magic, that is, are excluded from it. Nesbit's follower, the American Edward Eager, pursues similar lines in *Half Magic* (1954), *Magic by the Lake* (1957), and *Seven-Day Magic* (1962). The tendency to bring magical agents into the everyday life of ordinary children rather than transporting them to secondary worlds has been developed by many twentieth-century fantasy writers, notably Pamela Travers in *Mary Poppins* (1934) and sequels. In these, the magical agent, a true heir of Nesbit's Psammead, although superficially human, is arrogant and conceited, repeatedly reminding the children of her own superiority, not merely because of her magical abilities but in the first place as an adult. This power hierarchy between the adult author and the child protagonist and reader, clearly visible already with Carroll and MacDonald, is the foremost token of early twentieth-century children's fantasy. Empowered temporarily, the child protagonists are inevitably brought back into dependency upon the adults.

In James M. Barrie's *Peter Pan* (1911), an early secondary-world fantasy for children, the tension lies in the child's wish to remain a child for ever and the insight about the inevitability and necessity of growing up. Many critics assess Barrie's novel as the adult author's nostalgic longing for the lost childhood.[4] Notably, the secondary world is presented as a realm of endless play and adventure, and the struggle against an evil foe is a game rather than a matter of life and death. Death is in fact reversible in the Neverland; while the secondary world is interpreted as the land of death; it precludes maturation and inclusion in the natural cycle of life. Some considerably later fantasy novels, such as Antoine Saint-Exupéry's *The Little Prince* (1943) and Nathalie Babbitt's *Tuck Everlasting* (1975), investigate further the blessings and curse of eternal childhood.

A different strategy for power negotiations is maintained in Frank L. Baum's *The Wonderful Wizard of Oz* (1900), one of the first American children's fantasy novels. Dorothy finds herself in a foreign country where she performs deeds impossible in her everyday life in Kansas. Characteristically, she considers herself weak and powerless, as well as dependent on someone else's help. Her three companions, who can be interpreted psychoanalytically as three projections of her inner self, seek the three different qualities – brain, heart and courage – which Dorothy repeatedly reveals during the journey: she is clever, caring and brave, yet she believes that only an adult can send her back home, and as a very young child, she longs for the protection of her foster parents. Neither Dorothy nor the readers are informed that from the first day in the land of Oz she has the power to go back home unassisted: the silver shoes. It is repeatedly hinted that the shoes have many wonderful qualities, and as the Wicked Witch of the West tries to get them from Dorothy, it should be obvious that they are an instrument of power, yet the secret of this power is kept from Dorothy. She is further empowered by the Golden Cap that governs the Winged Monkeys, but she has to give it to the Witch of the South in exchange for the secret of the silver shoes.

Finally, as Dorothy is sent back to Kansas, she is stripped of her power (she loses her silver shoes during the flight), and in this book we never learn whether she can use her newly gained insights. While in the Land of Oz she was respected and even feared by adults, including Oz the Great and Terrible himself, as a powerful witch, in Kansas she returns to the position of a child and female, doubly oppressed.

Time displacement

Time-shift fantasy seems a more prominent subgenre in children's fantasy than in mainstream fantasy. It allows a considerable educational impetus, presenting a credible and edifying picture of certain historical epochs and famous people. It also offers a gratifying narrative device building up suspense and empowering protagonists with the knowledge that their associates in the past lack. Not least, time displacement focuses on change, growth, ageing and death, major issues in serious children's literature. Yet more than any other fantasy motif, time distortion is influenced by contemporary scientific thought, especially the theory of relativity, and the scope of problems which fantasy authors meet when they venture on the exploration of time patterns allows deep philosophical contemplations: the questions of predestination and free will, of the multitude of possible parallel times, of time going at a different pace or even in different directions in separate worlds, the mechanisms of time displacement, and the various time paradoxes.

Edith Nesbit is given credit for inventing time displacement as a motif and narrative strategy; at least *The Story of the Amulet* seems the first known example of this subgenre addressed to the young audience (H. G. Wells's science fiction novel *The Time Machine* was published ten years earlier and supposedly inspired Nesbit). Following the didactic purpose of children's fantasy, Nesbit proposes a number of rules concerning time travel, which have been faithfully adhered to by many children's writers. Thus, for the sake of convenience, time in the primary world stands still (a principle also employed in secondary-world fantasy, such as the Narnia novels). The time traveller cannot affect the past or bring objects from the past. It is, however, possible – and gratifying from the narrative viewpoint – to bring people from the past, so that displacement becomes bilateral. Nesbit also cleverly circumvents the issue of communication often neglected in secondary-world fantasy; her characters' ability to understand any language in the past is part of the magical set-up. Time travellers, endowed by historical knowledge, gain supremacy over adults in the past, yet lack power to make use of their knowledge. Moreover, the narrator repeatedly ridicules her protagonists' inadequate education, thus exercising the adult narrator's power over her young characters. Adults are also used, in Nesbit's works as well as in her successors', to explain the nature of time to ignorant children.

Later fantasy writers employ the time-shift device for a variety of purposes. Mary Norton offers an entertaining, yet rather mechanical transportation in time in her *Bonfires and Broomsticks* (1947), in which a bed with a magic knob is the agent, previously applied in *The Magic Bedknob* (1943) for spatial dislocation. Penelope Farmer follows Nesbit's Arden novels, letting the protagonist of *Charlotte Sometimes* (1969) change place with a girl in another historical time in order to discover her own identity, not unlike the eponymous protagonist of Barbara Sleigh's *Jessamy* (1967). A considerably more challenging time dislocation appears in Alison Uttley's *A Traveller in Time* (1939), Lucy M. Boston's *The Children of Green Knowe* (1954), Philippa Pearce's *Tom's Midnight Garden* (1958) and Ruth Park's *Playing Beatie Bow* (1980). While all these texts partly retain Nesbit's educational aspects of time travel, significant psychological and ethical aspects are added. None of the protagonists use any explicit magic agent for their time travels, even though these may be discovered by a keen reader, and they have no control over the magical gadgets; mostly they are not even aware of displacement at the beginning. Their experience is far from playful and pleasurable, rather, especially in Uttley's and Pearce's novels, highly traumatic. The time travellers are lost in the past, uncertain whether they will be able to return to their own time, and as their own time seldom promises anything enjoyable, they often consider staying in the past. Tolly in the Green Knowe series initially finds himself a passive observer, frustrated by his inability to interact with the children of the past. The strong involvement in the past and the emotional bands with people in the distant epoch produce a disturbing effect. Tolly realizes that his friends are long dead. Penelope in *A Traveller in Time* becomes marked for the rest of her life by her time-shift experience. Like Nesbit's characters, she discovers that she cannot change the past and warn Mary Queen of Scots of imminent danger. Abigail in *Playing Beatie Bow*, on the contrary, learns that the purpose of her displacement is to alter the past, a direct transgression of Nesbit's laws. Her ethical choice reverberates in her own situation as she returns to her own time. Yet it is possible to conclude that Abigail does not have a choice after all, that her fate is predetermined, that is, her role is similar to the chosen child in secondary world fantasy. While Penelope definitely is disempowered by her experience, Abigail may have come to terms with herself.

More recent time-shift fantasy is primarily employed as an artistic device for the characters' self-exploration rather than for educational purposes. Consequently, the destination of time travel is no longer an exciting and exotic historical setting featuring famous figures, but instead a period some-how connected with the protagonists' family history or, as in *Tom's Midnight Garden*, with an actual person in his surroundings. The young protagonist of *Tom's Midnight Garden* discovers that his nightly excursions into the past are caused by an old woman's nostalgic memories. The focus is thus transferred from a child's experience of a remote epoch to an adult's fear of ageing and death. Tom fails to notice that the little girl Hatty, whom he meets in the enchanted garden, grows up between his visits. What promised to be a welcome escape from dull everyday life turns out a highly traumatic realization of the necessity of growing up.

Animal, toy and miniature people fantasy

Already *The Nutcracker* introduced a popular theme in children's fantasy hardly appearing in the mainstream: stories of anthropomorphic animals, animated toys and dolls, miniature people and mythical creatures. The boundary between toys and animals is fluid, for instance in A. A. Milne's *Winnie-the-Pooh* (1926), and a talking baby dragon appearing in the everyday is in its function hardly different from a talking puppy. The motif goes back to literary fairy tales, notably Hans Christian Andersen. The use of such characters empowers the readers since a child is usually bigger and stronger than a toy, a midget or a mouse. If a toy or animal character is featured in symbiosis with the child, the latter can act as a wiser and protective adult. In *Winnie-the-Pooh*, the child who is helpless and frequently humiliated in his own world becomes omnipotent in the world of his toys, transferring his own shortcomings onto them.

Stories of animated dolls are habitually harmless domestic adventures, even though some elements of quest and maturation may be present. These include *Memoirs of a London Doll* (1846) by Mrs Fairstar, *Hitty, Her First Hundred Years* (1929) by Rachel Field, *The Doll's House* (1947) by Rumer Godden, *Rufty Tufty the Golliwog* (1952) by Ruth Ainsworth, and *Five Dolls in a House* (1953) by Helen Clare. Clare also wrote, as Pauline Clarke, *The Twelve and the Genii* (1962), involving toy soldiers.

Stories such as *Stuart Little* (1945) by E. B. White, or *A Bear Called Paddington* (1958) by Michael Bond, abound in comic situations and border on nonsense in their clash between reality and the absurd toy/animal figure. Paddington is an archetypal foundling, while Stuart has in some inexplicable way been born to a human family. Apart from anthropomorphism, these characters do not possess supernatural traits; thus it might be argued whether such books belong to fantasy or are a genre of their own. In most animal and toy stories, however, the non-human character is rather a companion to the lonely child, a role similar to the magic animal helper in folk tales. The function of the fairy-tale magic helper can also be performed in humorous fantasy by miniature people, dragons, wizards, witches, angels, fairies, brownies, elves, kelpies and other mythical creatures. Usually, the mythical nature of these creatures is reversed: they are harmless and benevolent toward their human friends and frequently inferior to them. The appearance of supernatural beings in an otherwise ordinary world creates a comic effect reminiscent of Nesbit, such as oriental genies in George Selden's *The Genie of Sutton Place* (1973) and Robert Leeson's *The Third Class Genie* (1975). When all such are the human protagonists' secret companions, the boundary between imaginative, and often therapeutic, play and actual magical events is blurred. Mythical creatures, such as fairies, gnomes or dragons, can be portrayed either in contact with humans or in communities of their own, such as Juliana Horatia Ewing's *The Brownies* (1879) and B. B.'s *The Little Grey Men* (1942). Such comic and idyllic stories become rare toward the second half of the twentieth century as they provide no room for moral and existential issues emerging in children's fantasy during the 1960s and onwards.

What may be more rightfully called animal fantasy features talking intelligent animals living within realms of their own without any contact with the humans, such as Kenneth Grahame's *The Wind in the Willows* (1908). Originating from fables and thus allowing vast possibilities for allegory and satire, such stories juxtapose human and animal traits in a fascinating manner. The four characters in *The Wind in the Willows* are hybrids of animal and human, and can therefore be read on different levels. The novel thus appeals to both young and adult audiences. *Charlotte's Web* (1952), by E. B. White, brings together an unlikely company of a pig, a spider and a rat involved in a complicated endeavour to save Wilbur the pig's life. A child's fear of death and coming to terms with death is the underlying theme of this otherwise both comic and sad story.

In toy fantasy, the objective of the toys is often to come alive or at least become independent. [5] The most poignant portrayal of a toy's longing is to be found in Russell Hoban's *The Mouse and His Child* (1967), seemingly a traditional fairy-tale quest after a better life, but in fact a tragic allegory on everything's inevitable decay. The eternal wish to become alive, inherent in toy fantasy, is represented more symbolically as striving to become self-winding. The toys' adventures are full of suffering, but there is no happy ending, no return to the nursery when they were new and enjoyed. Yet in all its gloom the novel asserts traditional values such as love, family bonds, friendship and mutual support, and the triumph of good over evil, although on moral rather than physical premises.

Mary Norton's *The Borrowers* series (1952–61) depicts a world of miniature people living isolated from humans, but finally befriending an ordinary boy. The three last surviving members of a once flourishing community are eventually forced to leave the temporal security and venture on a long and dangerous journey. The curiosity and resilience of the child, Arietty, is promptly emphasized in the series. A secret and secluded community of tiny people eventually saved by a human child appears also in T. H. White's *Mistress Masham's Repose* (1947). The isolation motif is echoed much later in *The Mennyms* (1993) and sequels, by Sylvia Waugh, featuring full-size rag dolls. These novels differ from earlier works as they allow more room for the fictive child's – and thus the reader's – moral choices while presenting adults as threatening and corrupted.

Alternative worlds

While time displacement and animated toys are significantly more prominent in fantasy for children, secondary-world fantasy is less original and shows more similarities with the mainstream. After Tolkien's *The Hobbit* (1937), published as a children's book, and C. S. Lewis's Narnia novels (see Chapter 5), which closely follow the Romantic tradition of the innocent chosen child, the most consistent secondary world addressed to a young audience appears in the American Lloyd Alexander's Prydain Chronicles (1964–8). Based on the medieval Welsh myth collection *The Mabinogion*, the series features the archetypal hero of unknown parentage destined to save the world from evil. The ending is similar to Tolkien's epic, as the magic forces abandon the world, leaving it to humans to attend to their matters. The hero is given the choice of remaining or following his fellow wizards.

The construction of the alternative world is still more subtle in Susan Cooper's series *The Dark is Rising* (1965–77). Their sources in the Arthurian legends, the five quest novels both bring magic into the everyday and contain parallel worlds and times with boundaries barely tangible. An ordinary eleven-year-old boy discovering on his eleventh birthday that he is a powerful magician is a distinct forerunner to Harry Potter. Will Stanton, however, is involved both in the struggle against evil in the world of magic and in protecting the real world from dark forces. The threat of evil magic penetrating into the everyday is a token of later fantasy for children (cf. the discussion of Alan Garner's works in Chapter 20). Cooper's *Seaward* (1983) presents the alternative world as an inner landscape, a mindscape, all the more elaborate as it is shared by the two protagonists, a boy and a girl, adding the gender-related experience of the fantasy world ostensibly based on the diverse male/female initiation and maturation patterns. The novel resists a straightforward reading and encourages complex psychoanalytical interpretations. Like much contemporary children's fantasy it rejects a happy ending. The two characters are given the option of forgetting their painful experiences, but prefer to keep them, while the children in *The Dark is Rising* forcibly have their memories erased.

The Australian Patricia Wrightson's Wirrun trilogy (1977–81) also presents a fluctuant boundary between the magical and the ordinary, incorporating Aboriginal lore into the story of a young person's quest, with animated nature and indigenous creatures as helpers and adversaries. Many writers, however, employ the classical device of sending the protagonist to an alternative world by means of some magic agent, with the purpose of temporary empowerment. Lloyd Alexander's *The First Two Lives of Lukas-Kasha* (1978) transposes the character into a world inspired by Arabian Nights, where he transforms from a good-for-nothing street urchin into a full-fledged hero who, on returning to his own world, is, unlike C. S. Lewis's children, allowed to retain his new qualities. The title of the novel points at heterotopia that emerges clearly in later fantasy writers such as Diana Wynne Jones and Philip Pullman.

Another typical secondary-world fantasy is the German Michael Ende's *The Neverending Story* (1979), which bears considerable traces of post-modern influences in its metafictive nature, as the protagonist eventually is drawn into the book he is reading. The novel demonstrates both the power of imagination, as the child is allowed to re-create a dying world, and its escapism and corruption, reminiscent of Tolkien's ring. Yet it is common for children's writers to bring their characters back to the security of home and of adult protection, following the tradition of Nesbit, C. S. Lewis and not least Tolkien with his 'There and Back Again'. This concession to the convention of children's literature is breached by the Swedish writer Astrid Lindgren in her two fantasy novels *Mio My Son* (1954) and *The Brothers Lionheart* (1973), both featuring lonely boys who escape into imaginary worlds from a bleak and hopeless reality. Rusky in *The Brothers Lionheart* is mortally ill, and his adventures in the alternative world may be interpreted as death agony. In both novels, the protagonists never return to the primary world and remain the heroes they have become due to their magical journeys.

A highly original and enigmatic fantasy novel is Catherine Storr's *Marianne Dreams* (1967) in which the protagonist's actions in the secondary world affect another person's condition in her real world. Although the title suggests a simple interpretation of the story as the character's dreams, or rather nightmares, the metafictive frame-breaking makes it complex and engaging, anticipating sophisticated fantasy from the 1980s and beyond.

Most other mid-twentieth century alternative-world fantasies are, however, quite repetitive, focused on the motifs of either quest or struggle between good and evil, or both, even though the nature of the alternative worlds as such can be imaginative and diverse. Erik Linklater's *The Pirates in the Deep Green Sea* (1942) takes the characters into an underwater realm. In Barbara Sleigh's *Carbonel* (1955) and sequels, a cat leads the protagonists into the secret nocturnal realm of the felines. Norton Juster's playful *The Phantom Tollbooth* (1961) introduces a bored boy to the exciting worlds of words and numbers. Roald Dahl's *Charlie and the Chocolate Factory* (1964) replays the theme of the virtuous hero winning over the less worthy rivals in a world of a gastronomic utopia. Dahl's *The BFG* (1982) features a land of giants who kidnap and eat children from England, while his *Witches* (1982) depicts an invasion of the ordinary world by evil magic powers. The original feature of this particular novel is that the protagonist wins over his adversaries while transformed into a mouse, and, unlike most conventional endings, he does not return to his human appearance. Otherwise, the majority of fantasy novels seldom go beyond action-oriented plots. While the protagonists gain some wisdom from their experiences, on a deeper level they stay unaffected, unlike some of the time travellers discussed above.

Visual fantasy

Children's picturebooks are normally treated as a separate category, while in fact some of them not only display characteristic features of fantasy, but provide vast possibilities for the hesitation that lies at the basis for the fantastic. There are numerous picturebooks employing anthropomorphic animals, animated toys and objects, and supernatural characters as children in disguise, from *The Tale of Peter Rabbit* (1901), by Beatrix Potter, to *The Little Train* (1973), by Grahame Greene and Edward Ardizzone. In such stories, an animal or toy, fairy or dragon have the same function as in ordinary fantasy: either a protagonist or a helper. Most of these stories hardly add anything substantially new to the range of fantasy motifs, even though the visual element offers more detailed setting and characterization and frequently creates a comic effect through word/image counterpoint. More challenging are the many picturebooks justifiably comparable to some major works of fantasy, where the interaction of word and image creates a synergy of meaning allowing various levels of interpretation. The best-known example is *Where the Wild Things Are* (1963), by Maurice Sendak, a typical secondary-world fantasy, in which a child escapes into an imaginary world from a conflict with his mother. He becomes a hero, conquers monsters, is enthroned but eventually returns to his ordinary world and is stripped of his tokens of power, much like the characters of the Narnia series. The images add to the sparse description of the gradual transformation of the everyday into the fantastic, but they also create a sense of uncertainty about the nature of events, since words and images are not quite in accordance with each other. In Anthony Browne's *The Tunnel* (1989) a portal connects two worlds, and expands on a scant verbal narrative of a girl following her brother to rescue him from danger, with images that contain secondary world of horror and enchantment as close attention reveals wolves and bears in the trees, and we are in a story shaped by very old tales, the most obvious of which is Red Riding Hood. In David McKee's *Not Now, Bernard* (1980), which features metamorphosis, a symbolic rather than a literal interpretation of the supernatural event is prompted by the words, while the images sustain the literal interpretation. Bernard is eaten by a monster who then does the things Bernard longs to do, but as none of the victims ever turn around, that the monster both is and represents Bernard *might* be assumed. Or it might not. Babette Cole's *The Trouble With Mum* (1983) brings the magical into the everyday and grants to the protagonist and the reader a sense that it is the 'real' world that is abnormal and the witch family of the story (much like The Addams Family) are the ones with ordinary lives. *The Trouble with Mum* plays with a comic contradiction of the matter-of-fact text and the most extraordinary events presented visually. In all these books, images play a central role in the construction of the fantastic.

If we regard picturebooks as a medium rather than a genre, many texts should be rightfully included among fantasy for children and are by no means less complex than novels.

Conclusion

Going back to some principal differences between fantasy for children and fantasy for adults, it is not sufficient to state that the former has a child as protagonist. At its best, fantasy for children provides moral and spiritual guidance for young people, addressing an audience that has yet not any firm distinction between reality and imagination; that does not dismiss magical worlds and events as implausible; that has stronger potential for secondary belief. The best examples of classical fantasy for children use the fantastic form as a narrative device, as a metaphor for reality. The fantastic mode allows children's writers to deal with important psychological, ethical and existential questions in a slightly detached manner, which frequently proves more effective with young readers than straightforward realism. For instance, the battle of good and evil may be less disturbing, yet more persuasive, when described within an imaginary world than in the reader's immediate surrounding. The spiritual growth of the protagonist can be presented more tangibly when depicted in terms of struggle with external magic forces than in terms of inner tension. In particular, fantasy can empower a child protagonist in a way that realistic prose is incapable of doing. In this respect fantasy has a huge subversive potential as it can interrogate the existing power relationships, including those between child and adult, without necessarily shattering the real order of the world.

The remarkable feature of fantasy for children is that it has always enjoyed a higher status within children's literature than fantasy in general literature where it is frequently treated as formulaic fiction. Apparently, fantasy is considered suitable for children on the same premises as folk and fairy tales, mostly as a socialization vehicle. Yet, paradoxically, the best examples of children's fantasy have always been questioned as books for children, such as *Alice in Wonderland*, *The Wind in the Willows* and *Winnie-the-Pooh*. This trend has culminated in the contemporary phenomenon of cross-over, best illustrated by Philip Pullman and J. K. Rowling.

NOTES

1 See Roger Sale, *Fairy Tales and After* (Cambridge, MA: Harvard University Press, 1978); and Jack Zipes, *When Dreams Came True. Classical Fairy Tales and Their Tradition* (New York and London: Routledge, 1999).

2 Barbara Wall, *The Narrator's Voice. The Dilemma of Children's Fiction* (London: Macmillan, 1991).

3 Marcus Crouch, *The Nesbit Tradition. The Children's Novel 1945–1970* (Tonbridge: Ernest Benn, 1972).

4 Jacqueline Rose, *The Case of Peter Pan, or The Impossibility of Children's Fiction* (London: Macmillan, 1984).

5 Lois Kuznets, *When Toys Come Alive. Narratives of Animation, Metamorphosis and Development* (New Haven, CT: Yale University Press, 1994).

5

EDWARD JAMES

Tolkien, Lewis and the explosion of genre fantasy

J. R. R. Tolkien said that the phrase 'In a hole in the ground there lived a hobbit' came to his unconscious mind while marking examination papers; he wrote it on a blank page in an answer book.[1] From that short sentence, one might claim, much of the modern fantasy genre emerged. Tolkien's *The Lord of the Rings* (1954–5) (henceforth *LOTR*) looms over all the fantasy written in English – and in many other languages – since its publication; most subsequent writers of fantasy are either imitating him or else desperately trying to escape his influence. His hold over readers has been extraordinary: as is well known, and to the annoyance of literary critics, three major surveys of public opinion in Great Britain around the turn of the millennium placed him as the 'author of the century' or his book as the most popular work of English fiction, beating Jane Austen's *Pride and Prejudice* into second place. In 2004, Australians and Germans both voted *LOTR* their nation's favourite book. *LOTR* has been translated into all the world's major languages; and film director Peter Jackson's loving re-creation of Tolkien's world (2001–3) is the most profitable trilogy in cinema history, grossing nearly three billion American dollars.

The fantasy novels of C. S. Lewis – in particular his so-called 'Space Trilogy' (1938–46) and the seven Narnia books (1950–56) – have not had quite that impact, but have nevertheless reached a large audience, and, as Lewis's status as a Christian writer continues to grow, so that audience expands. The Narnia sequence has become one of the best loved and most enduring series of fantasies for children, currently reaching a wide cinema audience: the first three adaptations were released in 2005, 2008 and 2010, and the fourth is in planning: it is *The Magician's Nephew*, based on the sixth book which Lewis published.

It is natural to consider the two men together, not just because they were close friends, who offered both criticism and encouragement on each other's fantasy writing, but because they stand together at the origins of modern fantasy, mediating the fantasies of earlier generations and both, in their own very different ways, helping to give modern fantasy its medievalist cast.

Tolkien was born in South Africa, but brought up as a Catholic in the English Midlands; Lewis was an Ulster Protestant from Belfast, and although educated (very unhappily) at an English public school always thought of himself as an alien in England. Both fought in the trenches in the First World War and both had been invalided out before the end; experiences which affected them profoundly. They both became professional medievalists, and both of them spent most of their academic lives at Oxford (although for the last nine years of his life (1954–63) Lewis was the Professor of Medieval and Renaissance English at Cambridge). Tolkien had been appointed to the first of his two Chairs of English at Oxford as early as 1925; he retired in 1959 and outlived his younger friend Lewis by ten years. Although they both taught medieval English, they came at it from very different angles. As Lewis put it in his autobiography, 'Friendship with [Tolkien] marked the breakdown of two old prejudices. At my first coming into the world I had been (implicitly) warned never to trust a Papist, and at my first coming into the English Faculty (explicitly) never to trust a philologist. Tolkien was both.'[2] Ironically, Tolkien was one of those instrumental in converting Lewis, from atheism to Christianity (though not to Catholicism), in 1931. However, the two of them remained on opposite sides in the academic warfare between literary scholars and philologists in the Oxford English Faculty. Lewis was above all interested in medieval literature, and in what the stories revealed about the way in which medieval people thought; Tolkien was fascinated by the languages of the past, and by what language revealed of the way in which medieval people thought. As a child, Lewis invented stories about people who lived in the fantasy world of Boxen, while Tolkien invented languages. In 1955, Tolkien wrote to his American publishers that all his works were *'fundamentally linguistic* in inspiration . . . The invention of languages is the foundation. The "stories" were made rather to provide a world for the languages than the reverse. To me a name comes first and the story follows' (*Letters*, 219). While still at school he had studied Gothic, Welsh and Finnish; but he also made a start on the invented languages of his fictional Middle-earth: Quenya, Sindarin and Dwarvish. When he said that the word 'hobbit' came to his unconscious mind while marking exams, it is worth noting that his unconscious mind was by no means blank. The hobbits were, in fact, the last of the denizens of Tolkien's fantasy world to be created: by then he had been writing unpublished stories about the elves, dwarves, wizards and men of Middle-earth for two decades.

In order to understand how profoundly Tolkien influenced the growth of the modern fantasy genre, it is necessary to comment briefly on the text. It starts in the Shire, a haven of rural normality, except for one thing: the existence in the pocket of Bilbo Baggins of the Ring into which Sauron has poured all his evil power. Bilbo leaves the Shire and, with great reluctance, leaves the Ring behind for his nephew Frodo. The wizard Gandalf warns Frodo that Sauron has learned the whereabouts of his lost ring, and that he must leave and take the Ring from the Shire. The first half of the first volume of the trilogy, *The Fellowship of the Ring*, takes Frodo and his three hobbit companions out of the Shire and into the relative security of Rivendell, one of the homes of the elves. The second half of the volume sees the Fellowship being formed (four hobbits, one elf, one dwarf, Gandalf and two men, one of whom is Aragorn, heir to the great kingdom of Gondor). At the end of the volume the Fellowship is broken up, and the second volume (*The Two Towers*) follows the separate adventures of Frodo and Sam, as they head towards the volcano in Mordor, Sauron's own territory, which alone can destroy the Ring, and the others, who begin to accumulate support for the defence of their lands from the increasingly aggressive actions of Sauron. In the final volume, *The Return of the King*, Frodo and Sam manage to destroy the Ring, just before Sauron launches his final attack on their friends and allies. Sauron's power vanishes; Aragorn is crowned king; a new age begins; and the hobbits go home, to clear the Shire of the last remnants of the evil powers. Frodo himself, along with some of the greatest of the elves, takes ship for the mysterious lands of the West, which is analogous to the journey from Earth to Heaven.

LOTR establishes many of the characteristics of genre fantasy, some of which can be indicated by terms that John Clute has introduced into fantasy criticism. (I capitalize certain words below, following the conventions of Clute and Grant's *Encyclopedia of Fantasy*, to indicate that these are entries in the *Encyclopedia*.) Middle-earth is subject to THINNING, a decline from its former state, partly due to the actions of Sauron, the *Dark Lord*. The sense of WRONGNESS in the world demands *Healing*, and that is the purpose of the QUEST on which our heroes embark. It is typical of the portal-quest, in Mendlesohn's definition, that the heroes (in this case hobbits) move from a familiar world into an unfamiliar one, and learn about that unfamiliar world largely through the uncontested explanations of a mentor-figure (in this case Gandalf). In the course of this quest, the characters reach RECOGNITION, an awareness of their own role in the story of the world, and finally achieve EUCATASTROPHE, a term which Tolkien himself invented to describe the uplifting characteristics of fairy tale. It is the final turn in the plot, which brings 'a catch of the breath, a beat and a lifting of the heart, near to (or indeed accompanied by) tears, as keen as that given in any form of literary art, and having a peculiar quality'.[3]

These elements are part of the basic structure of many fantasies; but Tolkien also indulged in various PLOT DEVICES which are commonly found in subsequent fantasies. These include the Cook's Tour (a journey around the MAP OF FANTASYLAND); Escape (such as Gandalf's escape from the Balrog, which Tolkien probably intended to recall Christ's Resurrection); Separation (when COMPANIONS are able to have different adventures, embarking on different Cook's Tours, thus enabling a trilogy to expand into a twelve-volume series if the readers so demand); Temptation (which brings drama into the confrontation between good and evil); and Walking (which means that characters travel slowly through LANDSCAPES and have to solve problems rather than ride away from them).

Tolkien's greatest achievement, however, in retrospect, was in normalizing the idea of a secondary world. Although he retains the hint that the action of *LOTR* takes place in the prehistory of our own world, that is not sustained, and to all intents and purposes Middle-earth is a separate creation, operating totally outside the world of our experience. This has become so standard in modern fantasy that it is not easy to realize how unusual it was before Tolkien. John Clute described it thus: '*LOTR* marked the end of apology.'[4] After 1955 fantasy writers no longer had to explain away their worlds by framing them as dreams, or travellers' tales, or by providing them with any fictional link to our own world at all.

The best introduction to Tolkien's own thinking is provided by his essay 'On Fairy-Stories', which was printed in his book *Tree and Leaf*. Fairy stories, he said (and in Tolkien's terms we may justifiably regard *LOTR* as a giant fairy story) should take themselves, and above all their Magic, seriously. 'If there is any satire present in the tale, one thing that must not be made fun of, is the magic itself' (15). If it is framed as a dream or a traveller's tale, the writer cheats the reader of 'primal desire at the heart of Faërie: the realization, independent of the conceiving mind, of imagined wonder' (16). He famously denies that fairy stories should be restricted to children; indeed, it demeans the fairy story to think that it needs a child, with credulity based on lack of experience, before the marvels of a fairy story can be appreciated. God has created the Primary World; but a writer can be a 'sub-creator' of a Secondary World (Tolkien's capitals).

> Inside it, what he relates is 'true': it accords with the laws of that world. You therefore believe it, while you are, as it were, inside. The moment disbelief arises, the spell is broken; the magic, or rather art, has failed. You are then out in the Primary World again, looking at the little abortive Secondary World from outside. (36–7)

One might say that Tolkien lapses on a number of occasions in *LOTR*. When, very near the beginning, one of Gandalf's fireworks is described as being like an express train, the spell has broken, as happens when Sam Gamgee mentions that his favourite food is fish and chips.[5] The reader is jolted out into the Primary World again. However, what Tolkien did to give readers that necessary sense of belief in Secondary World was to provide enormous historical and cultural depth to Middle-earth. *LOTR* came equipped with maps and appendices, but it also came after nearly forty years' work of sub-creation of the world which preceded the action of *LOTR*. Sometimes the depth is established simply by allusion. Aragorn says of Gandalf 'he is surer of finding his way home in a blind night than the cats of Queen Beruthiel' (303). Beruthiel is not otherwise mentioned in the trilogy at all. 'Who cares about the cats of Queen Beruthiel?' cried one early critic of Tolkien. Tolkien's insight was that most readers do, and it is a crucial insight into what is needed to make a 'full' fantasy world, as complex and intriguing, and hence as believable, as our own.

Tolkien suggested that there were four essential elements of fairy story: Fantasy, Recovery, Escape and Consolation. Fantasy was the result of sub-creation: the creation of something which is not in our world, but which has the consistency of reality. 'Fantasy (in this sense) is, I think, not a lower but a higher form of Art, indeed, the most nearly pure form, and so (when achieved) the most potent' ('On Fairy-Stories', 45). Fantasy, he continues, aspires to Enchantment. 'Enchantment produces a Secondary World into which both designer and spectator can enter, to the satisfaction of their senses while they are inside; but in its purity it is artistic in desire and purpose' (49). Fantasy brings us Recovery: the cleansing of our eyes so that we can see our world more clearly. Fantasy brings us Escape: not escapism, in a derogatory sense, which is the Flight of the Deserter, but (and here I summarize a long and complex argument) a mental escape from the ugliness and evil around us. And finally Fantasy brings us Consolation, above all the Consolation of the Happy Ending: Eucatastrophe, as described earlier.

Arguably this essay has been as influential as *LOTR* itself in the construction of modern fantasy. But in fact the two are inseparable. *LOTR* is Tolkien's realization of the principles he laid down in 'On Fairy-Stories', and arguably helped him to carry on *LOTR* to the end. As he himself noted, he wrote it in 1938/9, at a time when the hobbits had reached Bree (that is, only a few chapters into *LOTR*) 'and I had no more notion than they had of what had become of Gandalf or who Strider was; and I had begun to despair of surviving to find out' (*Tree and Leaf*, 5). The process of working out his philosophy of fantasy cleared the way to his completion of the work: one can easily see from the early drafts which Christopher Tolkien has published that until Bree (Chapter 9) Tolkien was indeed floundering.[6]

Whether Tolkien's friend Lewis had any input into the development of these ideas cannot be determined for certain, but it is highly likely. The two were still close friends in the late 1930s, and Lewis listened to the chapters, and the drafts of chapters, of *LOTR* as they were written. One of the keys to the friendship between Tolkien and Lewis was the fact that their background reading in fantasy was very similar. They both loved the Victorian fantasies of George MacDonald and William Morris, the fairy stories assembled by the Grimm brothers and Andrew Lang, the mythological operas of Wagner and the illustrations by Arthur Rackham of Wagner, Shakespeare and others. Like William Morris, they both found inspiration in the medieval Icelandic sagas. There were some differences, however. Tolkien was fascinated by the *Kalevala*, the Finnish epic; Lewis found Graeco-Roman mythology even more interesting than Norse mythology. And their academic interests were different, and that influenced the fantasies they wrote. Lewis was an enthusiast of the chivalric romances of the later Middle Ages, and Tolkien was inspired by the culture and languages of the early Middle Ages. In 1965 Tolkien described a couplet by Cynewulf, the tenth-century Anglo-Saxon poet – 'Hail, Earendel, brightest of angels / Over Middle-earth sent unto men' – as the 'rapturous words from which ultimately sprang the whole of my mythology'.[7] Eärendil became the subject of a poem in *LOTR*, and was a character in *The Silmarillion*, the posthumous publication of Tolkien's earlier mythological writings.

In 'On Fairy-Stories' and in his work on the Middle English poem *Sir Gawain and the Green Knight* – a wonderful work of supernatural fantasy – Tolkien argued forcibly and entirely successfully that works of imaginative creation, that fantasies, can express real and important truths – truths that were regarded as worthy of an adult audience in the Middle Ages, and should be now. The American medievalist Norman Cantor in his controversial book *Inventing the Middle Ages*, which looks at the achievements of many medievalists in the last century, including Lewis and Tolkien – 'the Oxford fantasists' as he called them, wickedly linking them with the eminent medieval historian Sir Maurice Powicke – claimed that Tolkien expressed three important truths in *LOTR*.[8] He showed us the real fear felt by those in the early Middle Ages of marauding bands of soldiers that frequently terrorized the countryside; he illustrates the problems faced by those little men, ordinary people, virtually unarmed and certainly unprotected by trained soldiers, as they made their journeys through the perilous countryside, as they often did; and he showed us that it is not just the knights who displayed courage in the Middle Ages, but the little men too, as can be seen in many of the court cases which survive from the later Middle Ages.

There may be something to be said for Cantor's third and final point, but the first two are simple banalities. Tolkien certainly valued the courage of 'the little men'; he once said that in the trenches of the First World War he saw far more courage from the ordinary soldiers than he did from the officers. In *LOTR* it is the courage of the little man – or, rather, the hobbit – that eventually saves the world. We have the courage of Frodo Baggins, Peregrin Took and Meriadoc Brandybuck, but they – despite their short stature – are not 'the little men' of whom Tolkien speaks. They are the officer class of the Shire: they are the well-to-do, the so-called 'born leaders'. It is Samwise Gamgee whose courage ultimately saves Middle-earth; and he, the gardener's son, is precisely the kind of man Tolkien was thinking about. In the book he has just the kind of relationship to Frodo that a British army batman has with his officer, or a man-servant with his gentleman. Tolkien also, of course, celebrates the courage of the great men, such as Gandalf, and of professional warriors and leaders like Aragorn and Faramir and many others, not forgetting Éowyn, the woman who stood up against the Lord of the Nazgûl when men had failed. 'She did not blench: maiden of the Rohirrim, child of kings, slender but as a steel-blade, fair yet terrible' (*LOTR*, 823).

Tolkien did, of course, bring to the composition of *LOTR* his profound knowledge of medieval literature. Of all the medieval texts that inspired Tolkien, the Old English poem *Beowulf* is the most important. His paper '*Beowulf*: The Monsters and the Critics', delivered to the British Academy in 1936, still remains, three-quarters of a century later, essential reading for the student, an astonishing achievement which has probably no parallel in any other corner of humanities scholarship.[9] Tolkien was preparing it at the same time as he was writing *The Hobbit*, the first major publication of any of his Middle-earth material, and it is interesting to see how it prefigures and parallels both that children's book and the later *LOTR*.

Tolkien's main point in his paper was not a philological one: it was to rescue the great Old English poem *Beowulf* from those who wished to view it as everything *except* a great poem: as a repository of historical facts, as a store of old words not found anywhere else, as the expression of the opinions of the whole committee of people who, it was once believed, constructed the poem. Earlier critics had tended to find stories about monsters and dragons terribly silly and concluded that a poem about them could not be any good. Tolkien argued that it *was* very good, that it was by a single author, and a great author, and that through the fantastic events of the poem – the killing of the monster Grendel, and then of Grendel's mother, and then of a dragon – the poet could express real truths about courage, and loyalty, and duty, as well as express those truths in gloriously complex and beautiful poetic form. Fantasy, for Tolkien, was a way of getting closer to the important things of life than the realistic novel ever could.

What the *Beowulf*-poet, whoever he was, did with *Beowulf* was very similar to what Tolkien did with *LOTR*. Tolkien called his fantasy 'a profoundly Catholic work', yet, as in *Beowulf*, the 'specifically Christian was suppressed, so also were the old gods'. Middle-earth is surprisingly unreligious – a very poor re-creation of the medieval world, but a very precise re-creation of the world of Beowulf. In *LOTR* the character Denethor is referred to as 'heathen', an anachronistic reference in a pre-Christian context, and 'heathen' appears once in *Beowulf*, in a similarly inappropriate context, a little in-joke which Tolkien must have known only *Beowulf* scholars would have appreciated. Yet although the specifically Christian is suppressed, Tolkien's book is full of subtle references to Christianity, showing how his fictional world prefigures Christianity just as medieval biblical scholars saw Old Testament stories as prefiguring Christ. Tolkien himself admitted that *lembas*, Elvish waybread, was intended to recall the Eucharist; Frodo triumphed over Sauron on 25 March, the date of Christ's conception, the traditional day for the crucifixion, and the beginning of the New Year in the Middle Ages (and, after Frodo's victory, on Middle-earth too). Frodo himself is a Christ figure, just as the hero Beowulf is; the final stages of the carrying of the Ring up Mount Doom are very like Christian accounts of Christ carrying the cross up Mount Calvary. Frodo is not the only Christ figure, however; Gandalf, dying in his fight with the Balrog, taken into the depths of the earth and then being reborn and clothed in white, is another. The whole discussion about the nature of evil is, as Tom Shippey has shown, couched in very Christian terms.[10] Like *Beowulf*, *LOTR* is a Catholic epic that is successful in part because it is so subtle and understated.

Tolkien believed that *Beowulf* critics, as well as misreading the Christianity of the text, were guilty of marginalizing the fantastic, 'putting the irrelevances at the centre and the serious things on the outer edge'. Nothing shows this better than R. W. Chambers's comment on the passing allusion by the *Beowulf*-poet to the story of Ingeld: 'In this conflict between plighted troth and the duty of revenge we have a situation which the old heroic poets loved, and would not have sold for a wilderness of dragons' ('*Beowulf*: The Monsters...', 108–9). Who wants to hear about *dragons*, Chambers was saying, when we could be hearing an epic love story? As Tolkien pointed out, Chambers is in effect blaming the *Beowulf*-poet for the accident that we have lost almost all the rest of Anglo-Saxon poetry, including all the songs about Ingeld, but he also misses the point that one of the things that gives

Beowulf its depth, and makes it so poignant, Tolkien thought, was the poet's frequent allusion to stories and characters which were familiar to the audience but not to us. The unexpanded reference to Ingeld may be frustrating, but it gives the story great depth and richness. As we have seen, in *LOTR* Tolkien frequently makes allusion to the epic history of the centuries that had passed before the events described in the book, and some of Tolkien's critics were as annoyed by this as Chambers was at the *Beowulf*-poet.

The final contribution made by Tolkien to later twentieth-century fantasy was that the default cultural model for the fantasy world was the Middle Ages. For Tolkien it came naturally, and he must have seen *LOTR* as in some sense a commentary upon things medieval. But in the hands of people who were not professional medievalists, medievalism could quickly become a cliché, and one that would be mercilessly parodied by the children's author Diana Wynne Jones (taught as an undergraduate at Oxford by Tolkien himself) in her book *The Tough Guide to Fantasyland*.

C. S. Lewis's take on the Middle Ages, in his own fantasies, was very different, partly because of his own spiritual journey. Lewis, ever since that conversion in September 1931, had been a convinced Christian even if not, to Tolkien's disappointment, a Catholic. Although he became Britain's best-known popularizer of Christianity, through radio talks and best-selling books, his conversion had been unusual. He had become convinced, as a result of his talk with his friends Tolkien and Dyson, that the Christian myths were actually as powerful as the Graeco-Roman myths that had so fascinated him, with the added advantage that they were true. He had already turned from atheism to theism, but this is what persuaded him to return to Christianity. Like a medieval Christian intellectual, he believed that God had given partial visions of the truth to Greeks and Romans, and that their myths reflected part of that truth. The pagan gods were not, thus, demons to him; stories about them, at least, could be prefigurations of Christ. When he went to Greece with his dying wife in 1960 he was sorely tempted to pray to Apollo the Healer: 'somehow one didn't feel it wd. have been very wrong – wd. have only been addressing Christ *sub specie Apollinis*'.[11] His last fantasy novel was *Till We have Faces* (1956), which retells the story of Cupid and Psyche, a classical myth which had been seen in the Middle Ages as expressing profound truths about the nature of Christian love.

The first fantasy books that Lewis wrote at first sight have nothing to do with Lewis the medievalist. The so-called Space Trilogy consists of *Out of the Silent Planet* (1938), *Perelandra* (aka *Voyage to Venus*, 1948) and *That Hideous Strength* (aka *The Tortured Planet*, 1945). They are generally regarded as science fiction, but they are clearly far removed from the science fiction of their day. The planets are governed by angelic beings, and the space between the planets is filled with spirits. In the final volume, the evil scientists are crushed by Merlin, who calls to his aid various of the planetary rulers, including Jupiter. The meaning of the trilogy is clear to readers of Lewis's book *The Discarded Image: An Introduction to Medieval and Renaissance Literature* (1964): Lewis is writing science fiction in which the familiar 'what if?' is the playful 'what if medieval cosmologists were right?' Some of this playfulness appears also in Lewis's more famous fantasy sequence, about the magical land of Narnia.

Of the first of Lewis's Narnia books, *The Lion, the Witch and the Wardrobe* (1950), Tolkien said to Roger Lancelyn Green, 'It really won't do!'[12] Tolkien was probably alluding to Lewis's apparently slapdash world-building, which was as far from Tolkien's laboriously constructed universe as it could possibly be. When the Pevensey children reached the fantasy world, through the portal in the wardrobe, they found it populated by a strange mixture of beings. Given that Narnia was an ancient Etruscan town in our world, perhaps it was not too surprising to find fauns, centaurs, dryads and even Bacchus in the fantasy Narnia. But there are also talking beavers, Father Christmas, a Snow Queen straight out of Hans Christian Andersen, and a lion called by the Turkish word for 'lion', Aslan. The lion turns out to be a Narnian version of Christ, and three of the seven books provide us with Narnian versions of Christian mythology: the Creation (in *The Magician's Nephew*, 1955), the death and resurrection of a god (*The Lion, the Witch and the Wardrobe*) and the end of the world (*The Last Battle*, 1956). The Christian is thus interwoven with the pagan, in a way that seems typical of Lewis. Those three books rework Genesis, the Gospels and Revelations; the remaining four in the sequence may be intended to recall classic Christian fantasies – *The Voyage of the 'Dawn Treader'* reworks the medieval *Voyage of St Brendan*; *The Horse and his Boy* may be a version of the popular parable, 'Footprints in the Sand' first credited to Mary Stevenson in 1936.[13] *The Silver Chair*, with its catechisms, may well be Bunyan's *Pilgrim's Progress*;[14] and so on.

Efforts have also been made to explain the seven books of the sequence in terms of Christian numerology: the Seven Virtues, the Seven Deadly Sins, even the Seven Sacraments. But the most plausible and exciting is that offered by Michael Ward, who links the Narnia books with the Space Trilogy, by considering it as a tribute to the seven heavenly bodies of medieval cosmology.[15] The mood of the first book, as beautifully expressed in the original Pauline Baynes cover picture of Susan, Lucy and the lion romping together in a meadow, is joviality. Peter constantly swears 'By Jove!'; and the coming of spring is associated with Jove/Jupiter in medieval tradition. Jupiter's colour is red (as in the costume of Father Christmas). Once that code is cracked, the other novels easily fall into their correct place. *Prince Caspian* (1951) is presided over by Mars: there is warfare, swords and armour, and Peter is portrayed as a paragon of chivalry. *The Voyage of the 'Dawn Treader'* (1952) is dominated by the Sun: gold and light appear throughout, and at one point Lucy sees Aslan in a shaft of sunlight. *The Silver Chair* (1953) is suffused with imagery of the Moon, of water, of silver, and of dark night; Prince Rilian has become a lunatic, and the children are helped in their quest to find him by an owl. *The Horse and His Boy* (1954) is probably the most difficult to fit into this schema. It has to be Mercury; and the twins associated with Mercury are everywhere. *The Magician's Nephew* (1955) is about love, creativity and fertility, all aspects of Venus; *The Last Battle* (1956) is about time, age and death, the attributes of Saturn. It is, surely the only children's book in which all the major child characters are killed off at the beginning of the book, and in which many other protagonists are consigned to oblivion while the chosen few finally progress to Heaven. It is a tactic that infuriated Philip Pullman, as Catherine Butler explains in a later chapter.

The influence of Tolkien and Lewis was partly positive: admirers were keen to write more of the same. But the negative influence has perhaps been just as important. Michael Moorcock wrote of *The Lord of the Rings* in a chapter called 'Epic Pooh' and claimed that his prose was 'the prose of the nursery-room ... meant to soothe and console ... It is frequently enjoyed not for its tensions but for its lack of tensions. It coddles, it makes friends with you; it tells you comforting lies.'[16] When Moorcock came to develop his own epic fantasy, in the 1960s, it centred on an amoral albino, Elric of Melniboné, whose magical sword had a thirst for blood: deliberately as far from Tolkien's aesthetic as Moorcock was able to manage. Likewise, in the 1990s, Philip Pullman was inspired in part by his distaste for C. S. Lewis to imagine his sequence called His Dark Materials, in the third volume of which God dies.

It must be remembered, however, that commercial viability is an important element in the development of new genres. C. S. Lewis's Narnia books sold well in hardback and then, from 1959, they began to appear as paperbacks and continued to sell steadily for the next fifty years, reinforced by BBC productions in the 1980s and a series of films beginning in 2005. But they were eclipsed by the huge sales occasioned by the paperback versions of *The Lord of the Rings*, which appeared in both the UK and the USA in 1965. As is well known, Tolkien became a cult classic in the later 1960s, and publishers began to realize the commercial potential of fantasy. The first to cash in on this were Ian and Betty Ballantine, whose imprint Ballantine Books in New York, had long been published science fiction. They had printed the first official paperbacks of Tolkien in 1965, which were followed up by reprints of E. R. Eddison, Mervyn Peake and others. In 1969 they created an imprint called Ballantine Adult Fantasy, which started reprinting classic fantasy: William Morris, Lord Dunsany, James Branch Cabell, and many others. Ballantine published eighty-five fantasy paperbacks in all, between 1965 and 1974; many of the titles had been out of print for years. They introduced readers to the rich variety of the English and American fantasy tradition, and they also showed one indication of the future: between 1970 and 1973 they published the first new fantasy trilogy since the paperbacking of Tolkien: Katherine Kurtz's sequence beginning with *Deryni Rising*. Thereafter fantasy trilogies began to make their appearance in the bookshops, slowly at first, but in a torrent in the 1980s and 1990s. Kurtz's own Deryni books, about magic in a secondary world closely based on north-west Europe in the high Middle Ages, became a whole sequence of trilogies. So far four trilogies have been published, and a fifth is almost complete.

There had always been some fantasy on the market, and there had even been trilogies before Tolkien. In 1946 the first volume of Mervyn Peake's astonishing Gormenghast trilogy was published, *Titus Groan*, which explored the grotesque world of Gormenghast castle; in 1938 T. H. White published *The Sword in the Stone*, a very new take on the Arthurian story, which, with its two sequels, appeared in 1958 as *The Once and Future King*. Other modern fantasy materials available in the 1960s were reprints of Robert E. Howard's Conan books, with additional material supplied by L. Sprague de Camp and others; and two volumes of Michael Moorcock's Elric sequence, originally published in *Science Fantasy*, a British magazine devoted to fantasy and outré science fiction, appeared between hard covers in the mid 1960s. Fantasy was beginning to emerge as a market challenger for the attention of science fiction writers: in the 1960s Andre Norton, a best-selling author of children's science fiction, turned to fantasy (or fantasy with science-fictional trimmings) in her Witch World sequence. Even more significant, however, was the number of children's writers who, in the wake of Lewis's Narnia books, published fantasies in the late 1950s and 1960s: the names include Joan Aiken, Lloyd Alexander, Susan Cooper, Alan Garner, Ursula K. Le Guin, Mary Norton and Philippa Pearce. By the 1970s, the generation who had read Tolkien, Lewis and these other writers of children's fantasy had become adult readers and, in some cases, writers. With the realization by publishers that fantasy had emerged as a commercial and recognizable genre, the fantasy boom began. At the same time, and related in many ways, came the horror boom. The origins of this may be dated to 1974, with the publication of *Carrie*, Stephen King's first novel. King himself, and numerous imitators, won a significant proportion of the market for popular fiction, and much of this horror contained elements of the fantastic. By the twenty-first century, horror had merged even further with fantasy, indicated in the appearance of new marketing labels: dark fantasy and paranormal romance.

1977 has often been taken as a crucial year in the development of the fantasy market. This saw the publication of the first volume of Stephen Donaldson's Thomas Covenant trilogy, *Lord Foul's Bane*; there were eventually to be two trilogies featuring the trials and tribulations of Covenant, a leper from our world, in a fantasy world which, initially at least, looked very like Middle-earth. In that year too the first of Terry Brooks's Shannara series appeared: *The Sword of Shannara*. To date Brooks has completed five trilogies set in the same world, and one tetralogy. *The Sword of Shannara* was little more than a reworking of *The Lord of the Rings*, although subsequent volumes moved away from slavish imitation. These books sold extremely well, presumably to people starved of new Tolkien. Ironically, this was also the year in which *The Silmarillion* appeared: Tolkien's stories of Middle-earth in its early years, put together by Tolkien's son, with the help of future fantasy writer Guy Gavriel Kay. It is also worth noting that 1977 was the year in which two science fiction movies were released: *Star Wars* (dir. George Lucas) and *Close Encounters of the Third Kind* (dir. Steven Spielberg). These were the first of many science-fictional blockbusters, but their feel, and part of their appeal, may derive from the fact that they occupied a half-way house between science fiction and fantasy. *Star Wars* in particular, with its sword-fights, knights, princesses and a sinister Emperor, was reminiscent of fairy tale, and it drew its structure, as George Lucas admitted, from Joseph Campbell's book *The Hero with a Thousand Faces* (1949; and subsequently reprinted with an image of Luke Skywalker on the cover). The aliens of *Close Encounters*, kidnapping humans who live with them without aging, are science-fictional reworkings of the fairies of medieval tradition.

By the late 1970s, it was clear that the new demand for fantasy was affecting the ways in which science fiction writers were working. Marion Zimmer Bradley, who had written a number of novels about the rediscovery of the abandoned colony planet Darkover by newly colonizing humans, began to write books about the centuries before the rediscovery which, with their magic and medieval trappings, were indistinguishable from fantasy. Anne McCaffrey's colony planet of Pern, with its dragon-riders and castles, likewise won a large following of readers who were able to discard the science-fictional framework and think of the books as fantasy. In 1982 (1980) the best-selling science fiction author Robert Silverberg published *Lord Valentine's Castle*, the first of a series set on the planet of Majipoor, which had the same crossover appeal to fantasy readers; and there are other examples.

Although reader surveys were not done at the time, it seems generally accepted that many of the readers of fantasy at this time were female. For female writers, fantasy appeared an obvious venue for working out ideas about feminism and utopian feminist possibilities. One of the earliest was Elizabeth Anne Lynn, whose trilogy beginning with *Watchtower* (1979) explored the possibilities of gender equality in a medieval-style society. In 1982 Marion Zimmer Bradley published *The Mists of Avalon*, the story of Arthur viewed from the point of view of Guinevere and the other women in his life, and portraying the king as struggling to impose patriarchal Christianity on the worshippers of the Mother Goddess. It was, and remains, enormously popular. But the period also saw more thoughtful explorations of gender, such as Samuel R. Delany's Nevèrÿon sequence, which began in 1979, which also began to deconstruct some of the assumptions behind the medieval or pre-industrial worlds of most fantasy.

Another sign that fantasy had achieved some sort of coming of age was the publication of parody that assumed some knowledge of the field. Terry Pratchett's *The Colour of Magic* (1983) and *The Light Fantastic* (1986) lampooned some of the best-known fantasy characters, notably Conan the Barbarian, who appears here as the toothless and cynical Cohen the Barbarian. These books were set on the Discworld, carried through space on the back of a turtle, a venue for magic, the home of trolls, dwarves, vampires, werewolves and other non-human species, and a place which has a strange resonance with the Earth that we know, making the books an ideal setting for satire and wry humour, although they have long gone beyond the parody of the earliest books. To date thirty-nine Discworld books have been published. Until he was displaced, at the very end of the 1990s, by another fantasy writer (J. K. Rowling), Pratchett was Britain's best-selling author (in any genre), and even now he sells some 2.5 million books a year in the UK.

It is important to recognize that fantasy also developed in new ways through the impact of other media. Although it is not within the remit of this book, gaming has been particularly important. The first version of the Dungeons and Dragons role-playing game (RPG) appeared in 1974. The fantasy setting was inspired initially by Tolkien, but RPGs have taken their fantasy settings from other novels, and they have also been the core texts upon which novelizations have been based. Dragonlance, for instance, is a shared universe created by Laura and Tracy Hickman, and developed, like Dungeons and Dragons, by TSR (Tactical Studies Rules, Inc.). In RPGs, the players develop their own characters, and a game master (GM) creates the setting and to some extent controls the narrative; in LARPs (live-action RPGs) the characters physically act out their adventures. Considerable invention and imagination is required for a successful RPG, and it is hardly surprising that players and GMs have gone on to write novels, developing their stories for a much wider audience. The first Dragonlance book was published in 1984; by now nearly 200 novels have been published within the Dragonlance universe.

A significant development of the 1990s was the appearance of the series novel on the best-seller lists. Robert Jordan, who had in the 1980s written seven new Conan books, published the first volume of his Wheel of Time series, *The Eye of the World*, in 1990. Each successive volume was 1,000 pages or more in length, and by the time of his death in 2007 he had published eleven of them; the twelfth and last is being finished by an author chosen by his widow. Another such prolific, and very popular, author is Terry Goodkind, whose Sword of Truth series (beginning in 1994 with *Wizard's First Rule*) has now reached its eleventh volume. Worldwide sales are estimated as twenty-five million.

One of the most unexpected developments of the last decade has been the domination of the popular fantasy genre by Australian women (and some Australian men). The first of these was Sara Douglass, whose first novel, *BattleAxe* (US: *The Wayfarer Redemption*) was published in 1995, and who has to date completed five fantasy trilogies. Others include Cecilia Dart-Thornton, whose novels make extensive use of English folklore; Caisel Mor, who is inspired by Irish folklore; Ian Irvine, whose Three Worlds Cycle is on the borderlands of science fiction; and Glenda Larke, whose well-imagined fantasy world is inspired by Indonesia where she has lived for some years. Some New Zealanders have gained prominence also, notably Russell Kirkpatrick and Juliet Marillier. These writers have only been a success because they have been able to market their books to publishers in the UK and USA; the Australian market remains far too small to sustain such a significant output of books.

Fantasy has become big business, for better or worse. J. K. Rowling's Harry Potter books, aimed at children but read by adults as well, have set numerous commercial records. The seventh and last book, *Harry Potter and the Deathly Hallows* (2007) sold 11 million copies on its first day of publication, 2.7 million copies in the UK and 8.3 million in the USA. The marketing impetus is sometimes sustained by the appearance of movies. The commercial potential of fantasy movies was established by Peter Jackson's *Lord of the Rings* trilogy (2001–3), and by various directors' adaptations of the Harry Potter books (2001 onwards). The film version of Stephenie Meyer's vampire novel *Twilight* (2005) was released in 2008, and in that year Meyer became the best-selling author in the USA, with sales of 22 million. At the time of completing this chapter, *USA Today*'s list of best-selling books (which includes cookery and self-help books) had five vampire novels in the top ten, four of which were by Meyer.[17]

It is remarkable that throughout this period *The Lord of the Rings* remained in print, and saw a new surge of popularity (as measured by sales) in the first years of the new millennium. C. S. Lewis's fantasies, likewise, have risen in popularity in recent years, as he has been taken up, particularly in the USA, as a Christian writer.

The current state of fantasy is to a large extent described in the last section of this book. Fantasy makes up a considerable proportion of the market for popular fiction, and although Tolkien-inspired quest fantasies dominate the bookshelves the field is not defined by this one form. There are many ways of writing fantasy, and many places to set it. There are many subgenres, and many ways in which fantasy tropes have leaked into the domain of mimetic fiction; fantasy has had a considerable impact on the genre often referred to as 'literary fiction'. Indeed, from Salman Rushdie's 1981 novel *Midnight's Children* onwards, there have been numerous award-winning books by major literary writers which could be described as 'fantasy'. In the chapters that follow, the traces of Tolkien's and Lewis's influence will always be visible, through both emulation and rejection, but while the two are giants in the field, the possibilities of fantasy are not confined by their works.

NOTES

1 Humphrey Carpenter (ed.), *The Letters of J. R. R. Tolkien* (London: George Allen and Unwin, 1981), p. 215.

2 C. S. Lewis, *Surprised by Joy: The Shape of My Early Life* (1955) (London: Fount Paperbacks, 1977), p. 173.

3 'On Fairy-Stories', in J. R. R. Tolkien, *Tree and Leaf*, 2nd edn (London: Unwin Hyman, 1988), pp. 62–3.

4 John Clute in Clute and John Grant (eds.), *The Encyclopedia of Fantasy* (London: Orbit, 1993), p. 951.

5 J. R. R. Tolkien, *The Lord of the Rings*, revised one-volume edn (London: HarperCollins, 1994), pp. 27, 640.

6 See Christopher Tolkien, *The History of Middle Earth II. VI. The Return of the Shadow* (London: HarperCollins, 2002), for the 'doubts, indecisions, unpickings, restructurings, and false starts' (p. 5).

7 Quoted in Douglas A. Anderson (ed.), *The Annotated Hobbit*, revised edn (Boston: Houghton Mifflin, 2002), p. 4.

8 Norman F. Cantor, *Inventing the Middle Ages: the Lives, Works, and Ideas of the Great Medievalists of the Twentieth Century* (New York: Morrow, 1991), p. 231.

9 Tolkien, '*Beowulf*: the Monsters and the Critics', *Proceedings of the British Academy* (1936), pp. 245–95, and reprinted many times, as in Daniel Donoghue (ed.), *Beowulf: A Verse Translation*, trans. Seamus Heaney (Norton Critical Edition) (New York: W. W. Norton, 2002), pp. 103–30.

10 Tom Shippey, *J. R. R. Tolkien: Author of the Century* (London: HarperCollins, 2000), chapter 5, pp. 241–2.

11 'under the guise of Apollo': Letter 23 May 1960, in Walter Hooper (ed.), *C. S. Lewis: Collected Letters, Volume III. Narnia, Cambridge and Joy 1950–1963* (London: HarperCollins, 2006), p. 1,154.

12 Humphrey Carpenter, *J. R. R. Tolkien: A Biography* (London: George Allen and Unwin, 1977), p. 201.

13 See http://www.wowzone.com/fprints.htm for three versions.

14 A suggestion from Farah Mendlesohn.

15 Michael Ward, *Planet Narnia. The Seven Heavens in the Imagination of C. S. Lewis* (New York: Oxford University Press, 2008).

16 Michael Moorcock, *Wizardry and Wild Romance: A Study of Epic Fantasy* (London: Gollancz, 1987), pp. 122–4.

17 *USA Today*, 19 March 2009, p. 4D.

PART II

Ways of reading

6

BRIAN ATTEBERY

Structuralism

Although structuralism is no longer the fashionable critical mode it was in the 1960s and 1970s, it still underlies most theoretical discourse (everything labelled 'poststructuralist', 'semiotic' or even 'deconstructionist' builds upon structuralist concepts) and is of particular relevance to the study of fantasy. The very origins of the structural analysis of literature are tied to traditional fantastic genres such as fairy tale and myth, and structuralist approaches remain useful as correctives to critical assumptions about the pre-eminence of realism as a literary mode.

Most histories of structuralism trace it back to linguistics. Ferdinand de Saussure's lectures on language, assembled by his students as the influential *Course in General Linguistics* (1916), sorted out syntax, speech sounds and even the generation of meaning into orderly systems of parts and features.[1] Saussure's scientific approach to language was imitated by other disciplines, including anthropology, art history, psychology and literary criticism. In each case, the approach was to break down a cultural product or expression into a set of constituent parts and then examine the way those parts were articulated, like boiling a body down to a set of bones and then assembling the bones into a skeleton. One might as easily describe the structure of a skyscraper or a psyche; a kinship system or a myth. This approach was both liberating and limiting: liberating because it did not assume that the essential structure of a thing was related to its apparent form or to the conscious intentions of its creator, and limiting because it tended to flatten out differences and to mistake the structure for the functioning whole.

One of the most influential applications of Saussure's ideas to narrative was Vladimir Propp's *Morphology of the Folktale* (1928). Though Propp is known as a formalist – one of the so-called Russian formalists – his major work is a model of structuralist practice. His chosen genre, the kind of magical folk tale usually called *fairy tale* in English, had previously been studied historically and thematically, but not until Propp outlined the form's grammar-like structure did it become obvious that nearly all fairy tales share a basic outline. Propp's book sometimes looks like a mathematics textbook, bristling with algebraic shorthand, yet Propp's system is not as formidable as it looks. At its core are four laws:

1. Functions of characters serve as stable, constant elements in a tale, independent of how and by whom they are fulfilled. They constitute the fundamental components of a tale.
2. The number of functions known to the fairy tale is limited.
3. The sequence of functions is always identical.
4. All fairy tales are of one type in regard to their structure.[2]

By functions, Propp means significant actions or conditions such as the testing of a hero or violating an interdiction. He finds thirty-one such functions, which can be grouped into larger movements such as preparation, complication, struggle, return, and recognition of the hero. Tales may not contain all thirty-one, and some functions may be doubled or tripled, but the order in which they appear is invariable.

The significance of Propp's morphology to the study of fantasy can hardly be overstated. It is not just that many modern fantasies conform to the pattern he identified in traditional tales – examples include *The Wizard of Oz*, *The Hobbit* and *A Wizard of Earthsea* – but also that Propp's way of looking at structure inverts the usual critical approach to fiction. For instance, before E. M. Forster, in his *Aspects of the Novel*, can get to the discussions of character, motivation and plot that he is really interested in, he has to acknowledge with an almost audible sigh, that 'Yes – oh, dear, yes – the novel tells a story.' For Forster, stories are 'this low atavistic form' that the novelist would dispense with if only he could,[3] whereas plots, made by characters working out their own fates, are organic, mysterious and in some way truthful (87–95). Propp, however, says nothing about plot and much about story. His close attention suggests that such a 'primitive' structure might have its own kind of power. In modern fantasy, typically, the fairy tale structure is not only present but is highlighted by such narrative devices as prophecy and providence. Prophecy says, in effect, 'here's the shape of the story you are about to read'. It subordinates the characters to the roles they are to play. Providence, or fate, shows up in many a realistic tale in the guise of coincidence. As Northrop Frye points out, though, 'In displaced or realistic fiction the author tries to avoid coincidence. That is, he tries to conceal his design, pretending that things are happening out of inherent probability.'[4] By 'displacement' Frye means 'the adjusting of formulaic structures to a roughly credible context' (36), implying that the structures of fantasy and its oral traditional ancestors are primary and inescapable, while the novelistic techniques that mask them are later, secondary developments.

The vogue of realism did not replace the fantastic; it merely drove it underground.

Another implication in Propp's work, one which is developed further by A. J. Greimas, is that fairy-tale characters are not people, but rather, as Propp put it, 'spheres of action'. It may not matter so much whether a given character harbours a secret passion or prefers cold toast to warm – the sorts of data that help readers feel they are getting to know characters as friends and that add up to our sense of them as 'round' or 'developed' – but rather how that character moves the story forward. Such a conception of character is not, as some critics would have it, aesthetically inferior. Greimas divides all characters into two aspects. First, characters can stand for the conceptual categories that play out their oppositions in the story: this aspect he called the *actant*. Examples of actants include the Hero, the Giver, and the desired Object.[5] But these roles can be overlaid with specific character traits until we barely recognize them as story functions. Instead we view them as believable individuals, as what Greimas called *acteurs* or actors.[6] A typical character in a fairy tale is more actant than actor – a fairy-tale hero is an abstraction, an outline that we can fill in with our own sense of selfhood.[7] A typical character in a realistic novel is more actor than actant. In *Pride and Prejudice*, our attention is drawn more to Elizabeth Bennet's history, relationships, motives, habits, ethical dilemmas, quirks and even internal contradictions than to her role as the hero of a fairy-tale quest for love and fortune. Yet every character is both actor and actant; the difference between a novel and a tale is the relative emphasis on one or the other. Structural analysis suggests that fairy tales are not inferior to realist fiction just because they favour the actant over the actor. Modern fantasies are free to draw on both traditions and to create complex characters that are nonetheless acknowledged as 'spheres of action' in service to the story. This is especially evident in fantasies explicitly based on traditional tales, such as Sheri S. Tepper's *Beauty* (1991).

Propp's morphology turns out to be useful in analysing many forms of fiction, not just fairy tales and their literary imitations. John Cawelti's *Adventure, Mystery, and Romance*, for instance, finds similar patterns in popular genres such as the romance, the detective novel and the Western.[8] Propp and Greimas also provide an important corrective to the notion that good fiction is some sort of unstructured reproduction of reality. The story bones are always there, as Frye points out, if sometimes well hidden by fictional flesh. One difference between fantasy and the genres of realism and naturalism is that fantasy typically displays and even celebrates its structure. If it were a shirt, the seams would be on the outside. This tendency is one reason that fantasies often take on a metafictional dimension. John Crowley's novels *Little, Big* (1981) and *Ægypt* (1987), for example, are as much commentaries on stories and storytelling as instances of them.

Propp was not the only scholar to apply structuralist methods to folk narratives, nor is the fairy tale the only genre to come under such scrutiny. In the 1930s the folklorist Lord Raglan took up the hero's life story, as recounted in sacred myths and legends. Raglan's analysis resembles Propp's morphology, though without the algebra. He outlines a sequence of events in the typical hero's life, from conception to death, and then compares the outline with a number of traditional heroes including King Arthur, Oedipus and Moses. Though Jesus is never mentioned, many of the incidents are described in such as way as to invite the reader to apply the missing instance: for example, Raglan's list includes number 18, 'He meets with a mysterious death'; 19, this death is 'Often at the top of a high hill'; 21, 'His body is not buried'; and 22, nevertheless 'He has one or more holy sepulchres'.[9]

Raglan's explanation for this recurring pattern was that the heroes of legend represent memories of sacred practices: ritual ordeals and sacrifices transformed into narrative. In this belief, Raglan is following Sir James Frazer and the myth-ritual school. He does not address the question of why rituals themselves take such form, nor why people find it necessary to impose the ritual pattern on cultural heroes of all sorts, even historical personages like Charlemagne. To answer these questions, other myth scholars, such as Otto Rank, turned to psychological theory.

Rank was a colleague of Sigmund Freud, and his approach to the hero narrative in *The Myth of the Birth of the Hero* (1914) explained the cross-cultural similarities in Freudian terms of early traumas and family dynamics. His work is not overtly structuralist, but his and other psychoanalytic approaches share with structuralism the goal of examining the human mind scientifically, and all end up positing structural divisions within the psyche. Freud's distinction between conscious and unconscious is a structural move, and so is Carl Jung's sorting the self into the various components he called archetypes. Indeed, the list of Jungian archetypes, such as the hero, the shadow, the wise old man, and the anima, resembles Propp's 'spheres of action' and Greimas's list of actants. For evidence, Freud, Jung and their followers turned to fantastic narratives: myth, fairy tale and the recounted dreams of their patients. Psychoanalysis became explicitly structural with the contributions of neo-Freudian Jacques Lacan, whose theory combines Saussurean linguistics and psychology. Though, unfortunately, Lacan's provocative ideas are rarely articulated as clearly as those of Propp or Raglan, his famous dictum that 'the unconscious is structured like a language' is relevant to fantasy studies, and would be even more so if amended to state that 'the unconscious is structured like a story'.

Such a statement summarizes much of the work of Joseph Campbell, whose synthesis of structural and psychoanalytic approaches to myth has influenced not only the study of fantasy literature but also the creation of particular fantastic texts. This influence has not always been a positive one. Campbell's first major work, *The Hero with a Thousand Faces* (1949), introduced his concept of the *monomyth* – the single narrative plan that, according to Campbell, underlies pretty much everything narrative, from tragedy to comedy, myth to modern novel. Campbell borrowed the word *monomyth* from James Joyce, and his idea owes as much to early twentieth-century literary mythmaking as to scholarship in traditional narrative. It comes in three parts: separation, initiation and return.[10] Each of these in turn is divided into small movements, such as the stages of separation, which are

> (1) 'The Call to Adventure', or the signs of the vocation of the hero; (2) 'Refusal of the Call', or the folly of the flight from the god; (3) 'Supernatural Aid', the unsuspected assistance that comes to one who has undertaken his proper adventure; (4) 'The Crossing of the First Threshold'; and (5) 'The Belly of the Whale', or the passage into the realm of night (36).

Even this small sample shows both Campbell's strengths and weaknesses. It is compellingly written – 'Belly of the Whale' is a lot more vivid than something like 'a period of testing in a dark place'. It simultaneously suggests the opening of a fairy tale and a mythic narrative such as Jonah's call to prophecy in the Bible. It harks back to Arnold van Gennep's studies of rites of passage, Freud's Oedipal pattern, Jung's archetypes, and folk tale scholarship (though Propp is not cited). The monomyth is an enormously suggestive idea: once you are alerted to it, it is hard to avoid seeing it everywhere. The trouble with the pattern is that Campbell insists that it is the only one. Whereas Raglan looked among traditional hero tales for a common pattern that was nowhere enacted in full, Campbell seems to start with a plan and to adjust the evidence accordingly. He retells numerous traditional myths in such a way as to make them fit, fudging the descriptions of characters and actions, leaving out details that do not correspond, and avoiding the many equally important myths that do not concern heroes. Campbell should be taken with a grain of salt, which is not to say that his work is unimportant. His is one of many structural schemata that can help illuminate fantasy, and, because of his direct influence on writers from George Lucas to David Zindell, he is essential to an understanding of the revival of interest in mythic structures and their use in late twentieth-century fantasy.

Another charismatic figure in structuralism and myth is Claude Lévi-Strauss. Trained in philosophy, Lévi-Strauss remade himself into an ethnologist and did fieldwork among tribes along the Amazon that resulted in his first major work, *The Elementary Structures of Kinship*. As that title indicates, his approach to culture was structural. In this, he was influenced by Roman Jakobson, a Russian formalist who pioneered the application of Saussurean linguistics to the study of poetry. Unlike Propp, Jakobson's critical method was not based in grammar so much as phonology: the study of sound systems and meanings. Meaningful sounds in any language can be categories by the presence or absence of certain features, such as voicing or the use of the lips to stop the sound: the letter *b* represents a voiced bilabial stop. Lévi-Strauss adapted this methodology in order to identify within various cultural products, including myth, the presence or absence of particular qualities such as rawness, straightness and liveliness. The method is demonstrated most succinctly in his 1955 essay 'The Structural Study of Myth'.

In that essay, Lévi-Strauss claims to be working inductively, first identifying all the motifs within a particular myth – he focuses mostly on the story of Oedipus – and then grouping them into 'bundles' of relations.[11] In practice, though, his groupings depend upon the particular binary oppositions that his previous structural studies have led him to expect. He innocently 'finds' in the Oedipus story just what he expected to find: oppositions such as life and death, kinship and strangerhood, human parentage and monsters born directly from the earth. Thus, 'the myth has to do with the inability, for a culture which holds the belief that mankind is autochthonous . . . to find a satisfactory transition between this theory and the knowledge that human beings are actually born from the union of man and woman' (91–2). Furthermore, he finds these oppositions at all levels of the narrative, from names of characters to aspects of the setting to significant actions. The same message is given many times over, because 'repetition has as its function to make the structure of the myth apparent' (105).

Lévi-Strauss has been criticized for privileging the researcher over the culture-bearer: he seems to be able to find meanings that no one within the society that tells the stories is conscious of. It is unlikely that oral storytellers in ancient Greece would have singled out the same meaning that Lévi-Strauss does. Certainly when Sophocles dramatized the story, his version did not invite the spectator to focus on autochthony as a key theme, nor do Aristotle or Freud emphasize it in their readings of the story. However peculiar his reading of Oedipus may be, Lévi-Strauss's central insight that meaning, as well as narrative, might be structural, is a powerful tool for studying all kinds of literature and especially fantasy.

Fantasy is often criticized for being too obvious in its oppositions. Light versus dark, good versus evil: such pairings seem glaringly evident, even simple-minded, compared to the intricately intertwined betrayals and bene-factions of the great characters of realist fiction. But Lévi-Strauss says, not so fast. There are different sorts of complexity. A myth is complex vertically, as it were; it lays out its pairings again and again, piling opposition upon opposition. The same binary pair might show up on one level as eternally battling forces; on another as complementary components of a whole, like the Taoist model of yin and yang. Finding the binaries is only the first step. Then one must look for the way they are bundled, and for the ways the groupings change throughout the narrative.

One of Lévi-Strauss's great insights is to see the Trickster figure in struc-tural terms, as both the mediator between polar opposites and the disruptor of all binaries. Loki, in Norse myth, and Coyote, in south-west Indian tales, are both good and evil, both divine and mortal, both creator and destroyer. Tricksters typically change form, confusing the distinctions between male and female or human and animal. A fantasy story that might have been written to illustrate just this sort of disturbance of binary thinking is Ursula K. Le Guin's 'Buffalo Gals, Won't You Come Out Tonight' (1987), in which animals are also people, past is present, and Coyote both dies horribly and rules supreme. Lévi-Strauss's version of structuralism does not work only in fantasies based on Native American myths, however. Le Guin's major fantasy sequence, the Earthsea tales beginning with *A Wizard of Earthsea* (1968) and concluding with *The Other Wind* (2001), starts out looking like a typical good-versus-evil-light-versus-dark fantasy, but ends up incorporat-ing those binaries and a number of others into a startlingly new structure of meaning. Even Tolkien's *The Lord of the Rings*, which keeps its good and evil pretty much corralled separately, can be read, through a Lévi-Straussian lens, as offering multiple and contradictory versions of the same basic oppo-sitions. We may have angels in disguise at one end of the scale and a wholly evil Dark Lord at the other, but in between there are alternative versions of the same characters that, among them, demonstrate how nuanced struc-tural thought can be. Sneaky Gollum is paired with loyal Samwise; both are matched at different times with Frodo; unheroic Frodo is contrasted with the human warrior Boromir; Boromir serves as a binary contrast sometimes with his brother Faramir and sometimes with the kingly Aragorn. Once alerted to this mode of doubling, the reader can see unlikelier but suggestive pairings such as the elf queen Galadriel with the loathsome spider Shelob, or the persuasive Gandalf with the skulking Wormtongue – the range of poten-tial meanings is vast and far from the simple either-or that first appears to be the message.

All of the versions of structuralism discussed so far were developed as approaches to oral genres, though they may work with written literature, but there are also structuralist ways to look at features peculiar to written narratives. Gérard Genette's *Narrative Discourse* (published in French as part of *Figures III* in 1972), takes up questions of storytelling technique in the novel, focusing especially on Proust's *Remembrance of Things Past*. While Proust might be considered the opposite of a popular, story-oriented tale-teller, the features that Genette finds in Proust's narrative actually turn out to be present in many recent works of fantasy. Genette is particularly interested in the way time is represented in fiction: in the fact that a narrator can disrupt the orderly flow of time by flashing forward or back, by freezing time while contemplating a tableau, by treating a series of similar actions as if they were one action repeated. Oral narratives do not do these things; they generally proceed from beginning to end at a steady pace.

The significance to fantasy is that the same sorts of intervention in the flow of time are frequent in fantasy narratives. In fantasy, however, they typically occur not at the level of narrative discourse but at that of the story itself. Rather than having a narrator artfully rearrange time in order to heighten suspense or anticipation, fantasy can move its characters into the past or future. A magic spell can literally freeze the moment, as in Delia Sherman's *The Porcelain Dove* (1993), or lay out multiple alternative timelines, as in Sean Stewart's *Nobody's Son* (1993) or create *Groundhog Day*-style time loops, as in Diana Wynne Jones's *Archer's Goon* (1984). One effect of moving such manipulations from the level of discourse to that of story is to invite metafictional readings. The examples just mentioned are all strongly metafictional. Unlike some versions of metafiction, however, metafictional fantasy tends not to close in on itself, implying that there is no connection between discourse and reality, nothing outside the text, as deconstructionist readings sometimes claim. Rather, fantastic metafictions tend to open up the text, inviting us to see the degree to which reality itself is structured like a story – or indeed, because much of the reality we live in is of human making, is constructed through the act of storytelling.

Early structuralists often made grandiose claims about their method, which was going to discover the universal and unchanging principles of all human activity and expression. The most recent versions of structuralism in the academy are tempered by poststructuralist scepticism, framed within specific cultural contexts, and tested against history. These versions of structuralism are still useful to the study of fantasy, especially fantasy written by artists who are themselves aware of the force of history and the limits of knowledge and communication. We are overdue for an extended structuralist/poststructuralist reading of China Miéville, Kelly Link, Michael Swanwick, Jeanne Larsen, Geoff Ryman and other self-aware fantasists.

Most theoretical works on fantasy to date have incorporated structuralist insights. These include Rosemary Jackson's *Fantasy: The Literature of Subversion* (1981), Christine Brooke-Rose's *A Rhetoric of the Unreal* (1981); Robert Scholes's *Structural Fabulation* (1975); Brian Attebery's *Strategies of Fantasy* (1992); Kathryn Hume's *Fantasy and Mimesis* (1984); and Farah Mendlesohn's *Rhetorics of Fantasy* (2008). Tzvetan Todorov does not belong in this grouping, though Todorov is among the major narrative theorists and he did write a study called *The Fantastic: A Structural Approach to a Literary Genre* (1973). The genre Todorov examines in this book is not what most English-speakers call fantasy; rather it is a rather specialized brand of eerie fiction in which the reader never knows for sure whether events are natural or supernatural. Todorov's title and his reputation as a theorist have given this work a greater prominence than its relevance warrants. In contrast, Northrop Frye's useful *The Secular Scripture: A Study of the Structure of Romance* (1976) – perhaps because the title does not contain the words *fantasy* or *fantastic* – has had little influence on fantasy scholarship despite Frye's fame as the author of the monumental (and structuralist) *Anatomy of Criticism* (1957). Another source of structuralist insights into fantasy and related genres is *The Encyclopedia of Fantasy*, edited by John Clute and John Grant. The format of this work means that the reader must go in quest of entry titles and cross-referenced clues to discover the underlying theory of fantasy and its structures of story and meaning. A good (and in proper fairy-tale fashion, highly unlikely) place to begin is with Clute's entry on WAINSCOTS. A wainscot is a world in miniature, hidden in the gaps or 'interstices in the dominant world'[12] whose structure it replicates. The same might said of every fantastic narrative.

NOTES

1 Ferdinand de Saussure, *Course in General Linguistics*, ed. Charles Bally and Albert Sechehaye with Albert Reidlinger, trans. Wade Baskin (New York: Philosophical Library, 1959).
2 V. (Vladimir) Propp, *Morphology of the Folktale*, trans. Laurence Scott. 2nd edn, rev. and ed. Louis A. Wagner (Austin and London: University of Texas Press, 1968), pp. 21–3.
3 E. M. Forster, *Aspects of the Novel* (1927) (Harmondsworth: Penguin, 2000), p. 40.
4 Northrop Frye, *The Secular Scripture: A Study of the Structure of Romance* (Cambridge, MA: Harvard University Press, 1976), pp. 46–7.
5 Robert Scholes, *Structuralism in Literature: An Introduction* (New Haven and London: Yale University Press, 1974), p. 105.
6 *Ibid.*, p. 103.

7 A good discussion of abstraction and its role in reader identification can be found in Scott McCloud's *Understanding Comics: The Invisible Art* (New York: Harper, 1994), which takes a partly structural approach to a genre related to fantasy, the comic book or graphic novel; see, for instance, pp. 36–7.

8 John Cawelti, *Adventure, Mystery, and Romance: Formula Stories as Art and Popular Culture* (Chicago and London: The University of Chicago Press, 1976).

9 Lord Raglan (Fitzroy Richard Somerset), 'The Hero of Tradition', *Folklore* 45 (1934), pp. 212–31; reprinted in *The Study of Folklore*, ed. Alan Dundes (Englewood Cliffs, NJ: Prentice-Hall, 1965), pp. 142–57 at p. 145.

10 Joseph Campbell, *The Hero with a Thousand Faces* (Bollingen Series 17), 2nd edn (Princeton University Press, 1968), p. 30.

11 Claude Lévi-Strauss, 'The Structural Study of Myth', in Thomas A. Sebeok (ed.), *Myth: A Symposium*, 2nd edn (Bloomington: Indiana University Press, 1958), pp. 81–106, at p. 87.

12 John Clute and John Grant (eds.), *The Encyclopedia of Fantasy* (London: Orbit, 1997), p. 991.

7

ANDREW M. BUTLER

Psychoanalysis

There is a moment in an essay by Ursula K. Le Guin when she argues that: 'Fantasy is the language of the inner self.'[1] Not least because of the multiple meanings of the word 'fantasy', psychoanalysis is a very useful theoretical approach in analysing fantasy: not just the mode of fictional narrative (and the narrower genre of the Fantastic)[2] but also desires, drives or unconscious fears – which I will refer to as 'phantasies'. Rosemary Jackson's *Fantasy: The Literature of Subversion* (1981) owes its subtitle in part to Sigmund Freud's and especially Jacques Lacan's notions of the divided self: fantasy 'has a subversive function in attempting to depict a *reversal* of the subject's [self's] cultural formation'.[3] Unities of space, time and character – and the attempt to represent them – are questioned both by fantasy and psychoanalysis. For Jackson, fantasy is 'a literature of desire, which seeks that which is experienced as absence and loss' (3) and the reader who associates fantasy just with Tolkien and his successors is likely to be disappointed by her literary choice of exemplars. At the same time, psychoanalysing genre fantasy risks tautology: since Freud draws upon myths such as that of Oedipus and stories such as Hoffmann's 'The Sandman' (1815) to formulate his theories, it is hardly surprising that the theories seem to work well with fantasy narratives which look back to such sources for inspiration. This chapter will outline part of the thought of three major figures in psychoanalysis – Freud, Lacan and Jung – in relation to analysing fantasy.

Freud is credited with being the proposer of the existence of the unconscious mind, an overstatement since he was just one explorer of the human psyche in the second half of the nineteenth century. From his earliest publications in the 1890s to his death in 1939 he moved through a number of different descriptions of the mind, which may be designated as his topographic, economic and dynamic models. The earliest, outlined in *The Interpretation of Dreams* (1900), divided the psyche into the conscious (*das Bewusste*) – that what it knows about – the preconscious (*das Vorbewusste*) – what it is has forgotten about – and the unconscious (*das Unbewusste*) – what it has repressed. The unconscious may be glimpsed in dreams, artworks and jokes, or may manifest itself as neuroses or psychoses. Sometimes the phantasies may be reversed or displaced onto something other than what the desire is really for, or several phantasies may be condensed into one. The role of psychoanalysis is to discuss with the patient the apparent (manifest) content of their dreams and through that get to the hidden (latent) content, and the making of connections should relieve the symptoms.

By 1911, Freud had rethought his model to pit two 'economic' forces against one another. On the one hand there was the unconscious mind (which included the preconscious and part of the conscious) which was the source of sexual and sadistic drives or the libido, and on the other there was the will as an internalized part of a social network which held such drives in check so as not to offend taboos. This lined the Pleasure Principle up against the Reality Principle, with the repressed once more able to manifest itself in disguised form. Finally, in 1923, Freud outlined his dynamic model, in which, for our purposes, the Id and Ego map onto the unconscious and conscious mind (although not all of the Ego is conscious). The emergence of the Ego leaves what forms the Id behind. To this Freud adds a third figure, the Super-Ego, the parent-like mechanism which allows or forbids phantasies to be acted upon, and in a crisis can reassure the Ego.

The Super-Ego is formed out of the residue of the Oedipus complex, in which the child desires his or her mother, but is prevented from acting out this phantasy by the fear (or the imagined fear) of castration by the father. The male child should then realign himself with the father, and seek in time for a woman to replace his mother. The female child may realize she is already castrated, and desire her father's penis – in time this may be displaced onto a desire for a child[4] – or reproaches the cruelty of her mother and aligns herself with the father.[5] Neither explanation is without its problems from a feminist point of view – which is not to say that all feminists have rejected Freud's ideas.[6]

These processes of repression and their dangers can be seen in Charlotte Perkins Gilman's 'The Yellow Wallpaper' (1892). The unnamed narrator has been prescribed a rest cure, which is more or less house arrest, mostly in a former nursery which is described as if it were a prison. She is forbidden from writing, and to see anyone but her immediate family and the household staff and nurse. Repressed, she begins to project her phantasies onto the titular wallpaper: 'when you follow the lame uncertain curves for a little distance they suddenly commit suicide – plunge off at outrageous angles, destroy themselves in unheard-of contradictions'.[7] Before long she has begun to discern another woman, trapped in the wall as she herself is in the marriage and house. The narrator's biggest fear is that the other will escape; and, at the end of the story, either this has happened, or she has taken on the identity of a woman who she imagines has escaped. "'I've got out at last . . . in spite of you and Jane. And I've pulled off most of the paper, so you can't put me back!'" (19). The 'you' here is the husband, the target for her anger caused by the repressing of her emotions and imagination, which has been directed inwards and now is directed at him; 'Jane' is less clear, given it is the first mention of the name. Most likely it is the narrator's name, who has dissociated herself into her Id from her Ego. Her husband has tried to castrate her, and she has struck back.

Samuel R. Delany offers a knowing Freudian parable in his 'The Tale of Old Venn' (1979), in a section that begins with a citation of Lacan about Freud. A girl and a boy are comparing their naked bodies to each other, in particular their genitalia, and in turn comparing it to their father, Arkvid's, who is sitting there, carving a penis-sheath or rult. The genitalia are referred to as 'gorgis', especially when applied to a male's, a term which immediately recalls the name of Gorgik, the tough, liberating hero of a number of stories in the *Tales of Nevèrÿon* collection (1979). The rult is both a functional and a symbolic object: "'They are considered very strong hunting magic. Girls do not get them. Indeed, girls are not even supposed to touch them.'"[8] The rult demarks the sexes, and a social distinction between them in a post-hunter-gathering society. At the same time it is something which is not spoken about, associated with a series of taboos. Arkvid suggests that the women are envious of the men's possession: "'The little girl sees that her brother and her father have rults . . . and she is jealous and envious of the rult – as she does not possess one . . . [T]he rult is strong, full of powerful magic . . . [T]he little girl will put this jealousy down in the dark places below memory'" (137). After describing penis envy and the female's alleged repression, Arkvid goes on to suggest that the female phantazises the child as a rult, and, in time, a male child will be given a rult by his father. This notion is disputed by Venn, who argues that the rult is associated with death (through the killing committed by the wearer), rather than new life, and it is noted that the twelve-year-old Arkvid had found the bloodied, broken pieces of his murdered father's rult, something which has clearly stayed in his unconscious. It is clear that such overvaluations of the penis are contingent on a given society rather than universal. Later in the volume, in 'The Tale of Potters and Dragons' (1979), a creation story is told which reverses the sexes of the Garden of Eden, and privileges the female: the male is a damaged woman, prevented from child-bearing, rather than female being castrated and enforced to bear children; such a society seems unlikely to have penis envy. The displacement of power onto the rult rather than the penis is suggestive of Lacan's notion of the phallus, which I shall return to later in this chapter.

According to Freud's theories, a matured child needs to have put the fear of castration behind them, although a reminder of the possibility of castration may result in their reinfantilization. Usually the castration works on symbolic level in terms of a loss of potency and power, but it may be displaced onto blinding ('The Sandman'), a damaged hand (Frodo, Thomas Covenant) or a damaged leg or foot (Mark in Catherine Storr's *Marianne Dreams* (1958), Paul Sheldon in Stephen King's *Misery* (1987), Kira in Lois Lowry's *Gathering Blue* (2006)). In Robert Holdstock's *Mythago Wood* (1984), war veteran Steven Huxley is trying to understand his father Henry and his brother Christian's obsession with nearby Ryehope Wood. The father has discovered and is trying to generate 'mythagos' – myth imagos – from the ancient woodland: apparently entities projected from the unconscious mind of humanity. One of these mythagos is Guiwenneth, also known as Guinevere or Gwyneth, and Henry has fallen in love with her. In his obsession he has neglected his wife, Jennifer: 'J arrived in the study and was very distraught. The boys have begun to be very upset by J's decline. She is very ill… When S and C around, she remains coldly silent, functioning as a mother but no longer as a wife.'[9] In time Jennifer kills herself, allowing Henry to continue his studies. Even without the etymological link between 'Gwyneth' and 'Jennifer', it is hardly surprising that Henry's sons would have had Oedipal urges for the mythago after their mother's death. After the death of the father, and the removal of the castrating figure, Steve and Christian become rivals in their desires for her. To win her, they have to defeat the Urscumug, a boar-human mythago with the face of their father. Even after death, their father is able to police their desires.

Fairy tales often offer parables of the child's repression or sexual awakening. The stories became increasingly sanitized through the editorial adjustments of first Charles Perrault and then the Brothers Grimm, but as a result became increasingly open to psychoanalytic readings. Modernizations of the tales have moved subtext to text. 'Little Red Cap' is the tale of a young girl who meets a wolf on the way to see her grandmother. Rather than eat her straight away, the wolf makes a deal with her to see who will first reach the grandmother. The wolf wins, and disguises himself as the old woman. In the Perrault version, the girl is eaten up; in the Grimm versions, the child and grandmother are rescued by a passing hunter. In *The Uses of Enchantment* (1976), Bruno Bettelheim suggests that she is 'already struggling with pubertal problems for which she is not yet ready emotionally because she has not yet mastered her oedipal conflicts'.[10] She has sexual experiences, but is not yet mature enough to deal with them successfully. Female figures are either useless – her mother offering ignored advice, her grandmother easily overcome – or are seen as sexual competitors – Bettelheim suggests the girl is suggesting the wolf would be better off with the more mature and (sexually) experienced grandmother. Little Red Cap faces a male world alone, with masculinity represented by 'the danger seducer' of the wolf and the 'responsible, strong, and rescuing father figure' of the hunter. She learns that it is dangerous to deviate from the straight and narrow and to yield to apparently innocent desires.

Angela Carter's 'The Company of Wolves' (1979) offers several versions of the Little Red Cap story, but without the condemnation of female and male sexuality. In the girl's encounter with the wolf in human form, there is almost the sense that she is an old hand at courting, as he is favourably compared with the 'rustic clowns of her native village'.[11] She seems desirous of being seduced by the wolf – the narrator speculates that she may be 'a little disappointed to see only her grandmother sitting beside the fire' (116). The wolf disguises himself, and he gets her to strip for him – but she then strips him. The story ends with her 'sleep[ing] in granny's bed, between the paws of the tender wolf' (118). The paws here contrast with the accounts related earlier in Carter's story, where paws are cut off and metamorphose (back) to human hands. Whereas these werewolves are castrated and stripped of power, here his paws, power and potency remain. The fantasy form allows the telling of an otherwise taboo narrative.

Whilst the child who correctly navigates their way through the Oedipus complex to maturity is no longer consciously afraid of castration, the fear may return. Freud describes certain phenomena which (re)invoke the infantile fears as the Uncanny (*unheimlich*): 'an uncanny experience occurs either when infantile complexes which have been repressed are once more revived by some impression, or when primitive beliefs which have been surmounted seem once more to be confirmed'.[12] Frequently the Uncanny is invoked by a liminal or hybrid figure, which is neither one thing nor another: living/dead (vampires, zombies, ghosts), natural/supernatural (witches, voodoo), human/animal (werewolves, familiars). Anxiety may derive from the protagonist's double: a guardian angel, a soul or a ghost. Freud speculates that the double was initially imagined as something reassuring, to ward off the fear of death; ironically the comfort figure ends up as frightening because the necessity to be reassured reminds the Ego of death.

Examples within fantasy are legion. Freud discusses Hoffmann's 'The Sandman', in which a mother warns young Nathaniel about the Sandman, who steals children's eyes; Nathaniel associates the bogey-man with Coppelius, a lawyer. At university Nathaniel buys a pair of spectacles from a pedlar, Coppola, and sees Olympia, his professor's beautiful daughter. Olympia, however, is an automaton, whose eyes were supplied by Coppelius. Freud focuses not upon the artificiality of the doll, but on the removal of eyes: 'A study of dreams, phantasies and myths has taught us that anxiety about one's eyes, the fear of going blind, is often enough a substitute for the dread of being castrated' (352). Tolkien's *The Lord of the Rings* (1954–5) contains the lidless eye of Sauron, as perhaps the only material element of the antagonist of the story, looking out from Mordor across the west, and the eye is doubled in the scene when Tom Bombadil – a spirit of the English countryside transplanted into Middle-earth – looks through the Ring. The ringbearers themselves act as doubles – Bilbo/Gollum, Bilbo/Frodo, Frodo/Sam, Frodo/Gollum, Gollum/Smeagol and so forth. The ring wraiths, or Nazgul, may be thought of as uncanny, being shadows of the men who once carried the nine rings of men, and echoes of the nine members of the fellowship. They move between natural and supernatural realms – Frodo is more visible to them when wearing the ring. It is also worth noting the constant swinging of locations between comfort and discomfort, between *heimlich* and *unheimlich*.

Freud's ideas were challenged and modified by a number of his followers, and it is perhaps most helpful to move first to Jacques Lacan. Freud's analysis of dreams already seemed to echo the structuralism that emerged from academia during the First World War – after all one dream could represent a number of different desires or a number of different dreams could represent the same desire, equivalent to the relationships between signifier (a means of representation) and signifieds (a concept being represented). Lacan wanted to combine the insights of psychoanalysis with those of structuralist anthropology and argued that the unconscious was structured like a language. In his revisioning of the Oedipus complex, the father was replaced by the father's functions – the Name of the Father – with the phallus or symbol of power being given centre stage. The child here desires to be desired by the mother, but fails because the mother desires the phallus. The male child attempts to become a phallus for the mother, but is prevented from doing so by the threat of castration. He knows that he will succeed in due course, but in the mean time has the compensations of (structured) language or the Symbolic Order. The female child attempts to do the same, but realizes she is always already castrated and so can only retreat into a nostalgia for the time before castration. She cannot fully enter the Symbolic Order as it is marked as masculine and structured around the phallus, so she may retreat into babble. The upside of the model is that it can be stretched to cover families other than the standard nuclear one – single-parent families, cases with lesbian or gay parents – but it risks being as misogynistic as Freud's. Nevertheless. it has been used by various feminist thinkers rather than rejected out of hand.

Lacan describes a psychosexual trajectory for the child, who only becomes gendered on reaching the Oedipus complex. The individual is born too soon, unable to fend for itself, to walk or even to see properly. But although the child is 'still in a state of powerlessness and motor incoordination, the infant anticipates on an imaginary plane the apprehension and mastery of its bodily unity. This imaginary unification comes about by means of identification with the image of the counterpart as a total *Gestalt*; it is exemplified concretely by the experience in which the child perceives its own reflection in a mirror.'[13] The Mirror Phase locates the individual in time, space and, perhaps more significantly, in *language* as an I which may be addressed. However this identification within what Lacan calls the Imaginary sphere is necessarily incomplete – the image of the other is imagined as greater than the self and so there is a disunity or lack at the heart of everyone's self identity. Identification also becomes alienation. It is only after the Imaginary has been located that the child may pass into the Oedipus complex and the Symbolic sphere; a third sphere, the Real, is that which cannot be imagined or symbolized, a term peculiarly resistant to definition. Not to be confused with 'reality', 'It's a relation to something which always lies on the edge of our conceptual elaborations, which we are always thinking about, which we sometimes speak of, and which, strictly speaking, we can't grasp, and which is nonetheless there.'[14] It seems to be glimpsable in sex and death, in the state of being a child and even in femininity – it feels almost like a version of the sublime.

Lacan's works, yet to be fully translated into English, have had a significant influence upon the theoretical reading of fantasy – for example in Jackson's work. Shoshana Felman reads Henry James's 'The Turn of the Screw' (1898), Todorov's most solid example of the fantastic, through Lacan's ideas, noting the impossibility of deciding between the possibilities of the narrating governess or the ghost-seeing children being mad.[15] The more populist end of the genre can be read through an exploration of shift from lack to the fulfilment of desires – movements from poverty to riches, from singleness to marriage. Strictly speaking, Lacanian desire can never be satisfied – he sees it as the distinction between need (for food, accommodation and clothes which may be temporarily satisfied) and demand (for love, which can never be fully satisfied). The quest narrative – for the Holy Grail or equivalent – becomes a narrative dependent on the frustration of desire, the postponement of possessing the phallus.

Lacan's ideas are also instructive in reading the quasi-fantastic *The Wasp Factory* (1984) by Iain Banks. We have a family open to recurring Oedipus complexes: Angus is father to Eric (hospitalized by the start of the novel) and Frank (the narrator who informs us that he has been castrated). Angus's dead wife has been replaced by Agnes, who potentially becomes a locus of desire for Frank and not only desires Angus but has a child, Paul. At Paul's birth, their dog Old Saul is choked to death by Angus for biting off Frank's genitals. Frank is literally separated from the phallus – and has been further unmanned by Angus's destruction of the castrator. Frank can kill the rival heir, Paul (note the echo of the Biblical Saul/Paul shift), but this does not satisfy his desire. Frank's entry into the Symbolic Order is thus problematic and he produces his own substitute – the elaborate wasp factory which, by killing wasps in a variety of ways, is able to divine the future and suggest actions. The revelation towards the end of the novel that Frank is in fact Frances and was born female does not negate the psychological structure of the novel, but rather suggests the structured nature of gender. Frank's genitalia, kept in a jar in his father's study, are fakes – 'a pink ball, like plasticine or wax'[16] – which recall his glimpse of his father's 'rather greasy-looking cock and balls' (174). It would not matter if Angus had faked his genitalia, too: the phallus in Lacan's Oedipus complex is connected to function rather than biology.[17]

Carl Jung was a Swiss psychoanalyst who split from Freud over the importance of the libido and the concept of a collective unconscious. In his analytic psychology, he notes that the individual psyche is made up of a number of different elements which need to be brought in to balance or individuated. The Ego, as in Freud, is only part of the self. Each male and female psyche has an anima and animus respectively: an unconscious feminine or masculine element which, if repressed, may be projected onto others. In Philip Pullman's His Dark Materials (1995–2000) we see a version of this in which male characters have female daemons and vice versa; these are mutable in appearance until the individual reaches maturity. (On those rare occasions where the two are of the same sex, it is regarded as mildly sinister.) Another component is the shadow, which is the repressed, animal and sexual instincts of the individual – this should not be viewed as purely negative and can be seen as the source of creativity. Again there is a tendency to project the figure onto others – in dreams (especially nightmares) and within waking life.

Jung's ideas have been a frequent inspiration for Ursula K. Le Guin in her writing of and thinking about fantasy. She notes how individuation can be represented as a journey across a landscape: 'fantasy is the medium best suited to a description of that journey, its perils and rewards'.[18] In A Wizard of Earthsea (1968) Ged/Sparrowhawk is showing off about his magical abilities when he conjures up a malevolent spirit, which scars him before being driven off. This spirit remains as a threat through his early career as a wizard, until he decides to go and confront it head on.

The final meeting comes in open seas which Ged transforms into land by magic:

> Ged spoke the shadow's name, and in the same moment the shadow spoke . . . 'Ged.' And the two voices were one voice.
> Ged reached out his hands, dropping his staff, and took hold of his shadow, of the black self that reached out to him. Light and darkness met, and joined, and were one.[19]

Through this acknowledgement (which occurs in a different form in Frodo's relationship with Gollum), Ged comes of age as a self.

The Ego, anima/animus and shadow are all part of an individual unconscious, in fact archetypes which express particular complexes. There were also many other archetypes which again represent certain behaviours, desires and relations. These include the hero, the wise old man, the mother, the trickster and so on, and these appear to be part of what Jung calls the collective unconsciousness. Such archetypes occur throughout fiction but especially in fantasy – see for example *Mythago Wood* and its follow-ups – where the archetypes shade into stereotypes and even cliché.

In part thanks to developments in structural anthropology (including James Frazer's *The Golden Bough* (1890–1915), which noted repetitions between different myths), certain patterns of hero and narrative began to be recognized within fiction. Joseph Campbell's *The Hero with a Thousand Faces* (1949) describes a monomyth which has proved most visible (because intended) in *Star Wars* (1977). Northrop Frye's archetypal literary criticism noted the birth, life, death and rebirth of the hero which (like Frazer) he saw as representation of the cycle of crops or the seasons. Frye even identified modes (comedy, romance, tragedy, satire) with the seasons (spring, summer, fall, winter). Again Frye isolated archetypes which can be recognized with fantasy as well as other fiction, but he was less interested in the Jung explanation for why we share such archetypes.

Psychoanalytic criticism has of late focused more on filmed than written fantasy. This includes notions of the Uncanny, especially as developed by Julia Kristeva and then Barbara Creed, and Slavoj Žižek's Marxist-Lacanian analysis has included work on popular film.[20] The feminist exploration of psychoanalysis has explored notions of the mother and motherhood (rather than the father) and alternatives to the Symbolic Order, whilst less well-known psychoanalysts (especially Melanie Klein)[21] still need to be thought through in terms of what insights they hold for understanding fantasy – especially at the more commercial end of the genre. There is still much work to be done.

NOTES

1 Ursula K. Le Guin, 'The Child and the Shadow', *The Language of the Night: Essays on Fantasy and Science Fiction*, ed. Susan Wood (London: The Women's Press, 1989), pp. 49–60, at p. 55.

2 Tzvetan Todorov, *The Fantastic: A Structural Approach to a Literary Genre* (Cleveland and London: The Press of Case Western Reserve University, 1973). Though Todorov distances himself from Freud, Todorov's Fantastic is closer to Freud's Uncanny (*unheimlich*) than his definition of uncanny (*étrange*). See below for the Freudian Uncanny.

3 Rosemary Jackson, *Fantasy: The Literature of Subversion* (London: Methuen, 1981), p. 177.

4 Sigmund Freud, 'The Dissolution of the Oedipus Complex (1924)', in *On Sexuality: Three Essays on the Theory of Sexuality and Other Works*, ed. Angela Richards (Harmondsworth: Pelican, 1977), pp. 313–22, at p. 320.

5 Sigmund Freud, 'Female Sexuality (1931)', in, *On Sexuality*, pp. 371–92.

6 See, say, Juliet Mitchell, *Psychoanalysis and Feminism* (New York: Pantheon, 1974).

7 Charlotte Perkins Gilman, *The Charlotte Perkins Gilman Reader* (London: The Women's Press, 1981), p. 5.

8 Samuel R. Delany, *Tales of Nevèrÿon* (London: Grafton, 1988), p. 134.

9 Robert Holdstock, *Mythago Wood* (London: Grafton, 1986), pp. 115–16.

10 Bruno Bettelheim, *The Uses of Enchantment: The Meaning and Importance of Fairy Tales* (New York: Vintage, 1989), p. 171.

11 Angela Carter, *The Bloody Chamber* (London: Vintage, 1995), p. 114.

12 Sigmund Freud, 'The Uncanny', in *Art and Literature; Jensen's 'Gradiva', Leonardo Da Vinci and Other Works*, ed. Albert Dickson (Harmondsworth: Pelican, 1985), pp. 335–76, at p. 372.

13 J. Laplanche and J.-B. Pontalis, *The Language of Psychoanalysis*, London: Hogarth, 1973), pp. 250–1.

14 Jacques Lacan, *The Seminar of Jacques Lacan Book II: The Ego in Freud's Theory and in the Technique of Psychoanalysis 1954–1955*, ed. Jacques-Alain Miller, trans. Aylvia Tomaselli with notes by John Forrester (New York: Norton, 1991), p. 96.

15 Shoshana Felman, 'Turning the Screw of Interpretation', *Yale French Studies* 55–6 (1977), pp. 94–207.

16 Iain Banks, *The Wasp Factory* (London: Macdonald, 1984), p. 178.

17 For more on the doubles in the novel – Agnes/Angus, Saul/Paul, Frank/Frances, etc. see Andrew M. Butler, 'Strange Case of Mr Banks: Doubles and *The Wasp Factory*', *Foundation* 76 (1999), pp. 17–27. The notion of Frank and Eric being doubles – indeed the same person – I owe to Kev P. McVeigh, 'The Weaponry of Deceit: Speculations on Reality in *The Wasp Factory*', *Vector: The Critical Journal of the British Science Fiction Association* 191 (1997), pp. 3–4.

18 Le Guin, *The Language of the Night*, p. 55.

19 Ursula K. Le Guin, *The Earthsea Trilogy* (Harmondsworth: Penguin, 1979), p. 164.

20 Julia Kristeva, *Powers of Horror: An Essay on Abjection*, trans. L. S. Roudiez (New York: Columbia University Press, 1982); Barbara Creed, *The Monstrous Feminine: Film, Feminism, and Psychoanalysis* (London: Routledge, 1993); for example, Slavoj Žižek, *Looking Awry: An Introduction to Jacques Lacan Through Popular Culture* (Cambridge, MA: MIT Press, 1991).

21 See, for example, Melanie Klein, *Envy and Gratitude and Other Works 1946–1963* (London: Virago, 1988).

8

MARK BOULD AND SHERRYL VINT

Political readings

All fantasy is political, even – perhaps especially – when it thinks it is not. From the abstruse literary confection to the sharecropped franchise series, a fantasy text at the very least functions like any cultural text to reproduce dominant ideology. This essay is concerned with some of the ways in which fantasy has been theorized as being political, and with the ways in which some authors have utilized fantasy for explicitly political ends. Rosemary Jackson's *Fantasy: The Literature of Subversion* (1981) established the association between fantasy literature and resistance to the dominant social order, arguing that fantasy 'characteristically attempts to compensate for a lack resulting from cultural constraints: it is a literature of desire, which seeks that which is experienced as absence and loss'.[1] Fantastical intrusions into bourgeois reality are thus seen as the return of the repressed into the realm of representation.[2]

Jackson characterizes this in Lacanian terms: the Symbolic (the law, the signifier, subjectivity) constrains and is disturbed by the Imaginary (delusion, the signified, the Other), exhuming 'all that needs to remain hidden if the world is to be comfortably "known"' (65). Fantasy opens 'for a brief moment, on to disorder, on to illegality, on to that which lies outside the law [and] dominant values systems' and thus 'reveals reason and reality to be arbitrary, shifting constructs and thereby scrutinizes the category of the "real"' (4, 21). For Jackson, fantasy's subversiveness lies in its disruption of the smooth surface of the bourgeois social order as constructed in the mimetic novel. It does not constitute an escape into a made-up realm different from taken-for-granted reality, but constructs fictional worlds that are 'neither entirely "real"...nor entirely "unreal"...but [are] located somewhere indeterminately between the two' (19). Such indeterminate imaginary spaces implicitly comment on the taken-for-granted as an ideological construction, and suggest those things, both threatening and promising, typically marginalized in or excluded from consensual bourgeois reality: it unleashes monsters from the Id, as in Bram Stoker's *Dracula* (1897), but also offers connections to the non-alienated subjectivity that exists before our entry into the Symbolic, as in the longed-for 'pleroma', the otherworldly realm known as the Couer, in M. John Harrison's *The Course of the Heart* (1992). However, as Jackson notes, 'nearly all literary fantasies eventually re-cover desire, neutralizing their own impulses towards transgression' (9).[3]

José Monleón's *A Specter is Haunting Europe* (1990) argues that 'one of the basic mechanisms of the fantastic is to question the premises of the natural'.[4] For him, fantasy emerges from the dialectic of reason and unreason that arose with modernity – with the establishment of an episteme which suppressed feudalism and irrational structures of knowledge in favour of mercantilist and industrial orders which valorized reason. He stresses, however, that 'the exposition of the repressed is not necessarily a subversive act, if by subversion is meant a challenge to the causes of repression' and that fantasy can as easily serve in 'the defense of the status quo and the preservation of economic order' (14) by channelling and managing the eruption of the irrational it depicts. Central to Monleón's discussion of nineteenth-century fantasy is the insight that 'unreason was now the product of society' rather than a foreign intrusion into it (67).

A recent example of this dialectic of containment and critique, and of the strategies by which fantasy texts might produce political commentary, is Kit Whitfield's *Benighted* (2006), set in a world recognizably our own – except for the fact that 99 per cent of the population are werewolves. This 'lycanthrope' majority discriminates against the 'bareback' minority of mutant (i.e., normal) humans. Lycanthropes pursue lives indistinguishable from human lives in our world, but when transformed into wolves – 'luning' – they lose their sense of human identity and become violent. During such periods, law and convention require them to isolate themselves within their homes so as maintain a stable social order. The bareback population is so small that they all must work for the bureaucratic Department for the Ongoing Regulation of Lycanthropic Activity (DORLA), which responds to possible problems during luning. They organize patrols to tranquillize and detain any loose lycanthropes, and shelters for those away from home.

This fantastic social structure facilitates a critique of our own taken-for-granted social structures and relationships. While barebacks are discriminated against, subjected to racialized slurs and restricted civil liberties, DORLA operates within a 'state of exception' – situated between the political and the legal, it produces unnameable, unclassifiable beings whose existence outside of established institutional frameworks removes them from all juridical protections and subjects them to arbitrary violence.[5] Outside DORLA, barebacks have little authority; within its ambit, they exercise unquestioned and unchecked power. DORLA agents are required to treat dehumanized, dangerous lycanthropes as citizens while detaining them, but they resent a social order that places such civil liberties above their own safety. Thus lycanthropes who violate the rules enabling the stable, bourgeois order are subjected to the retaliatory violence of frustrated, overworked, physically-at-risk barebacks. Criminalized lycanthropes are refused contact with lawyers or family members and often beaten, not necessarily for information. As the bareback protagonist reflects, 'The horror doesn't leave me. I don't understand how it is that a nursery rhyme enables me to sit back and watch one man beat another. But a childish slur is a hard one to deal with . . . I am ashamed of myself. I am holding a nursery rhyme as a talisman against torture. There is no excuse for what we do to him.'[6]

The source of disruption in *Benighted* is not the existence of the werewolves but government plans to sabotage certain pregnancies in order to cause more bareback births and thus ensure proper staffing of DORLA, thus maintaining the social order. Unlike the fantasy Jackson focuses upon, which establishes 'reality' through mimesis 'but then move[s] into another mode which would seem to be marvellous [i. e., supernatural] . . . were it not for its initial grounding in the "real"' (20), Whitfield upsets mimesis in her first paragraph, referring to 'furring up' and 'lunes' within a narrative context that creates a world both like and unlike our own: dominated by bureaucratic institutions and the policing of 'normal' and 'marginalized' subjects, yet putting humanity in the category of those who fail to meet the cultural norms.

Benighted locates its politics firmly within bureaucratic institutions of governance, focusing on the mechanics of how such legal institutions would manage a world of multiple human-like species and thereby drawing our attention to the roles of such institutions in managing subjectivity in our own world. Fantasy which begins from the premise that the supernatural is an acknowledged part of the day-to-day world can effectively draw attention to the cultural politics of daily life even without such explicit focus on governance. For example, the popular Anita Blake series by Laurell K. Hamilton and Hollows series by Kim Harrison both posit worlds in which vampires, were-creatures, witches, fairies and the like are 'normal' and include agencies similar to DORLA (although not staffed exclusively by humans). The politics of everyday life as much as those of official institutions inform these visions. Hamilton's work focuses on the modes of governance internal to the social structures of vampires and were-creatures, political structures that exist on top of those which govern all species and whose rules do not necessarily coincide with the latter's standards. The existence of supernatural creatures with non-human 'natures' enables Hamilton to overtly explore social structures based on dominance and submission, offering a vision of social order that exists in uneasy tension with the dominant culture's investment in liberal humanist notions of equality. Further, political order and sexuality are complexly entwined in Hamilton's world, drawing attention to ways in which dominant (human) notions of 'normal' subjects privilege heteronormativity and marginalize a variety of queer subjectivities. From this point of view, Hamilton's work critiques our 'common sense' about sexuality and power and invites us to think about the way that ideas about gender and sexuality inform human cultural politics.

Harrison's work explores our mundane ideas about morality and ethics through structures of 'white' and 'black' magic that inform the social order in the Hollows. When the series begins, protagonist Rachel Morgan, recently gone freelance from work in the FIB (Federal Inderland Bureau), which polices non-human species and acceptable relationships among species who do at times prey upon one another, is adamant that she will perform only white magic. Yet as the series progresses and Rachel finds herself confronted with difficult choices that require compromise or the use of more powerful 'black' magic in order to prevent what she sees as greater harm, this ideological distinction begins to blur. Harrison's work encourages us to ask, with Rachel, if the relevant criterion for determining the ethics of a choice should be the action performed or the outcome of this action· can the ends justify the means? In this way, the very political institutions that Harrison sets up in her world are scrutinized, inviting us to view them as contingent structures that have their own politics and ends as much as do individuals such as Rachel.

Such fantasy, in which 'normal' and supernatural subjects exist in a quotidian world which does not perceive this multiplicity as a break with 'reality', points to one of the limitations of Jackson's analysis, which defines fantasy in terms of the 'paraxial' function of fantasy existing alongside a recognizable mundane reality in certain literary fantasies by already-canonical authors, such as Mary Shelley, Charles Dickens, Julio Cortázar, Italo Calvino and Thomas Pynchon, and thus excludes most genre fantasy. Monleón also focuses on a specific type of fantasy, predominantly the Gothic tradition which arose with modernity, but acknowledges that his analysis reveals 'monsters of a material and social reality' tied to a particular time and place, not 'existential abstractions [or] expressions of some sort of human (psychological) attributes'. He concludes that 'new relations of power, the creation of a hierarchy of first, second, and third worlds, the supremacy of corporations, the existence of a nuclear threat – all would be elements that would contribute to a different social order' than the one he examines, and that 'the rich production of the fantastic that invades our most recent past thus requires the tracing of another history' (*Specter*, 139–40).

Farah Mendlesohn's *Rhetorics of Fantasy* (2008) provides a taxonomy of a much broader range of texts – portal-quest, intrusion, immersive and liminal fantasies – and suggests the various sorts of politics each type enables and constrains. The intrusion fantasy roughly corresponds to Jackson's paraxial fantasy. Portal-quest fantasies, which typically 'reconstruct history in the mode of the Scholastics, and recruit cartography to provide a fixed narrative',[7] and restore rather than transform the fictional world, suggest its social order is natural and given rather than historical and contingent, reflecting the tendency Monleón notes to contain rather than release subversive energies.

The protagonist of the intrusion fantasy succeeds 'by challenging the rules or changing them – usually in the face of the pessimism of their colleagues from the fantastical lands. This is of course the colonialist fantasy of rescuing the natives from themselves.'[8] Not all intrusion fantasy yields equally to this imperative, and awareness of it can become the grounds for political engagement, as a comparison of two time-slip intrusion fantasies will illustrate. In Mark Twain's *A Connecticut Yankee in King Arthur's Court* (1889), Hank Morgan finds himself inexplicably transported back to Arthurian Britain. His scientific knowledge and Yankee knowhow save him from execution and elevate him to Arthur's right hand. His industrial rationalism and meritocratic aversion to privilege prove generally superior to feudalism and medieval superstition. He is on the verge of recreating Camelot as a capitalist democracy when his bitter enemy Merlin succeeds in putting him to sleep to awaken in the present day. While Hank's bluff republicanism remains largely unscathed, one can sense in Twain's depiction of his slaughter of 25,000 knights – using electrified fences, Gatling guns, explosives – an ambivalence about the benefits of modernity. However, because Hank visits a past to which he is only tangentially connected – America's founding myths stress its break with Old World values and social structures – the novel, whatever its doubts and hesitations, tends to valorize his colonial perspective on the 'inferior' past.

In Octavia Butler's *Kindred* (1979), the African-American Dana time-slips from bicentennial California to ante-bellum Maryland because of some fantastical connection with her slave-owning ancestor, Rufus. When his life is threatened, she is pulled into the past, enabling her to see him grow into adulthood; when hers is threatened, she returns to 1976. Dana struggles to manipulate the past, not only because her status – a black woman – transforms her from person to property but also because Butler refuses the notion that the future is *necessarily* superior to the past. Familiarity with slave narratives and American history gives Dana no advantage over the plantation's inhabitants, whose material experiences have better shaped them to survive its vicissitudes. Instead, her own understanding is challenged, eventually leading her, for example, to sympathize with the cook, Sarah, who 'had done the safe thing – had accepted a life of slavery because she was afraid. She was the kind of woman who might have been called a "mammy" in some other household. She was the kind of woman who would be held in contempt during the militant nineteen sixties.'[9] Unlike Twain's Hank, Dana becomes wary of intervening in the past even though she can see its failings all too clearly. She tries to educate Rufus about the wrongs of slavery, but is ultimately defeated by the ideological and material forces of his culture. Consequently, she recognizes that killing him would not prompt any structural change and might in fact put the slaves she has come to know in greater jeopardy.

Butler uses time travel to stress continuity between past and present, rather than to replicate the myth of progress. Dana's relative independence and career in 1976 is an improvement over slavery, but at the same time her personal and bodily connections to the past – on her final return to the present, after stabbing Rufus, she loses the part of her arm he was gripping – emphasize the extent to which it continues to have material effects in the present. Far from intruding the 'superiority' of the colonial explorer, *Kindred* instead requires us to rethink the relationship between 'official' discourse and 'reality'.

Within Mendlesohn's scheme, the immersive is perhaps the type of fantasy most amenable to political readings. If done skilfully, the construction of an entire other world in which to set the narrative – often working out detailed maps, charts, languages, lineages and bestiaries – focuses the reader's attention on the necessary interdependence, and radical contingency, of its elements.[10] Immersive worlds thus function to convey 'reality' in a manner similar to the way in which, according to Roland Barthes's *Mythologies* (1957), everyday semiotic structures convey reality; but unlike 'myth today', which obscures contingency by transforming 'history into nature',[11] immersive fantasy potentially lays bare the operation of world-building. An exemplary text in this regard is China Miéville's *Iron Council* (2004).

Perhaps more than any other contemporary fantasy writer, Miéville exploits the power of imagining otherwise for the purpose of social change. His embrace of meticulous world-building is central to this project. *Iron Council* recounts the genesis of a socialist revolution through the serendipitous alliances formed among workers laying railway tracks (including the normally shunned Remade, former criminals whose punishment by the state was to be transformed into machine/human/animal hybrids), prostitutes and other camp followers. While magic is important to reshaping and transforming the social structures of his fictional world, Miéville gives equal emphasis to these material struggles among people of many classes, all of whom have different experiences of and investments in both the existing social order and the revolutionary Iron Council. Mendlesohn sees protagonist Judah Lowe's magical abilities as metonymic of his political activism: he 'intervenes in the world. He finds its cracks and twists; to do this, like all scientists, he must stand back and regard the world while remaining fundamentally of it. The attitude to the physics of the world in Miéville's work becomes a metaphor for politics: there is nothing predestined, there is only what we work out' (65).

Perhaps the most stunning of Miéville's images comes at the end of the novel. The revolutionaries, racing aboard their train towards New Crobuzon, have been arguing about whether to continue their approach to the city – a prospect that will result in almost certain death, since the revolution there has been all but crushed – or to retreat, regroup and wait for a more promising conjuncture. They cannot reach a consensus, but Judah refuses to allow the revolutionary energies to be 'wasted' in defeat. Instead, he traps the train within a time golem, locking it in a moment of forever approaching but never arriving. Within Bas Lag, the fantastic appears not as the Remade or the magic or even the revolution but in this temporal disruption: 'a terrible intrusion in the succession of moments, a clot in diachrony, and with the dumb arrogance of its existence it paid the outrage of ontology no mind'.[12] The train, frozen in immanence, is thus transformed into a powerful metaphor of the revolutionary impulse itself, 'from some angles the train was hard to see, or hard to think of, or difficult to remember, instant to instant' (542), perpetual and always coming. The novel leaves the morality of Judah's decision unresolved: he insists 'History had gone on. It was the wrong time' (548) and that he saved the Iron Council, but another revolutionary, Ann-Hari, is equally adamant, 'You don't *know* . . . You don't get to choose. You don't decide when is the right time, when it fits your story. *This was the time we were here*. We knew. We decided' (551, 552). By enabling Judah to trap the Iron Council in '*the perpetual train, truly perpetual now perhaps poised always poised forever just about its wheels just about to finish turning*' (562) the novel thus gestures beyond Bas-Lag and into our extratextual world, in which the revolutionary impulse is similarly deferred but not destroyed, and in which history is always open, never foreclosed.

The tensions between fixedness and contingency, formula and innovation, closing-down and opening-up, the world-as-it-is and the word-as-it-might be are common to fantasy texts of all types. In conclusion, we will consider Gwyneth Jones's *Bold As Love* series (2001–6), which illustrates the political potential of self-consciously negotiating these dialectical relationships.[13]

These five novels are science-fictional inasmuch as they are set in the near future and involve the development of cutting-edge physics and new technologies. They are simultaneously fantasy novels which rework the legend of King Arthur in a setting in which magic works.

Drawing on even older mythic structures, the legend of Arthur dates from medieval literature and continues to shape 'literary' and genre fantasy. Overtly political retellings are common, probably the most influential being T. H. White's *The Once and Future King* (1958), which stresses the need to prevent violence, and Marion Zimmer Bradley's *The Mists of Avalon* (1979), whose focus on Morgaine recasts the legend as a struggle between matriarchal and patriarchal forms of government. Gwyneth Jones plays on two major aspects of the legend: the promise of Arthur's messianic return in England's hour of greatest need; and the destruction of Camelot's perfect government because of sexual infidelity in the relationship between Arthur, Guinevere and Lancelot. The *Bold As Love* series follows the 'triumvirate' of rockstars: Ax Preston, who becomes king of England; his girlfriend, Fiorinda Slater, who has magical powers; and his knight errant, and – later – their boyfriend, Sage Pender. At one point, a Hollywood producer pitches a film about the triumvirate in specifically Arthurian terms: 'The rockstar king, who rode out the storm, and kept the lights burning. With his queen, the heroine of the resistance, and the very perfect knight who hath achieved the Grail' (*Midnight Lamp*, 132), told in a tone of 'triumph that foreknows its fall, a sense that great deeds are evanescent as a dream, and that's the way greatness should be' (2). The novel, however, refuses such familiar forms: as Ax replies, 'But first we have to create those fictional characters' (132).

The story begins at a rock festival marking the dissolution of the United Kingdom of Great Britain and Northern Ireland into four separate nations. The future government of independent England recruits a number of popular countercultural musicians onto an advisory council. Things, however, do not go as planned. England goes through a succession of governments in the decade the series narrates: a countercultural declares himself President in a bloody coup leading to a period of 'deconstruction' and anarchic violence; when he falls from grace, Ax establishes a dictatorship without recourse to violence; a Green Nazi occupation follows, aided by the reactionary Celtic tendency and Fiorinda's magical, evil father; Ax returns, like a promised Arthur, to reconquer England from these dark forces; the triumvirate, now officially monarchs, live under house arrest and effectively without power; and finally, Chinese forces, come to suppress what they call the 'pernicious delusion' (a combination of neuroscience, immersive media technology and magic which enables those in a certain brain state to 'hack the game' (*Rainbow Bridge*, 347) and reorder the physical construction of reality at the atomic level), invade and occupy the country. As this suggests, the construction of a better world is not as easy as utopian and sf traditions might lead us to believe.

From the beginning, Ax insists that his utopia will be, at best, 'partial, fucked-up and temporary' (*Bold As Love*, 82); but also, and equally, that this is good enough: 'We must not be afraid of quirky small-scale initiatives, partial solutions, the piecemeal of many ideas and techniques' (*Band of Gypsys*, 119). This, he believes, is the only way to prevent utopia from turning into totalitarianism, and it is modelled in the series' own resistance to the legend of Camelot's inevitable fall because of Guinevere and Lancelot's infidelity to their king. Ax, Sage and Fiorinda form a ménage-à-trois, which is often partial and fucked-up, but only temporary in the sense that its precise nature changes through their ongoing willingness to negotiate difference among themselves. Their residence, dubbed 'our post-modern Camelot', offers 'a glimpse of a compromised and *possible* Utopia... A life of recreation. Of making art, with people you both love and hate (often equally, and at the same time)' (*Castles*, 139, 140).

The series concentrates its own utopian energy in the images of the Zen Self and of magic, both ways of reaching an altered state of consciousness which creates the possibility of transforming the world. The Zen Self project is a technology concerned with enabling the subject to gain direct access to 'information-space' and thus to grasp 'all the ways in which Self and the world are connected, and how those connections can be reconfigured toward our final goal' (*Bold As Love*, 75). If one can achieve the Zen Self – when Sage does so, it is called 'achieving the Grail' – then one can 'truly forgive and understand the whole terrible world... It's like getting back to that state where everything is right, via the tech, and making it physical reality' (*Castles*, 213). The Zen Self can 'manipulate this solid world as if it were the environment of a fantasy game' (*Castles*, 305), making the Zen Self – and Fiorinda, whose magical abilities enable her to do this without technology – analogous to the fantasy writer, able to posit the rules for reality and build a world using them. Politics then becomes, quite literally, the act of world-building. Yet Jones cautions us against too blithely using such power or assuming that we can know in advance how things might turn out. For example, a group called the A-Team uses the Zen Self to transform all the world's oil resources into crude slime, falsely believing this will contribute to world peace. The Chinese call this power a pernicious delusion because they fear 'playing games with the stuff of reality' will cause 'the universe to dissolve into primordial information soup' (*Rainbow Bridge*, 172).

The series as a whole, however, while sympathetic to such concerns and thus deeply aware that we always face a situation of complex over-determination in which the outcome of any change cannot be predicted in advance, nonetheless celebrates the power of literatures of the fantastic to help us see the world anew and to engage responsibly in the creation of better futures. Like Miéville's time golem, an image that captures the continual presence of the utopian impulse and thus sustains hope for the coming revolution, Jones's Zen Self technology reminds us that 'there is one code uniting mind and matter, the perceived world and the consciousness that perceives it. We have learned to read that code, and the future opens, stranger than imagination could devise' (*Rainbow Bridge*, 259). This is the political potential of, and ever-present trace within, fantasy.

NOTES

1 Rosemary Jackson. *Fantasy: The Literature of Subversion* (London: Methuen, 1981), p. 3.
2 Cf. Chapter 5, 'The American Nightmare: Horror in the 70s', in Robin Wood, *Hollywood from Vietnam to Reagan – and Beyond* (New York: Columbia University Press, 1986), pp. 63–84.
3 As Mark Bould argues, in 'The Dreadful Credibility of Absurd Things: A Tendency in Fantasy Theory', *Historical Materialism* 10.4 (2002), pp. 51–88, the primary focus of Jackson's work is the subversion of realist codes of representation rather than any overtly political project, and her psychoanalytic paradigm tends toward the individual-therapeutic rather than the social-political. But if, in Althusserian terms, mimetic realism captures our imaginary relationship to our material conditions, fantasy arguably has the potential to capture the real relationship.
4 José B. Monleón, *A Specter is Haunting Europe: A Sociohistorical Approach to the Fantastic* (Princeton University Press, 1990), p. 9.
5 See Giorgio Agamben, *State of Exception*, trans. Kevin Attell (University of Chicago Press, 2005).
6 Kit Whitfield, *Benighted* (New York: Ballantine Books, 2006), p. 102.
7 Farah Mendlesohn, *Rhetorics of Fantasy* (Westport, CT: Wesleyan University Press, 2008), p. 14.
8 *Ibid.*, p. 148. This is inverted in such narratives of invasion and contamination from the colonies as *Dracula* and Richard Marsh's *The Beetle* (1897).
9 Octavia Butler, *Kindred* (1979) (Boston: Beacon Press, 1988), p. 145.
10 Bould argues that the construction of a fictional totality so that it possesses internal consistency, regardless of any disparities it must persuasively yoke together, is common to all fantasy texts, whether driven by a franchised series' 'writer's bible' or the author's own design. While 'the specific *contents* of fantastic fiction are various and defy generalisation', the 'baroque paranoia of the *form*, however, embeds an austere realism' ('Dreadful Credibility', p. 84) that parallels the subject's negotiation of his or her own subordination to power and to the phantasmagoric irreality of social relations under capital. Fantasy always thus models the relationship between free-will and determinism – or, more precisely,

between complex over-determination and linear determinism – it also frequently narrates.

11 Roland Barthes, *Mythologies*, trans. Annette Lavers. (New York: Noonday Press, 1972), p. 129.

12 China Miéville, *Iron Council* (New York: Ballantine Books, 2004), p. 541.

13 Gwyneth Jones, *Bold As Love* (London: Gollancz, 2001); *Castles Made of Sand* (London: Gollancz, 2002); *Midnight Lamp* (London: Gollancz, 2003); *Band of Gypsys* (London: Gollancz, 2005); *Rainbow Bridge* (London: Gollancz, 2006).

9

JIM CASEY

Modernism and postmodernism

Jorge Luis Borges's flash fiction story 'On Exactitude in Science' ('Del rigor en la ciencia') features an incredibly detailed, albeit cumbersome map, similar to the one in Lewis Carroll's *Sylvie and Bruno Concluded* (1893), that is drawn exactly to the same scale as the world itself, matching the terrain 'point for point'.[1] As Alfred Korzybski notes, however, 'A map *is not* the territory.'[2] Even when a cartographer precisely records the exact dimension of every twig and pebble in the empire, s/he will fail to capture the unique character of the mapped terrain itself. This is especially true when mapping abstract, epistemological or metaphysical countries. Critics of fantasy are continually mapping the territories of the fantastic, and this essay represents a foray into the critical and generic landscape of modern and postmodern fantasy, all the while recognizing the futility of an expedition that obsesses over the precise demarcation of boundaries and borders. Even if we could produce an exact map of the Fantastic (Post)modern Empire, adding landmarks work by work until the map becomes as big as the empire itself – *this* is modern fantasy; *that* is postmodern fantasy – we would fail to capture the *qualia* (the essential, defining quality) of the territory itself. Such a perfect, meticulously drafted, scale map would ultimately prove useless, good only when ripped into tatters for critics and scholars to huddle under in the deserts of literary criticism, like the beasts and beggars in Borges's story.

Brian Attebery describes fantasy as a 'fuzzy set',[3] and the same might be said of both modern and postmodern literatures. Fantasy, modernism and postmodernism are all disputed territories, and the boundaries of each vary from map to map, depending upon the cartographer-critic. (Post)modern fantasy then comprises one of the fuzziest of all sets. Considering this imprecision, this essay might be subtitled 'On *In*exactitude in Criticism'. Nevertheless, critical maps are useful, as long as they are used not by conquistadors trying to claim modernism for the kingdom, nor by priests trying convert postmodernism to the religion of fantasy, but by explorers who recognize the power of maps to shape conceptual experience. Critics may disagree about the particulars of modernism and postmodernism, but the ideas of these critics may still be applied to an exploration of the fantastic. Fantasy has always been marginal, on the edges of maps, beyond the well-defined kingdoms, in the areas marked 'Here be Dragons'.

In 1922, the same year that James Joyce's *Ulysses* and T. S. Eliot's *The Waste Land* appeared, E. R. Eddison published *The Worm Ouroboros* and Lord Dunsany produced his first novel, followed in 1924 by *The King of Elfland's Daughter*. Robert Howard, J. R. R. Tolkien, and C. S. Lewis also all developed within the milieu of modernism, and many of their works, as we shall see, feature attributes common to modernist literature, but none of these fantasy writers is generally discussed alongside recognized modernist authors such as Virginia Woolf, Gertrude Stein or Joseph Conrad. Jürgen Habermas argues that 'the project of modernity' may be traced back to the philosophical, social and political values of the Enlightenment (reason, equality, justice) and represents an effort to 'develop objective science, universal morality and law, and autonomous art'.[4] For modernist literature, the last of these goals is of particular importance, and works of fantasy would appear to be a logical medium for 'autonomous art', but many early twentieth-century critics were unprepared to deal with fantasy for fantasy's sake. Marshall Berman describes modernism as the 'amazing variety of visions and ideas that aim to make men and women the subjects as well as the objects of modernization, to give them the power to change the world that is changing them, to make their way through the maelstrom and make it their own'.[5] Today, Frodo and Samwise might be seen as subjects trying to make their way through the maelstrom in order to change the world, but many of Tolkien's contemporaries dismissed these characters as unrealistic or irrelevant and condemned works of fantasy, such as *The Lord of the Rings*, as mere escapism.

In his influential article on *Beowulf*, Tolkien suggests that his critical peers had been misreading the poem because they were trying to evaluate a poetic, heroic elegy as a historical document: 'It has been said of *Beowulf* that its weakness lies in placing the unimportant things at the centre and the important on the outer edges.'[6] Similarly, modernist critics criticized the work of Tolkien for not being what it was not, for placing the unimportant things at the centre and the important on the outer edges. As Brian Attebery notes, Tolkien's 'work showed virtually none of the signs of excellence that critics ... looked for, and they were unprepared to see the sorts of excellence he had achieved.'[7]

For more than fifty years, Tolkien's work has been one of the most powerful models for (post)modern fantastic literature. As a result, most works of fantasy, even those written during the heyday of modernism, resist the appellative designation of modernist literature because they are Tolkienesque rather than modernist, although they may share common attributes with modernist texts. For example, although fantasy, like modernism, rejects the restrictions imposed upon the narrative by Realism, fantastic works do not always reject the Romantic subjectivity of experience. Moreover, fantastic works may feature modernist techniques such as stream of consciousness, parallax (differing narrative points of view) or metafictional experimentation, but they rarely embrace modernism's avid rejection of tradition. Tolkien and other fantasy writers drew heavily on myth, history and fairy tale, and the formal considerations of these earlier narratives helped to shape the face of the genre. In contrast, modernism, with its emphasis on freedom of expression, experimentation, radicalism and primitivism, was founded on an emphatic disregard for conventional approaches. Modernist literature has been described as elitist; modern novels often reject intelligible plots and modern poetry can be surreal or incomprehensible. Fantasy (even recent fantasy) often bears an affinity to the symbolic, hierarchical and formally conjunctive bases of modernism, but fantasy has almost always been considered popular literature, a 'low' art form concerned with play and desire. In this way, fantasy is itself postmodern. Attebery has observed that 'Tolkien is not a postmodernist',[8] and neither were his contemporary fantasists, but fantasy, by its very nature, challenges the dominant political and conceptual ideologies in a manner similar to that of postmodernism.

In his 'Postface' to *The Dismemberment of Orpheus*, Ihab Hassan presents a table that neatly presents the 'schematic differences' between modernism and postmodernism, suggesting that modernism produces *Lisible* (Readerly) Art Objects/Finished Works created through an attention to (conjunctive, closed) Form with specific Purpose, Design, and Hierarchy, whereas postmodernism constructs *Scriptible* (Writerly) Processes/Performances generated through a focus on (disjunctive, open) Antiform and characterized by Play, Chance, and Anarchy; Hassan's table presents modernism as founded on the Interpretation and Reading of the transcendental Signified (a timeless mental or metaphysical idea or concept) and privileging the Centring, Totalization and Determinacy of vertical Roots which present a unified Narrative/ *Grande Histiore*, whereas postmodernism works Against Interpretation (may actually produce Misreadings) of the Signified, concentrating instead on historically and culturally malleable Signifiers (spoken or written expressions of the Signified) and privileging the Dispersal, Deconstruction, and Indeterminacy of horizontal Rhizomes (metaphorical root-systems that have no one central point but rather multiple nodes that spread out, sending up shoots from myriad points) which allow for the possibility of decentralized

Anti-narrative/*Petite Histoire*.[9] Few critics accept Hassan's clear-cut division. Countless examples of modernist literature display characteristics that Hassan attributes to postmodernism (and vice versa). In fact, some critics oppose the very category of postmodernism; Habermas, for example, argues that 'the project of modernity has not yet been fulfilled' and should not be abandoned.[10] Most critics, however, recognize that postmodernism – whatever its qualities, and whether in opposition to modernism or as a continuation of it – forms and informs the current world-experience. Since the first popular use of the term in Arnold Toynbee's *A Study of History* (1947), postmodernism has become a buzzword of remarkable flexibility. In fact, postmodernism may be best understood in the plural, and the remainder of this essay will examine the way various postmodernisms may be applied to the fantastic.

Jean-François Lyotard suggests that postmodern works stress the 'incommensurability' of human existence, putting 'forward the unpresentable in presentation itself; that which denies itself the solace of good forms',[11] but modernist works often consider the incommensurability of human existence as well and postmodern works sometimes embrace the 'solace of good forms'. The difference, perhaps, is in the self-reflexive awareness of the postmodern text. Zygmunt Bauman defines postmodernity as 'modernity conscious of its true nature'.[12] For example, modern and postmodern works both grapple with the problem of a decentred world, as expressed in William Butler Yeats's 'The Second Coming', where 'Things fall apart; the centre cannot hold.' For the older waiter of Ernest Hemingway's 'A Clean Well-Lighted Place', for instance, a decentred, potentially Godless world produces insomnia, perhaps over the realization that

> It was all a nothing and a man was nothing too . . . it was all *nada y pues nada y nada y pues nada*. Our *nada* who art in *nada*, *nada* be thy name thy kingdom *nada* thy will be *nada* in *nada* as it is in *nada*. Give us this *nada* our daily *nada* and *nada* us our *nada* as we *nada* our *nadas* and *nada* us not into *nada* but deliver us from *nada*; *pues nada*. Hail nothing, full of nothing, nothing is with thee.[13]

In his own confrontation of the potential nothingness/emptiness of the universe, the eponymous protagonist of John Gardner's *Grendel* makes similar biblical substitutions when he asserts, '*The world is my bone-cave, I shall not want*'[14] and 'I saw long ago the whole universe as not-my-mother, and I glimpsed my place in it, a hole. *Yet I exist*, I knew. *Then I alone exist*, I said. *It's me or it*. What glee, that glorious recognition! (The cave my cave is a jealous cave.)'[15] Although expressing the same existential angst as the Hemingway story, *Grendel*'s self-reflexive narrative opens the novel to a remarkable amount of deconstructive play. For example, Grendel contends throughout that the world is 'nothing: a mechanical chaos of casual, brute enmity on which we stupidly impose our hopes and fears'. All actions are equally 'meaningless' and all events are 'Blind, mindless, mechanical. Mere logic of chance', where even Grendel's death is simply an 'Accident'.[16] Yet the entire novel is organized by the zodiac, itself a testament to the ordered-ness of the universe. Within the postmodern apparatus of the novel, the organizing structure may contradict the nihilism of Grendel and the dragon, or it may simply position the author as yet another of the human 'pattern makers'.[17] In this way, the potential decentring of the universe becomes reflected in the decentring of language and interpretive meaning.

As a postmodern novel, *Grendel* co-opts one of the most influential post-modern concepts, Jacques Derrida's *différance*, which notes that because words generate meaning through a comparison to other words (difference), absolute understanding is always postponed (deferred). This linguistic ambi-guity creates a situation where ultimate meaning is always uncertain and preliminary, as exemplified by the very word *différance* (a word coined by Derrida), which sounds exactly the same as *différence* (difference), but has a different meaning. In *Grendel*, Gardner exploits Derridean linguistic play to undermine the notions of textual unity, totality and mastery through the denial of a transcendental signified.

This postmodern unbalancing act in *Grendel* displaces not only the cen-trality of order and meaning, but also challenges the stability of traditional form (the first-person narrative splinters into third-person, verse, and a scene with play-like structure) and the primacy of the dominant narrative (the narrator Grendel is, after all, the same demon-monster who terrorizes Heo-rot in the Anglo-Saxon poem *Beowulf*). According to Lyotard, postmod-ernism encourages the discrediting of grand narratives and the retextual-ization of history and reality so that overarching metanarratives, or *grands récits*, become replaced by micronarratives and multiple perspectives. From a critical standpoint, the legitimization of alternate narratives allows for the serious reconsideration of modern and even pre-modern texts, such as in Jane Chance's examination of Grendel's mother and the critically marginal-ized women of *Beowulf*.[18] From a creative standpoint, postmodern fantasy allows for the production of various parallax retellings and expansions: Carole Nelson Douglas' *Good Night, Mr. Holmes* (1990) gives Irene Adler's version of Arthur Conan Doyle's 'A Scandal in Bohemia'; Tad Williams' *Cal-iban's Hour* (1994) retells portions of Shakespeare's *The Tempest* through Caliban's perspective; Mary Stewart's *The Wicked Day* (1983) recounts the events of Thomas Malory's *Le Morte D'Arthur* from Mordred's eyes; and Anne Rice's *The Vampire Lestat* (1985) refigures her own *Interview With the Vampire* (1976) from the point of view of the earlier novel's villain. More broadly, marginalized narrative groups have greater representation in postmodern fantasy. Othered voices have always spoken in fantasy through the masks of elves, dwarves or dragons, but recent vampire novels alone demonstrate how fantasy – even in a white male, Dracula-centred genre – can produce remarkable ethnic variety, such as the seemingly prepubescent African-American girl of Octavia Butler's *Fledgling* (2005), the Soucouyant Caribbean vampires of Nalo Hopkinson's *Brown Girl in the Ring* (1998) and 'Greedy Choke Puppy' (2000), or the Ethiopian immortal of Tananarive Due's *My Soul to Keep* (1997). In addition, postmodern fantasy provides increased access to vampires from non-English speaking cultures, as with Hideyuki Kikuchi's Japanese series, *Vampire Hunter D* (1983–), John Ajvide Lindqvist's Swedish story *Let the Right One In* (2004) and Sergei Lukyanenko's Russian *Night Watch* tetralogy (1998–2006).

But postmodern fantasy represents more than just a shift from white, Western, patriarchal culture. Brian McHale describes postmodernism as the shift from 'problems of *knowing* to problems of modes of being – from an epistemological dominant to an *ontological one*'.[19] In other words, post-modernism moves from epistemology (theories of knowledge) to ontology (theories of being). Of course, the ontological imperative can be seen in modernist literature's elevation of art for art's sake, as in Archibald MacLeish's 'Ars Poetica', which asserts, 'A poem should not mean / But be.' But post-modernism's insistence on epistemological rupture (through the repeated explosion of theories of being) and ubiquitous indeterminacy (through the ever-present possibility of multiple interpretations of a text) reifies modernism's artistic ontological foundation into an integral tenet, producing an episteme (a system or collection of beliefs regarding the present human understanding of knowledge) of anti-episteme. In other words, postmodernism's central system of knowing affirms the impossibility of knowing anything for certain.[20]

McHale argues that 'Science fiction, like postmodern fiction, is governed by the ontological dominant. Indeed, it is perhaps *the* ontological genre *par excellence*.'[21] In fact, science fiction has provided the site for some of the most interesting and important postmodern theories, including what Jean Baudrillard and Umberto Eco call 'hyperreality', which Baudrillard defines as 'the generation by models of a real without origin or reality'.[22] Baudrillard uses Borges's map from 'On Exactitude in Science' to demonstrate the process through which simulacra (likenesses or imitations of the real) become interchangeable with reality, so that the map becomes more 'real' than the territory itself: 'Henceforth, it is the map that precedes the territory – *precession of simulacra* – it is the map that engenders the territory and if we were to revive the fable today, it would be the territory whose shreds are slowly rotting across the map.'[23] This idea, similar to that of Eco's 'Absolute Fake',[24] has been applied most often to science fiction works by authors like Philip K. Dick, William Gibson, Bruce Sterling or Pat Cadigan and has been popularized by films such as *Blade Runner* (1982), *Total Recall* (1990), *Ghost in the Shell* (1995) and *The Matrix* (1999). It makes sense that science fiction, and especially cyberpunk, should be connected to postmodern hyperreality, where as Baudrillard notes, 'The real is produced from miniaturized units, from matrices, memory banks and command modules – and with these it can be reproduced an indefinite number of times.'[25] But hyperreality may be useful when applied to fantasy as well.

Eric Rabkin describes the 'anti-expected' as fantastic, 'even if it takes place in a work that is not itself a fantasy'.[26] This is true not only in works that Attebery refers to as 'science fantasy',[27] but in cyberpunk fiction and stories purporting to be straight science fiction. For example, in the *Babylon 5* episode 'Fall of Night' (1995), when Kosh the Vorlon leaves his encounter suit to reveal his appearance as an angelic-looking creature, each race identifies him as one of their own deities or supernatural beings. Although this moment presents a scientific explanation for human (and alien) myth – Vorlon manipulation of younger races – the revelation of Kosh's true appearance is itself quite magical, almost spiritual. Similarly, the apparent advent of technological Singularity in Vernor Vinge's *Rainbows End* (2006) has an element of the fantastic in it, even if science may one day make artificial intelligence a reality. In film, computer animation/special effects have made it harder to differentiate between the fantasy world of the movie and the real world of the audience. Fantasy becomes easier to (hyper)realize when dinosaurs, trolls and giant gorillas appear almost more real than their human counterparts. Even in traditional fantasy novels, the hyperreal abounds. More than in any other genre, the maps actually do precede the territory: the reader experiences the '*precession of simulacra*' when s/he encounters Middle-earth, Pern or Gwynedd on maps before reading a single word.

Farah Mendlesohn notes that in stories with differentiated 'real' and 'fantasy' worlds, the fantastic is generally segregated from the real. In 'portal-quest fantasies', for example, 'Although individuals may cross both ways, the fantastic does not.'[28] Similarly, in 'intrusion fantasies', such as H. P. Lovecraft's 'The Call of Cthulhu', 'The division between the outer story and the inner one is almost absolute'.[29] Yet hyperreality still occurs in either of these types of stories when the fantasy world becomes more real than the real. For example, both Gordon R. Dickson's *The Dragon and the George* (1976) and Joel Rosenberg's *The Sleeping Dragon* (1983) begin with characters from our world being transported into a fantastic one; as each series progresses, however, the 'real' world becomes all but forgotten. Unlike the hyperreal in cyberpunk, however, where 'there is no *there* there',[30] the lands of Phantásien in Michael Ende's *The Neverending Story* (1979) and Narnia in C. S. Lewis's *The Lion, the Witch and the Wardrobe* (1950) are in many ways more *there* than here is. This aspect of fantastic hyperreality may account for one seemingly un-postmodern trait of the genre. Fredric Jameson describes 'flatness or depthlessness' as 'perhaps the supreme formal feature of all postmodernisms'.[31] Cyberpunks, for whom 'hipness is all',[32] inhabit a world of style and surface. They are often apathetic, self-centred-but-cool slackers whose world-weary cynicism obviates any personal connection to their worlds. In contrast, even the most unbelieving of anti-heroes, such as Stephen R. Donaldson's Thomas Covenant, fight with passion and love for their deeply developed lands. Even in hell – or a suburb of hell, as in Andy Duncan's 'Beluthahatchie' (1997) – hope is not abandoned. Cyberpunk stories are often dystopian nightmares but few fantasy tales are, even when they end with destruction. According to Attebery, the 'essential content' of fantasy's 'fuzzy set' includes instances of 'the impossible', experiences of 'wonder', and a characteristic structure that is 'comic'.[33] As Tolkien asserts, fantasy often depicts 'eucatastrophe' (literally a 'fortuitous unravelling').[34] Alan Moore explores this seeming-paradox of a happy end-of-the-world in his comic book series *Promethea* (1999–2005). Noting the etymological connection between revelation and apocalypse, he explains that Promethea is 'the Apocalypse. She is Revelation. It's what Apocalypse is. Apocalypse is Revelation... that ends the world.'[35]

Neil Gaiman ties the hyperreal and Baudrillard's Borgesian map to storytelling: 'One describes a tale best by telling the tale... The more accurate the map, the more it resembles the territory. The most accurate map possible would be the territory, and thus would be perfectly accurate and perfectly useless. The tale is the map that is the territory.'[36] Just as hyperreality confuses the real with the simulacrum, metafiction complicates the division between the story and the real. Attebery suggests that 'Fantasy, by its structure, emphasizes the difference between fiction and life',[37] but he acknowledges the interpenetration of fiction and life through metafictional narrative in works such as John Crowley's *Little, Big* (1981):

> Whereas Tolkien upholds a fast distinction between what he called primary creation (the world we live in) and secondary (the world of story), and his metafictional devices serve chiefly to establish the importance of storytelling in its own secondary sphere, Crowley indicates that there is no primary creation in that sense, or that it is approachable only through the imagination.[38]

In fact, *Little, Big* itself blurs the distinction between stories and histories when Alice Drinkwater observes that 'People in tales *don't* know, always [that they are in a tale]. But they are.'[39] Narrative confusion and the subversion of traditional plot and character are hallmarks of literary postmodern fiction, such as Thomas Pynchon's *Gravity's Rainbow* (1973), or John Barth's *Lost in the Funhouse*, which begins, 'Once upon a time there was a story that began,' or Italo Calvino's *If on a Winter's Night a Traveler*, which opens with 'You are about to begin reading Italo Calvino's *If on a winter's night a traveler*.'[40] Samuel R. Delany's *Tales of Nevèrÿon* foregrounds the theoretical scaffolding of postmodern literature through a preface by the fictitious K. Leslie Steiner, which describes Delany's work as 'a narrative hall of mirrors', and through an appended article by the equally fictitious S. L. Kermit, which references the work of Derrida and remarks on the fact that written signification is a 'signifier of the signifier, a model of a model, an image of an image, the trace of an endlessly deferred signification'.[41] In *Flight from Nevèrÿon* (1985), Delany problematizes narrative provenance by having a character who appears to be Delany himself produce a journal entry recounting an encounter that mirrors a clearly fictional tale about a young smuggler told earlier in the book. Except for minor disparities, each story features a scene that mimics its analogue, with sentences that are exactly the same or differ by only a word or two. Like the film *Adaptation* (2002), which overlays Charlie Kaufman the writer with Charlie Kaufman the writer/character, the *Nevèrÿon* stories offer a postmodern interrogation of authorship and narrative, providing Delany the opportunity for 'continuous, open-ended, self-critical dialogue' with his own novels.[42]

The extensive footnotes of Susanna Clarke's *Jonathan Strange & Mr. Norrell* (2004) or Mark Z. Danielewski's *House of Leaves* (2000) allow a similar metatextual effect, as does the form of Milorad Pavić's *Dictionary of the Khazars: A Lexicon Novel* (1984). Gérard Genette notes that rather than forming 'a boundary or a sealed border', postmodern paratext creates a 'threshold' to be crossed.[43] Postmodern fantasy bursts narrative boundaries in myriad ways. Jon Scieszka and Lane Smith's children's book *The Stinky Cheese Man and Other Fairly Stupid Tales* (1992) features a falling Table of Contents and a loquacious Little Red Hen whose blather overwhelms the normal paratextual space; David Mack's mixed-media *Kabuki* comic series (1994–) consistently disregards the accepted conventions of frame and gutter and often must be turned sideways or upside down to be read; Nick Bantock's *Griffin & Sabine* (1991) transcends the limits of the page so that characters' correspondence may be removed and postcards may be seen from both sides. Not only do each of these works represent what Espen Aarseth terms 'ergodic' literature – literature requiring 'nontrivial effort' from the reader[44] – they also provide rhizomic narratives similar in multiplicity to the conceptual rhizomes of Gilles Deleuze and Félix Guattari, which allow for multiple, non-hierarchical nodes of meaning and interpretation (rather than one centralized, hierarchical system of base and branches).

Jameson believes that cultural rhizomes have created Babel-like divisions, with each separate group speaking 'a curious private language of its own, each profession developing its private code or ideolect, and finally each individual coming to be a kind of linguistic island, separated from everyone else'.[45] According to Jameson, this dislocation and fragmentation of language communities allows for 'pastiche', which he defines as the 'neutral practice' of stylistic mimicry 'without the satirical impulse, without laughter, without that still latent feeling that there exists something normal compared to which what is being imitated is rather comic. Pastiche is blank parody, parody that has lost its sense of humour.'[46] Like hyperreality, Jameson's pastiche becomes more real than the original. Referents have been lost, so history and nostalgia are experienced '*metonymically*', as when the film *Star Wars* (1977) resurrects the 'long extinct' Buck Rogers-esque serial without direct reference or allusion.[47] Pastiche is one of the most visible forms of late postmodern fantasy, although a distinction might be made between a *bricoleur*, who uses whatever is at hand, and a *pasticheur*, who borrows specifically from earlier sources. Works such as Terry Pratchett and Neil Gaiman's *Good Omens: The Nice and Accurate Prophecies of Agnes Nutter, Witch* (1990), the film *Mystery Men* (1999) or the internet movie *Dr. Horrible's Sing-Along Blog* (2008) fail without an audience's awareness of the hypotext (the earlier text alluded to by the later hypertext). Similarly, pasticcios like Alan Moore's *League of Extraordinary Gentlemen* (1999–) benefit from but do not require knowledge of the work's inspiration. Such reimaginings/homages/reinventions extend the borders of postmodern fantasy independent of history, nostalgia or the knowledge-base of the reader. This allows for an ever-expanding kingdom. Colin Manlove describes the definitive 'character of fantasy' as '*A fiction evoking wonder and containing a substantial and irreducible element of supernatural or impossible worlds, beings or objects*'.[48] But Andy Duncan's lovely short story 'Unique Chicken Goes in Reverse', about a young Mary (Flannery) O'Connor and her frizzled chicken named Jesus, has no substantial and irreducible element of supernatural or impossible worlds, beings or objects, but was nonetheless nominated for the 2007 Nebula Award. The borders of postmodern fantasy expand daily and perhaps, like Clive Barker's *Weaveworld*, 'having no beginning, will have no end'.[49]

NOTES

1 In Jorge Luis Borges, *A Universal History of Infamy*, trans. Norman Thomas di Giovanni (New York: Dutton, 1972), p. 141.

2 Alfred Korzybski, *Science and Sanity: An Introduction to Non-Aristotelian Systems and General Semantics*, 4th edn (International Non-Aristotelian Library) (Lakeville, CT: Institute of General Semantics, 1958), p. 750.

3 Brian Attebery, *Strategies of Fantasy* (Bloomington and Indianapolis: Indiana University Press, 1992), p. 12.

4 Jürgen Habermas, 'Modernity – An Incomplete Project', trans. Seyla Ben-Habib, in Hal Foster (ed.), *Postmodern Culture* (London: Pluto, 1983), pp. 3–15, at pp. 8–9.

5 Marshall Berman, *All That Is Solid Melts Into Air: The Experience of Modernity*, 2nd edn (London: Penguin, 1988), p. 16.

6 J. R. R. Tolkien, '*Beowulf*: The Monsters and the Critics' (1936), in Daniel Donoghue (ed.), *Beowulf: A Verse Translation* (Norton Critical Editions) (New York: Norton, 2002), pp. 103–30, at p. 103.

7 Attebery, *Strategies*, p. 39.

8 *Ibid.*, p. 41.

9 Ihab Hassan, *The Dismemberment of Orpheus: Toward a Postmodern Literature* (New York: Oxford University Press, 1982), pp. 267–8.

10 Habermas, 'Modernity', p. 13.

11 Jean-François Lyotard, *The Postmodern Condition: A Report on Knowledge*, trans. Brian Massumi (Manchester University Press, 1984), p. 81.

12 Zygmunt Bauman, *Intimations of Postmodernity* (London: Routledge, 1991), p. 187.

13 Ernest Hemingway, 'A Clean, Well-Lighted Place', in *The Complete Short Stories of Ernest Hemingway: The Finca Vigía Edition* (New York: Scribner's, 1987), pp. 288–91, at p. 291.

14 John Gardner, *Grendel* (New York: Vintage 1989), p. 170.

15 *Ibid.*, p. 158.

16 *Ibid.*, pp. 21–2, 110, 173.

17 *Ibid.*, p. 27.

18 Jane Chance, 'The Structural Unity of *Beowulf*: The Problem of Grendel's Mother', in Donoghue, *Beowulf*, pp. 152–67.

19 Brian McHale, *Postmodernist Fiction* (New York: Methuen, 1987), p. 10.

20 Hassan, *The Dismemberment of Orpheus*, p. 269.

21 McHale, *Postmodernist Fiction*, p. 59.

22 Jean Baudrillard, 'Simulacra and Simulations', in Mark Poster (ed.), *Jean Baudrillard: Selected Writings* 2nd edn (Stanford University Press, 2001), pp. 167–87, at p. 169.

23 Baudrillard, 'Simulacra', p. 169.

24 Umberto Eco, *Travels in HyperReality: Essays*, trans. William Weaver (San Diego: Harcourt Brace Jovanovich, 1986), p. 35.

25 Baudrillard, 'Simulacra', p. 170.

26 Eric S. Rabkin, *The Fantastic in Literature* (Princeton University Press, 1976), p. 10.

27 Attebery, *Strategies*, p. 106.

28 Farah Mendlesohn, *Rhetorics of Fantasy* (Middletown, CT: Wesleyan University Press, 2008), p. 4.

29 *Ibid.*, p. 135.

30 William Gibson, *Mona Lisa Overdrive* (London: HarperCollins, 1995), p. 55.

31 Fredric Jameson, 'Postmodernism, or the Cultural Logic of Late Capitalism', *New Left Review* 1.146 (1984), pp. 53–92, at p. 60.

32 Istvan Csicsery-Ronay, Jr. 'Cyberpunk and Neuromanticism', in Larry McCaffery (ed.), *Storming the Reality Studio: A Casebook of Cyberpunk and Postmodern Science Fiction* (Durham, NC: Duke University Press, 1991), pp. 182–93, at p. 184.

33 Attebery, *Strategies*, pp. 14, 16, 15.

34 J. R. R. Tolkien, 'On Fairy-Stories', in *Tree and Leaf* (Boston: Houghton Mifflin, 1965), pp. 3–84, at p. 68.

35 Jon B. Cooke and George Khoury, 'Alan Moore and the Magic of Comics', *Comic Book Artist* 25 (2003), pp. 8–45, at p. 33.

36 Neil Gaiman, Introduction, in *Fragile Things: Short Fictions and Wonders* (New York: William Morrow, 2006), pp. xvii.

37 Attebery, *Strategies*, p. 141.

38 *Ibid.*, p. 47.

39 John Crowley, *Little, Big: The Fairies' Parliament* (New York: Bantam, 1981), p. 17.

40 John Barth, *Lost in the Funhouse* (New York: Bantam, 1969), pp. 1–2; Italo Calvino, *If on a Winter's Night a Traveler*, trans. William Weaver (New York: Harcourt Brace Jovanovich, 1979), p. 1.

41 Samuel R. Delany, *Tales of Nevèrÿon* (1979) (Hanover, CT: Wesleyan University Press, 1993), pp. 14 and 260.

42 Samuel R. Delany, *Silent Interviews: On Language, Race, Sex, Science Fiction, and Some Comics* (Hanover, CT: Wesleyan University Press, 1994), p. 48.

43 Cited by Richard Macksey, "Foreword", in Gérard Genette, *Paratexts: Thresholds of Interpretation* (Cambridge University Press, 1997), p. xvii.

44 Espen J. Aarseth, *Cybertext: Perspectives on Ergodic Literature* (Baltimore, MD: Johns Hopkins University Press, 1997), p. 1.

45 Fredric Jameson, 'Postmodernism and Consumer Society', in Hal Foster (ed.), *Postmodern Culture* (London: Pluto, 1983), pp. 111–25, at p. 114.

46 Jameson, 'Postmodernism and Consumer Society', p. 114.

47 *Ibid.*, p. 116.

48 Colin Manlove, 'Introduction to Modern Fantasy', in David Sandner (ed.), *Fantastic Literature: A Critical Reader* (London: Praeger, 2004), pp. 156–65 at p. 165.

49 Clive Barker, *Weaveworld* (New York: Poseidon, 1987), p. 584.

10

FARAH MENDLESOHN

Thematic criticism

Thematic criticism is a form of archaeology that excavates the layers of a text and compares that text with those found in other excavations: it is almost always comparative. As such, thematic criticism can be powerful and threatening, and sometimes limited and self-limiting. Thematic criticism is not a theoretical approach to fiction in itself, but can be situated within theoretical approaches such as modernism, deconstruction, postmodernism and structuralism; it is very strongly linked to psychoanalytic and political interpretations of fantasy. It is discussed in this book because thematic criticism may be the most common approach to the literature of fantasy among both academics and fans.

Thematic criticism can focus on just one text, but is far more often deployed in comparative work, in order to create clusters of texts which can be discussed together. In a field where tropes, style, fantastical location and magical systems vary widely, thematic criticism has proved a very powerful way of creating a collectivity of texts. For example, in John Clute and John Grant's *Encyclopedia of Fantasy*,[1] the thematic essay on reincarnation by Brian Stableford (808) or the essay on story, by John Clute (899–901) lay the basis for further exploration, offering a variety of pathways through a diverse field and demonstrating the multiplicity of pathways through individual texts, as different thematic filters open different windows into books, and different clusters emerge. The result, when thematic criticism is collected together, is a mosaic of fantasy.

The process of thematic criticism can be understood as a deconstructionist route into a text's deeper meaning, finding it richer and more meaningful than it might otherwise be read. This notion of the deeper, often metaphorical meaning in the fantastic is one of the classic defences of fantasy to the outside world.

Thematic criticism is also, however, a mode of reader response criticism and as such contributes an extra layer to the text, the role of the reader who brings to the text his or her own prior reading and may slot the text into a pattern of thematic reading which the author did not envisage.

One particularly good example of the role of thematic criticism in intensifying the reading of a set of fantasy texts can be found in Charles Butler's *Four British Fantasists*.[2] Butler considers the ways in which an understanding of the authors' context, and particularly the landscape of their lives, inflects a reading of the text. Butler demonstrates that thematic criticism can be a powerful way to understand fantasy texts because the relationship between metonym and metaphor in the fantasy literature is almost directly reversed from that in mimetic forms. He demonstrates through themes such as 'Longing and Belonging' and 'Myth and Magic' how to figure out what is metaphor and what is the mimetic, because in fantasy literature obvious metaphors may be explicitly literalized. Thus, in a variety of texts, 'he's an animal really' gains a mimetic as well as a metaphoric form. In George MacDonald's *The Princess and Curdie* (1883), Curdie is given the power to know people's character when he shakes their hand, by a physical manifestation of the animal nature inside them; Philip Pullman manifests this idea externally with his daemon companions, which settle to reflect the true nature of the individual, in *Northern Lights* (1995; US: *The Golden Compass*), while Terry Pratchett, in *Witches Abroad* (1991), introduces us to a wolf which has been made to think of itself as a person and suggests that the horror of such transformations may not be only one way, consequently interrogating a metaphor that is by now rather taken for granted.

Many writers deliberately build their metaphor into their magic. For Diana Wynne Jones, control over magic is always related to other issues of agency for her (mostly child) protagonists, and almost always to their characters. Barbara Hambly's protagonists frequently use magic in ways that metaphorize rifts in their societies. Stephen Donaldson and Steve Cockayne both construct worlds in which the magical nature of the Land can be understood as metaphor. Other authors are more critical of this approach: of Terry Pratchett's major characters, neither Captain Vimes of the City Watch nor Granny Weatherwax, greatest witch on the Ramtop Mountains, have much time for people who read great lessons into magic. The themes of the everyday are to be understood in the way people paint their houses (poverty and pride) and understand the world (where posh words for water make it sound medicinal to effect a cure).

Thematic studies of single texts are not particularly common outside the undergraduate essay, because the very advantage of a thematic approach is that it can link a cluster of texts and allow each to be used as a foil or as a tool of criticism for the other. A classic approach to thematic criticism can be found in Maria Nikolajeva's *The Magic Code*.[3] In this book, Nikolajeva identifies a theme, selects a number of texts and then rigorously examines the ways different authors make use of the theme, trope or device. In her Chapter 3, 'The Magic Time', we are asked to consider linear time, parallel time, time slips, ellipses in time and pocket universes, each carefully described, with examples. Nikolajeva's approach avoids reductiveness and demonstrates the fractal nature of the form which can be twisted and turned to achieve new perspectives. Nikolajeva is able to avoid generalizations and promotes a critical approach to fantasy as a conversation in which ideas are tried, tested and modified.

In the collection *Diana Wynne Jones: An Exciting and Exacting Wisdom*,[4] several of the articles use the 'foil/tool' approach in a range of ways that demonstrate the pitfalls of the thematic approach: Sarah Fiona Winters's 'Good and Evil in the Works of Diana Wynne Jones and J. K. Rowling' struggles because it compares a very subtle text to a very direct one, with the result that a single issue produces complex explanations for one book and description from the other. The 'comment' that one book ends up making on the other is not wholly complimentary, as one book inadvertently exposes the weaknesses of the other. In contrast, the single-text thematic essays – Donna R. White's 'Living in Limbo: *The Homeward Bounders* as a Metaphor for Military Childhood' and Sharon M. Scapple's 'Transformation of Myth in *A Tale of Time City*' – demonstrate the complexity of two texts and uncover an archaeology of the tales. White's essay is particularly interesting because it demonstrates the degree to which thematic reading is closely tied to reader response. White argues that *The Homeward Bounders* functions very well as a text for military children – pushed from pillar to post, never fully in play – but never once claims that this is an intention of the author. Here, a thematic reading is a self-conscious filter, in which the reader-critic understands reading as an active experience. Alice Mills's 'The Trials and Tribulations of Two Dogsbodies: A Jungian Reading of Diana Wynne Jones' *Dogsbody*', on the other hand, makes it clear that Mills is trying to dig under the skin of the writer and peel back the layers of psychological complexity behind a novel that, on one level, is the story of an orphaned girl and her dog and to look at issues of empowerment, protection and responsibility as well as at the construction of femaleness and relationships. Mills uses a thematic approach to scrape away at areas where she, as a reader, feels uneasy. In this sense there is a continued link with the notion of reader response. One thing we can see clearly from this cluster of essays is that the scope of a thematic essay, and the depth to which it wishes to dig, can vary greatly.

The best thematic critics have approached their chosen texts with questions. William A. Senior's *Stephen R. Donaldson's Chronicles of Thomas*

Covenant is predominantly concerned with Donaldson's reworking of landscape and language, and with structure and poetics – with the bones of the book rather than its flesh. In Chapter 2, however, Senior takes on one of the major themes of fantasy and of fantasy criticism, 'the hero', and subjects it to an interrogation that is concerned with establishing what questions Donaldson set out to ask of fantasy and the relationship of his own work to the wider body of fantasy.

Senior is one of the rare critics to find an absence of his theme, and in doing so, to find something else. A great deal of 'hero' studies have gone little further than the imposition of the Campbellian hero structure upon a text, or to work out how the text benefits from the author's own reading of Campbell, or to study the variations played on the notes. Senior uses thematic criticism to deepen his consideration of Donaldson's technique, by refusing to take the Campbellian model, point by point, as a template for critical analysis. Instead, Senior demonstrates the way in which the thematic issue of the hero is wound into the structure of the plot, and into the construction of the metaphoric landscape.

Senior's critique observes the degree to which all of this – the notion of hero as *superhero* – is rejected by Donaldson at both the micro and the macro scale. In Donaldson's work the protagonist is mostly impotent against the invader (a thematic parallel with Covenant's leprosy) but so too are other figures and so too is the shape of the war. In Donaldson, Senior argues, there are no grand battles, great units are disbanded or never meet their chosen enemy, and many characters meet the evil in their own homes.[5] The world of Donaldson is a world in which ordinary people try, but often fail, to be heroes, and the war is far more the unpleasant and unheroic scurrying of modern warfare than it is the staged epic of the eighteenth and nineteenth centuries. Later, Senior demonstrates the degree to which Donaldson turns Campbell's ideas inside out, so that Covenant is continually engaged in a refusal of the heroic path: 'he acquires no magic sword or steed (in fact, contrary to the paradigm, he rejects the Ranyhyn, the supernatural horses of the Land, as well as the *krill* of Loric)' (47), but Covenant's refusal becomes the means by which he resists. Senior's critique is essentially political and is motivated by questions: How does one relate to a destructive hero? How, technically, can Donaldson compel the reader with such an unforgiving and relentless character and convince him/her to continue to regard as hero a character who rejects both the term and the consequences, and in doing so, effectively rejects the reader conditioned to look for the hero? As Senior explores this, he takes the critical reader into an understanding of the way Donaldson uses a very common theme as a tool, deployed to expose the ease with which the 'theme of the hero' has been absorbed into the bones of the fantastic.

As Senior demonstrates, thematic criticism can encompass and embrace political criticism. However, this can be turned around. Political criticism may take a thematic mode for its structure and, by exploiting its possibilities as a form of reader response, demonstrate how a reader may be in charge of thematic interpretation. In this mode, a particular political stance is deployed as a filter through which to understand a text. Eliza T. Dresang's 'Hermione Granger and the Heritage of Gender'[6] considers only momentarily whether we can find feminist themes, dismisses the notion of Rowling as in any way writing a self-consciously feminist text and focuses instead on how the feminist reader can work her way through the sense of uneasiness that the Harry Potter novels – with their often marginalized female characters, and unexpectedly weak characterization of the main female character, Hermione – engender.

Dresang's article stands out because she chooses to offer not one 'feminist' filter, but several 'feminisms'. This creates a polysemic approach, which challenges the problem outlined earlier of finding what one seeks: Dresang is able to take a single incident – the treatment of Hermione when she attempts to stand up for the house elves – and demonstrate how it can be seen both as sexist from one angle and as an opportunity for empowerment from another. Similarly, Dresang is able to separate the language with which Hermione is described from Hermione's own character ('Her hysteria and crying happen far too often to be considered a believable part of the development of Hermione's character and are quite out of line with her core role in the book' (223)) to draw attention to what might be interpreted as Rowling's own ambivalence about female empowerment and its associated behaviour which (and this Dresang does not say) is replicated in Rowling's own 'narrative of an author': the 'lone mother strikes lucky', rather than the 'woman with drive works incredibly hard'.

Thematic criticism is powerful, and can feel genuinely threatening to authors, who may feel that they are being required to consider theme as an element in the writing of the text. As the writer Kelley Eskridge says:

> I despise conscious theme, the great battering ram on the literary war machine. It subverts story. It renders characters nearly non-dimensional. It makes for some truly terrible dialogue. Good writers smile a polite 'no' when the theme tray is passed around, and instead allow theme to emerge from a well-told story about people who engage us because their choices, fears and hopes seem real, even if they are as strange to us as the surface of Pluto.[7]

Thematic criticism risks giving the impression that the aim of the critic is to dismantle a text into its component parts. For both author and reader, thematic criticism can feel like a challenge to the 'ownership' of the text.

Take, for example, Patricia Monk's article 'Goddess on the Hearth'.[8] Monk is interested in the degree to which images and figures of the cat function as 'aspects of self... deeply repressed by processes of feminine acculturation in patriarchal society' and begins with a survey of the many ways cats are deployed in fantasy, ranging from the cat in the author blurb ('... lives with her partner and ten cats'), the role of the cat as host for the soul of the powerful, cats as friends to mythic animals such as dragons, as teaching animals, a representatives on earth of goddesses and of the moon, as magical servants and as symbols of wildness. 'The cat also takes on, from time to time, the role of psychopomp' (313). After defining each category, Monk lists a number of authors who use the cat in such a way. Having completed her survey, Monk picks out one aspect of these uses on which to focus, the cat as 'a representation of the woman's supra-ordinate self', and asserts, 'Everything said about the cat in modern fantasy by women, moreover, bears out the constellation of the archetypal essential feminine Self in the cat. Even the multiple relationships between cats and women writers of fantasy bear this out' (315).

Monk has a very specific interest, 'the cat', and in her explorations of 'the cat' she is open both to the charge of reductiveness – losing track of the story of the texts she studies – and of appropriation, in that she is insistent that her understanding of this trope and her valorizing of this trope among the texts she studies are correct. Monk's writing inadvertently insists on the rightness of her interpretation, but the article also exemplifies other potential weaknesses of thematic criticism: the first, to reduce criticism to cataloguing the manifestation of a theme; the second, to assume for one's theme too great a universality, so that all uses of a trope or icon (in this case a cat) can be tucked neatly into the thematic paradigm.

A further difficulty with the construction of thematic criticism is that it frequently rests on a pre-ordered understanding of the text. This paragraph from Kath Filmer is not untypical:

> It seems that fantasy literature does two things: it comes to terms with the existential *angst* of the twentieth century, and accepts the reality of the skepticism that pervades the external world... I believe that fantasy is skeptical only superficially; if one looks more deeply at the texts of fantasy, one finds unmistakably the articulation of hope.[9]

As Stanley Fish might have said, what Filmer is looking for, she finds.[10] It is almost unheard-of for a critic taking a thematic approach to the text to discuss texts that do *not* respond to their chosen filter. Filmer, for instance, does not examine the work of Edith Nesbit, who may articulate hope, but whose model of hope is entirely secular, and not one which in any way intends to re-image the spiritual. Had Filmer done so, it would have wrecked her thesis.

Yet despite these pitfalls, when thematic criticism assumes the self-consciousness of the author it can acquire a meta-critical edge. Ulrike Borgman's 'King Arthur of Britain in the Nineties: Just Like a Man'[11] is an interesting approach to thematic criticism, and one that chimes with Kelley Eskridge's fears, cited earlier. Borgman, as a critic, is concerned with precisely the over use of theme-as-structure and theme-as-political-stance. After considering the Arthurian fiction of Persia Woolley, Helen Hollick, Rosalind Miles (and in an aside, Marion Zimmer Bradley), Borgman concludes that each has set out rather too ostentatiously to 'rewrite the Guinevere figure' in terms of 1980s values in which a man's inability to communicate emotion becomes the crux of the political tale, and the author attempts 'to inscribe contemporary ideals of feminism... onto this figure who is simply undeveloped or downright condemned in most Arthurian sources' (162). The attempt at rescue, Borgman argues, produces three remarkably similar models of Guinevere, because the thematic thread she is intended to weave is so consistent and so insisted upon. Borgman ends with a challenge to the authors to rethink masculinity as much as femininity, to create the reasonable men who must exist. Ulrike Horstmann, in '"Boy!" – Male Adolescence in Contemporary Fantasy Novels', takes up this challenge. Horstmann argues that across fantasy novels we can trace a model of what it is to be a boy, how to handle issues of growing up, the role of male mentors and the constructed relationships between young men and women. Horstmann moves a thematic critique into a discussion of inherent ideology to show how easily fantasy can obscure very conservative values and transmit them as true lessons.[12]

While thematic criticism can arouse hostility among some authors, others have been comfortable with the thematic messages of their work being brought to the fore. J. R. R. Tolkien's *The Lord of the Rings* is perhaps one of the most studied texts in the genre. As Meredith Veldman has pointed out in *Fantasy, the Bomb and the Greening of Britain*, Tolkien understood his work as a vehicle for a cluster of messages (even while he condemned Lewis for too-obvious advocacy). Veldman, in her chapter 'Middle-earth as Moral Protest', uses Tolkien's own letters, which describe noise and air pollution as 'Mordor in our Midst',[13] and those he wrote to his son Christopher of his role in the RAF: 'My sentiments are more or less those Frodo would have had if he discovered some Hobbits learning to ride Nazgul-birds for the liberation of the Shire.'[14] Tolkien understood the world in binaries, some of which are, as Veldman delineates, clear in the text: good characters and species such as the elves and the hobbits are nature worshippers, whereas evil characters and species such as Saruman and the orcs are those who have become infatuated with science and technology, which, while not in themselves evil, 'are pretty certain to serve evil ends.'[15] Tolkien compares the latter to Catholics who engage in research on poisonous gases.[16] In Tolkien's case, the critic need not be concerned about deconstructing the text in terms of themes, because Tolkien in his own writings has already validated the project.

NOTES

1 John Clute and John Grant (eds.), *The Encyclopedia of Fantasy* (London: Orbit, 1997).
2 Charles Butler, *Four British Fantasists: The Children's Fantasy Fiction of Penelope Lively, Alan Garner, Diana Wynne Jones, and Susan Cooper* (Lanham, MD, Toronto and Oxford: Children's Literature Association and Scarecrow Press: 2006).
3 Maria Nikolajeva, *The Magic Code: The Use of Magical Patterns in Fantasy for Children* (Stockholm: Almqvist and Wiksell International, 1988).
4 Teya Rosenberg, Martha P. Hixon, Sharon M. Scapple and Donna R. White (eds.), *Diana Wynne Jones: An Exciting and Exacting Wisdom* (New York and Oxford: Peter Lang, 2002).
5 W. A. Senior, *Stephen R. Donaldson's Chronicles of Thomas Covenant: Variations on the Fantasy Tradition* (Kent, OH: Kent State University Press, 1995), pp. 44–5.
6 Eliza T. Dresang, 'Hermione Granger and the Heritage of Gender', in Lana A. Whited (ed.), *The Ivory Tower and Harry Potter: Perspectives on a Literary Phenomenon* (Columbia: University of Missouri Press, 2002), pp. 211–42.
7 Eskridge in Nicola Griffith and Kelley Eskridge, 'War Machine, Time Machine', in Wendy Gay Pearson, Veronica Hollinger and Joan Gordon (eds.), *Queer Universes: Sexualities in Science Fiction* (Liverpool University Press, 2008), pp. 45–6.
8 Patricia Monk, 'Goddess on the Hearth: The Archetypal Significance of the Cat in Modern Fantasy', *Journal of the Fantastic in the Arts*, 12 (2001), pp. 309–21.
9 Kath Filmer, *Scepticism and Hope in Twentieth Century Fantasy Literature* (Bowling Green, OH: Bowling Green State University Popular Press, 1992), p. 2.
10 'Theories always work and they will always produce exactly the results they predict, results that will be immediately compelling to those for whom the theory's assumptions and enabling principles are self-evident. Indeed, the trick would be to find a theory that *didn't* work': Stanley Fish, *Is There a Text in This Class? The Authority of Interpretive Communities* (Cambridge, MA: Harvard University Press, 1980), p. 68.
11 Ulrike Borgman, 'King Arthur of Britain in the Nineties: Just Like a Man', in Susanne Fendler and Ulrike Horstmann (eds.), *Images of Masculinity in Fantasy Fiction* (Lewiston, NY, and Lampeter: Edwin Mellen Press, 2003), pp. 145–63.
12 Ulrike Horstmann, '"Boy!" – Male Adolescence in Contemporary Fantasy Novels', in Fendler and Horstmann, *Images of Masculinity*, pp. 81–102.

13 Meredith Veldman, *Fantasy, the Bomb and the Greening of Britain: Romantic Protest, 1945–1980* (Cambridge University Press, 1994), p. 87.
14 *Ibid.*, p. 89, discussing Tolkien's letter of 29 May 1945.
15 Tolkien, to Peter Hastings, September 1954, in Humphrey Carpenter *The Letters of J. R. R. Tolkien*, ed. Humphrey Carpenter (London: George Allen and Unwin, 1981), pp. 187–96.
16 Veldman, *Fantasy*, p. 89.

GREER GILMAN

The languages of the fantastic

Any fiction – but above all a work of fantasy – is a world made of words, 'A world,' as Ursula K. Le Guin has said, 'where no voice has ever spoken before; where the act of speech is the act of creation.'[1] There is no Middle-earth, no Dorimare that lies beyond a barrier, a veil of words; no window heaped with goblin fruit for sale. No 'faery-lands forlorn' exist unless the casement is the spell. The glass is language; and the glass is all there is.

For the most influential of modern fantasists, that glass was a telescope, trained on origins.

Etymon

Fairy tale and philology have been entwined since Jacob Grimm first studied both, the linguistic root-stock inextricable from Briar Rose's hedge. The sleeping beauty of the past awaits the scholar seeking it, undaunted by the thorns. Grimm's study, etymology, derives from *etymon*: the true name of a thing, its first form. Origin is seen as authenticity; the eldest is most true.

J. R. R. Tolkien conceived of Middle-earth as a reconstruction of a lost world. Philology, he thought, 'could take you back even beyond the ancient texts it studied. He believed that it was possible sometimes to feel one's way back from words as they survived in later periods to concepts which had long since vanished, but which had surely existed, or else the word would not exist.'[2] He hung his mythology on these *-words – the asterisk marks conjecture – in the spaces between words, as if imagining his constellations from a scattering of stars.

Silent etymologies construct his world. So Gríma (as in Wormtongue) has the same meanings in Anglo-Saxon as 'larva' in Latin – ghost, spectre, hobgoblin; also, a mask or guise or helmet (think of Sutton Hoo). His new-invented languages – Sindarin, Quenya – are reported as of ancient lineage: as old as galaxies, old as creation.[3]

There is a backward-yearning branch of fantasy in Tolkien's descent that is all about the once and future: a lost nobility and purity, a restoration of words, worlds. Its concern is with authenticity.

> This is a rock; *tolk* in the True Speech . . . By the Illusion-Change you can make it look like a diamond – or a flower or a fly or an eye or a flame –' The rock flickered from shape to shape as he named them, and returned to rock. 'But that is mere seeming. Illusion fools the beholder's senses; it makes him see and hear and feel that the thing is changed. But it does not change the thing. To change the rock into a jewel, you must change its true name. And to do that . . . is to change the world.[4]

Imago

Writers are illusionists. They spell.

To speak with dragons, says the lore of Earthsea, one must call them by their true names: by their *etymons*. And yet the writer's craft is jugglery, a dazzle of mere seeming:

> All the myriad material things that we, in our universes, touch and use and love and hate and depend on – our food, our flesh, our breath; cities and towns, roads and houses, dogs, stars, stones, and roses – in a book these things have no true reality at all. They're just nouns.[5]

To name an eye, a flame, a flower on the page is to summon, not the thing itself, but its *imago*: in the oldest senses of that word, its ghost, shade, effigy. Its fetch.

The art is in the summoning, or what the linguist Karl Bühler called 'Deixis am Phantasma': the calling into mind of absent or imagined objects or the projection of the self elsewhere, as in a dream. When we speak of fantasy, so many of the terms are spatial: ecstasy, estrangement, transport, rapture, repulsion. The elves are leaving us; the fairies bid us come away. The Other sends us dreams and visions: we must let them in.

Contemporary realists – and writers of a kind of fantasy – may slip at will into an off-the-peg consensus reality: we know what a cocktail party or a quest is like. The writer may concern himself with other things, with story or psychology, and leave the setting – like the dull bits of a tapestry – to the imagination. But set a story farther off in time or space – on Neptune or in Heian Japan – and words must make the world. Readers of a tale are present at a world's creation – its cosmopoiesis – and sometimes even at its making over. In Diana Wynne Jones's *The Spellcoats* (1979), Tanaqui encodes her world as text(ile), weaving and reweaving as she comes to understand, to shape the story that she's in, the shifting story that we read: the fabric of her myth.

It may be that intensely worked language in itself fantasticates, that a Nabokov or a Joyce rebuilds the world we thought we knew. Great words re-estrange.

In Linnaeus, the *imago* is the true essential form of insects, their emergence from their larval guise in their proper shape and colours: the perfected metamorphosis, the butterfly, in myth called *Psyche*.

Mimetic fiction is a mirror playing at transparency: its text reflects for us the cities and the fields we know. But fantasy 'construct[s] an irony of mimesis':[6] its mirror is a Looking-glass, inverting the literal and metaphoric. A raven is not *like* a writing desk, but *is*. A leaf takes wing.

'When a butterfly has to look like a leaf, not only are all the details of a leaf beautifully rendered but markings mimicking grub-bored holes are generously thrown in,' writes Nabokov. In the language of fantasy, its readers find 'mimetic subtlety, exuberance and luxury' to match its non-existent worlds. We may discover in imagined nature 'the non-utilitarian delights that [Nabokov] sought in art. Both were a form of magic, both were a game of intricate enchantment and deception.'[7]

Strategies of style

Works of fantasy can make unusual narrative demands. Their writers may need to call forth spirits from the vasty deep; or convincingly record a dialogue of dragons; or invent the tongues of angels and of orcs. There are many strategies of style. One may tell a story in the timeless vernacular of 'Once upon a time'; or speak of marvels in a slangy cool demotic or in the dispassionate prose of scholarship, with footnotes; or employ – as Joyce did – a knot intrinsicate of tongues to wake the mythic echoes in banalities. And there are writers who evoke the languages of worlds removed from us: of Heorot or Nightmare Abbey or the Shakespearean stage. Yet we know those cadences: they are the language of madness and of vengeance, of courtiers and witches, Puck and Prospero; the language of ghosts.

Hieratic language

To speak of the unseen – of ghosts, gods, spirits – or evoke another world, we often use a language set apart from the vernacular. It may be simple ('Once upon a time...' or 'Hwaet!'); it can be formally elaborate, with masks, dance, music, and archaic speech. It is always stylized. As ritual, such language sets apart: chalks out a circle for a game, a stage, a conjuration. It creates a holy ground on which the numinous can be. A teller of sacred mysteries is a hierophant; her style of language – intricate, incantatory, ceremonious – is called hieratic.

Like song in theatre – irrational, sublime – hieratic language may be heard as artifice or as the true speech of aliens, mimesis of an otherworld. So even as a creature may appear in faultless evening dress with sword and wig, or wings and talons, or a robe and crown, so his demotic may be poetry: the music of estrangement.

The Archaic

Readers of immersive fantasy must navigate an alien new world; must learn the element they're in or drown. For them, this voyage of discovery, the joy of mastering the unfamiliar, is a prime aesthetic of the genre: their delights are dolphin-like.

If science fiction is a literature of the transcendent, then fantasy is a literature of immanence, of the indwelling or upwelling of an otherness: of time, of etymology. The past bleeds through the distemper. But even in a fantastic setting that is like the here and now there is a spring of strangeness – an elsewhere or an otherwise – beneath the fields (or city streets) we know, upwelling. The language of the past is one such spring, a medium of dissolution and of transport.

In *Ulysses*, each chapter's imagery is matched with a rune of Ogham, of the alphabet of trees – birch, rowan, alder – so that an unseen forest rises up through the cityscape, drowning the clatter of the streets in green.[8]

A writer may draw echoes and allusions from a single style – epic gravitas, Gothic hysteria, Austenian elegance – or many, as did E. R. Eddison, to tell a history of neverwhen. In *The Worm Ouroboros* (1922) and his unfinished Zimiamvian trilogy, he inlaid verses culled from Dunbar to the metaphysicals, from Sappho and the Elder Edda. His style – archaic, ink-horn, sonorous – is a rich mélange of periods, a moiré. Now one, now another strand of language catches the light: now Malory, now Webster, now Burton or Browne. In the trilogy, his players all are gods, mythic creatures speaking in the high mimetic, which is irony to them. His world is soaked in time, all rivers mingling; he writes, not pastiche, but 'like a creature native and indued / Unto that element' (*Hamlet* iv.7, 178–9).

Creators of a world begin, like Shakespeare's fellows, with an empty stage. Echoes of his world-engendering voice are potent. Alien and yet familiar, Shakespeare's language overwhelms us with its sheer intensity, and yet we're carried by the music of it, swept along. His words are both the tempest and the raft.

Iambics, the measure of blank verse – one TWO – the beat of Shakespeare's plays, are twice hieratic, the exalted language of an age long past. My own books are written largely in that cadence, 'a high Jacobean iambic, endlessly enjambed'.[9] But changes in signature are subtly important. Iambics mark displacements: a character immensely old, or alien, unmoored in time or space; a deity, a ghost, a sovereign. In John M. Ford's *The Princes of the Air*, iambics are the tricky language of diplomacy, neurologically coercive. Iambics mark a shift in mood or mode: the coin stamp of authority; the descent into madness.

Mervyn Peake's unfinished *Gormenghast* trilogy is a babble of voices: a mad Goth Dickensian, patter song, twitterings. It is an *Odyssey* which goes nowhere, a static chaos that is all the world. But here is Sepulchrave, the mad Earl of Gormenghast. His library has been burned; he is turning into an owl; he speaks measured mad soliloquy: 'each flint a cold blue stanza of delight, each feather, terrible'.[10]

His vast languid Countess is given to brusque spondaic and trochaic utterance:

> 'Slagg,' said the Countess, 'go away! I would like to see the boy when he is six... Take this gold ring of mine. Fix a chain to it. Let him wear it around his wry little neck. Call him Titus. (45)

But when she rouses herself, takes on authority (in vain: the upstart kitchen boy, Steerpike, holds the power), her metrics flip. She speaks iambically – one TWO – like one of Shakespeare's queens.

> God shrive my soul... God shrive it when I find the evil thing!... For every hair that's hurt I'll stop a heart. If grace I have when turbulence is over – so be it; and if not – what then? (374)

Against them Steerpike wields a voice like a blunted kitchen knife, just equal to its task, to pry and topple: in the war of words, the triumph of the prosaic.

Ecstasy

There are works of dark fantasy that seek to clothe the primal in hieratic ecstasies: to masque. Archaic language is for them a ritual disguise, a costume for an anti-carnival: 'grave-cerements and corpse-like mask... untenanted by any tangible form'.[11] For the nakedness of what they crave – the unspeakable *it* – appals them. Against it they must wield a language glutted and engorged – atrocious! eldritch! ichor! (a text-cloud of Lovecraft is like a flock of bats) – a high Baroque frenzy swirled about a central absence.

At its root, ecstasy is a dislocation of the self: a state of rapture, awe, despair, dread, madness, longing. The ecstatic speaker is beside himself, de-centered. His language is the shadow inverse of hieratic; he is not the magus calling up the tempest, but the ship that's wrecked. His circle is a vortex, like Poe's Maelström: its surfaces dark-dizzying, but for 'the gleaming and ghastly radiance they shot forth . . . in a flood of golden glory along the black walls, and far away down into the inmost recesses of the abyss'.[12]

For some writers, that language verges on hysteria, a babble of adjectives which must surround, though not at last contain, the unspeakable. Sense vanishes in sensibility, and reason is blinded by 'the general burst of terrific grandeur.'[13] For others, grammar and vocabulary are at odds; their style is almost ritually formal, like a charm to ward off what it summons: an apotropaic patterning, a litany of fear. Here is Thomas De Quincey, in a trance of opium:

> I was stared at, hooted at, grinned at, chattered at, by monkeys, by paroquets, by cockatoos . . . I came suddenly upon Isis and Osiris: I had done a deed, they said, which the ibis and the crocodile trembled at. I was buried for a thousand years in stone coffins, with mummies and sphynxes, in narrow chambers at the heart of eternal pyramids. I was kissed, with cancerous kisses, by crocodiles; and laid, confounded with all unutterable slimy things, amongst reeds and Nilotic mud.[14]

De Quincey – the authentic voice of derangement – is a taproot text for dark fantasists. A river runs from him through William Hope Hodgson to Lovecraft, and beyond:

> And round by the House of Silence, wound the Road Where The Silent Ones Walk. And concerning this Road, which passed out of the Unknown Lands, nigh by the Place of the Ab-humans, where was always the green, luminous mist, nothing was known.[15]

*Un*known, *un*speakable, *un*canny: this language works by paradox, denying what it names. It finds estrangement in a throng of words.

> And a great and painful excitement came upon the people of the lesser pyramid; for the loneliness of the world pressed upon them; and it was to them as though we in this age called to a star across the abyss of space.[16]

At its uttermost, it is a dissolution:

> In that instant it was as though her entire being was burned away, skin hair lips fingers all ash; and nothing remained but the butterflies and her awareness of them, orange and black fluid filling her mouth, the edges of eyes scored by wings.[17]

Contemporary writers – Jeff VanderMeer, China Miéville – play with ecstasies, but in a cooler vein and self-aware: baroquing the familiar and writing of the marvellous with wilful nonchalance. In Lucius Shepard's

'The Jaguar Hunter', a huddle of widows watching a cop show are seen as an invasion, 'a covey of large black birds with cowled heads, who were receiving evil instruction from the core of a flickering gray jewel'.[18] Contrariwise, Miéville speaks jadedly of monstrous chimaeras, atrocious cruelties: 'It was a childish excitement, like that of boys and girls who burnt insects with magnified sun.'[19] His voice is cool as Mephistopheles – 'Why this is hell, nor an I out of it' – at home in the abyss.

Irony

One may – with perfect self-possession – set a story in the past or in a distant country. There is a cool ironic style of fantasy that sets *then* and *elsewhere* on a footing with the *otherwise*.

Here is a kingdom of Elfin in Northumberland:

> The gipsies had come to announce the death of Queen Jocasta and to convey her dying command that the obsequies should be held in front of the Castle of Catmere. Queen Coventina had ordered that her whole court should attend the ceremony. As a mark of respect, visibility would be worn.[20]

Sylvia Townsend Warner writes of Elfin with a silver-eyed dispassion, and a beauty like a killing frost. Others, entomologists of faerie, turn a merciless clear lens on the astonishing, dissect the non-existent. Lord Dunsany, Elinor Wylie, David Garnett – and latterly Susanna Clarke and Theodora Goss – all write an elegant and unbedizened prose, like dry white wine and a biscuit, very English in its understatement.

Such works of the fantastic are an interplay of now/here and nowhere as figure and ground; but edgier texts, like Michael Swanwick's *The Dragons of Babel*, play with contrariety, dazzle with dissonance.

> The dragons came at dawn, lying low and in formation, their jets so thunderous they shook the ground like the great throbbing heartbeat of the world.[21]

In 'From Elfland to Poughkeepsie', Le Guin argues that an otherworld that can be disenchanted at a strikethrough is none (85). But here you could change a single word and change everything, and that's the point of it: Poughkeepsie with intent. Swanwick writes the language of the night with neon, Elfland with mean streets: a chimaera of awe and irony.

It is a style for satire, shading from comedy of manners to the darkest of political charges. One may argue with the censors: *But I write of nowhere.* Yet Le Guin's *Orsinian Tales* show the state erasure of a *was*, of memory; Geoff Ryman's 'The Unconquered Country', the annihilation of a *here*.

Absurdity

Mirrors are uncanny. In reflecting, they estrange. The object in the mirror ought to be the object mirrored; yet is not. The literal can disconcert; as the Mad Hatter insinuates, to say that '"I see what I eat" is the same thing as "I eat what I see"'[22] threatens to devour table, child, and all.

Absurdity – that which goes contrariwise to reason – can be whimsical; but often there is method in its madness. It plays with linguistic forms – inversion, metamorphosis, deletion – to generate unreason, making paradox of laws.

Such games with language, from anagrams and puns to Dadaist bricolage, may seem capricious or bedazzling, but there's matter in their mischief. The banning of the letter O in James Thurber's tale (*The Wonderful O*) erases what it spells: no dogs, stones, roses, moon, bassoon. No nothing.

Wordplay is refractive. It rejoices in distortion; but it also tells: it clinches. The riddle 'what has it got in its 'pocalypse?'[23] may truly be answered: 'String, or nothing!'[24] There is wordplay which reflects an alternate reality (Lost Angeles, Parisn't in Miéville's *Un Lun Dun*); there are even transformative puns: quibbles which can (literally) reshape a world, can turn misprision into prophecy. In John Crowley's *Little, Big*, a mistranscription of the phonebook – 'the Seventh Saint Bar and Grill and the Church of All Streets'[25] – is seen as mere computer-generated noise. Caught and corrected, these forms will later re-emerge as true and emblematic names. Nonsense – the 'bizarre witlessness' of the machine – is a cause or mirror of the transmutation of the City in its latter days.

Diana Wynne Jones's *Fire and Hemlock* is built on linguistic metamorphoses. The title of each part, its epitome, kaleidoscopes into the next: *new hero, now here, where now? nowhere*. As in fugue, the formal bounds enhance inventiveness. Each variant respells the world.

The demotic

Words are like bright stones that you have to put in your mouth, to taste the curve and edge of them, their cool. Spoken language – the sung tales of the scalds, the cradle rhymes, the vaunts and taunts of city youth, the mad songs, the ballads – is a living river.

Listen to Nalo Hopkinson's island patois or Russell Hoban's post-English, or to Joan Aiken's raucous and rackety play of voices: they must be read aloud.

[T]he more she'd wheedle, the rustier he'd get, and tell her to shab off, or she'd get a clump on the lughole. Once in a blue moon if summat had put him in a good skin, he'd play for her, but not if she asked.[26]

Scraps of allusion fly about some fantasies like autumn leaves. Sometimes a flickering from lyrical to louche – a wilful dissonance – makes time vertiginous or wads it up: 'Hasten, Mirth, and bring with thee a host of furious fancies whereof I am commander, which will be on sale for three days only at bargain summer prices.'[27] Peter Beagle's flitterwitted butterfly is a scrap of anywhen: a creature of a day, of centuries. Language possesses him.

More quietly: take note of hobbits talking. Amid all the lofty cumulonimbus of warriors and elves, their vernacular grounds us: 'Sam, what about a bit of rope? You'll want it, if you haven't got it.'[28]

In his *Outline of English Speech-Craft* (1878), the poet William Barnes forbade outlandish Roman words. His passion was the rootedness of Saxon English, its power to create ungrafted words, of its own thorny and inalienable stock. There is a Barnesian thread inweaving still, through Morris and Tolkien, into fantasy's common tongue: runesmiths and riddlemasters, werelights and wolfsheads.

It resonates in Alan Garner, in the bare-bones demotic of his patch of Cheshire. His stories have an intensity of *hereness* that is timedeep, footprints overlaid on footprints: room to rhyme. He writes with the mastery of a smith or mason – 'turning, tapping, knapping, shaping'[29] – in the cadences of work. He drives wordnails. His old words are not about revival but a stubborn persistence: stumps of old rootstock that refuse to be howked up.

Mary in *The Stone Book* cannot read; but she knows the glyphs her forebears cut in stone, the bull they smutched in soot and raddle on a cavewall under the hill. Her father makes for her a prayer-book of stone with a fossil in it: 'It's better than a book you can open . . . A book has only one story.' This has 'all the stories of the world and the flowers of the flood' (58, 61). In Garner's world, a pebble is the word, and the true speech is silence.

Re-estrangement

Garner finds the numinous in commonplace, in the here and now (which is many-layered): in work. So in another medium, Vermeer's woman with a milk jug seems holy, as if she were pouring stillness into stillness from an endless spring of grace. Nothing in the room, no title hints at this transfiguration: only the quality of light.

There are writers whose fantastic is oblique: it changes in a slant of light.

In Hopeless Mirrlees' *Lud-in-the-Mist*, Master Chanticleer is haunted by metaphor:

> He might dream that his own old nurse was baking an apple in her own cosy room, and as he watched it simmer and sizzle, she would look at him with a strange smile ... and say, 'But of course, you know it isn't really the apple. *It's the Note.*'[30]

Not *like* but *is*. A threat of magic hangs like thunder in the air, an undischarged sublimity. Against which he will set his counter-rhetoric: the equivocations of the law, which decrees that yellow is 'a *blackish* canary' (38), that fairy fruit is silk tuftaffity. Words in Dorimare are edgy. The out-walled Silent People are the plague-rats of poetry. Here the coupling of the lyrical and louche is both comic and sinister: 'to hear such high-flown oaths as: by the Sun, Moon, and Stars ... come tumbling out in the same breath with such homely expletives as Busty Bridget; ... by my Great-Aunt's Rump; or to find names like Dreamsweet, Ambrose, Moonlove, wedded to such grotesque surnames as Baldbreech, Fliperarde, or Pyepowders' (26). An unholy coupling: the Sublime will ask no leave of commonplace but lay it down, begetting chimaeras.

Other tactics may create unease: odd capitals; off-paragraphing; shifts in person.

John Crowley's quartet of novels, *Ægypt*, is in part another history of the world, infolding in its tesseract the art of memory, gnosticism, Giordano Bruno, Hermes and John Dee, who takes young Shakespeare's photograph. A *roman fleuve*. His manner is his own, a glassy, cool, translucent medium: refractive. 'Oh. Oh yes: oh yes of course,'[31] his characters will say. *I see*: but their epiphanies are writ in water. *Sure*: the momentary ripples where a trout has risen fading as they spread.

Even his punctuation refuses closure: cascading chains of : : : : : create a *mise en abyme* of uncertainty. Endless things.

Contrary to his grand design, his writing seems Æolian, a wind-played instrument. But like an anamorphic painting – seemingly a swirl of colours until a mirror set upon it draws an image out of chaos – it transmutes. It gathers to a final image of a wind-harp on a hill: round which his world rings, newly Copernican.

Some texts by Kelly Link 'resemble those random scratchings made by common use that you only see when you lift your wineglass up to the light'.[32]

There are three kinds of food.

> One is the food that your mother makes for you. One is the kind of food that you eat in restaurants. One is the kind of food that you eat in dreams. There's one other kind of food, but you can only get that in the underworld, and it's not really food. It's more like dancing.[33]

Seemingly, her text is all of tangents; bring a candle to the glass, and all its multitudinous fine scratches are revealed as pattern, haloing the light. But that is not the writer's task; it is the reader who must bring the ordering intelligence – or not – the reader who must find a spectrum and a centre. Where I stand is why.

Deixis

Words create perspectives, setting us in space and time and selfhood. In linguistics, this mapping is called deixis. It is marked with small words: I, you, it; here, now; then, elsewhere; this world and that other. Small words, but they conjure, summoning 'within *this* wooden O' the histories of an elsewhere, here and now. The speaker casts the circle; all things else are planetary to the I. 'Shine here to us,' Donne bids the sun, 'and thou art everywhere. This bed thy centre is.' And Prospero, himself the centre of his island world, its I and everywhere, is one with what he practices: 'But this rough *magic I here* abjure.' Three words are at the focus of his charm; which in the next word he dissolves.

By nature, works of fantasy engage in deictic paradox. Imagine, if you will, the now and here of nowhere. Tell a *never was* that is. Or wake, translated and confused: *But this is none of I*. Time, space, and person are the reveries and riddles of the literature. Each story that I've cited plays with one or more of these dimensions.

'Come away, O human child,' the faeries bid in Yeats's song; and he is stolen from himself. His *I* becomes peripheral.

In Gaiman and Vess's *Dream*, an imp in the audience cries out, '*Peaseblossom!* That's meant to be *me*, that is. Iss nuffink *like* me!'[34] And shortly Bottom will awake, confused: not I, this ass's head.

These stories play – no trick, but a marvel of perspective, so that the farthest yonder is *this*-most; the oldest new forever; and the alien the most myself.

One of the great *topoi* in fantasy is LITTLE BIG: 'almost anything that can be entered... may well be bigger inside than out'.[35] 'The further in you go, the bigger it gets,' says Crowley, over and again in *Little, Big*: the stranger and more intimate, the more sublime.

In her fantasia on the *Dream* wood, 'nowhere near Athens', Angela Carter wrote about that *further in*:

> The English wood is nothing like the dark, necromantic forest in which the Northern European imagination begins and ends, where its dead and the witches live... An English wood, however marvellous, however metamorphic, cannot, by definition, be trackless, although it might well be formidably

labyrinthine. Yet there is always a way out of a maze ... But to be lost in the forest is to be lost to *this* world, to be abandoned by the light ... That forest is haunted; this wood is enchanted.[36]

Reimagining

Wood, hill, water; stars, stones, roses; eye and flame: creation's endless things inspire us to subcreate. But as writers, we have only words to summon them: 'We translate a hill into a tale, conceive lovers to explain a brook, turn the perfect into imperfect.'[37]

But you, you readers – all unconscious masters of illusion – reverse that, recreate a world within your heads. Together, we are demiurges, synergistic. Look now.

In the turning of a leaf, the printed page becomes a green hill in another world, the other now is I. The lovers will resolve into their element, undrowning in themselves: the Erl-King 'dresses me again in an embrace so lucid and encompassing it might be made of water. And shakes over me dead leaves as if into the stream I have become ... '[38] The river rushes to the sea:

> The mind, that Ocean where each kind
> Does straight its own resemblance find;
> Yet it creates, transcending these,
> Far other Worlds, and other Seas;
> Annihilating all that's made
> To a green Thought in a green Shade.
>   (Andrew Marvell, 'The Garden')

The real is shadow to the word.

NOTES

1 Ursula K. Le Guin, 'From Elfland to Poughkeepsie', in *The Language of the Night: Essays on Fantasy and Science Fiction* (New York: Putnam, 1979), p. 95.
2 T. A. Shippey. *J. R. R. Tolkien: Author of the Century* (Boston: Houghton Mifflin, 2000), p. xiv.
3 Fossils and all.
4 Ursula K. Le Guin, *A Wizard of Earthsea* (London: Gollancz, 1978), pp. 53–4.
5 John Crowley, *Endless Things* (Northampton, MA: Small Beer Press, 2007), p. 171.
6 Farah Mendlesohn, *Rhetorics of Fantasy* (Middletown, CT: Wesleyan University Press), p. 59.
7 Vladimir Nabokov, *Speak, Memory*, rev. edn (New York: Putnam, 1966), p. 125.
8 Cf. Guy Davenport, 'Joyce's Forest of Symbols', in *The Geography of the Imagination* (San Francisco: North Point Press, 1981), pp. 286–99.

 9 Greer Gilman, 'A Conversation with Greer Gilman: An Interview with Sherwood Smith', *The SF Site*, February 2004. www.sfsite.com/02b/gr170.htm.
10 Mervyn Peake, *Titus Groan* (Woodstock, NY: Overlook Press, 1992), p. 334.
11 Edgar Allan Poe, 'The Masque of the Red Death', in *Poetry and Tales* (New York: Library of America, 1984), p. 490.
12 Edgar Allan Poe, 'A Descent into the Maelström', in *Poetry and Tales*, p. 444.
13 *Ibid.*
14 Thomas De Quincey, *Confessions of an English Opium-Eater and Other Writings* (Oxford: Oxford University Press, 2008), pp. 73–4.
15 William Hope Hodgson, *The Night Land and Other Perilous Romances* (San Francisco: Night Shade Books, 2005), p. 25.
16 *Ibid.*, p. 42.
17 Elizabeth Hand, 'Cleopatra Brimstone', in *Saffron and Brimstone* (Milwaukie, OR: M Press, 2006), p. 2.
18 Lucius Shepard, 'The Jaguar Hunter', in *The Jaguar Hunter* (New York: Four Walls Eight Windows, 2001), pp. 9–10.
19 China Miéville, *Perdido Street Station* (London: Macmillan, 2000), p. 189.
20 Sylvia Townsend Warner, 'The Climate of Exile', in *Kingdoms of Elfin* (New York: Viking Press, 1977), p. 164.
21 Michael Swanwick, *The Dragons of Babel* (New York: Tor, 2007), p. 11.
22 Lewis Carroll, *Alice in Wonderland: Authoritative Texts of Alice's Adventures in Wonderland, Through the Looking-glass, The Hunting of the Snark: Backgrounds, Essays in Criticism*, 2nd edn, ed. Donald J. Gray, Norton Critical Edition (New York: W. W. Norton, 1992), p. 55.
23 Greer Gilman, *Moonwise* (New York: Roc, 1991), p. 231.
24 J. R. R. Tolkien, *The Hobbit, or, There and Back Again* (Boston: Houghton Mifflin, 1966), p. 90.
25 John Crowley, *Little, Big* (New York: Bantam, 1981), p. 7.
26 Joan Aiken, *Dido and Pa* (Boston: Houghton Mifflin, 2003), p. 20.
27 Peter S. Beagle, *The Last Unicorn* (New York: Viking Press, 1968), p. 12.
28 J. R. R. Tolkien, *The Fellowship of the Ring*, 2nd edn (Boston: Houghton Mifflin, 1965), p. 294.
29 Alan Garner, *The Stone Book* (London: Collins, 1976), p. 58.
30 Hope Mirrlees, *Lud-in-the-Mist* (New York: Knopf, 1927), p. 16.
31 John Crowley, *Ægypt* (New York: Bantam, 1987), p. 99.
32 Angela Carter, 'Alice in Prague *or* The Curious Room', in *American Ghosts & Old World Wonders* (London: Chatto & Windus, 1993), p. 125.
33 Kelly Link, *Stranger Things Happen* (Brooklyn, NY: Small Beer Press, 2001), p. 242.
34 Neil Gaiman (w), Charles Vess and Malcolm Jones III (p), 'A Midsummer Night's Dream', *The Sandman #3: Dream Country* (New York: DC Comics, 1991), 3:18.
35 John Clute and John Grant (eds.), *The Encyclopedia of Fantasy* (New York: St. Martin's Press, 1997), p. 586.
36 Angela Carter, 'Overture and Incidental Music for *A Midsummer Night's Dream*', *Black Venus* (London: Picador, 1986), pp. 67–8.
37 Arthur Machen, *The Great God Pan* (London: Simpkin, 1916).
38 Angela Carter, 'The Erl-King', in *The Bloody Chamber and Other Stories* (London: Gollancz, 1979), p. 110.

12

KARI MAUND

Reading the fantasy series

When one thinks of fantasy, it is often the series novel that springs first to mind. Fantasy is a very broad church, yet the series is close to being its dominant form. Why should this be? This chapter aims both to address the question of the appeal of this mode of writing within the genre and to offer a preliminary typology of the form.

Series fiction is, of course, found over the full range of literature, but most particularly within genre fiction – detective novels, historical and military novels, science fiction and fantasy – and in children's books. And in all cases, series are popular. What is the reader looking for when he or she opens a series novel? In *Reading Series Fiction*, Victor Watson proposed that 'Reading a series involves a special relationship between reader and writer which the reader has made a conscious decision to sustain.'[1] Watson was writing about children's fiction, but his observation applies equally to fantasy, and indeed to other forms of series fiction. In writing, any author is effectively promising to provide her readers with adventure, pleasure, exploration and experience. But the series author holds out an often reassuring offer of familiarity and continuity. The series reader undertakes to stay with a group of characters or a place or a problem over a prolonged period. There is thus a commitment on both parts of the relationship. How is this relationship built and sustained? How do authors create familiarity and continuity without destroying suspense or becoming overly predictable? Are there any strategies specific to fantasy? And how do readers respond? Creating a sense of familiarity and continuity within a fantasy (or indeed a science-fictional) context presents certain genre-specific problems. The writer of a detective series, say, or a school series, must build and sustain the particular setting of their story – the Californian hinterland, the English village, the large comprehensive or selective private school. But they can assume a certain amount of pre-existing knowledge in their audience. The reader may not know the precise geographical details of California, but they know about cars and malls and police officers. This is not so in a fantasy world: there are some tropes which have grown familiar over time, as Diana Wynne Jones has observed,[2] but there will be many elements which will have to be explained, a challenge also faced by writers of stand-alone fantasies. Some of the strategies for overcoming this difficulty – the use of plentiful description, the provision of an expert guide or teacher, the construction of an ideal or mode of history – have been expertly analysed by Mendlesohn.[3] But it should be noted that series fantasies in particular often employ tropes and images derived from other forms of series fiction.

Not all series take the same form. Some are mainly character-dependent. The stories that make up such series may take place over a long period of time, occur in a number of settings and present the protagonists with a variety of problems and challenges. As a form it is open-ended. Each of the exploits and adventures is largely self-contained: although there may also be an overarching plot, this is not usually the focus of any one adventure or episode. I have chosen to refer to this form as the *classic* series, as it is the one most characteristic of early fantasy. The most famous example is, of course, the Conan series, which has grown out of the original work of Robert E. Howard into a franchise; others would be the Fafhrd and the Grey Mouser series by Fritz Leiber, and, more recently, the Taltos books of Steven Brust. The classic series is reader-accessible: each book or tale does not have to depend on earlier ones in the series and the author reintroduces his characters and setting briefly in each, perhaps because this form is deeply rooted in the pulp magazines. An author could not assume that his or her readers had read earlier stories when he wrote each new one. The heroes are often wanderers – mercenaries, assassins, thieves, swordsmen – with few personal ties, and supporting cast members come and go. It is perhaps of note that the classic series lends itself most readily to sword-and-sorcery fantasies – the Conan stories, the Elric books (Michael Moorcock), the Kane books (Karl Edward Wagner), amongst many others. More recently the classic series has re-emerged within urban fantasies, also. Series such as Tanya Huff's Blood books or The Dresden Files by Jim Butcher present as semi-independent novels with continuing characters, but can be read out of order without too much difficulty and over-plot, if present, is frequently not the focus of the immediate story arc.

A second series type we can identify is the *scripted* series. These books also have continuing characters, but the main driving force is plot. How will the heroes and their society survive? Will the quest be achieved or the antagonist defeated? Will the hero fulfil her potential? The scripted series is perhaps the most common form within fantasy: in the first volume the author presents a situation, a problem, a conflict and a cast of characters whose task it to resolve it. The middle volumes provide obstacles and short-term successes, often followed by further obstacles. The final volume contains resolution and character reward. This is the form of Roger Zelazny's Amber series, Robert Jordan's Wheel of Time books, the Belgariad by David and Leigh Eddings, and Barbara Hambly's Darwath books, amongst many others. The scripted series is essentially closed and self-limiting, although it should be noted that reader demand can lead and has led to expansion of some series beyond their original plot arc. Thus Eddings returned to the Belgariad with the successor series, the Mallorean, and Hambly extended her original trilogy with two further novels connected mainly by character to the original three.

The third form is the *thematic* series or series of *place*. In such a series, books are bound less by plot arc or continuity of character than by a common theme or setting. Thus, the Deryni novels by Katherine Kurtz are arranged as a sequence of thematically linked groups, exploring the history of a people with inherited telepathic abilities. Certain characters link specific groups of books but become ancestors or descendants of others, and the whole builds towards a history of both setting and people. M. John Harrison's Viriconium books and stories share a common landscape, but their over-arching theme is the questionability of fiction: characters, items, settings and events appear, disappear and reappear within the sequence, binding the sequence together through its very fictionality. The Books of Paradys and The Books of Venus, two series by Tanith Lee, are linked by the idea of a city as character – the books have separate characters and plot-lines, but at their core is an exploration of the changing nature of the urban. Cherry Wilder's Rulers of Hylor series is linked by both place and theme (in this instance the nature of responsible and irresponsible uses of power).

It should be stressed that none of these types are mutually exclusive. Thus, within the Deryni series, subgroups of books have a scripted plot and the groups form an extension out from the original trilogy. The same process can be seen in Mercedes Lackey's Valdemar books, the Avaryan novels of Judith Tarr and many others. In both the Taltos books and the Fafhrd and the Grey Mouser series, place – the cities of Adrilankha and Lankhmar – is a powerful unifying factor. The Taltos and Dresden series both have long over-plots which play out through their course, but each book usually has its focus on a single-volume problem. The Hylor books present aspects of all three types and will, later in this chapter, be used as a short case study.

How is familiarity built within the fantasy series, and do the methods vary between series types? Perhaps the most obvious method is foreshadowing: we are told of prophecies that foretell a particular character's fate – Oedipus will kill his father and marry his mother; or of circumstances that will trigger a particular crisis – a man is betrayed by his best friend and vows revenge.

The examples given here derive from Greek tragedy and *The Count of Monte Cristo*, but this technique is peculiarly suited to series fantasy. The Belgariad begins with a prophecy concerning the young hero, Garion: the five volumes follow his path to fulfilling it. The use of a cliff-hanger at the end of an episode is perhaps now mainly associated with film, but as a form was pioneered in nineteenth-century magazines by Alexandre Dumas, Victor Hugo and others. Hence, at the end of *The Time of the Dark*, the first volume of Darwath, the heroes are losing against their antagonists but have reached a place of safety. Volume two, *The Walls of Air*, provides them with more of the information and equipment they need to fight back, but progression is inhibited and thwarted by political and religious divisions between characters, and success seems a long way away. The final part, *The Armies of Daylight*, brings resolution not only of the over-plot but of the various character relationships, frictions and tensions that Hambly has built up over the series.[4]

Continuing characters are another method of binding together the series. The classic series in particular is heavily dependent upon this: reader investment is mainly in the personalities and abilities of the main characters. Protagonists in classic fantasy are often strongly drawn, almost archetypical, and weak series can descend into cliché. But the presentation of such characters in the hands of a good writer is sophisticated, and the reader's desire for more adventures takes him or her on a journey, too, through maturation. Hence Fafhrd and the Grey Mouser age from their late teens to their late forties across the stories, and it is a tribute to Leiber's writing that their reactions and behaviour mature without ever becoming predictable, dull or inappropriate. In the earlier stories, the two pass from place to place and girl to girl, but over the course of the tales they become more tied to certain locations (notably the city of Lankhmar and Rime Isle), becoming more merchant-adventurers than wanderers. Scripted series may have larger casts of characters, presenting what are essentially braided narratives as we follow the adventures of many different heroes (as with Robert Jordan's Wheel of Time and Kate Elliott's books). At the end of any given volume one character may have achieved resolution, but others are in flux or in danger. The extended form of the scripted series – where an author adds new books after the end of the first plot arc – often follow the fortunes of characters who were secondary or historical in the earlier books. Thus Lackey followed her initial Valdemar trilogy with a further series set in the same world but detailing the life of a character (Vanyel) who was seen as legendary by the characters in her first books. The author both relies on reader recognition of the fantasy world here and satisfies reader desire for more by relocating focus onto new protagonists.

As mentioned above, one method is to borrow tropes from other forms of series fiction and in particular from juvenile and genre fiction. Huff's Blood books and Butcher's Dresden Files both present us with the hero-as-detective: Vicky Nelson is a P.I., Harry Dresden a Wizard-for-Hire. Both, moreover, take place in recognizable urban environments (Toronto and Vancouver for Huff, Chicago for Butcher). The fantastical elements of both – vampires, werewolves, magic – become normalized both through location and through the provision of a familiar narrative style, the mystery. The Valdemar novels – which are largely female focused – draw considerably on the tradition of animal stories aimed at children. Any female reader familiar with pony stories will have an instant sense of recognition for the intelligent Companion horses of Valdemar. School narratives, familiar to many readers from experience as well as reading, might seem to be mainly appropriate to young adult fantasy – one thinks particularly of Harry Potter. But Mages' Colleges, warrior schools and guilds and apprenticeships are common in fantasy and provide a means whereby the author may guide the reader alongside the character into the new world and teach them about it. Hence the training of Heralds is a trope repeated throughout the Valdemar series, while the education of wizards is a trope Hambly employs not solely in Darwath but in several of her other fantasy series.

Characters like Conan, Fafhrd and the Mouser, Vlad Taltos or Elric are in themselves conveyors of familiarity. The classic series in particular has its roots in pulp magazines, which presupposed a largely male audience, and the heroes of this type often conform to adventurous archetypes. The swashbuckling behaviour of such heroes, combined with adventures which frequently occur in exotic locales (jungles, ruined temples, harems and whore-houses), recall the adventure novels of Rider Haggard, Robert Louis Stevenson and Edgar Rice Burroughs or the imagery of Westerns and pirate movies. The Black Company series by Glen Cook plays to another familiar adventure story style: the military novel. The setting and trappings of Cook's world are fantastical, but his heroes operate in a context that will provide immediate recognition and reassurance to a reader who is interested in military history or historical war novels.[5]

I propose in the remainder of this paper to offer a brief study of a specific series – Cherry Wilder's Rulers of Hylor – chosen for a number of reasons, not least that it is short. Hylor is a thematic series, but it presents many aspects of the other series' types, and makes use of a variety of strategies to build familiarity and depth. Each book operates as a biography of a protagonist – Aidris am Firn (*A Princess of the Chameln*, 1984), Yorath (*Yorath the Wolf*, 1984) and Sharn am Zor (*The Summer's King*, 1986) and can be read alone. They overlap both in chronology and in plot, and the over-plot – which is depicted largely in the interstices of the personal tales – can only be fully understood across the three books as a whole. But the over-plot is not the core, and the characters who carry it – the mage Rosmer, the margrave Kelen and his mother Guenna, the healer Jalmar Rais and his son Raff – are not central. Wilder's concern is not linear plot – which could be defined as 'how the margravate of Lien extended its territory' – but *theme* and the focus of the books is on the effects of this ambition on those around Lien whose lands are threatened. Wilder uses her over-plot both as the background and the glue to tie together her stories. Thus Aidris's story is a narrative of exile and return and her understanding of Rosmer's activities limited: she glimpses him in a stone, she is aware of him as the enemy of her ally, Guenna. Her narrative is told in third-person limited viewpoint – we are able to follow Aidris and learn what she learns but no more, and what she does not understand is not explained, but left to later volumes. Like Garion in David Eddings's Belgariad series and so many other hero/protagonists of this kind of fantasy, Aidris carries expectation with her – she is the heir to Chameln – but she is dependent on others. Yorath's tale, told in the first person, is that of the lost heir and military hero. Where Aidris knows herself born to rule, Yorath rejects power: he is offered a wide world but chooses a small one which is largely outside the wider canvas of the series. To him Rosmer is both tempter and antagonist, met several times face-to-face. His experiences serve to illuminate Aidris's, and his exploits make her reconquest of Chameln possible, while her interactions with Guenna provide depth to Yorath's back story. *The Summer's King* by contrast, is told in multiple view-point and switches back and forth between present and past tense, telling Sharn's story almost as a series of snapshots. We watch him mature episode by episode and through other eyes (including Aidris's). It is Sharn who holds the key to the over-plot but our experience of him is intermittently distanced. (Sharn is that rare thing in series fantasy, the unreliable narrator.) Yorath's actions have determined Sharn's course, but the two are barely aware of each other. Wilder provides us with reassurance by the use of familiar tropes – the training narratives in *Princess* and *Yorath*, the romance sub-plots, the trappings of courts and battles and magic – but she does not over-narrate, and our view of people and events are nuanced by our varied narrators. The three narratives are bound by the reader's recognition of the continuing characters (who dip in and out) and of events told from many sides. And these markers of familiarity are drawn both from within reader expectations of fantasy – Sharn's quest for a bride, for instance – and from the wider literary world.

The fantasy series thus constructs itself both from elements that are part of the assumed common culture of reader and writer – school or training environments, animal stories, coming of age – and from elements specific to the genre – magic, prophecies. Reader involvement is built by the layering of new narratives over these tropes and by the expansion out from the story's core (the quest, the swashbuckling hero, the city) into surrounding land-scapes, into fictive history and into character growth, thereby encouraging the reader on from tale to tale and book to book. The result is – can be – the creation of a rounded, exciting and satisfying world to which the reader is drawn to return over and over again.

NOTES

1 Victor Watson, *Reading Series Fiction: From Arthur Ransome to Gene Kemp* (London and New York: Routledge, 2000), p. 1.
2 Diana Wynne Jones, *The Tough Guide to Fantasyland* (London: Vista, 1996).
3 Farah Mendlesohn, *Rhetorics of Fantasy* (Middletown, CT: Wesleyan University Press, 2008).
4 The two later volumes, *Mother of Winter* (New York: Ballantine, 1996) and *Icefalcon's Quest* (New York: Ballantine, 1998), have self-contained plots and are tied to the first three by character.
5 It is interesting to note in passing that military fiction is much more common in science fiction than fantasy: this is perhaps because sf is popularly perceived as a more male genre. Armies and navies are common in fantasy, but they are seldom the main focus of the story.

13

GREGORY FROST

Reading the slipstream

As a definition of a category of fiction, 'slipstream' is abused as much as it is applied. Part of this is due to the subjectivity of its definition and its implementation – as originally coined by author Bruce Sterling circa 1989 it referred to contemporary literature that utilized certain modalities of genre fiction in building a new postmodern extra-genre creation, but in practice it has long since abandoned the limits of this definition, with cross-pollination blowing furiously in both directions, because of which, like the category of magical realism before it, the term has become a confused plurality. As with the nature of the fictive reality slipstream describes, it is itself inconstant.

My sense also is that slipstream is not a new tradition so much as a new alloy, mercurial and shape-shifting. The reader, in approaching something so slippery, must come prepared to submerge in layers of possible meaning. The skimming reader who only engages with surfaces may find some purchase but will miss the breadth of examination, meaning and resonance, and probably come away dissatisfied.

The alloy that is slipstream requires of the reader an ability to roll with the punches, to shift through a kind of multitasking approach to the story. The reader must come at the story with a willingness to flow with such shifts even if unaware of the sources. Like someone from the pen and paper universe forced to interact with a computer for the first time, readers versed only in traditional, unadorned narrative may feel they are leaping into a void. Readers familiar with the likes of Borges – who have sifted through metafictions and magical realism in its various guises – will have a much easier time of it because stories like Borges's 'Tlön, Uqbar, Orbis Tertius' have already taught them to expect intrusive unreality awaiting its cue in the wings. For them it might be no more than stepping off an already deranged sidewalk into a still more unpredictable flow of traffic in a world at play, where the characters, the landscape, the narrative can turn trickster at any instant, and the surface of the story, actively self-aware, might shuffle its component parts and slyly and quietly enclose the reader.

Points of origin

In his influential book *How to Read and Why*, educator and literary critic Harold Bloom identifies two 'rival traditions' from which all contemporary short fiction springs.

The first of these he characterizes as Chekhovian. This, the classic unadorned tale, speaks to the truth of the human heart most directly. Bloom lists both Hemingway and Flannery O'Connor among the Chekhovian canon. The list might easily expand to include Updike, Cheever and Carver. Chekhov, says Bloom, 'expects you to believe in his realism, his faithfulness to our ordinary existence'.[1] And while we might quibble that O'Connor isn't *exactly* a realistic writer, for the purposes of Bloom's distinctions her adornments nevertheless suit the category as outlined.

His competing tradition has something other than the truth of the human heart in mind. It comprises the Borgesians: Jorge Luis Borges himself, as well as Kafka, Calvino, Cortazar and the rest of the intrepid band of magical realists, with Nabokov a liminal ringer (there's always one who refuses to conform). These authors, Bloom states, 'invest in phantasmagoria' (65). In this group, truths of the heart take a decided backseat to a kind of gamesmanship, a tendency to pull the rug out from under reality if not the reader. These authors are tricksters, and the fabric of reality in their hands as malleable as modelling clay. Nothing can be trusted.

We plunge into these separate streams for different reasons: the Chekhovian tradition 'gratifies our hunger for reality' while the Borgesian 'teaches us how ravenous we still are for what is beyond supposed reality' (67). As the earliest recorded fictions are of a fantastic nature, we may assume that the desire for the phantasmagoric is hard-wired into us on a level more primal than that which engages consciously with the real world.

While Bloom makes no mention of the publishing genres of mystery, science fiction, fantasy and so on, those of the fantastic – fantasy, science fiction and (if we dare still use the term) horror – in particular stand oddly against these identified streams in that despite their unrealities and phantasmagoria, they descend from the Chekhovian tradition. Their concern remains the telling of a story about humans in crisis, solving problems, as often as not with an entire universe hanging in the balance. However decked out in fantastic garb, they nevertheless use the methods of 'realism'. They might present and establish an alternate reality, but they don't violate the rules by which that new reality runs once it's established. In fact, the new reality has quite familiar facets. The fantasy is not absurdist. The stories remain, ultimately, stories of the human heart.

One place we might locate the Borgesian stream flowing into the fantastical genres is through the works of Philip K. Dick and others who followed him in creating unreliable realities. However, close inspection shows these fantastical realities to be the result of chemically altered perceptions or false presentations that are, ultimately, technologically derived – instrumentalities of man that distort the world if only to shield humankind from its sorry state. The purpose of such fiction is not to play with reality as the Borgesian model would; while the two share certain elements, the Borgesian stream remains not fully reflected in or represented by the Dick model because with the latter it is still not the reader but the *characters* in the story who are affected by the revelation that theirs is at best one layer or one possible reality among many. We can perhaps propose that the paranoiac works of Dick are essential forebears of a Borgesian science fiction, but that is a topic for someone else to tackle elsewhere.

In its infancy, then, slipstream was a uniting of the two streams identified by Bloom: human stories but in a shape-shifting world.[2] In most cases the reader can draw the human story from the text; however, to 'get' everything going on, that reader must have read outside the Chekhovian tradition, and must, again, know to read for possibilities beneath the surface that might even undermine the surface.

Science fiction and fantasy readers familiar with Philip K. Dick and films like *Dark City* and *The Matrix* were already equipped with a recognition that capricious and illusory reality can fracture at any moment. For such a reader, the jump from category fantasy fiction into slipstream is not so extreme. One thing such genre fiction can prepare the reader for is the puzzle box aspect of slipstream: this notion that reality, while it isn't reliable, does assemble into a recognizable 'other'. Someone who, for example, knows only the fictions of Chekhov and Cheever, and who reads strictly for the quiet story of the human heart, will likely be grasping for a lifeline almost immediately. In part this is because trickster texts intend to make the reader lose her footing if not her trust of the very fabric of the fictive reality itself. The unease produced by the text is capable of bleeding off the page and shaking the reader's reality, much the way the angst produced by a terrifying film can follow the audience out of the theatre and into the night.[3]

Slipstream, then, is not a new stream at all, but an effect produced by genetic modification, a recombinant organism.

Definitions and debates

Slipstream as a category, never mind as an approach to interacting with a text, is problematic in the same way that the term 'magical realism' became problematic soon after its coinage. Initially applied to a specific Central and South American fiction that blended together Catholic and folkloric modalities, it was emulated with varying success by North American writers and, more to the point, embraced by reviewers and critics. Fiction that fit no easily identifiable category of genre but included some fantastical element was, ipso facto, suddenly magical realism, by which argument, Thorne Smith could be hailed as one of our great magical realists. Topper, after all, lives right alongside his ghosts very much as does the heroine of Jorge Amado's *Dona Flor and Her Two Husbands*.

'Slipstream', coined by author Bruce Sterling (with Richard Dorsett) in an article in 1989, focused upon – at that moment in time – contemporary extra-genre fiction that was trolling in the genres for tropes and modalities that hadn't previously been used much less sought after by writers of realism.[4]

In all likelihood this unintentional 'movement' was an attempt on the part of non-fantasists to charge their fiction with new life, new excitement. New blood. When Robert Olen Butler extols the virtues of genre fiction because those authors have never forgotten that the engine driving all great writing is desire,[5] he is perhaps inadvertently acknowledging its appeal to writers tired of a staid plodding contemporary story where '[w]hen blame has been assigned, the story is over'.[6] In 1989 Sterling compiled a solid list of books and stories that included Steve Erickson's *Days Between Stations* and Paul Auster's *New York Trilogy*, and which suggested that something interesting and fantastic was going on in the margins of contemporary fiction. The levee that kept out those riff-raff genres had cracked, and genre elements were swirling into the larger pool of contemporary fiction.

Sterling, it should be noted, was not attempting to stamp a date upon the beginning of this phenomenon. He was merely observing how common the experiment had become in American literature; he was noticing something that had been going on for some time. Slipstream, whatever else it is, doesn't rise to the level of a literary movement. It's more an expression of a literary zeitgeist. Or perhaps, like horror – if one accepts the 'feeling very strange' feature an essential component – an identifiable effect. What may have begun as the world of the reader has become . . . peculiar.

Over time, Sterling's initial definition has mutated and been recast still closer to this idea of effect. Works like Margaret Atwood's *The Hand-maid's Tale* that *might* have fit the definition initially don't belong in the revised canon. Atwood is not 'making the familiar strange or the strange familiar'.[7]

According to the editors of the slipstream anthology *Feeling Very Strange*, John Kessel and James Patrick Kelly, slipstream fiction can be identified by a characteristic of ontological distress existent in the story. The reader is never certain of the nature of reality – what writer Carol Emshwiller calls 'estranging the everyday'.[8] Ever-present is the possibility that the story's reality is unlike the reality known to the reader. It may mimic it, it may undermine it or it may promise that we are in this world; but, like an unreliable narrator who can't quite maintain the façade he's promoting, it reveals its falsity in subtle ways.

At about the same moment that Bruce Sterling was formulating the slipstream category, John Clute reviewed for *Interzone* another of Steve Erickson's novels, *Rubicon Beach* (1986). Clute's compressed summary of that novel is itself a concise description of slipstream construction:

> The book begins in a surrealist near-future police-state America obscurely defined by its relationship to earlier states of the land, which are called America One and America Two. Just out of prison for telling a betraying joke about a chthonic tree – a tree full of Americans who live in its highest branches and who, it may be, have crossed each others' Rubicons and now share one growth, one inextricably intertwined reality – a man named Cale haunts a drowned Ballardian Los Angeles, and is haunted in turn by Catherine, whom he cannot reach, any more than Lou Reed could. The book approaches its close through episodes set in England, where an old man named Lake ('Cale' reversed) slips deathwards on the wrong side of the beach of dreams; and yet another character – a mathematician who has discovered a secret number between 9 and 10 – travels into America, taking a train which crosses a river without a further shore, and which stops only to deposit him in the bole of a great tree, whose highest branches are full of Americans. He sees Catherine in the distance, and steps her way. She is the secret number, the lost chord, the Rubicon. The novel ends.[9]

Clute's descriptive summary itself can generate that ontological distress named by Kessel and Kelly. The word 'slipstream' was unavailable to Clute, and he had to make do with earlier markers in noting that the book could be multiply interpreted as 'an essay in magic realism', as 'a quasi-Pynchonesque fantasy of quest', as 'an archaeology of dreamed America', as 'a jape', as 'Escher-like spirals of storyline' (155). It is all of these, and the reader must at least approach the book open to the multiple facets and comfortable with a self-aware trickster text; comfortable also with non-conforming realities. The summary is also suggestive of those sliding, perfectly aligned surfaces of the puzzle box.

Like *Days Between Stations*, or like Hal Duncan's *Vellum*, it is a dream-text providing the reader with sufficient material from which to build his own dream landscape in response. And so one way of collectively describing works of slipstream might be to call them oneiric texts. That does not convey the element of distress that Kessel and Kelly attribute to slipstream save in suggesting the fragmentation and shape-shifting that dreams are prone to, which *is* an element in many (but not all) slipstream stories; even within the confines of their own anthology, that distress is a debatable and debated point. One reader's distress is another reader's farce.

Consider, for example, the brilliant satire 'Sea Oak' by George Saunders. The world seems to be ours, with a family living a dead-end life in an urban environment where gun battles over drugs go on in the streets, and the family's aunt has taken the helm because her sister is addled and useless. This would be a believable, unhappy portrait of a family except that the narrator works at a restaurant called 'Joysticks', modelled loosely on the 'Hooters' franchise with its scantily clad waitresses. 'Joysticks' features nearly naked male servers catering to a mostly female clientele. The aunt soon dies, leaving the family – the brother and his two directionless sisters – with no idea what to do, trapped as they are by their own indolence, lack of education and no-exit options. But the aunt returns. Fresh from the grave, she directs the family to act, to pull together and get out of their hopeless situation: It takes the supernatural to overcome the limitations of such a life. The trouble is, auntie is a decomposing zombie, and after a week has gone by her overly ripe body parts are decaying and falling off. She dies a second time, leaving the narrator with the unanswerable question of why some people have good lives and others pointless existences, getting nothing for all their effort. He, in what can only be seen as a parody of a Joycean epiphany, embraces the revelation that, to save his family as instructed, he will expose himself to his tipping customers in order to get enough money to go to law school. Out of the mouths of zombies comes the sly, ugly essence of the American Dream.

Analyses and conclusions

To read slipstream, then, is to read texts that will play loose with the rules of reality. Some of them will wink at reality to let you know the game is on, as Saunders does. Some of them will quietly lead you from the world you know into the one where the watch spring has snapped, and time gone out of joint, as Kelly Link does in her story 'Lull'. The story begins with a collective narrative identity: we. The 'we' is a group of poker players who, during a lull in the game, call a very odd sex chat line to ask the sex worker, 'Starlight', to tell them a story 'that goes backward'.[10] Her story begins:

> So the Devil is at a party at the cheerleader's house. They've been playing spin the bottle. The cheerleader's boyfriend just came out of the closet with her best friend. Earlier the cheerleader felt like slapping him and now she knows

why. The bottle pointed at her best friend who had just shrugged and smiled at her. Then the bottle was spinning and when the bottle stopped spinning, it was in her boyfriend's hand.[11]

Time is already running backwards.

From here the narrative shifts to just one of the poker players, Ed, and a series of impossible things – notably his estranged artist-wife Susan making copies of herself that are green, duplicates that seem to be all the various possibilities of her – some young, some fat, some ancient – and who are building a machine for aliens that keeps getting larger and filling their house, all seemingly with the goal of bringing back Susan's drug-addict brother. This story unfolds like a spiral galaxy. It never returns to where it began, but ultimately throws off story strings of ejecta, culminating with Ed and his wife alone, in a very late phone conversation that reconciles nothing. Has Ed gotten drunk at the poker game? Has everything up to this final section been a fractured and nightmarish dream? The power of this and many other Link stories is that you don't have to resolve these questions to enjoy or understand the story. It floats in at the level of fairy tale, under the conscious radar that scans for textual clues in linear 'Chekhovian' stories. That part of the brain won't necessarily come to the reader's aid with works of Emshwiller, M. Rickert, Link and others operating in this curious territory.

The Kelly Link story included in *Feeling Very Strange*, 'The Specialist's Hat', likewise makes everything uncertain. It's a ghost story of a sort. The two little girls in it *seem* to have the ghost of a former inhabitant of their house for a baby-sitter. Dad, a widower, *seems* to be so disconnected from his daughters' world that he doesn't notice this. The girls play act that they are dead, inventing the rules for what life is like when you are dead, but by the end they are 'made' dead by the sitter, and have integrated into the house, up the chimney. Link, a supreme trickster, celebrates unreliability and eschews explanation. In her hands, we are anchored in a universe knitted of weird waves and peculiar particles.

'The Specialist's Hat' is a haunted house story, and not surprisingly the haunted house as a supernatural locus if not trope seems inherently appropriate for slipstream investigation – by the house's very nature the world of reality and unreality have slid over each other like warring tectonic plates. Nothing can be trusted, and the fictive enclosure is a kind of puzzle – structurally, through its language, or simply through the treachery of the house described.

In 'What We Know About the Lost Families of — House' Christopher Barzak delivers a story that stands where Shirley Jackson's *The Haunting of Hill House*, Julio Cortázar's 'House Taken Over' and Thornton Wilder's *Our Town* overlap. As in 'Lull' a collective voice tells the story. The collective narrative is reminiscent of Wilder, whose town citizenry, many of them dead in the third act, narrate the play, reflecting upon their own nature, prejudices, attitudes; of Jackson ('Hill House, not sane, stood by itself against its hills... and whatever walked there, walked alone');[12] and of Cortázar ('We would die here someday, obscure and distant cousins would inherit the place...'),[13] whose narrator lacks any explanation for what progressively invades the tranquillity of his and his unwed sister's home – 'they' have arrived, knocking over chairs, whispering conversations, and the narrator and his sister are steadily driven into smaller and smaller spaces, and finally into the street. Barzak's story, then, is descended from a type of story already predisposed to the uneasiness of slipstream.

His craft permits you to read the story without awareness of its antecedents, but recognizing how he riffs on them makes the experience richer. A town's collective memory recalls specific events, explaining how a family died, one by one, by manipulations of the house. Some take their own lives. Others are chased out into the snow and vanish. And others still are absorbed into the house with no explanation. There are no elements of pseudo-science, no alembics, Ouija boards, or other technological trappings of the supernatural that populate many haunted house tales. Barzak draws you into the story through the authority of voice alone. That voice, however, contains a further tilt off-centre.

While the names of the earliest individuals are lost and forgotten, their actions – even their thoughts – have been preserved in some timeless aspic, and the unlikeliness of this suggests that the collective narrator telling this story is unreliable. We have to doubt what we're being told and will never know for certain what has happened. The edginess runs through the story to the very end. At every moment we anticipate a narrative deception will be revealed, as if the town, having ignored the evil house for so long, will now absorb it into themselves. Perhaps they have done already.

Other works of slipstream emerge out of the 'allegorical/metaphorical made real' school of the fantastic. Out of my own body of work, 'Collecting Dust' is such a story. Ted Chiang's 'Hell is the Absence of God' is another. The world is and isn't ours. Chiang plays out a reality where our unseen, mythological angels actually, corporeally appear – not just to those in crisis, but to everyone, randomly. Quite often Chiang's angels arrive in non-human forms, and the manifestations are as random as miraculous cancer remissions. However, instead of this phenomenon aiding us to make sense of God's plan and God's love, the angels make it even more incomprehensible, and for that matter dangerous. Those witnessing the appearance of an angel might be driven mad, might have their eyes erased entirely, might be healed, might be mutilated as collateral damage, all of it providing at best a subjective sense depending upon which precepts one embraces. 'No love's this random,' sings Wilco of God's affection, and Chiang establishes that even if the miraculous becomes the norm, the interpretation remains fuddled and divine love utterly impossible to countenance. Applying the literality of biblical angels to a realistic world only makes the world more unreal and terrifying. It is a strangely tender story, not anti-Christian but rather pushing one element of Christianity into the open and then watching what happens.

Michael Chabon is surely slipstream in thought even when not in deed. His novel *The Yiddish Policeman's Union* unites elements of alternate history (the failure of the state of Israel causes a Jewish province to arise in Alaska), Tony Hillerman novels (the partnering of Meyer Landsman with the half-Tlingit Berko Shemetz), and pulp-era noir fiction. This yoking of elements – this borrowing from across the aisle – is the *single* most distinguishing feature of slipstream as tagged by Sterling. It's the sign directing the reader down the rabbit hole. Chabon's 'The God of Dark Laughter' was originally published in *The New Yorker*, and one can only delight that this author managed to slide the Cthulhu Mythos past the editors of that august magazine. Here the world of William Faulkner is rocked by that of H. P. Lovecraft. Someone is killing and skinning the faces off clowns, all part of a monstrous ritual to bring back the old gods, and the main character – like the Texas cop in Cormac McCarthy's *No Country for Old Men* – is out of his depth in confronting this abomination.

Debate will continue to rage as to what is and isn't slipstream. Is T. C. Boyle's 'Modern Love' slipstream? By the ontological distress definition it isn't, but in terms of absconded material it meets the litmus test. Boyle's satire operates entirely within the tried-and-true science fictional 'if this goes on' approach, building to the point where the two central characters' pathological terror of pathogens is so intense that they can only have sex while wearing clear, giant condom suits, like two lusting astronauts in freefall. There's no more distress than in Saunders's story, but surely this is science-fictional enough to qualify as material dragged across the aisle.

Ultimately, however one chooses to define or quantify slipstream, the task of the reader remains the same – to find the truths being spoken while the shape surrounding those truths transmutes and teases in an act of literary sublimation.

NOTES

1 Harold Bloom, *How to Read and Why* (New York: Touchstone, 2001), p. 65.
2 For this reason we find Gabriel García Márquez and others among the magical realists (as that term originally applied) on most slipstream reading lists.

3 See for example 'Continuity of Parks' by Julio Cortázar, in *End of the Game and Other Stories*, trans. Paul Blackburn (New York: Harper Colophon Books, 1978).

4 Bruce Sterling, *SF Eye #5*, 1989: 'It seems to me that the heart of slipstream is an attitude of peculiar aggression against "reality".' To be fair, Sterling does also say that this fiction 'makes you feel very strange', but it has always seemed to me he's commenting here on the result of genre tropes having been lifted out of their context and repurposed, and not insisting that this is an essential ingredient of the resulting story. Strangeness is something of an inevitability. (Catscan 5, Slipstream Article currently resides at http://w2.eff.org/Misc/Publications/Bruce_Sterling/Catscan_columns/catscan.05.)

5 Robert Olen Butler, *From Where You Dream* (New York: Grove Press, 2005), p. 41: These 'writers who aspire to a different kind of fiction – entertainment fiction, let's call it, genre fiction – have never forgotten this necessity of the character's yearning'. He adds that maybe that's why the genre fiction sells books, adding, 'You cannot find a book on the best seller list without a central character who clearly wants something, is driving for something, has a clear objective.'

6 Charles Baxter, *Burning Down the House: Essays on Fiction* (St Paul, MN: Graywolf Press, 1997), p. 10.

7 James Patrick Kelly and John Kessel (eds.), *Feeling Very Strange* (San Francisco: Tachyon Publications, 2006), p. xiii.

8 Kelly and Kessel, *Feeling Very Strange*, p. xiii. The editors call Emshwiller an author 'central to any understanding of slipstream'.

9 John Clute, *Look at the Evidence* (Brooklyn, NY: Serconia Press, 1995), pp. 154–5.

10 Kelly Link, *Magic for Beginners* (Northampton, MA: Small Beer Press, 2005), p. 250.

11 *Ibid.*, pp. 250–1.

12 Shirley Jackson, *The Haunting of Hill House* (New York: The Viking Press, 1959), p. 5. In the 1963 film, the voice-over of Eleanor, now dead, delivers much the same speech, but with a collective narrative twist at the end: 'We who walk here, walk alone.' As Link's little girls have done, she, too, has joined her house.

13 Cortázar, *End of the Game*, p. 11.

PART III

Clusters

14

SHARON SIEBER

Magical realism

What is realism? When we examine the cultural conventions which have developed around the concept of realism in the Western world, we see an emerging standard which is allied ever more closely to scientific explanations of reality, widely accepted as the 'official' view. Such views have determined and structured, to a large extent, the modern way in which we 'read' reality. The many different kinds of realism are of course a way of communicating the current agreed-upon interpretation, or interpretive consensus, of a given reality in a given place and time, and as filtered by the current view of accepted science. Rosemary Jackson in *Fantasy: The Literature of Subversion* gives us a working basis from which to begin:

> As a literature of 'unreality' fantasy has altered in character over the years in accordance with changing notions of what exactly constitutes 'reality'. Modern fantasy is rooted in ancient myth, mysticism, folklore, fairy tale and romance. The most obvious starting point for this study was the late eighteenth century – the point at which industrialization transformed western society.[1]

Paradoxically, each generation seems to define its version of realism differently, even when literature arises from an oral tradition in which the most important element is continuity and history. The Surrealists were famous for communicating realism as a vision that went beyond the outer appearance of things, more so even than the Romantics desired to communicate the inner essence of things. Ken Booth, citing the legendary story of Picasso painting a portrait of Gertrude Stein, argues that 'Gertrude Stein is fixed in our minds as Picasso, not nature, made her.'[2] If we carefully examine the many realisms that manifest in different cultural milieu, times and geographies, one thing is certain: the concept of verisimilitude itself will always be replaced, or deconstructed, by a new hierarchy of verisimilitude, a concept that resonates with a particular readership in a definite place in space and time.

What gives magical realism the appeal of the twentieth century so that it becomes a dominant movement of the modern period? One of the most frequent and perplexing questions asks just why it is that magical realism is so often considered by Latin American critics, authors and theorists to be the artistically spiritual property solely of Latin Americans? Perhaps the larger question is whether this trend did actually begin in Latin America. In any case, Latin American critics assert that it is a certain combination of a political, social and mythical reality that creates what is known as magical realism in such canonical Latin American authors as Alejo Carpentier, Gabriel García Márquez, Julio Cortázar, Mario Vargas-Llosa, Jorge Luis Borges, Isabel Allende, José Lezama Lima, Miguel Angel Asturias, Carlos Fuentes, Juan Rulfo, Maria Luisa Bombal, Laura Esquivel, Rosario Castellanos and Elena Garro, to name a few.

Maggie Ann Bowers in *Magic(al) Realism* summarizes the difficulty in defining the term: 'The one thing that the majority of critical works about the related terms "magic realism", "magical realism" and "marvellous realism" agree upon is that these terms are notoriously difficult to define.'[3] She asserts that magical realism is not a recent phenomenon, but dates back to the 1920s (4). In a meticulously argued presentation, she considerably narrows the playing field for the terms magic and magical realism, and differentiates both from the term magic(al) realism as well: 'An umbrella term used in this book when discussing the artistic concept that encapsulates aspects of both magic realism and magical realism' (131). Finally, she bans the fantastic from consideration in the same category with magic(al) realism altogether.

> The fantastic is a genre of art and literature in which there is a constant faltering between belief and non-belief in the supernatural or extraordinary events presented. The critic Tzvetan Todorov identifies the key characteristic of the fantastic as the reader's hesitation between natural and supernatural explanations for the fictional events in the text (130).

While Bowers may be faulted for structuring the terms in question to fit her argument, her attempt to define, differentiate and refine the phenomenon represents a wider disagreement among theorists from all over the world who are either inclusive in their definitions or are exclusive and adhere to the argument that magical realist writings reflect a period and a place located in Latin America. This conflict would seem to indicate that literary critics are as consumed with literary genealogy as any family seeking to find its 'roots' and prove its importance through proximity to long-dead royalty. This phenomenon certainly suggests that the concept and literary movement of magical realism does not and cannot belong to a single author or tradition; however the site may be defined, it constantly changes and interacts with other 'sites', and yes, regrettably, even becomes 'other' to itself.

Good literary criticism, like all great literature, is multi-faceted and layered; its meaning flickers and changes and is couched in ambiguity: it is both a particle and a wave. The wonderful thing about literary definitions is that, like science, they never seem to gain permanent status. How do the two combine with fantasy? Here again Rosemary Jackson wisely notes that 'the value of fantasy has seemed to reside in precisely this resistance to definition, in its "free-floating" and escapist qualities' (1).

The question to ask here is why the magic of magical realism has become so important in twentieth- and twenty-first-century literature, particularly at a time when hard-line, linear scientific discoveries seem to diminish in importance and reality next to the fantastic discoveries of physicists such as Hugh Everett III regarding the many-worlds interpretation of quantum mechanics. This development was also taking root at just the time when the two literary movements which had become paradigms of the Western world, modernism and postmodernism, have affirmed the random nature of existence and events, twentieth-century alienation and fragmentation, assembly-line mass production, lack of free will and self-determination, identity disintegration, chaos, dysfunction and dystopia.

The desire to communicate difference, common to each generation of authors and artists, here is centred around the novel, which has become the symbol of the rise of the individual in literature.[4] Also, the desire for difference is mirrored in the change of the connotations of the word 'novel', which in the past meant in keeping with tradition in order to distinguish its historical and realist value. The 'new' form bore the burden of responsibility to tradition, that is, to history, mimesis and realism, in a way that oral traditional narratives and romance did not.[5] This demonstrates the changing values of the literary community, since oral literature valued the epic storyteller's ability to re-create exactly (especially in a pre-literate society) and is certainly reflected in the language surrounding the new novel in the 1960s regarding the 'bold, new realism' of French author Alain Robbe-Grillet. It is also no accident that Robbe-Grillet accomplishes this bold, new realism through another retelling of the *Odyssey*, coming out of the twentieth-century fascination and obsession with the mystery and detective genre combined with the return to ancient Greek myth. But what about realism is bold or magical? Doesn't the phenomenon of magical realism belong to the wide world in spite of the fact that it is the result of non-duplicable cultural, political and historical phenomena? Widely recognized as a genre of the fantastic that combines dream, magic and prosaic reality, magical realism has come to be part of the iconic representation of twentieth-century paradoxes that postmodernism embraces.

The term 'magic realism' was first applied to painting, in Franz Roh's 1925 essay 'Magic Realism: Post-Expressionism', although this essay has been widely quoted as describing magical realism in the form in which we understand it today:

> It seems to us that this fantastic dreamscape has completely vanished and that our real world re-emerges before our eyes, bathed in the clarity of a new day. We recognize this world, although now – not only because we have emerged from a dream – we look on it with new eyes.[6]

When Roh wrote this about painting, he could hardly have expected it to be applied to literature on another continent. Although the Latin American critic and historian Angel Flores is credited with first applying the term to Latin American literature, Miguel Angel Asturias is said to have popularized the term when he applied it to his own fiction, particularly *Men of Maize*, after he was awarded the Nobel Prize for literature in 1967.[7] Though it is one of the lesser-known novels, probably because of its excruciating complexity, this work presents one of the most interesting and powerful examples of magical realism in terms of perspective, point of view, and elements of postmodern and fragmented narrative techniques to tell what is basically an epic story. Part myth and part historical fact, the main character is a Mayan Indian chief, Gaspar Ilóm, who resists the forces of the Spanish colonial empire, here represented by Guatemalan government soldiers, and defeats death when officers with whom he has shared hospitality trick him into ingesting poison. A complex layering of realism, magic and the fantastic, the novel presents a narrative that is faithful to the spirit of the original event, portrayed as though told from an indigenous perspective and means of representation.

It seems apt that a term originally applied to painting would come to be known as a continent-wide movement in Latin America. The magical realism seen in *One Hundred Years of Solitude* resembles the hybridity of painting, since the representation of painting and literature make use of entirely different conventions and value structures. If one thinks of this novel in terms of the kinds of brush strokes used by the author, it is clear that so much is suggested or implied, in the same way that movement or light is implied in a canvas. The novel is such a visual experience that the author has refused to sell the movie rights to the book in spite of many requests. A moving visual picture would set the images and characters in stone; the moving picture of the imagination is far more flexible and pliable in the creation of the corresponding images.

Curiously enough, something that almost all the Latin American works of fiction have in common is the suggestion of another medium of the arts imposing on the novel, which has an impact on the representation of motion and emotion. Juan Rulfo's *Pedro Páramo* (to whom García Márquez pays appropriate homage) portrays ghost-like images fading in and out of view, while the one living character, the sometime narrator, wanders through a maze of past personal and archetypal memories, some his own and others not, and finally ends in a crypt in a mass burial area of a cemetery, his thoughts and the thoughts of other decomposing corpses mixing together so that they are almost indistinguishable as in a painting.[8]

Certainly the concept term 'still-life' defies the reality, as paintings may portray fluidity as well as tense and frozen action at the same time. Just as the corpses in *Pedro Páramo* are far more alive than the single living character who appears in the story, we see the magical real at its best – the fantastic is portrayed as ordinary so that the reader suspends disbelief beyond the necessary parameter to enjoy the 'fiction'. In Elena Garro's *Recollections of Things to Come*, Martín Moncada remembers far better things that never happened – or that happened outside of time – than the things he did the day before, all the while making a political commentary on the Mexican Revolution and the Cristero War (as does *Pedro Páramo*).[9] Of course, the indigenous influence everywhere apparent in mainstream Mexican and Latin American writing is a part of the native mysticism that is especially apparent in the treatment of time and space. North American native mysticism does not meet mainstream tradition until the 1960s, but when it does, the magical realism in the writings of Louise Erdrich, M. Scott Momaday and Leslie Silko is as prevalent as in their Latin American counterparts.

Magical realism: that two words can contain, capture and project so much in imagination, theory and definition is nothing short of amazing. Critics have researched, written and devoted careers and tens of thousands of pages to getting this definition right, in fact, 'just right', the reason being that we, as a modern reading public, are immediately intrigued by the mystical paradox of the term. While we may argue the genesis and proprietary rights to magical realism, we immediately recognize that magic cuts across national and linguistic boundaries, gender, age and social class and mores, un/natural boundaries of life and death, communicating the territories of this world and the next (or another world), and belongs as a birthright to all peoples. Children especially have not lost their magical connection to the universe. For all of us, it is a part of our identity in the same way that magical realism belongs to the identity of Latin Americans, but is shared with those who come to it later. Magic belongs to everyone, including those who are dismissive of it.

So it is with magical realism; the many definitions springing up around the term and its variations are intriguing. Wendy B. Faris in *Ordinary*

Enchantments: Magical Realism and the Remystification of Narrative discusses one of the most important, not to mention useful, aspects of magical realism as the 'irreducible element' in a narrative which has to be accepted at face value and cannot be broken down further:

> The 'irreducible element' is something we cannot explain according to the laws of the universe as they have been formulated in Western empirically based discourse, that is, according to 'logic, familiar knowledge, or received belief', as David Young and Keith Hollaman describe it. Therefore, the reader has difficulty marshaling evidence to settle questions about the status of events and characters in such fictions. We must take Gabriel García Márquez's very old man with enormous wings, for example, 'as a given, accepted but not explained'. The narrative voice reports extraordinary – magical – events, which would not normally be verifiable by sensory perception, in the same way in which other, ordinary events are recounted.[10]

The conflict that ensues comes from the fact that Western society defines itself, through its over-reliance on science as a means of explaining the universe (and human existence), as reductive. When we attempt to use science as a means to explain the 'irreducible' part of this element, we must take into account the modern tendency of science to reduce everything to the knowable through a deductive or inductive explanation.

Why is this term, magical realism, so seemingly simple and relevant at once so evocative and resonant? I trace the history of this phenomenon back to Octavio Paz's discussion of analogy in *Children of the Mire*; his analysis of the Baudelairian correspondences which govern the nature of the interaction of things, which he uses as an analogy for magic in that instant feeling of connectedness and the inner working of events. Paz refers to this magic as a tradition which 'crosses the eighteenth century, penetrates the nineteenth, and reaches our own. I am referring to analogy, the vision of the universe as a system of correspondences, and of language as the universe's double.'[11] These correspondences link every human being with every other human being on this planet (and the next if we include magical realist authors of science fiction such as Daína Chaviano, Rosa Montero and Yoss). Jorge Luis Borges firmly believed in the so-called 'interconnectedness' of events, so much that every quotidian, personal and individual act of the day had an impact on every other event, both great and small, in the life of the planet. We see this manifest and acted out in intricate design in his short stories and essays.

It is my own belief that magical thinking is the underpinnings for magical realism, and that magical realism is tied to the dream world in that it represents the site where the conscious and unconscious worlds meet. This is the very definition of magical 'place', and the magical realists have taken the mirror held up to nature one step further, in what I would call the mirror turned lamp turned projection. This is evident in Márquez's 'spoken mirror' in *One Hundred Years of Solitude*; life interacts with the mirror of *mimesis* and changes the mirror; as Octavio Paz states in *Children of the Mire*, 'If art mirrors the world, then the mirror is magical; it changes the world' (60). Magic is myth not yet ritualized; magical thinking resonates in us as readers and reminds us of the fresh perception(s) of childhood, where reality is magic and magical all by itself, and not through some slight of hand or efficacious altering of appearance through a clever *trompe l'oeil*.

Latin Americans who claim sole proprietorship of magical realism point out that Latin America does not share the history of the Occident, that neither the Enlightenment nor the Industrial Revolution ever came to Latin America, nor did either of the world wars, which saw human mass destruction and murder on a colossal scale, and as such, Latin America did not undergo any of the precursors for postmodernism.[12] A Colombian colleague once confided that 'Colombians are postmodern without ever having been modern.' The trajectory for the Latin American author cannot be described in the same terms as authors undergoing the reality and basis for postmodernism.

Hence the direct link of magical realism to the Baroque as the one continuity in Latin America that prevailed through colonialism and postcolonialism, leading to a different literary expression than the modernism and postmodernism expressed in North America and Europe. Latin Americans come to magical realism from an entirely different cultural milieu than that of Europe and North America, never having experienced the cultural relativism of mass production and the events leading up to postmodernism in the West. How interesting, then, that another of the elements common to magical realism as analysed by Wendy Faris in *Ordinary Enchantments* is that 'in addition to merging worlds, these fictions disturb received ideas about time, space, and identity' (23). Further, she explains that 'Magical realism reorients not only our habits of time and space but our sense of identity as well. The multivocal nature of the narrative and the cultural hybridity that characterize magical realism extends to its characters which tend toward a radical multiplicity' (25).

Through asserting its difference, the New World could establish its importance *vis-à-vis* the Old World, not weighed down by the burden of tradition. Alejo Carpentier is recognized by some as the first author who saw the potential of the new world for the old world imagination – the author didn't have to invent a 'fantasy', he only needed to record what he actually saw. He is also credited with the invention of the phenomenon and its (until recently) largely synonymous term the 'marvellous real' in the introduction to his 1949 book *The Kingdom of This World*. However, it is one of his other lesser-known books, *The Lost Steps*, that is more indicative of magical realism through its experiment with musical form, imposed on the novel from another precursor to magical realism: French Symbolism. Literary theorists and critics of magical realism have to acknowledge its sources in other literary traditions; likewise, although it may be a movement coming from Latin America, like every other literary event, it travels quickly and manifests in different ways on different continents.

In her introduction to Jorge Luis Borges's *The Book of Fantasy* (with Silvina Ocampo and A. Bioy Cásares), Ursula Le Guin traces the history of the word *fantasy* in the Oxford English Dictionary: '"A making visible" . . . or in Late Greek, "to imagine, have visions" and "to show" . . . "an appearance, a phantom, the mental process of sensuous perception, the faculty of imagination, a false notion, caprice or whim"'. She laments that 'the tracks of the word *fantasy* have been complicated still further by the comings and goings of psychologists'. Finally, she adds, 'And so it is that the "magical realists" of South America are read for their entire truthfulness to the way things are, and have lent their name as perhaps the most fitting to the kind of fiction most characteristic of our times.'[13]

Borges certainly recognized the importance of the ludic as he played with the reader in a cat and mouse game. However, he also aided the reader in transversing a complex inter-dimensional and seismic shift in understanding through playing on reader expectation. Further, Borges develops the ground for magical realism through his new fiction or *nueva narrativa*, which sets the stage for the boom literature in which magical realism finds its most formidable expression. Borges is perceived as far too cerebral for magical realism, but just the opposite is the case – magical realism cannot *be* too cerebral – it is the very definition of aware-ized and self-conscious literature, a tale aware of itself and devouring its own tail as it unravels, as in the 'spoken mirror', Melquíades's manuscript as doubled representation or a copy of reality (copying itself) in *One Hundred Years of Solitude*. Borges understands that his character Pierre Menard, in writing the Quixote in another century, using exactly the same words, has produced a different and completely unique text. Of course, these 'characters' in Márquez's 'spoken mirror' seem to spring forward in much the same way as the aquatic green plants grow from Melquíades's dentures in the glass by his bedside, following a cause and effect which is recognized but not understood.

Another Argentine author, Julio Cortázar, is at almost the same time producing short stories in which the narrative is continually turning back on itself and, in this case, devouring its own tale, overlapping planes of fiction and reality as seen in 'Continuity of the Parks', where the story ends where it begins, but not exactly in the same place or space (a space, perhaps, 'contaminated by literature').[14] The reader/character believes that he is reading – an act that catches the reader of this plane unaware since s/he reads over the shoulder of the main character and forgets about the primary narrative while Cortázar catches him/her in a moment of carelessness. This inattentiveness makes the reader accomplice to the murder of the reader/character who has settled down for the evening in a green, high-backed velvet chair, engulfed in a detective thriller in which the distance between reader and character is emphasized. Like the use of defamiliarization in Dostoevsky, Cortázar makes the reader unfamiliar with territory that should be very well known, and makes him/her question whether s/he is awakening from a dream with a corresponding disorientation and ambiguity of overlapping planes.

In writing about magical realism and children's literature, Maggie Ann Bowers asserts that 'fairy tales are not "magical realist", since the stories take place on another plane of reality from our own', and that critics of children's literature have pointed out that 'young children often prefer texts to resolve unusual situations and restore normality' (104). All fiction by definition, however, places us on different planes of reality, and some even leave us there, as Cortázar's 'Continuity of the Parks' does. It is important to remember that what we think of as consensus reality is not composed of merely one level or plane – literature itself is another plane or dimension which impinges on our own and changes both our world and the universe of fiction. Children want 'stability' in literature precisely because they think adults want that; yet creatively they are far more willing to play with concepts. Adults cannot see magic in reality because they refuse to see it, but the child observing the same event might take away a very magical interpretation – especially if we take into account modern psychological studies of eidetic imagery in children. All is not lost for adult readers, however; the modern authors of magical realism do take us there.

Magical realism underlies a process of magical thinking as an accepted cultural consensus. This same magic can be seen as the blurring of boundaries between fantasy, realism and magical realism. The best examples of many of the precursors to magical realism are to be found in a site other than Latin America; the German author E. T. A. Hoffmann's short stories, particularly 'The Golden Flower Pot', and Franz Kafka's 'Metamorphosis' certainly fit under the larger umbrella of fantasy, realism and the supernatural. The description of Gregor's disorientation in trying to figure out the mechanics of moving each of his insect legs to get the comforter positioned over his body is a perfect match for all of the descriptions of Latin American magical realism. This literary movement is far too creative to be contained on a single continent; if Salman Rushdie can re-ignite Don Quixote's imagination and so lessen the pain of this enormous loss to literature, and Italo Calvino can create tales that share magical realist qualities as well, the world is all the richer.

Perhaps one of the richest sources for magical realism does date back to that inimitable knight with a vivid, alive imagination and his fascination with tales of chivalry and a code of honor, of value. Italo Calvino calls upon the incipient image of this magical world of knights, which seemed at one time to belong to the world of human beings, but negates its existence through another parody of our love of chivalry.[15] While Don Quixote is occupied with the whole miraculous apparatus of madness, creativity and imagination, the ghost knight in *The Nonexistent Knight* busies himself, with of all things, daily ordinary details, the crushing minutiae precisely of things with which he no longer has any physical concerns. He 'occupies' his suit of mail, and strictly enforces knightly code or rather prosaic 'rules'. His 'appearance' may be magical, but his presence is about as far from the miraculous as it gets.

Yet the psychological concerns that brought him to the place or the site of chivalry, which is the battlefield, are precisely those things that allowed him to continue as a knight though he was long dead, and these other worldly concerns were best expressed through those things that most tie human beings to a physical world – everyday reality and the physical necessities that accompany it. This artificial separation of form and content are similar to the magic and the real; these are distinctions we make for theoretical arguments, for one cannot exist without the presence and/or structure of the other. The unknown is approached always through the known.

Salman Rushdie's *Shame*, similar to *One Hundred Years of Solitude*, likewise needs a genealogical tree at the beginning of the novel to assist the reader in sorting out family lines and serves as an orientation to the idea of family saga.[16] The three sisters who share one pregnancy to hide the identity of the sister who has a child out of wedlock even share the same cravings to prevent outsiders from recognizing which of them actually gives birth. The maternity continues to be concealed after the birth, and the closeness of the daughters allows them to share childrearing from the perspective of birth-mother. The fabric of everyday life is stitched together in such a fashion to reveal the 'marvellous real' within a time and space that are both distant and near.

Two other authors worthy of mention here are Angela Carter and Kurt Vonnegut, especially regarding their treatment of time and space. How interesting that these two representatives of countries colonized and colonizing should portray similarly pragmatic aspects of literature that share magical realist tendencies with the fantastic so that one might say there is at least a family resemblance. Vonnegut's Billy Pilgrim in *Slaughterhouse Five*, Kilgore Trout in *Breakfast of Champions* and Malachi Constant with his 'chrono-synclastic infundibula' in *The Sirens of Titan* represent a curiously American pragmatic expression of magical realism, a fatalist sense that its presence is part of the weight and inevitability of destiny. Perhaps in that way Vonnegut's work matches more closely the inverse of magical realism in America, a movement Rudy Rucker has designated the 'trans-real', which writes about everyday events as though they were fantastic. However, the magical realism surfaces in uncanny ways, and there is no return for the reader to the ordinary from Vonnegut's narratives.

Angela Carter's *The Infernal Desire Machines of Doctor Hoffman* most closely matches the achievement of García Márquez in the European embodiment of magical realism. If one closely follows the precision of the prose and the depiction of direct cognition in the presentation of analogy and symbol, the work is a reflection both on and of itself as it tells/shows the most inter-dimensional and miraculous tale. Her short stories, particularly 'The Bloody Chamber' and 'Reflections', are clear demonstrations that the magical real (working backwards from the prosaic to the Stepford wives, 'The Bloody Chamber' presents fantastic events that are both real and unreal at the same time) is alive and well in other parts of the globe.[17]

The reader is aware that it is in the arena of literature that a society first tries out new ideas, perceptions and realities. Then perhaps they are also experienced by the rest of the world, and a hundred years later, proven to be fact. So it is that magical realism is a branch of the fantastic, as in Borges's attempt to describe the unutterable Aleph: 'Perhaps the gods would not be against my finding an equivalent image, but then this report would be contaminated with literature, with falsehood.'[18] The falsehood to which Borges alludes is literature, or fiction, and, though made up, it is not a lie. Academics are singularly uncomfortable with this ambiguity; authors and artists thrive on it as an inherent part of the creative material of language. Literary movements are associative, not chronological; linear thinking insists they 'develop', 'progress' or, worse, 'evolve'. Fantasy and magical realism belong to the same guild. Both partake in Mikhail Bakhtin's carnival, Octavio Paz's fiesta, Rosemary Jackson's literature of subversion and Tzvetan Todorov's narrative of perception and imagination, and all of these elements come together in magical realist narratives. They comprise a process of magical thinking, on the part of not only the author, but an entire community – a community of writers resonating on many continents, crossing temporal borders and always creating new literary events.

NOTES

1 Rosemary Jackson, *Fantasy: The Literature of Subversion* (New York: Routledge, 1981), p. 4.
2 Ken Booth, *Theory of World Security* (Cambridge University Press, 2007), p. 247.
3 Maggie Ann Bowers, *Magic(al) Realism* (London: Routledge, 2004), p. 2.
4 See Ian Watt, *The Rise of the Novel* (Berkeley: University of California Press, 1957) for a more thorough discussion of the development of the novel as it coincides with the rise of the ordinary individual as the protagonist.
5 For a more in-depth discussion of the development of the empirical and the fictional in prose narrative, deriving from the epic synthesis of myth, history and fiction, see Robert Scholes and Robert Kellogg, *The Nature of Narrative* (New York: Oxford University Press, 1966).
6 Franz Roh, 'Magic Realism: Post-Expressionism' (1925), quoted in Lois Parkinson Zamora and Wendy B. Faris (eds.), *Magical Realism: Theory, History, Community* (Durham, NC: Duke University Press, 1995), p. 17.
7 Miguel Angel Asturias, *Men of Maize*, trans. Gerald Martin (University of Pittsburgh Press, 1995).
8 Juan Rulfo, *Pedro Páramo* (Madrid: Cátedra, 1992).
9 Elena Garro, *Recollections of Things to Come*, trans. Ruth L. Simms (Austin, TX: University of Texas Press, 1986).
10 Wendy B. Faris, *Ordinary Enchantments: Magical Realism and the Remystification of Narrative* (Nashville: Vanderbilt University Press, 2004), p. 7. See David Young and Keith Hollaman (eds.), *Magical Realist Fiction: An Anthology* (New York: Longman, 1984).
11 Octavio Paz, *Children of the Mire*, trans. Rachel Phillips (Cambridge, MA: Harvard University Press, 1974), p. vi.
12 Conversation with Fernando de Jesús, Bogotá, Colombia, December 1999.
13 Ursula K. Le Guin, 'Introduction', in Jorge Luis Borges, Silvina Ocampo, A. Bioy Cásares (eds.), *The Book of Fantasy* (New York: Viking Penguin, 1988), pp. 9, 10, 12.
14 Julio Cortázar, 'Continuidad de los parques', in *Ceremonias: Final del juego y las armas secretas* (Barcelona: Seix Barral, 1989).
15 Italo Calvino, *The Nonexistent Knight and The Cloven Viscount*, trans. Archibald Colquhoun (Orlando: Harcourt, 1977).
16 Salman Rushdie, *Shame* (London: Cape, 1983).
17 Angela Carter, *The Infernal Desire Machines of Doctor Hoffman* (New York: Penguin, 1994); *Burning Your Boats: The Collected Short Stories* (New York: Penguin, 1995).
18 Jorge Luis Borges, 'El Aleph', in *A Personal Anthology*, trans. Anthony Kerrigan (New York: Grove, 1967), p. 149.

15

NNEDI OKORAFOR

Writers of colour

'Writers of colo(u)r' is a term which has emerged in the United States as an extrapolation from 'people of color', which itself emerged as a response to two issues: first, that many people in the USA who do not identify as white do not identify as black either; and, second, this more expansive terminology 'acts as a recognition that certain people are racialized', and allows for wider coalitions and more complex discussions, in addition to moving from a 'negative' (non-white) to a positive description.[1] Writers of colour may be of African, Asian,[2] Indigenous Australian, Native American or other heritage not discussed here.

The term 'writer of colour' is not uncontested in terms of its application. To begin with, it is a term used by US and Canadian writers, and by Caribbean authors resident in those countries; it has not been widely used as yet in the United Kingdom or elsewhere. More important, it has to be used with caution when one is dealing with authors who, while presented as writers of colour in the USA or the European market, are members of the dominant, majority group in the land in which they were born, lived and wrote. Miyuki Miyabe is a Japanese author who continues to live in Japan, but whose work has been available in translation since 1999, and who some consider a 'writer of colour' within the Anglo-American market. Hayao Miyazaki, author of one of the great Japanese fantasy mangas, *Nausicaa of the Valley of the Wind* (1982–94), is similarly positioned, part of the hegemonic culture in which he lives, but potentially read as 'other' when read within the Anglo-American fantasy market. China is currently the largest market for sf and fantasy in the world: its main sf magazine, *SF World*, has a circulation in the region of 120,000, and it would be absurd to regard Chinese authors in this market as 'of colour' in the sense meant here, but when their works enter the Anglo-American market, the situation might be considered to change.

One of the more complex areas of definition because these writers are, after all, the indigenous peoples of their regions, are Native American and

Indigenous Australian writers. Owl Goingback has published fantastical novels such as *Crota* (1996), although his novels have more in common with genre horror than with genre fantasy, while Leslie Marmon Silko's much acclaimed *Almanac of the Dead* (1991) appears closer to the work of Latin American magic realists, where *belief* in the supernatural within the text suggests we should be cautious about understanding these texts as genre fantasy. For Indigenous Australian authors, the issues are even more complex. Yaritji Green writes of the complex negotiations with her elders over the 'ownership' of culture in a context in which stories belong to specific groups, and of her uneasiness over publishing even the results of these negotiations. Her short fiction is now in print, but she is still working on the differences between Indigenous copyright (which, for her peoples, follows land boundaries) and general Australian copyright (which follows date of written publication and doesn't give stories copyright, only the worlds of the telling).[3]

However, as I discussed in my article 'Can You Define African Science Fiction?', any definition that is imposed upon individuals is problematic: self-identification is really the only acceptable route.[4]

Among 'writers of colour', Indian writers writing in English form a specific group; they have long been important in the body of English-language literature. Among them is Amitav Ghosh, born in India, educated in India and the UK (winner of the Arthur C. Clarke award in 1997 with an sf novel heavily infused with the fantastic) and now resident in the USA; Salman Rushdie, author of *Midnight's Children* (1981) and *Haroun and the Sea of Stories* (1990); Suniti Namjoshi, author of *The Blue Donkey Fables* (1988) (who holds Indian, UK and Canadian citizenship); Indian writer Ashok Banker, author of the 'Ramayana Series' (2003–10); and Vandana Singh (Indian, resident in the USA). All of these authors work with both Indian and European traditions of fantasy, and all of them understand both traditions as their own.

For a long time, there were very few writers of colour specifically working in the field of fantasy, or of science fiction. Among African-American writers, the best known were Samuel R. Delany, Octavia Butler (both best known perhaps for their science fiction), Charles R. Saunders, author of a subversive Tarzan-style adventure series which began with *Imaro* in 1981, and the children's author Virginia Hamilton, whose *Justice and Her Brothers* (1978) and its sequels, all spiritual time-travel stories, once offered the only available African-American children's fantasy. Since the 1990s a critical mass of authors who identified themselves as writers of colour has emerged. Within the collective body of work are direct challenges to the outright racism of many fantasy texts,[5] manifested in, for example, the Nevèrÿon sequences from Samuel R. Delany through to the alternative fantasies of Nalo Hopkinson, Larissa Lai and Vandana Singh.

In my novel *Who Fears Death* (2010) there is a moment where the main character, Onyesonwu, meets a Masquerade (a spirit from the 'wilderness', the spirit world). This ethereal creature is as tall as a house, as wide as a car, and has a wooden head with an angry face and a body made of dried raffia. It lunges at Onyesonwu with long, needle-like claws. Though she is afraid, she does not flee. She looks it in the face, ready for whatever it will give.

> When I didn't run, the spirit stopped and stood very still. We looked at each other, my head tilted up, its head tilted down. My angry eyes staring into its wooden ones. It made a clicking sound that resonated deep in my bones. I winced but didn't move. Three times it did this. On the third, I felt something give inside of me, like a cracked knuckle.[6]

In this moment, Onyesonwu experiences a deep spiritual pain as she is changed forever by this creature in ways that she doesn't fully understand until later. When writing this scene, I drew this instance of pain that leads to enlightenment from my own experiences as a reader. I was recalling the way certain books I read affected me in profound ways. These narratives cut so deeply that they were uncomfortable to read; sometimes they even hurt.

Good fiction allows for easy suspension of belief. This can be used to help readers escape reality. It can also be used to help them understand abstract or difficult ideas. Such fiction can remind people of what they have lost and encourage them to go beyond what they have dreamed. I call this type of fiction 'Big Bang literature', for just as the Big Bang was a violent act that produced the universe and hence ultimately life, so these stories enact pain to produce an evolution of ideas. This is an extension of Darko Suvin's idea of the novum, as an object or idea from which the estrangement, central to the construction of the fantastic, begins.[7] Big Bang literature is rare. Big Bang fantasy literature written by people of colour is almost non-existent. Nevertheless, in this minuscule literary cabal, the resulting "life" often bears a deeper significance, one that addresses issues of race and culture. Big Bang fantasy literature by people of colour can be foreign to its majority Caucasian readers and displacing to its readers; in general, the cognitive estrangement Suvin argues for can be integral to the existence of the fiction as well as to the stories it tells. This is a good thing. This is also what makes it excellent material for college-level courses.

It is impossible to discuss the work of writers of colour, and particularly African-American writers, without discussing Octavia Butler. Butler's work is predominantly sf but has had such an important impact on younger writers of fantasy that it remains central to the discussion. *Dawn* (1987) is Big

Bang science fiction, as opposed to fantasy. I have taught it in one of my literature courses. My class consisted predominantly of African-American undergraduates, with two or three Caribbean and African students in the mix. After we finished the novel, my students came clambering to class eager to discuss it. Most had been exposed to fantasy and science fiction through films like *Star Wars* (1977), *The Matrix* (1999) and *Avatar* (2009), but, to all of them, *Dawn* was something new. To them, the book lived up to its title. 'I've never, ever, ever experienced anything like this,' one of my students said. Notice she said 'experienced' instead of 'read'. My students were especially surprised by the fact that such a novel had a black main character and was written by an African-American. After class, another student approached me with wide eyes, grinning from ear to ear, clutching her *Dawn* novel as if it would fly away if she loosened her grip. 'Professor Nnedi,' she said. 'Thank you so much for having us read this. This book has changed the way I *see* things. It's changed my life! And it's about aliens!' She said she planned to continue the series though the other books were not on the syllabus.

The significance of this moment of identification should not be underestimated. Deepa Dharmadhikari, in 'Surviving Fantasy Through Post-Colonialism', talks of growing up 'speaking Marathi with my family, and Hindi with schoolmates and neighbours, but the only children's books I read were in English . . . *I grew up with half a tongue*'.[8] Absent from her reading was precisely these moments of identification that white readers may take so much for granted that they do not recognize them. Samuel R. Delany began writing science fiction in the early 1960s: he has told the story that his moment of identification came with the sudden realization that the main protagonist in a novel by the (white) science fiction writer Robert A. Heinlein was black. It was the first black character he had met in science fiction. Over twenty years later, when the Jamaican-born Nalo Hopkinson realised that Samuel R. Delany himself was black, she cried. Delany was 'Company. My universe had doubled in size.'[9]

Octavia Butler uses the tropes of speculative fiction to revitalize topics that students will have discussed *ad nauseam* in other courses, such as slavery, issues of gender and assumptions we make about sex and relationships. Butler's prose is crisp and sparse, and the plot is swift; nevertheless, the apparent accessibility is a trap. *Dawn* will bring the 'pain' for student readers new to the genre (and those not so new to it, too). The themes Butler addressed in science fiction, she also brought to fantasy, with the fantasy time-travel novel *Kindred* (1979) which challenges readers to consider the complex choices of a woman who might prevent the rape of an ancestor only if she accepts that she herself will not be born, and also to her 'Patternist' series. *Wild Seed* (1980), the first novel in the series, follows the lives of two individuals who are essentially immortal. Doro, originally from Egypt, is 4,000 years old. He can transfer his 'life essence' into the bodies of others by sheer will, causing their souls or essences to die. Anyanwu, a 300-year-old Igbo (Nigerian) woman, possesses the power to heal and the ability to shape-shift into humans and other animals. The novel's story takes place between 1690 to 1840, following Doro and Anyanwu through the phases of slavery – from capture in Africa to the Middle Passage to enslavement in the New World, and finally to freedom. The plot centres on Doro's desire to create a race of immortals with amazing powers and Anyanwu's resistance to the cruelty of his methods. The journey of these African immortals from pre-colonial Africa to the 'New World' allows the reader to watch the transatlantic slave system from beginning to end. The continuity of view intensifies the brutality and impact of slavery. Only through a fantasy novel can slavery be presented in such entirety.

One of the most direct uses of fantasy to test ideologies and cultures of slavery was Samuel R. Delany's Nevèryon sequence, which consists of eleven stories, one of which is novel-length; they were published in four volumes between 1979 and 1987. The most recent edition, by Wesleyan University Press, emphasizes the cyclical nature of the sequence by reprinting the first story at the end of the fourth volume. These stories are a complex meditation on many things, including the nature of civilization, the nature of narration itself, sexuality and AIDS. Above all they form a dialogue with traditional 'sword-and-sorcery' fantasy, and they reverse one of the standard motifs: the dominant culture is brown-skinned, and the barbarians who form the bulk of the slaves come from the south, and are white. The sequence sees the growth of civilization, and the efforts to liberate the slaves, but it underlines the paradoxes of 'civilization', and the ambiguous nature of the power relationships set up by slavery and race.

Among more recent writers, Steven Barnes's *Lion's Blood* (2002) and *Zulu Heart* (2003) offer alternate histories of Europe in which Christianity gives way to Islam, and the European nations to the African. David Anthony Durham's *Acacia: Book 1. War with the Mein* (2007), deploys the structures of epic fantasy to tackle a slavery that is integral to the trading agreements between nations, institutionalized in the power structures of the governments. The alliances formed among the slaves are multiracial and multi-ethnic in a world that insists on racial divisions.

Carole McDonnell's *Wind Follower* (2007), Alaya Dawn Johnson's *Racing the Dark* (2007) and N. K. Jemisin's *The Hundred Thousand Kingdoms* (2010) intend to create fantasy worlds which distance themselves from the default whiteness of the Tolkien tradition. Jemisin's much-admired

The Hundred Thousand Kingdoms is a fantasy with strong overtones of *Gormenghast*. It is interested in issues of colonialism and the stagnation of a culture, but it is the corruption and renewal of the gods which takes centre stage.

Slavery, slavery's consequences and post-colonialism have been central to the work of Jamaican-Canadian author Nalo Hopkinson. In her first novel, the magical realist *Brown Girl in the Ring* (1998), privilege and refusal of privilege still affects the lives of a Caribbean family living in a futuristic Toronto. *Midnight Robber* (2000), ostensibly a planetary exploration novel, will have readers reading in tongues. Although the novel can be read as science fiction, the novel is filled with creatures concocted from Trinidadian folklore and Hopkinson's imagination (and who we see more of in her collection of fantastical tales *Skin Folk* (2001)). Hopkinson has created a world that is understood though the culture of the conquerors, so that a conquered culture becomes an imperialist culture. In Trini folklore, mako junbies are stilt walkers who represent spirit-like or god-like creatures. In *Midnight Robber*, mako jumbies are giant predatory birds with long, long legs. In Trini folklore, the douen are the lost souls of unbaptized babies. In *Midnight Robber*, they are a mysterious peaceful bird-/bat-/lizard-like people who live in the forest. The 'magical' sense of the world in which the reader moves is intensified by the Trini dialect of much of the narrative.

> Oho. Like it starting, oui? Don't be frightened, sweetness; is for the best. I go be with you the whole time. Trust me and let me distract you little bit with one anansi story: It had a woman, you see, a strong, hard-back woman with skin like cocoa-tea. She two foot-them tough from hiking through the diable bush, the devil bush on the prison planet of New Half-Way Tree.[10]

The reader is forced to 'hear' the story, a speculative tale set in a futuristic near utopian community which then follows a community of criminals full of fantastical beasts based on Trinidadian folklore. The result is beautifully jarring. Hopkinson, like Butler, explores the consequence of slavery and oppression through their impact on individual women. In *Midnight Robber*, it is Tan-Tan, raped and abused by her father, who uses the trickster tales of Trinidad to save her sanity and later her soul. In *The Salt Roads* (2003), the lives of three separate women are examined: Mer, a respected slave on a plantation in eighteenth-century St Domingue (Haiti), Merit, a Nubian prostitute in ancient Egypt, who becomes St Mary of Egypt, and Jeanne Duval, the black mistress of the poet Baudelaire. All are inhabited by incarnations of Ezli, the African goddess of love and sex. *The New Moon's Arms* (2007) explores the race and colour cultures and systems of oppression that structure the societies of the Caribbean. All of these novels are also interested in sexuality and economic oppression.

As Hopkinson demonstrates in *The Salt Roads* and *The New Moon's Arms*, and the Jamaican-British writer Ferdinand Dennis explores in the ghost story *Duppy Conqueror* (1998), the tools of the fantastic offer a powerful way to address the contemporary world as well as the distant past, and ghost narratives have been particularly important in the work of Caribbean and African authors.

Of African writers of fantasy, probably the best known is the Nigerian writer Ben Okri. *The Famished Road* (1991) is set at an unspecified time in an unnamed country, though it is obvious that the country is Nigeria and the time is in the 1960s. A boy named Azaro, about seven years old, narrates the story. Amongst the Yoruba, it is traditionally believed that there are children destined to move continually between the spirit and physical worlds in a cycle of infant death and rebirth, plaguing their mothers. These children are called abiku children (amongst the Igbo, these children are known as ogbanjes). Azaro is one of these children and has already been born to and died with the same mother a number of times.

> How many times had I been born and died young? And how often to the same parents I had no idea. So much of the dust of living was in me. But this time, somewhere in the interspace between the spirit world and the Living, I chose to stay.[11]

The story opens with Azaro deciding to stay in the world. To him, this is an act of compassion toward his mother. Along with evading his overzealous spirit friends who wish for him to return to them, Azaro and his parents must contend with disease, hunger, politics and a troubled personal life. Characters exist in both the spirit and the material worlds. Okri's imagery and poetic prose demonstrate the power of the fantastic as Big Bang literature.

> In the land of beginnings spirits mingled with the unborn. We could assume numerous forms. Many of us were birds. We knew no boundaries. There was much feasting, playing, and sorrowing. We feasted much because of the beautiful terrors of eternity. We played because we were free.   (3)

Almost every line of *Famished Road* is heavy with symbolism, story or imagery. Like Hopkinson, Okri brings mythology to life. In Okri's case, it is mostly Nigerian mythology.

> Shadows stormed past, giving off a stench of sweat and rage. Drums vibrated in the air. A cat cried out as if it had been thrown on to fire. Then a gigantic Masquerade burst out of the road, with plumes of smoke billowing from its head.   (11)

Okri was the first to show me Masquerades (spirits and ancestors from the spirit world) as I had always imagined them, as powerful monstrous real creatures. *The Famished Road* calls forth visions, dreams and nightmares. It places the reader equally within the physical and the spirit worlds, for Azaro's world is simultaneously alive, dead and something else, in the feverish dreams and nightmares of Nigeria.

The magical realist novel by Ngũgĩ wa Thiong'o, *Mûrogi wa Kagogo* (known outside Kenya as *Wizard of the Crow*, 2006) takes place during 'our times' and is set in the fictional African country of Aburiria. When Aburiria's ruler (a combination of Kenya's ex-President Moi, Uganda's Idi Amin and Zaire's Mobutu, who gives a new definition to the phrase 'god complex') cooks up a plan to build the tallest building in the world, bad things begin to happen, and a great battle between good and evil ensues.

There are vibrant characters, plot twists, back-stabbing government officials; powerful women who develop effective methods of terror; a body of water where time stands still; an illness rightfully known as 'whiteache'; and three corrupt government ministers who are like inverted forms of the mythical Three Wise Monkeys, each with their surgically enlarged eyes, ears or mouth. And there is the Wizard of the Crow, a wizard many believe is two-faced – one face female and one male. The 'Big Bang' power of this novel lies in its storytelling. The novel is physically and verbally heavy, over 700 pages long. The heart of the story is about globalization, corruption, the power of stories, the power of the people and love.

The novel was translated from Gĩkũyũ into English by the author. It draws on the African oral tradition, and to some extent stays within it. During a private interview in May 2006, Ngũgĩ Wa Thiong'o informed me that in Kenya people who could read were reading the books to those who could not. Because so many people were illiterate in Kenya, people were making plays out of the book, a novel so potent with story that it transcended the physical page.

Helen Oyeyemi, a British writer born in Nigeria, is also fascinated with ghosts and the spirit world. Her first novel, *The Icarus Girl* (2005), deals with Yoruba beliefs about twins, and dead twins, and involves a haunting at first welcomed and then rejected. *The Opposite House* (2007) told of a Cuban woman in London, possibly haunted by a goddess, striving to deal with the visceral experience of cultural alienation. Her most recent novel, *White is for Witching* (2009), is set in Cambridge and revolves around the haunting of Miranda Silver and the understanding and knowledge brought to the situation by her Nigerian friend, Ore.

Among Asian writers Vandana Singh's short story 'Delhi' (2004) is haunted by different kinds of ghosts. Aseem is a drifter with no real home or family. He used to be a university student but he left all this behind because he sees possible pasts and futures wherever he goes and no one can help him understand or stop it. Some of those Aseem meets are famous historical figures (including India's Emperor Mohammad Shah Rangila), and he wonders if by speaking with them he's changed the present and future in some minute way. Then one day he is charged with the task of finding a woman whose fate is supposedly profoundly connected to his. For years, he searches for her. When he finds her, she is a woman from the future. Thinking she was from the present, he accidently gives her incorrect information. She disappears before he can correct it. This leads him further into chaos. 'Delhi' is a genius mix of speculative fiction, strange destiny, actual history and civil duty. And the backdrop is the Indian city of Delhi.

> Tonight he is intensely aware of the city: its ancient stones, the flat-roofed brick houses, threads of clotheslines, wet, bright colors waving like pennants, neem-tree lined roads choked with traffic. There's a bus going over the bridge under which he has chosen to sleep. The night smells of jasmine and stale urine, and the dust of the cricket field on the other side of the road.[12]

The storytelling, in this, as in the stories in her collection *Distances* (2009), is lush and the juxtaposing of detailed Indian life, landscape and history with the speculative and the fantastical makes for a rare refreshingly dislocating read.

Writes of colour have done particularly well in the Tiptree Award, a juried award that is given for explorations of gender issues. Winners have included Larissa Lai, Andrea Hairston (both sf writers), Hiromi Goto and Nisi Shawl. Hiromi Goto, a Japanese-Canadian novelist, won the award with *The Kappa Child* (2002). This novel begins in the Canadian prairies exploring the life of the daughter of a Japanese immigrant, trapped in low-paying work and convinced she is undesirable, until a chance encounter with a kappa, a trickster figure, leaves her craving cucumbers. Writing for children, Laurence Yep has twice received the Newbery Honor Award, for *Dragonwings* (1975) and *Dragon's Gate* (1993), for stories which draw heavily on Chinese dragon mythologies.

One of the most successful Asian writers in the past decade is Ted Chiang, whose exquisitely crafted, prize-winning short stories have tackled religious belief ('Tower of Babylon', 1990; 'Hell is the Absence of God', 2001), alternative engineering ('Exhalation', 2009), communication with aliens ('Story of Your Life', 1998) and cultural notions of beauty ('Liking What You See: A Documentary', 2002). More recently, Aliette de Bodard, a French-Vietnamese writer, has begun producing a series of highly regarded short stories: in a context in which writers of colour are often expected to 'represent' their own culture for Anglo-American readers; de Bodard's *Servant of the Underworld* (2010) stands out because it is set in an alternate Aztec kingdom.

As the number of writers of colour has increased, so too has the body of critical work addressing issues of race, of all-white futures and complexities of cultural appropriation and problematizing common terms of engagement such as the injunction to 'write the other'. Samuel R. Delany, Octavia Butler, Deepa Dharmadhikari, Nisi Shawl, Isiah Lavender III and I have all offered significant contributions to the critical debate.[13] Works by writers of colour are critically engaged directly and indirectly with challenging the hegemonic givens of the field, and, furthermore, many of these authors are consciously addressing their own experiences of reading the fantastic as a reader of colour: of particular interest in these terms is Pulitzer-Prize-winning *The Brief Wondrous Life of Oscar Wao* (2007) by Junot Díaz, in which the engagement with fantastic fiction of the Dominican protagonist, living in New Jersey, is central to the text.

Writing 'Big Bang stories' is often just as much of a journey for the writer. I speak from experience. My own novel *Who Fears Death* is about how a woman named Onyesonwu becomes infamous enough to have to tell her story from a jail cell two days before her scheduled execution.

In this part of future Africa, many of the past and present problems remain. There is genocide in the West, like the genocide of today in the Sudan. Onyesonwu is Ewu, a product of this war, the result of 'weaponized rape'. In this world, familiar issues are further complicated by technology. There are old paper-thin computers that are durable enough to last centuries and tiny digital devices that hold e-maps and e-books, and ... can record. There is the capture station, a portable device that pulls condensation from the clouds to produce fresh water, the perfect tool to help Onyesonwu's mother survive alone in the desert ... after her brutal rape.

Writing this novel was a painful, mind-numbing, mind-stretching process. The novel's very inspiration was a deeply disturbing news story by Emily Wax, titled '"We Want to Make a Light Baby": Arab Militiamen in Sudan Said to Use Rape as Weapon of Ethnic Cleansing'. It appeared in the *Washington Post* on 30 June 2004. From this story, my main character was born.

Even while writing *Who Fears Death*, I knew this had to be more than a good speculative fiction novel. The story was dealing with issues that were very real, including female circumcision, genocide, 'weaponized rape' culture and the plight and struggle of powerful African women and men. I knew I was writing Big Bang literature and I had to strap on a seatbelt and hang on for dear life while writing it. I expect the same of readers.

NOTES

1 Naomi Zack (ed.), *American Mixed Race: The Culture of Microdiversity* (Lanham, MD: Rowman and Littlefield, 1995).

2 In the USA, 'Asian' usually indicates Japanese, Chinese or Korean heritage; in the UK it usually indicates Indian, Pakistani or Bengali. The term 'Oriental', used by many of Chinese or Japanese heritage in the UK, is considered offensive in the USA.

3 Gill Pollack, 2 May 1010, email.

4 'Can You Define African Science Fiction?' at www.sfwa.org/2010/03/can-you-define-african-science-fiction/.

5 See, e.g., Anderson Rearick, 'Why is the Only Good Orc a Dead Orc? The Dark Face of Racism in Tolkien's World', *Modern Fiction Studies*, 50 (2004), pp. 861–74, who absolves Tolkien of the oft-repeated charge.

6 Nnedi Okorafor, *Who Fears Death* (New York: DAW, 2010), p. 4.

7 Darko Suvin, *Metamorphoses of Science Fiction: On the Poetics and History of a Literary Genre* (New Haven: Yale University Press, 1979).

8 Deepa Dharmadhikari, 'Surviving Fantasy through Post-Colonialism', *Foundation: The International Review of Science Fiction*, 107 (Winter 2009), pp. 15–20.

9 Author profile, Nalo Hopkinson, *Quill and Quire*, November 2003. Quillandquire.com.

10 Nalo Hopkinson, *Midnight Robber* (New York: Warner, 2000), p. 1.

11 Ben Okri, *The Famished Road* (New York: Anchor, 1993), p. 5.

12 Uppinder Mehan and Nalo Hopkinson (eds.), *So Long Been Dreaming: Post-colonial Science Fiction and Fantasy* (Vancouver: Arsenal Pulp, 2004), p. 79.

13 Samuel R. Delany, *About Writing: Seven Essays, Four Letters and Five Interviews* (Middletown, CT: Wesleyan University Press, 2005); Deepa Dharmadhikari (already cited); Nnedi Okorafor-Mbachu, 'Stephen King's Super-Duper Magical Negroes', *Strange Horizons* (25 October 2004); Isiah Lavender III, *Race in American Science Fiction* (Bloomington, Indianapolis: Indiana University Press, 2011). See also E. Leonard, *Into Darkness Peering: Race and Color in the Fantastic* (Westport, CT: Greenwood Press, 1997).

16

W. A. SENIOR

Quest fantasies

The structuring characteristic of quest fantasy is the stepped journey: a series of adventures experienced by the hero and his or her companions that begins with the simplest confrontations and dangers and escalates through more threatening and perilous encounters. The narrative begins as a single thread but often becomes polysemous, as individuals or small groups pursue minor quests within the overall framework. Quest fantasies conventionally start in a place of security and stability, and then a disruption from the outside world occurs. The protagonist, generally an average person with hidden abilities, receives a call to action and reluctantly embarks on the first adventure. Choice is crucial in quest fantasy, so protagonists face several cruxes where their choices determine the fate of many. After the hero and company pass the first test and receive rewards such as magic items, a respite, often characterized by feasting and music in a haven under the protection of a wisdom figure, occurs during which the members of the company receive aid and knowledge.

The quest journey continues across a massive, wild landscape of forests, rivers, mountains, valleys, small villages and occasional cities. As in the American Western, the landscape functions as a character, here endowed with animate traits as the fantasy world itself seeks to heal the rift that threatens its destruction. The menace frequently comes from a Dark Lord, a satanic figure of colossal but warped power, who wishes to enslave and denature the world and its denizens and who lives in a dead land, often in the east or north, surrounded by a range of forbidding mountains and deserts. During the quest the pattern of an organic, moral world with directive purpose emerges. The final stage of the quest brings the hero into direct confrontation with the Dark Lord, whose defeat is a result of some action or decision by the hero. The conclusion reveals a recovery from the devastating losses that characterize this genre. However, quest fantasies also posit a cyclical history so that the possibility of the reappearance of the Dark Lord, or of another, in the future remains.

Stephen R. Donaldson's Chronicles of Thomas Covenant the Unbeliever present a particularly American version of quest fantasy. *Lord Foul's Bane* (1977) begins in a small Midwestern town where Thomas Covenant, a successful author, husband and father is living the American Dream. However, he discovers that he has leprosy: his wife leaves him, taking their son; the townspeople revile and reject him; and he lives isolated outside the town until he has an encounter with a mysterious figure, who turns out to be the Creator of this world and its mirrored version. The First Chronicles are portal fantasies in which Covenant is called from his primary world three times, one for each book in the trilogy, into a secondary world called the Land, which inheres to an American democratic tradition more than the hierarchal worlds of British fantasy. This world represents all the Covenant lacks: it is a living, breathing place filled with the magic of health and nature called Earthpower. Its Dark Lord is not the monolithic power of a Sauron, but an incarnation of Covenant's despite, hopelessness and inner hatred. *Lord Foul's Bane* presents Covenant's first test, a journey primarily of knowledge and revelation.

Covenant cannot believe that he is in an alternate world or that he can have a purpose in it because the stringencies of his leprosy demand that he examine everything objectively, thus the sobriquet 'The Unbeliever.' His reluctance to become involved mirrors in exaggerated fashion the conventional attitude of the fantasy hero, but his rationale springs from his leprosy, for any exercise of power could destroy him. However, he begins to regain his humanity after he is rescued by a young girl named Lena and accepted into the small rural village where she lives. As a result of the Land's restorative effects, he is overcome by lust and rapes her but rationalizes his actions by taking refuge in the belief that everything he experiences is a dream.

Nonetheless, he becomes embroiled in the Land because he resembles a mythic hero from the past, possesses a talisman, a ring of white gold, and fits a prophecy about a figure of power who will save or destroy the world. Covenant leaves the Stonedown and begins his first journey with Lena's embittered mother, Atiaran, as his first guide. Covenant witnesses the wonders of the Land but cannot accept them or even act when he is needed, leaving Atiaran in despair. So, during the second leg of this trip, Covenant receives a more powerful guide, Saltheart Foamfollower, a Giant, who takes him down a mighty river to Revelstone, where the Lords, wizards, live and guide the peoples of the Land. Members of the Bloodguard, a group of vaguely Asian warriors who do not age or weaken over time because of a magical vow, take Covenant under their control as the Lords explain much of the Land's history and enlist him in their quest to find the missing Staff of Law, an icon of power that embodies the magical laws of the Land. The quest is achieved, and Covenant fades back to the primary world to wonder about what he has experienced.

In this first instalment, Donaldson employs many of the conventions of quest or high fantasy and the scaffolding journey motif: the average person as unwilling hero, the mage or wisdom figure, the importance of companions, the acquisition of knowledge and discovery of self, the crux of choice and action, the rejection of passivity, the wonder of the secondary world and its organic, sentient nature, the deep mythic past of history and legends, the mixture of peoples, the rules and limits of magic, the machinations of the Dark Lord and his minions, the reality of evil and the final crescendo of battle and triumph, if only for a time.

As is usual in this genre, the events that occur in the secondary world take months; however, in the primary world, only moments have passed. The second book, *The Illearth War* (1977), occurs only weeks after the first in our world but a generation later in the Land. The primary action of *The Illearth War* centres on another staple of quest fantasy, a massive battle, as Lord Foul builds an army made seemingly invincible by his recovery of the Illearth Stone, a powerful talisman that warps all it comes into contact with, and by the destruction caused by Ravers, vampiric-like spirits who possess others' bodies. While Hile Troy, a character from the primary world, searches for a military solution and assembles his own army, Covenant goes on another lengthy quest across the Land with his companions in search of lost knowledge and power. Foul is defeated for the time, but at terrible cost, and Covenant returns to his world.

The Power that Preserves (1977) starts with Covenant's third summons into a preternatural winter that threatens to make a waste land of the Land. In addition, the Ravers have mastered the Illearth Stone and destroyed the natural law governing death to build an army of the dead. Covenant and his companions must take a night-sea journey across a frozen landscape in order to confront the demon Foul in his own stronghold while the embattled peoples of the Land struggle merely to survive the onslaught of his forces. Covenant's defeat of the Despiser, fittingly, is not a contest of might but one of spirit, in which the qualities of life – joy, hope, laughter – annul the forces of self-loathing, corruption and despair.

The Second Chronicles of Thomas Covenant (*The Wounded Land*, 1980; *The One Tree*, 1982; *White Gold Wielder*, 1983) witness Covenant's return to the Land after ten years in his world but thousands in the secondary world. Accompanied by a doctor, Linden Avery, Covenant finds Foul has returned and a Raver wields the force of the Banefire, a magical bonfire fed by blood that has created a hell of the Land: the Banefire blocks the health sense natural to the inhabitants of the Land, while standard weather patterns no longer exist, and there are wild swings from absolute drought to periods of rampant fecundity to violent, flooding storms. Covenant must discover what has happened since he left the Land and teach Linden Avery, whose health sense has remained intact. Their arduous journey leads them across the Land in search of knowledge and help, and in *The One Tree* Donaldson goes beyond one convention of quest fantasy and expands the geography of the series to include places in this world outside the limits of the Land. The search for the One Tree to find the wood for a new Staff of Law takes Covenant, Avery, their companion Giants and Haruchai to varied places beyond the sea; their return in *White Gold Wielder* concludes the Second Chronicles with another departure from the norm in Covenant's sacrifice and death as he defeats Lord Foul again.

If Donaldson explores primarily American dilemmas concerning the problems of power, its use and the reciprocal damage it can inflict on the user, Canadian Guy Gavriel Kay's Fionavar Tapestry offers a different focus within the framework of the quest fantasy. Kay, who assisted Christopher Tolkien in the editing and production of *The Silmarillion*, borrows heavily from Tolkien in such elements as the geography of Fionavar, the parallels of past history, the Dark Lord figure of Rakoth Maugrim, the *lios alfar* and their hidden land (elves and Lothlórien) and dwarves; yet other influences abound: Donaldson's wild magic in a magical ring, Norse and Celtic mythology, Arthurian legend, matriarchal-goddess cultures, Shakespeare's *Henry IV*, Part I and *The Tempest*, the traditions of Native American Plains Indians and others.

The Summer Tree (1984, first US edition 1985) introduces the main characters in our contemporary world, students of the University of Toronto: Kimberly Ford, a medical intern, and her roommate Jennifer Lowell; Kevin Laine, an attorney, and his friend Paul Schaffer; and Dave Martyniuk, a law student. At first, each seems to be no more than the average person common to quest fantasy, but their voyage to and experiences in Fionavar, the prime world of which all others are reflections, reveal that several have deeper mythic identities and functions which they can recognize and fulfil only in Fionavar. While the purpose of their individual journeys is the same, the defeat of Rakoth Maugrim, each has a separate quest, and rarely are they together. Through their trials and suffering, Kay generates the signature effect of most of his work, including such stand-alone novels as *Tigana* and *A Song for Arbonne*: an almost palpable weight of loss, nostalgia and sadness rooted in characters' choices, all of which are two-edged.

The five friends attend a lecture on Celtic studies, where they meet the keynote speaker, the mysterious Lorenzo Marcus, who turns out to be Loren Silvercloak, a mage in Fionavar, who has had a premonition about their importance. After a passage from the primary world, they find themselves guests in the royal household, but a terrible drought of unknown origin has afflicted it, turning all into waste land. Aileron, the High King of Brennan, is an avatar of the Fisher King; his elder son has been exiled for offering himself as a sacrifice, while the younger, Diarmuid, a clear referent to Prince Hal of *Henry IV*, seems little more than a wastrel and royal *fait-néant*. However, the roles of the five guests evolve quickly. Paul Schaffer, tormented by the death of a past lover and his potential culpability, offers himself as a sacrifice to hang on the Summer Tree, where he is accepted by the God, and the drought breaks; Kim stays with the Seer of Brennin, Ysanne, where the latter transfers her power and soul to Kim. Dave Martyniuk becomes separated from the rest during their passage and winds up among the Dalrei, a nomadic hunting group, where he establishes himself as a great warrior and has a confrontation with the goddess Ceinwein. Jennifer is kidnapped by a giant black swan and taken to Rakoth Maugrim, who has re-emerged after his defeat centuries ago and by whom she is raped and tortured. The end of the novel shows Kim, using the uncertain power of the Baelrath, her ring of power, reaching across the land to capture the dying Jennifer and transporting them all back to their world.

The Summer Tree encapsulates the standard elements of quest fantasy: the reluctant, average person as hero; the journey to the magical land populated by wizards, gods, demonic creatures, elves, dwarves, etc.; the threat from a Dark Lord; and the need for choice, action and community. These last three provide the transition into the second novel of the trilogy, *The Wandering Fire* (1986), a title that refers to Kim's ring. Its opening chapter reveals all five main characters' resolve to return to Fionavar and confront the evil that assails it, regardless of the cost. Jennifer decides to bear the child of her rape, while Kim has a vision of the hero they need in the battle against Rakoth. Using Stonehenge and Glastonbury Tor as portals, Kim sends the others back to Fionavar and, in an agony of self-recrimination for what she must do, raises the mythic hero who can fulfil the land's need: Arthur Pendragon.

Their return reveals a world in a preternatural winter, the result of the betrayal of Metran, a mage who has found and corrupted a magical cauldron. Rakoth has begun to assault the separate peoples of Fionavar, and war builds. Each of the main characters must go his or her way: Jennifer is revealed to be the current incarnation of Guenevere; Kevin Laine, whose name is revealed as a pun, sacrifices himself in a fertility ritual to the Goddess and ends the unnatural winter; Paul assumes his power as Lord of the Summer Tree, clashing further with Jaelle, the High Priestess of the Goddess; Kim as Seeress raises the Wild Hunt and leaves on a quest of her own to the trapped Giants, while Dave returns to the Dalrei to battle.

The action of the second book is marked by the traditional communion of groups. Aileron asserts himself as the leader of an alliance of the peoples of Brennin and Cathal, the neighboring country to the south, the Dalrei, and the *lios alfar*, leading them into the first battle against Maugrim's forces. Diarmuid emerges as a true royal son and leads a night-sea journey to the lost isle where he and his companions defeat Metran and raise the third of the inevitable triangle: Lancelot.

The core of the novel involves Darien, the son Jennifer has borne and abandoned so that he might choose his own road. He, as the son of a god, matures rapidly and begins the journey back to his father, bearing with him two magical icons, one a dagger with unknown power.

The Darkest Road (1986) concludes the trilogy; the major action involves the titanic battle before Starkadh, Maugrim's fortress, and its resolution fulfils the prophecies and visions from the past. Darien chooses to go to his father; in their confrontation the power of evil destroys itself and the armies of the dark lose their guiding purpose and flee. Arthur, Guenevere and Lancelot come to the end of their tribulations and are wafted to an Avalon of peace and serenity; the land is restored, and the High King rules over prosperity. However, the war has taken its toll – the destruction is incalculable and devastating, and it is virtually impossible to understate the poignancy of sadness and loss that Kay creates. The original five are divided forever: Kevin dead, Jennifer passed to an afterlife, Paul united with Jaelle as intercedents of the God and Goddess. Kim, who has forfeited her power, and Dave, who must leave Fionavar because of the decree of Ceinwein, return where they started, leaving the others to memory and to grief.

A third variation on the quest theme comes from British author Philip Pullman's His Dark Materials trilogy, which draws from the Bible, *Paradise Lost*, Blake's mythologies, the many worlds theory, Mary Shelley's *Frankenstein* and others to create a tale that moves across worlds and universes in which both magic and varied technologies exist, adding an element of science fiction. The title of trilogy comes from *Paradise Lost*, Book 2, lines 911–19, as Satan stands on the brink of the abyss and ponders his voyage to earth, there being no evidence of other worlds. *Northern Lights* (1995; US edition *The Golden Compass*, 1996) introduces one of the protagonists, a young girl Lyra Belacqua, from an Oxford and England parallel to our primary world, where people have daemons, embodiments of their souls, as companions. Lyra's upbringing and voyages inhere strongly to the monomyth since she seems to be an orphan with little promise or talent and is a riotous child always into mischief and uninterested in anything serious; however, it becomes clear that she has hidden depths and a mythic role adumbrated by different prophecies about her over the course of the trilogy. Her adventures will take her across oceans, between worlds and into the land of the dead before she can fulfil her destiny. In this first novel, she and her daemon, Pantalaimon, must travel with the gyptians to the north to rescue children kidnapped by agents of the Church bent on absolute dominion of others. Along the way she acquires friends and protectors such as Farder Coram, a sage of the gyptians; Lee Scoresby, a Texan balloonist; Iorek Byrnison, whom she helps recover his state as king of the bears; and Serafina Pekkala, a leader of a witch clan. She is also given a periapt, the alethiometer, a magical device that allows her to discover the truth by falling into a state of Keatsian 'negative capability' to interpret its arcane signs.

The other protagonist, Will Parry, lives in our primary world and conforms more to the pattern of fantasy hero as average person who overcomes terrible hurdles and crushing loss and makes dire choices. *The Subtle Knife* (1997) begins as Will searches for a refuge for his mentally distressed mother and goes on a search for his lost father. He enters into a crossroads between worlds, Cittàgazze, where Lyra has become lost after following her father, Lord Asriel, whom she had been told was her uncle; and the two become companions, both seeking reunion with their parents. He and Lyra survive various assaults, and he comes into possession of the Subtle Knife, another periapt, which can cut doorways between the different possible worlds.

Despite the trilogy's initial adherence to the outline of the quest fantasy, Pullman avoids the staples of much of that genre, especially commodified fantasy; there are none of the conventional dragons, dwarves, elves or wizards, no Dark Lords or their cruel slaves; at no point do the characters enter a polder, a magical land where time runs differently, and meet a protector or wisdom figure who offers aid and guidance. Pullman's witches, for instance, are young in appearance, beautiful and fierce and live apart, close to nature, in their own clans. Giant armoured bears who work metals with great craft live in the polar regions. Gallivespians, Lilliputian warriors who ride on dragonflies and possess deadly stings, serve as spies and shock troops. Billions of angels, drawn from Milton's vision, exist but differ in strength, corporeal nature, allegiance and courage. Spectres, vampiric entities, float through Cittàgazze and empty adults of mind and soul.

These spectres prey upon Dust, the crux upon which the narrative armature hangs. In Pullman's Blakean mythos, there is an Authority who claims to have created everything, yet factions within the various overlapping worlds oppose his authority; and the Church within Lyra's world has regressed to a medieval state, including a branch which recalls the Inquisition. The biblical story in which Adam is created from dust or clay takes on a different significance when it becomes apparent that what is called Dust is in fact a form of sentience which is drawn to consciousness, although Church authorities equate it to original sin. As Mary Malone, a scientist researching dark matter at Will's Oxford, comes to learn,

> Dust came into being when living things became conscious of themselves; but it needed some feedback system to reinforce it and make it safe ... Without something like that, it would all vanish. Thought, imagination, feeling, would all wither and blow away, leaving nothing but a brutish automatism.
>
> *(The Amber Spyglass, 451)*

In the place of a battle against a Dark Lord comes a clash between massive powers over the theology of Dust.

Lord Asriel, Lyra's father and a Byronic figure, assembles a vast military to combat the forces of the Authority, who are under the command of Metatron, an angel who was once human. Against the unfolding of this Miltonic background, Lyra and Will pass between worlds on their various quests and discover that there are rules to the use of magic tools and consequences of any such use. Their final epiphany results from their nascent adulthood and discovery of their feelings for each other as they enact a new Adam and Eve paradigm. However, Pullman provides little of the *evangelium* cited by Tolkien as the outcome of fantasy. Lyra and Will must separate because of the damage done by crossing worlds; Lyra's parents have sacrificed themselves, and she can no longer read the alethiometer; many of their friends have died; and the cosmic clash of powers has, again, resulted in an enormously destructive cataclysm and loss of life. Pullman's conclusion lacks the bitterness of Donaldson's or the pathos of Kay's, but the inexorable, cosmogonic forces of his worlds deny equally poignantly the escapist, happy conclusion that critics of the genre erroneously assert.

Robin Hobb's Farseer trilogy (*Assassin's Apprentice*, 1995; *Royal Assassin*, 1996; and *Assassin's Quest*, 1997) lacks the mythic gravitas of the three previous series but leads to another direction in the quest genre. Set in the quasi-medieval world of much commodified fantasy, the novels draw substantially from the Arthurian tradition for their foundation, but Hobb shapes the narrative into an intriguingly different pattern. *Assassin's Apprentice* sets the stage: the Six Duchies, a loose confederation of fiefdoms, is under siege from Red Raiders, reminiscent of Viking incursions into England. Shrewd, the current king of the Farseer line, is fast weakening and becoming ill, a variation on the Fisher King story. Into this growing crisis, the illegitimate son of Chivalry, the deceased heir to the throne, is brought to Buckkeep, the kingdom's centre, and becomes a stable (not kitchen) lad. Although he has no name and his parentage is hidden from others, almost everyone notices his similarities to his late father and his burgeoning talents and noblesse. FitzChivalry, as he comes to be known, possesses both of the primary magics of this secondary world: the Skill, a power that allows communication between those trained in it and the ability to farsee, among other potentialities; and the Wit, a despised ability to commune with animals. The story arc of the three novels relates Fitz's monomythic development and growth, but his task is not to defeat a Dark Lord: it is to restore the kingdom to its rightful ruler, after Shrewd's assassination, and its health.

In *Assassin's Apprentice* the six-year-old Fitz is brought to the court by his two uncles, Verity, the new heir, and Regal, Shrewd's son by his second wife, a conniving and embittered degenerate. The allegorical names of many of the characters are often ironic, and Regal, a Mordred figure who takes after his mother in outlook and habit, proves himself the opposite of his naming and sees Fitz's arrival as a threat to his dynastic plans. Fitz himself comes under the tutelage of three different kinds of wisdom figures: Burrich, the master of the stables and Chivalry's loyal retainer; Chade Fallstar, a mysterious Merlin figure and royal by-blow who becomes Fitz's mentor in the art of assassination; and Galen, Regal's warped half-brother who is the Skill master and instructor. This first book details Fitz's education and beginning tasks as stableboy, royal bastard and assassin. His first quest is to the Mountain Kingdom, where Prince Regal will stand in for Verity in a proxy wedding to Ketterick in hopes of creating an alliance to help against the Red Raiders. Betrayed by Regal and left for dead, Fitz is rescued by the wolf Nighteyes, to whom he has become bonded and by members of the nobility of the Mountain Kingdom.

Royal Assassin begins with Fitz's convalescence from Regal's assault and his return to the king's seat, Buckkeep, but the major story arc follows his continued training and opposition to the deteriorating conditions, or thinning, within the Six Duchies. The Forged, zombie-like victims of the Raiders, appear in greater numbers, attacking anyone in their way; the Raiders' attacks become more destructive and elusive; King Shrewd's health and mental state decline steeply; Regal continues to undercut authority and deplete the kingdom's riches. As a result, Fitz is put in the position of having conflicting choices, between his loyalty to others and needs for himself. His love affair with Molly, a local chandler, his link with Nighteyes, his friendships with Burrich, Chade and the Fool, his duty to his king and loyalty to his uncle Verity – all these invoke the necessity of choice so important to fantasy and take a terrible toll on him.

Verity proposes a quest to the wild lands north of the Mountain Kingdom to find the Elderlings, a mythical race who helped the people of the Six Duchies generations before. After his departure, the Six Duchies fall further into disorder and weakness as Regal's excesses increase. His coterie of those trained in the Skill drain the King of power and life, so Fitz kills several of them and tries to revenge himself on Regal. His capture and resultant torture brand him as a Witted one, for whom the penalty is a gruesome death. Fitz takes a potion which makes him seem as if dead and then merges his conscious with Nighteyes.

Assassin's Quest begins with Fitz's resurrection from the dead, his sundering from Chade and Burrich and the assumption with Nighteyes of his own quest to find Verity and the Elderlings. The two undertake a gruelling journey to the Mountain Kingdom, pursued by Regal's agents and soldiers once their identity is revealed. Fitz, again badly wounded, is discovered by the Fool, who has taken refuge in the Kingdom after helping Ketterick escape, and, after another lengthy recovery, Fitz joins a company with Ketterick, the Fool, the minstrel Starling Birdsong and a mysterious old woman, Kettle, who clearly has hidden power, to find Verity. Their quest reveals a hidden prophecy and their roles within it as it takes them deeply into the northern mountains and Fitz into a time out of time as he learns the true nature of the Skill. They discover Verity, who has been trying to rouse the Elderlings but finds he must become one of them through mastery of the Skill. In the battle that ensues with Regal's forces, Verity saves his queen and land but loses himself, while Fitz discovers how to awaken the Elderlings, who aid Verity in destroying his enemies. The recovery stage Tolkien proposes for fantasy ensues as Ketterick assumes the throne, and peace and prosperity are restored. The denouement finds Fitz living anonymously in a small village as a scribe with Nighteyes and recuperating from the heavy damage done by the past several years of his life. The story continues in the Tawny Man series (*Fool's Errand*, *Golden Fool* and *Fool's Fate*) as Hobb expands her secondary world and reasserts the cyclical nature of fantasy, and Fitz, the Fool, and Chade become involved in another threat to stability as they journey far to the south to a land only rumoured in the first trilogy to confront another enemy.

Far from a rigid formula, the quest fantasy is characterized by its protean quality, its ability to subsume and reflect varied purposes and narratives through the medium of Story, as John Clute asserts in the *Encyclopedia of Fantasy*. Its simplest form is the market-driven predictable and redundant formula of commodified fantasy; however, the work of more accomplished writers belies the limitations of such works. In the hands of Ursula K. Le Guin, Robert Holdstock, Ian Irvine, Robin McKinley, Elizabeth Hand, Neil Gaiman, Patricia McKillip and others, the quest fantasy is an ever-changing portal that leads us into the heart of the human condition.

17

ALEXANDER C. IRVINE

Urban fantasy

> For the city is a poem, as has often been said . . . but it is not a classical
> poem, a poem tidily centred on a subject. It is a poem which unfolds
> the signifier and it is this unfolding that ultimately the semiology of the
> city should try to grasp and make sing.[1]

A taxonomy of urban fantasy

The term *urban fantasy* initially referred to a group of texts – among whose early exemplars are the Borderlands series of anthologies and novels, conceived by Terri Windling, Emma Bull's *War for the Oaks* (1987) and Tim Powers's *The Anubis Gates* (1983) – in which the tropes of pastoral or heroic fantasy were brought into an urban setting. It quickly grew to encompass supernatural historical novels and overlap with the loosely defined literary phenomena known as new wave fabulism or the New Weird. It has also been retroactively extended to include virtually every work of the fantastic that takes place in a city or has a contemporary setting that occasionally incorporates a city, with the result that any particularity the term once had is now diffused in a fog of contradiction (and, it must be added, marketing noise; the writers of 'paranormal romance' have all but co-opted the term for the broad American readership). If it is applied to both *Perdido Street Station* and *The Night Watch* – not to mention texts as disparate as *Shriek: An Afterword* and *War for the Oaks*, *Neverwhere* and *The Physiognomy*, or *Mortal Love* and *The Iron Dragon's Daughter* – what can it possibly mean?

The elements common to all urban fantasies – a city in which supernatural events occur, the presence of prominent characters who are artists or musicians or scholars, the redeployment of previous fantastic and folkloric topoi in unfamiliar contexts – hint at a characterization if not a rigorous definition. Within those common elements, there are two fundamental strains of urban fantasy, which might be loosely differentiated as those in which *urban* is a descriptor applied to *fantasy* and those in which *fantasy* modifies *urban*.

In the first, a more or less recognizable city – New York or London, Minneapolis or Galveston, Newford or Bordertown – is revealed to be in contact with the realm of Faerie, or some magical realm, and the resultant narrative redeploys the tropes and characters of older fairy tales and folklore, forcing them into collisions with a contemporary urban milieu. These cities are recognizably taken from our collective history, and the attempt at historical verisimilitude (even in the cases of Newford or Bordertown, both recognizable mosaics of existing cities) creates a circumstance in which the irruption of the fantastic juxtaposes two common figurative and symbolic vocabularies: those of the fairy tale and the tale of urban initiation. In the second, the city is not a field on which the naturalist and fantastic play out a series of thematic collisions; it is a *genius loci*, animating the narrative and determining its fantastic nature. Cities of this kind include New Crobuzon, Ambergris, the Well-Built City and Ashamoil. Here, the city creates its own rules, independent from existing canons of folklore. In the purest examples of these stories, whatever fantastic elements exist derive from the nature and history of the city. These are stories of the fantastic city, distinguishable from stories of real or almost-real cities in which fantastic events occur.

This distinction does not imply a hard binary opposition. These two types of urban fantasy are best understood as the far ends of a literary axis, with *urban* as one terminus and *fantasy* as the other. Corresponding to this difference in emphasis, a difference in literary ancestry is also apparent. Urban fantasies of the folkloric type derive more closely from the literary fantasy tradition, from the fairy tale through the Victorian fantasists to the Inklings. Among these texts are *Mortal Love*, *The Iron Dragon's Daughter*, *Neverwhere*, *The Anubis Gates* and *War for the Oaks*. Behind the other urban fantasy form – exemplified here by *Perdido Street Station*, *Shriek*, *The Physiognomy*, *The Etched City* and the Viriconium tales, a different lineage appears: Dickens, Baudelaire, Machen, Peake, Céline, Robbe-Grillet. Or the great modernist novels of the City: *Ulysses*, *Berlin Alexanderplatz*, *Manhattan Transfer*. One comes from an exploration of the folkloric tradition and places it in an urban environment; the other derives from the tradition of exploration of urban existence and uses the devices of the fantastic to continue this exploration. Both trade in the sublime, but one locates the sublime in the irruption of reawakened supernatural powers into the urban landscape, whereas for the other, that urban landscape is itself the location of the sublime.

The city as text

'If the city is a text,' Joyce Carol Oates asked in 'Imaginary Cities: America', 'how shall we read it?'[2] Where the city itself is a literary artifact, we shall read it according to the genre codes and protocols we detect. But when the city is itself a genre protocol – when it is created out of the material of the fantastic – these codes become a little harder to tease out. A novel in which a definable space within a city is magically transformed, or in the city serves as a map of human consciousness, with Ego above and Id down in the subway tunnels, offers a solid base from which to diagram and analyse the intrusion or interpenetration of the fantastic. But what of Ambergris or New Crobuzon, in which the people are ordinary and their environment fantastic?

The fantastic city has roots in utopian and quest literature all the way back to the Ur of Gilgamesh, and the city as a literary trope has always been profoundly ambivalent, both the City of God and the City of Man. The explosion in the size of European and American cities that accompanied the Industrial Revolution, and the concomitant urbanizing migration on both continents, created a new kind of literature of the city. By the turn of the twentieth century, writes Christophe Den Tandt in *The Urban Sublime*, 'ambivalence toward the city expressed itself in the authors' tendency to describe the metropolis as a site of terror and wonder, in accordance with Edmund Burke's definition of the sublime'.[3] Den Tandt goes on to trace the process throughout the twentieth century, as various literary genres 'initiated what we might call in Bakhtinian terms a pattern of dialogization of the rhetoric of terror: in these texts, the investigation of the visible and hidden aspects of the metropolis is performed by the interplay of several idioms against each other – realism and romance, documentary narration and the sublime, positivism and the gothic' (xi). The development of the urban fantasy dialogizes the rhetorics of both fantasy and the literature of the urban, occasionally as pure bricolage but more interestingly as a form of artistic resistance to what recent writers have seen as the exhaustion of traditional modes of the fantastic.

'A large number of texts in the present corpus are novels of initiation to urban life in which protagonists stand on the threshold of the city,' Den Tandt continues, 'beholding it as a mysterious totality. The sublime is, I believe, historically tied to this initiation motif' (xi). In that strain of urban fantasy in which ordinary people encounter (often) creatures out of English folklore – the Seelie and Unseelie Courts, for example, as in *War for the Oaks* and *Bordertown* – the fey characters incarnate the sublime that the disaffected human protagonists desire, and for which they either came to the city or were attracted to music or art once they got there. The mysterious nature of the urban sublime is here given a face and a voice through the authors' repurposing of the same folkloric elements that animated and drove the pastoral fantasy in the nineteenth century.

A puzzling and occasionally self-indulgent predilection of urban fantasy – the use of idealized occupations such as artists, writers, musicians and scholars as protagonists – might also be illuminated by the historical development of city into metropolis, as Raymond Williams writes in 'The Metropolis and the Emergence of Modernism':

> The metropolis housed the great traditional academies and museums and their orthodoxies; their very proximity and powers of control were both a standard and a challenge. But also, within the new kind of open, complex and mobile society, small groups in any form of divergence or dissent could find some kind of foothold, in ways that would not have been possible if the artists and thinkers composing them had been scattered in more traditional, closed societies. Moreover, within both the miscellaneity of the metropolis – which in the course of capitalist and imperialist development had characteristically attracted a very mixed population, from a variety of social and cultural origins – and its concentration of wealth and thus opportunities of patronage, such groups could hope to attract, indeed to form, new kinds of audience.[4]

The metropolis, then, provides a field in which the recursive nature of writing about art and writing finds an aesthetic rationale. Williams's statement is particularly relevant, as we shall see, to the construction and intersection of art and politics in *Perdido Street Station*. The immensity of the metropolis provides cover for any and all activity, although this cover is never without risk; but this same immensity creates the cracks through which can seep the fantastic as well, since the metropolis by its very size becomes a kind of fantastic landscape. Fragmentation has negative consequences as well, of course, that the European modernists were quick to document and engage with such intensity that, as Michael Long writes in 'Eliot, Pound, Joyce: Unreal City':

> The Modernist, fragmented city is virtually the poem's protagonist. The city's dirty buildings and polluted river, sweating oil and tar, the city's canal, gashouses and rats, those scarcely living roots in the winter ground or under the city's stones: all go to make up one of the great wilderness images of Modernism. In English this is the classic image of the Modernist city, and when it ends with fragments shored against the ruins the stress is on the fragments and the ruins, not on any very successful shoring.[5]

Looking forward, it is not hard to detect this aesthetic at work in China Miéville; Long's details culled from *The Waste Land* read almost as a paraphrase of any number of descriptive passages in Miéville's *Perdido Street Station* (2000). Eliot himself traced ancestry of this vision of the city back to Baudelaire, as Peter Collier notes:

> It is not merely in the use of imagery of the sordid life of a great metropolis, but in the elevation of such imagery to the first intensity – presenting it as it is, and yet making it represent something much more than itself – that Baudelaire has created a mode of release and expression for other men.[6]

Eliot, Collier goes on, 'dissects the problems of the alienated city-dweller, with an irony made crueler by its insertion of the clutter of the city into a mythical, pastoral, and romantic tradition' (42). His characterization of this project, in which writers of Eliot's generation 'found themselves reenacting the nightmare visions of the nineteenth century on a new plane of intellectual and artistic sophistication' (43), usefully outlines the situation writers of urban fantasy find themselves in nearly a century later. The millennial visions of China Miéville, for example, reach back through their immediate predecessors – M. John Harrison, Tim Powers, Mervyn Peake – and themselves recapitulate a nightmare nineteenth century, only now through the prism of the twenty-first century's nightmares rather than those of the early twentieth. In Joyce Carol Oates's formulation, 'the contemporary City, as an expression of human ingenuity and, indeed, a material expression of civilization itself, must always be read as if it were Utopian (that is, "sacred") – and consequently a tragic disappointment, a species of hell' (11).

This utopian disappointment informs the ancestry of the fantastical city, and therefore that of the contemporary urban fantasy, which has at its centre the city transformed, either an existing city made fantastical or a fantastical city made real according to the narrative logic of the story in question. This city is descended not just from the London of Dickens and Eliot, but from the Prague of Musil and Kafka, the city which Edward Timms writes 'can only be glimpsed if we "go over" into that "other condition" which is "beyond"'[7] (one might add Rushdie's Bombay, Bulgakov's Moscow, even the fantastically anarchic Boston seen in Nathaniel Hawthorne's 'My Kinsman, Major Molineux'). For the urban fantasist, that 'beyond' can consist of a pocket fantastical universe, as in the underworld of Neil Gaiman's *Neverwhere* (1996), or it can be a location beyond a geographical border, as in Bordertown or the divided Canadian cities of Vancouver and Edmonton in Sean Stewart's *The Night Watch* (1997). Or we might find that the 'beyond' is everywhere and we are within it, as in New Crobuzon or Ambergris. Yet even in Ambergris there is a Below, and the scholar Duncan Shriek returns from it fearfully transformed.

Below, beyond, within

Every hero, in the Campbellian formulation, must journey to the underworld and return with a prize. Underworlds feature prominently in the texts of the urban fantastic, reconfigured and adapted to their new environments. In Neil Gaiman's *Neverwhere* (the novel version, not its television predecessor or comic successor), London Below is a fantastic world whose geography and nature reflect the names of various Underground stations. Knightsbridge becomes the perilous Night's Bridge, we meet an angel named Islington and a dangerous group of Black Friars, and so on. The protagonist of *Neverwhere*, Peter Mayhew, is drawn into a vengeful fallen angel's plot to reclaim his place in heaven; he meets a variety of magical characters and defeats the plot, returning to London Above. But there is nothing for him there, now that he knows of Below; unlike the traditional questing hero, Peter Mayhew does not want to return home, or at any rate doesn't want to stay there. At the end of *Neverwhere*, he has returned Below, in the company of the alluring Lady Door. *Neverwhere* thus neatly encapsulates several of the urban fantasy's constituent qualities: the fantastic pocket universe, the sense of alienation from city life that creates a desire that (in the urban fantasy) only the encounter with the uncanny can satisfy; and the flight from the city in the end.

London is also the focus of another Below, that of Tim Powers in *The Anubis Gates*. Here, a cabal of Egyptian sorcerers determines to reawaken their gods and unleash them on London as revenge for British suppression of pagan worship in the early nineteenth century. Their first attempt fails, and in the process creates the titular gates, which allow English professor Brendan Doyle to travel back in time in the company of an immortality-besotted millionaire. Doyle, a Coleridge scholar with a passion for the little-known (fictional) Romantic poet William Ashbless, undergoes a harrowing journey through a subterranean London presided over by the clown-wizard Horriban, who serves the Egyptians. Doppelgängers abound, and Doyle ultimately discovers that he has become Ashbless, as the Egyptian cabal runs afoul of the hunger of its deities, and London is saved. *The Anubis Gates* is at once a clever time-travel story and a prominent example of the intersection between urban fantasy and what might be called the magic historical, in which existing historical people and events are repurposed and given hidden fantastical motivations. It is also of interest because of the way it hearkens back to the tradition of novels in which a European city is under supernatural threat from a force that represents a less advanced or colonized culture. *Dracula* is the most prominent and influential of these, as the folk tradition of the Carpathians threatens the flower of English womanhood; but the motif, of the city under threat from a supernatural entity, resonates through the history of urban fantasy.

An American example of such a story is Emma Bull's *War for the Oaks*, in which the two courts of Faerie – Seelie and Unseelie – do battle for control of the city of Minneapolis. Eddi McCandry, an aspiring musician, is enlisted in the battle by a phouka, and plays a pivotal role in events while events play a pivotal role in shaping her into the kind of person and musician she has always wanted to be. Bull's Minneapolis is thoroughly infiltrated by fey creatures of every stripe, as are the various artistically inclined protagonists of Charles de Lint's novels. Newford, the mongrel city of de Lint's creation, incorporates elements of a number of North American cities, from Ottawa to Seattle, and, like Bull's Minneapolis, it is continually both threatened and enriched by the magical presence of fairy creatures. Urban fantasy's protagonists are often musicians or artists, but in the American urban fantasy of the 1980s and 1990s in which Faerie comes to the big city, the narratives' saturation in music is remarkable. Music – especially punk – becomes an emblem of alienation (as it was in the real world), but it is the punks and alienated dropouts who encounter the numinous (and perilous) presence of Faerie, whether in Minneapolis or Bordertown or Newford. In this way certain of these fantasies become consolatory, presenting the idea that the very qualities which unsuit the punk to bourgeois city life simultaneously give access to revelations that non-punks (or, more broadly, non-musicians) will never have. Incorporating a powerful wish-fulfilment fantasy, the Gaiman-Windling-de Lint strain of urban fantasy has attracted a passionate following.

In the novels of Elizabeth Hand, which often follow the trajectories of punk-inflected artists, the irruption of the fantastic is more likely to destroy the artist involved than point the way to any kind of emotional self-realization. The fey spirit-muse known as Larkin Meade in Hand's *Mortal Love* (2004) brushes across the emotional landscapes of her artistic paramours and leaves wreckage behind. She destroys Swinburne and Dante Rossetti and later battens on *Mortal Love*'s protagonist Daniel Rowlands, who in his research on Tristan and Iseult becomes a character in another doomed and dangerous romance. Like Powers in *The Anubis Gates* and *The Stress of Her Regard* (1989), Hand makes use of figures from English literary history, interpolating her created artists into this historical lineage and literalizing the relationship between artist and muse. Unlike Powers, Hand's demimonde is less indebted to the grotesqueries than to the historical excesses of the punk era and their consequences. Her literary reflexivity is of a different sort as well; where Powers's scholar Brendan Doyle becomes the poet he has always loved, the transformation is contained within the text. Eddi McCandry's transformation, too, is contained within the invented universe of Bull's novel. Hand's characters become iterations of previous stories, and her novels thus become conscious claims of a place in the lineage of such stories. (Powers too does this, but in later novels such as *Last Call*, 1992, an

Arthurian fantasy informed by chaos theory which is contemporary but not an urban fantasy.) In this self-conscious confrontation with (as opposed to continuation of) the literary tradition, Hand's work signals a more literary turn in urban fantasy.

The family romances, as John Clute has termed them, of Sean Stewart historicize and complicate the urban fantasy by rejecting the hero motif entirely in favour of deploying the fantastic as a way of investigating the vexed and dangerous bonds that hold families together. *The Night Watch* and *Galveston* (2000) occur in the aftermath of an event known as the Flood, in which various forms of magic returned to the world, taking on local inflections and sweeping away the technological society that existed before. In *The Night Watch*, Vancouver and Edmonton are divided, with pockets of ordinary humans trying to maintain what they can of their previous ways of living in the face of an overwhelming threat from the magical powers that surround them. The story pivots on the character of Winter, whose father has held together the Southside of Edmonton at the price of a terrible bargain with supernatural forces. The survival of her people demands a sacrifice of Winter that she never agreed to make, and this central theme of sacrifice pervades *Galveston* as well. Written after *The Night Watch*, *Galveston* is set some seventy years previously, in the immediate aftermath of the flood that caught the city in the middle of Mardi Gras revels. All of the half-believed carnivalesque absurdities of Mardi Gras have become real: magical Krewes control different aspects of the city, most prominently the Krewe of the lunar god Momus, whose underworld Carnival dictates much of what happens in the daylight city above. Opposed to him are Sloane Gardner and Joshua Cane, both of whom grapple with Momus for reasons of desperate love – Sloane for her dying mother and Josh for Sloane. In the end, whatever salvation they find is contingent; the sacrifices they make only enable a coming generation to make sacrifices of its own. Momus most clearly articulates the novel's disagreement with the closed returns to equilibrium that mark traditional genre literatures. '[L]ife is not fair,' he tells Sloane just before cheating on a bargain between them. 'The universe is not fair. The game is rigged. You can win for a time – find love, hope, happiness. But in the long run, the house always wins. It always wins. That's the truth.'[8]

While Hand and Stewart cast a more grounded and psychologically complex eye on the assumptions of urban fantasy, in the novels of Michael Swanwick, China Miéville and Jeff VanderMeer, both the wish-fulfilment and consolatory impulses found in the fantasy tradition are furiously repudiated. Inverting the fey-in-the-mundane-world default posture of much urban fantasy, Michael Swanwick startlingly reinvents the mode in *The*

Iron Dragon's Daughter (1993) Here a changeling girl, Jane, works in a Dickensian Faerie factory building cybernetic, intelligent mechanical dragons to fight in a war. Keeping her changeling status secret, she escapes with the aid of an obsolete, junked dragon on the edge of the factory grounds. Once she has found her way to the city, Jane manages to balance college with a whirlwind of sex, drugs and music – but all the while the dragon, Melanchthon, is waiting to call his favour in. Faerie here is not just dangerous, as it always has been, but deliberately debauched and horrible, as the residents well know. 'We are all of us living stories that on some deep level give us satisfaction. If we are unhappy with our stories, that is not enough to free us from them,' Jane's tutor Dr Nemesis tells her,[9] and her response is to acquiesce to Melanchthon's nihilistic plan to destroy the Spiral Castle, which holds the order of the universe together. This is the way out, *The Iron Dragon's Daughter* seems to say of the stories it recapitulates but refuses to keep living. The calcified dominant traditions of heroic fantasy (including as imported into many works of urban fantasy) are the Spiral Castle that the writer must confront and destroy.

Like Swanwick, Miéville is out to destroy a tradition, or the ruts it has fallen into, and his choice of milieu is not Faerie but the idea of the fantastic city. The assimilation of the rational into the supernatural, which in *Galveston* occurs against the backdrop of known history in a known city, expands to incorporate the idea of the city itself in *Perdido Street Station* and Jeff VanderMeer's *Shriek: An Afterword* (2006). *Perdido Street Station* is a steampunk extravagance, its city, New Crobuzon, rendered with brutal particularity as a mock-Victorian recreation of the stewing tensions of contemporary London: tensions between and among communities of immigrants (here Xenian, or non-human), simmering violent confrontation between an authoritarian militia and underground groups of political revolutionaries, the creation of a permanent underclass by the mechanisms of judicial punishment (here Remaking). The great cities of the heroic fantasy tradition are deliberately thrown on the literary junk-heap, and Miéville's attitude toward that tradition is perhaps aptly expressed in an interview between the khepri artist Lin and her gangster patron Motley:

> People were miserable, so communal art got stupidly heroic. Like Plaza of Statues. I wanted to spit out something … nasty. Tried to make some of the grand figures we all made together a little less perfect … [10]

Motley himself neatly diagrams the novel's overriding aesthetic in the same interview: 'Transition. The point where one thing becomes another' (40–1). Everything is always becoming something else in *Perdido Street*

Station, including Motley, whose body is a shambling, horrific explosion of Remaking. Through this bio-thaumaturgical process, the criminals of New Crobuzon are transformed either to inscribe their punishment into their bodies or to recreate them to perform a particular task. Transformation is inherent in the projects of Lin's lover Isaac Dan der Grimnebulin, a scientist whose Holy Grail is the control of crisis energy, a force latent in the forms of things but through which those forms can be forced into conflict with their own nature. The idea of crisis energy reflects through the entire construction of *Perdido Street Station*, which pushes the ordinary *topoi* of genre until they reach the point of crisis, where they are in conflict with themselves. What emerges is a new kind of fantasy – fantasy held in a shape to which it is unaccustomed. All of the elements of a fantasy are here: outrageous monsters, strange magics, a threatened city, a proliferation of non-human characters. Yet *Perdido Street Station* is also any number of other kinds of story. Grimnebulin's Faustian pursuit of crisis energy makes him careless and results in the deaths of a number of his friends and the maiming of Lin; a thoroughly Marxist worldview informs an extended sub-plot about a newspaper called the *Runagate Rampant* and its doomed editor and complicates the portrayal of the artistic bohemians; in the gradually exposed relationship between Motley and New Crobuzon's mayor, the brutality and corruption of government ramifies throughout every event in the novel. The slake-moths, dream-eating monsters from another dimension so terrifying that even demons from Hell won't confront them, are gleefully appropriated Lovecraftian plot devices around which the various genres of *Perdido Street Station* coalesce into a post-genre bricolage that remains in touch with its pulp roots.

The variety of races – some, such as the Russian vodyanoi, Egyptian khepri and Indian garuda, named from existing folklore and others invented from whole cloth – push the novel's genre status further, to a kind of crisis. They come to New Crobuzon, these various races and occupations, trailing the genre protocols that gave them life and creating in the process an urban fantastic in which urban is genus and fantastic species, instead of the other way around. But the characters we love are leaving the city; and it is guilty, mutilated, despised and heroic Yagharek alone who transforms himself to become a true citizen of New Crobuzon. The city is the place where all things are contingent, where Grimnebulin's logic might have produced a different result; but he was already gone when he made his choice. Yagharek, himself Remade, is fitted to New Crobuzon not just by his sin but by his twinned ambition to atone (by endangering his own life in pursuit of the slake-moths) and to assume responsibility for his own forgiveness (by regaining his powers of flight). New Crobuzon is where those people go who still believe they can transform themselves; New Crobuzon is where those people leave whose belief in transformation is broken. In the end, they leave the city – not for an imagined pastoral landscape, for none such exists in a world that can give birth to slake-moths – but for an indeterminate future.

And over it all preside The Bones, symbolic of the depthless history of the place now occupied by New Crobuzon. They occupy a superstitiously undeveloped parcel in the heart of the city, as if the prehistory of the site insists on a continuing presence (32). The Bones are ultimately meaningless; no one knows what animal they belonged to, or how long they have been there. What has happened before in the space now occupied by New Crobuzon (and, we are meant to understand, in the parts of the fantasy tradition against which *Perdido Street Station* rebels – no mention is ever made of an Old Crobuzon, or simply Crobuzon) survives only as monuments empty of meaning. New Crobuzon is the place where all things are not only possible, but mandatory. Everything has happened there.

Yet another tradition in the development of urban fantasy draws on metafictional innovations, characteristic of writers from Cervantes to Calvino, that continually complicate a text's fictional status and interrogate the reader's relationship to the events narrated. In Jeff VanderMeer's *Shriek: An Afterword*, the Victorian-hued and spore-besieged city of Ambergris becomes the central figure in the story of scholar Duncan Shriek, whose obsessive quest to discover the truth about the Gray Caps, a fungal race living in scheming exile below the city, is chronicled by his sister Janice in a narrative that was begun as an afterword to Duncan's own (never seen) *The Hoegbotton Guide to the Early History of Ambergris*. Janice's work is then heavily annotated by Duncan himself, whose version of events often contradicts Janice's. On one level, the story of *Shriek* is that of Duncan returning from his quest to find his sister gone and her book left behind. Through this filter, we read both of their versions of Duncan's life, and through those versions, we triangulate and infer much of the history of Ambergris itself. In the history of the city lurks the mystery of the Silence, the expulsion of the Gray Caps, the menace they pose in their desire to reclaim what was once theirs. The entire story is then recomplicated in 'A (Brief) Afterword' by a certain Sirin, who discovered the manuscript and undertook to publish it despite its dubious veracity. 'While many of the sections dealing with Ambergris' recent history had a general ring of truth to them,' we are told with a Cervantine flourish, 'these were inextricably interwoven with sections that contained the most outrageous accusations and assertions. What was true and what false, I might never know.'[11] The book ends with Sirin's summary of the difficulties involved in preparing the text for publication, complete with images of manuscript pages, and the editor's final speculations about the ultimate fates of Duncan and Janice Shriek.

What happens, then, in *Shriek* is not nearly as important as the manner of its telling. If *Perdido Street Station* is the hybridized apotheosis of genre heteroglossia, *Shriek: An Afterword* is the city fantastic reclaimed as the pure product of the formal innovations of Kafka, Calvino – and perhaps Robbe-Grillet, the title of whose *Topology of a Phantom City* offers a fine gloss on the narrative action of Shriek, as would Borges's 'Tlön, Uqbar, Orbis Tertius'. A third lineage is woven into the urban fantasy tradition here, alongside the previously incorporated folkloric-heroic and urban-sublime ancestries.

The waste land

In many contemporary urban fantasy texts, a tinge of German Expressionism shows through. Consider the demonic creatures of Heinrich Kley, or the titular figures in Georg Heym's poems 'Der Gott der Stadt' and 'Die Dämonen der Städte'. For the German Expressionists, there was something essentially infernal about the urban energies that drove their visions, and contemporary writers of urban fantasy adopt much the same ambivalence toward their own invented cityscapes. Edward Timms, writing about the fraught juxtaposition of Georgian pastoralism and German Expressionism, notes the 'myth of rural England' cultivated by British writers of the First World War generation.[12] Timms does not mention Tolkien, but the arcadian longings of *The Lord of the Rings* are of a piece with this tradition; much contemporary urban fantasy, rebelling against the consolatory impulse of the Tolkienian pastoral, rebels against the natural landscape as well. In *Perdido Street Station* and *Viriconium*, and to a lesser extent *Shriek*, the natural world is a source of horrors, and those who leave the city expose themselves to dangers whose incomprehensibility to a city dweller makes them more frightening than the known adversaries within the city proper.

But the city, perhaps, is no better. 'Civilization isn't what happens in the absence of barbarity,' one of Galveston's patron ghosts tells Joshua Cane. 'It's what we struggle to build in the midst of it.'[13] For the writer of contemporary urban fantasy (as for the various groups of writers before them who took up the problem of the urban), 'the city becomes the emblem of an insoluble historical crisis' (118), Timms writes. The fantastic, as it moves from an ahistorical arcadian past, encounters the contingent dread of the historicized urban present. In Harrison's Viriconium cycle, Tomb the Dwarf encounters this crisis most directly when he learns to tap into the technologies of the Afternoon Cultures and thus presides over the ominous reappearance of the Alstath Fulthor and the Reborn. The past coming to life hammers home the omnipresent sense that everything that might have mattered in Viriconium has already happened, that history is gone by, and that the Twilight people are fallen away from a past that must not only remain inaccessible, but has destroyed them by poisoning their world and littering it with incomprehensible and lethal technological remnants. They are dwellers in literal ruins, a literal waste land.

Even if not a waste land, the fantastic city is old, if not in its current incarnation then by virtue of being built on the remnants of preceding cities (and previous narratives). There is a consciousness in these stories of having come late to the party, of being interlopers into a story already written, of endlessly seeking after a meaning that would have been available had we only not arrived quite so far along in the history of the place whose essence we can never quite comprehend. Figurations of this sentiment abound in the texts of contemporary urban fantasy: the towering bones of New Crobuzon, the creeping fungal intrusions of Ambergris, the incarnations of historical Id in the subways of London. Most especially, perhaps, this sentiment pervades M. John Harrison's Viriconium, the setting of a story sequence whose science-fictional characteristics – lost technology and a post-apocalyptic setting – are forced into an uneasy co-existence with a storytelling mode that presents as fantasy. Although Viriconium proposes a technological origin for its uncanny phenomena, the nature of the characters' relationship to technology exemplifies Arthur C. Clarke's famous dictum that any sufficiently advanced technology is indistinguishable from magic. Thus a novel full of robots and powered weapons and human-made objects in the sky can read like a novel of fantasy, and from this collision between the nature of the narrative and the nature of its telling, a new and influential kind of text emerges.

In a 1921 review of Jean Cocteau's *Poésies*, Ezra Pound commented, 'The life of the village is narrative . . . In a city the visual impressions succeed each other, overlap, overcross, they are cinematographic, but they are not a linear sequence. They are often a flood of nouns without verbal relations.'[14] The fantastic tradition, coming from the enchanted village to the demonic city, itself becomes a palimpsest as the urban canvas explodes the conventions of the arcadian fantasy. The nineteenth-century *flâneur* is remade as the contemporary youth escaping adolescent alienation, and finding dangerous kindred spirits in the elven rebels and parading krewes of the fantastically colonized city. Then a second generation of urban fantasists overwrites the tradition yet again, this time locating the sublime not in the invasion of the city by the fantastic, but through a fantastic reconstitution of the nature of the city itself.

NOTES

1 Roland Barthes, 'Semiology and the Urban', in Neil Leach (ed.), *Rethinking Architecture: A Reader in Cultural Theory* (London: Routledge, 1997), pp. 166–72, at p. 172.

2 Joyce Carol Oates, 'Imaginary Cities: America', in *Literature and the Urban Experience: Essays on the City and Literature*, eds. Michael C. Jaye and Ann Chalmers Watts (New Brunswick, NJ: Rutgers University Press, 1981), pp. 11–33, at p. 11. (See now www.usfca.edu/~southerr/bellow03.html, retrieved 14 December 2008.)

3 Christophe Den Tandt, *The Urban Sublime in American Literary Naturalism* (Urbana: University of Illinois Press, 1998), p. x.

4 Raymond Williams, 'The Metropolis and the Emergence of Modernism', in Edward Timms and David Kelley (eds.), *Unreal City: Urban Experience in Modern European Literature and Art* (Manchester University Press, 1985), pp. 13–24, at p. 21.

5 Michael Long, 'Eliot, Pound, Joyce: Unreal City?', in Timms and Kelley, *Unreal City*, pp. 144–57, at p. 145.

6 Peter Collier, 'Nineteenth-Century Paris: Vision and Nightmare', in Timms and Kelley, *Unreal City*, pp. 25–44, at p. 37.

7 Edward Timms, 'Musil's Vienna and Kafka's Prague: In Search of a Spiritual City', in Timms and Kelley, *Unreal City*, pp. 247–62, at p. 262.

8 Sean Stewart, *Galveston* (New York: Ace, 2000), p. 194.

9 Michael Swanwick, *The Iron Dragon's Daughter* (New York: Avon, 1994), pp. 131–2.

10 China Miéville, *Perdido Street Station* (New York: Del Rey Books, 2000), p. 39.

11 Jeff VanderMeer, *Shriek: An Afterword* (New York: Tor, 2006), p. 341.

12 Edward Timms, 'Expressionists and Georgians: Demonic City and Enchanted Village', in Timms and Kelley, *Unreal City*, pp. 111–27.

13 Stewart, *Galveston*, p. 343.

14 Ezra Pound, Review of Jean Cocteau's *Poésies, The Dial* 70.1 (January 1921), p. 110.

18

ROZ KAVENEY

Dark fantasy and paranormal romance

The taxonomy of genres is always a work in progress. It is a way of describing empirical data, facts that may change across time. Dark fantasy, and the subgenres which can usefully be included within it – template dark fantasy and paranormal romance – are in some measure developments of the last two decades; they are publishing categories, but also ways of thinking about texts which already existed, or which were not automatically allocated to dark fantasy on their first appearance. Nothing that is said here is a criticism of earlier attempts at a taxonomy, so much as a clarification in the light of subsequent information and later texts.

John Clute in the 1997 *Encyclopedia of Fantasy* was almost sceptical about whether the term 'dark fantasy' was useful at all, pointing out that usage varied at that time to a remarkable degree, sometimes being used almost synonymously with 'Gothic fantasy', sometimes to sanitize horror fiction's perceived low-rent image. The *Encyclopedia* itself opts for a usage that this article will dispute:

> We define a DF as a tale which incorporates a sense of Horror, but which is clearly fantasy rather than supernatural fiction. Thus DF does not normally embrace tales of vampires, werewolves, satanism, ghosts or the occult, almost all of which are supernatural fictions (although such tales may include DF elements, while some DFs contain vampires, ghosts etc. . . .) (249)

Clute goes on to suggest that the term can be usefully applied to those heroic fantasies that include a serious possibility of the ultimate failure of that genre's usual positive resolutions, and, more usefully, that it can be used to describe those 'crosshatches in which the intersections between this world and an upswelling otherworld' are at least partly drawn from the vocabulary of horror fiction. It is quite specifically not a criticism of what Clute wrote in the 1990s to say that the greater part of what he says in his entry has become incorrect.

The rise of the paranormal romance, and of the template dark fantasy of which the paranormal romance is a subset (although a dominant strain), forces a reassessment of all of this. Template dark fantasy has in turn to be seen as part of a broader genre of dark fantasy, almost always set at the point where dark fantasy overlaps with the setting of urban fantasy. ('Template' is used here as a description of a mode of genre fiction in which a set of assumptions and characters are drawn out into the stuff of a series that need never end.) Most paranormal romances fall into this category with the stuff of the romantic novel thrown into the mix as well – as a general rule, template dark fantasy features male protagonists and paranormal romance female ones, but there are some clear exceptions to this. Lilith Saintcrow's Dante Valentine novels (2005–8), for example, though they contain erotic and romantic elements, can be argued, since those elements never dominate, to fall on the template dark fantasy side of a very loose boundary.

Dark fantasy needs in turn to be distinguished from horror, Gothic and the bleaker sort of heroic fantasy. Inevitably this involves arguing that some texts often seen in terms of those genres need to be reallocated to dark fantasy wholly or in part; part of literary taxonomy is always a matter of creating a canon. Clute's exclusion of vampires from dark fantasy is ironic given that template dark fantasy and paranormal romance, both clearly sub-sets of dark fantasy in the way it is understood in this essay, have been so totally dominated by a revisionist version of such creatures of the night. Fur-ther, paranormal romance has to be carefully disentangled from the more romance-oriented sort of space opera and planetary romance with which it is often classed by publishers and bookshops on the grounds that readers who like to mingle romantic fiction with genre elements, whether Gothic, sf or dark fantasy, do so irrespective of what the specific genre elements are. This is useful in terms of understanding the economics of the book trade, less useful when describing genre itself. Nonetheless, it is worth remem-bering that there are links across genres as well as lineages within them. It is also worth remembering that such mingling existed before deliberate attempts by publishers to create particular cross-over categories – a num-ber of the Darkover planetary romances of Marion Zimmer Bradley (1958 onwards) contain elements of romantic fiction, a genre in which Bradley also wrote.

Though this article concentrates on dark fantasy as a literary form, the influence on its development as a genre and publishing category of various television shows and a few films is undoubted and needs to be acknowledged. Crucially, *Buffy the Vampire Slayer* (1997–2003) and its spin-off show *Angel* (1999–2004) helped determine much of the vocabulary of the template form of the genre – both shows had an extensive range of spin-off novels and the original fiction of most of the writers who produced those spin-offs has tended to fall into the dark fantasy category. (At least one template dark fantasy series – Jim Butcher's Harry Dresden novels (2000 onwards) – and one paranormal romance series – Charlaine Harris's Sookie Stackhouse novels (2001 onwards) – have made it onto television, as *The Dresden Files* (2007–8) and *True Blood* (2008 onwards).) Similarly, certain comic books clearly belong to the genre and have influenced its development. If in what follows Angela Carter is to be seen as one of the prevailing influences on the evolution of dark fantasy, so too David Lynch, Chris Carter, Joss Whedon, Alan Moore and Neil Gaiman have to be seen as extremely influential as well. Their influence has been twofold, both in helping to create or refine some of the central tropes of the genre and in creating an appetite for it among an audience, particularly a young audience.

In retrospect, John Clute can be seen as excluding from dark fantasy several writers whom he particularly admired and whom he wished to describe in terms of his own preferred taxonomy of instaurational fantasy and so on. The Clutian taxonomy is often useful, but I would argue that it is not the only useful way to examine the work of, say, Elizabeth Hand or Jonathan Carroll, both of whom are central to a sense of dark fantasy as a genre within which work of real quality can be created. One of the major areas in which this article dissents from Clute is in his use of the term dark fantasy to describe those elements within heroic or high fantasy in which horror tropes are used, or in which the ultimate victory of good is not a coda towards which all else inevitably develops. Clearly, most of the key texts of high fantasy, as well as much third-rate and derivative work, are ones in which the quest for the cure to the world's pain is a successful quest, and in which the claims of the mundane and those of faerie, are successfully reconciled. Equally clearly, there are many texts of merit or interest in which this is not the case, because it was never the issue – obvious examples are the short fiction of Fritz Leiber, Lord Dunsany, Clark Ashton Smith and Robert E. Howard.

Those writers in particular, and a tradition deriving from them, largely precede the creation of high fantasy by Tolkien and his epigones, and there is an extensive tradition from Moorcock to Miéville which explicitly rejects Tolkien and his tropes, which indeed defines itself, to a large extent, through that rejection. I would argue that it is useful to see these traditions, which deal in rogues rather than unblemished heroes, and in the pursuit of hard cash rather than transcendence, as a separate genre, which one might usefully term low high fantasy or picaresque heroic fantasy. That element within otherworld fantasy which plays most extensively with both the imagery and the affect of horror fiction – much of Howard, say, and almost all of Smith – can be seen usefully as lodging within this genre.

Perhaps the most crucial distinction to draw, and in essence the hardest, is that between dark fantasy and horror. The two genres share much vocabulary and many key writers – there is always a sense in dark fantasy of its protagonists being in a jeopardy that is the default setting of horror. Part of the difference is that the central aim of horror is to create catharsis by confronting the reader with a world in which the worst thing happens to the characters with whom we identify, whereas the protagonist of dark fantasy comes through that jeopardy to a kind of chastened wisdom – the heroine of Elizabeth Hand's *Generation Loss* (2007), for example, comes to terms with the extent, but also the limits, of her failure as an artist. I acknowledge that this model of the difference means that many key texts which have always been considered as part of Gothic or of horror are annexed by dark fantasy – *Dracula*, for one. One of the reasons for this is the evolution of horror itself during the decades in which dark fantasy became discernible as a genre.

The early work of Clive Barker – whose mature, though less interesting, work clearly falls within dark fantasy – was instrumental in creating a particular flavour of horror which has been usefully termed 'splatterpunk'. His *The Books of Blood* (1984–5) defined a mode in which body-horror and a sense that nobody gets out of here alive fitted the zeitgeist – all humans are 'books of blood – wherever you open us, we're red'. There is a real contrast between this and his later work, the protagonists of which stand a reasonable chance of coming through with their souls intact, if not their bodies. Human existence was seen as a commodity traded by blind and uncaring forces – it is no coincidence that the rise of splatterpunk coincided with the 'triumph' of market liberalism under Thatcher and Reagan – and the only conceivable response was a hedonism of damnation, a relishing of the exquisite pain of one's own destruction. Amalgamated with the Lovecraftian tradition, and with an apocalyptic strain of urban fantasy that derives from psychogeography, a horror fiction that is explicitly and gloriously nihilist has its place still in the work of, say, Conrad Williams. Williams is a good example not only because of the extreme violence to which his characters are liable to be subjected, but also because those of his characters who make it through to the end of his novels without being killed will have made accommodations to evil that utterly destroy the people they used to be. In a very real sense, and without any eschatological dimension, they lose their souls.

There are individual texts whose genre attribution is contentious. When thinking through these necessary distinctions, it occured to me that Nicholas

Royle's *Counterparts* (1996) is just such a book. Most of Royle's work is readily placeable on the psychological horror side of the divide, but the use of Australian Aboriginal culture in *Counterparts* and in particular its use of spirit doubles would seem to place it on the dark fantasy side of the divide. *Counterparts* is the story of a rope walker who finds himself drawn to perform the sort of radical genital modification on himself common in some Australian cultures. It is a work which explores liminality in a splendidly terrifying way.

Luckily, I was able to interview Nicholas Royle over the internet almost immediately, and his responses were illuminating.

> I never knew what genre *C/parts* belonged to, but was not Splatterpunk. May have been Dark Fantasy. I did a story for Chris Morgan's anthology *Dark Fantasies* and that term enjoyed a degree of popularity for a while. I would use it to describe what I was doing. Most people thought *C/parts* was horror, just about. I always loved what you said about it, that it was on the cutting edge of genre and close to the border with something different. I do fear change. Clive Barker used to say that he embraced change in the stories in the *Books of Blood*. I felt as he said it that my own stories were limited because they tended to end in death, whereas his went on beyond death or beyond normality. In *Counterparts* I was always trying to have my cake & eat it. I wanted ambiguity to be right at the heart of it. I wanted the two characters to be one and two at the same time. I wanted to know what it was like to be here and there at the same time. I was scared of change and mutilation, yet attracted to it.

What then, is dark fantasy? I would argue that it is a genre of fantasy whose protagonists believe themselves to inhabit the world of consensual mundane reality and learn otherwise, not by walking through a portal into some other world, or by being devoured or destroyed irrevocably, but by learning to live with new knowledge and sometimes with new flesh – it is interesting how often and how positively physical revision of gender crops up as a theme, in say Carter's *The Passion of New Eve* (1977) or Hand's *Waking the Moon* (1994). Where splatterpunk sees all physical change as mutilation, in dark fantasy physical change may be a road to wisdom. Dark fantasy is a literature of accommodation and endurance, rather than of transcendence or despair; its intrinsic affect is the bitter-sweet and its presiding erotics the polymorphous. It is a genre to which a sense of the liminal is central and crucial and foregrounded, where in most other fantasy genres it is optional. Where splatterpunk saw change only in terms of mutilation and penetrative abuse, dark fantasy embraces change as the demon lover who brings wisdom as well as sensual bliss. Key modern texts in this version of the genre would include Fritz Leiber's *Our Lady of Darkness* (1977), Angela Carter's *The Infernal Desire Machines of Doctor Hoffman* (1972),

Elizabeth Hand's *Mortal Love* and *Generation Loss*, Jonathan Carroll's *The Land of Laughs* (1980), and M. John Harrison's *The Course of the Heart* (1992).

All of these texts fit my suggested pattern of the revelation to the protagonists of secret wisdom that nearly kills them, but which they survive. Leiber's drunk is haunted by a creature made of paper and despair, and saved by the heroine's invocation of logic and enlightenment, for example. Hand's photographer in *Generation Loss* learns to accept that there are limits to clear vision – we are never entirely certain that magic has actually been encountered and she is better off not knowing for sure. Sometimes survival is bought at the cost of corruption: the last line twist of *Land of Laughs* indicates as much. Sometimes survival involves a more complex transaction: engagement, in *The Course of the Heart*, with a lost European realm that opens Gnostic wisdom, brings with it death, entropy and the scent of roses.

What is particularly interesting is that most of the characteristics I have described persist even when the sexual and other politics of the writer are not the usual progressive and feminist values one can associate with most of the above writers – Carroll clearly belongs to the genre in spite of the reservations about female reproductive choice expressed in *A Child Across the Sky*, as does Tim Powers, in spite of his ultramontane Catholicism.

In what follows, the term template dark fantasy is used to describe that particular sort of dark fantasy which standardly consists of a series of thrillers/detective stories that are set in, and whose plots are determined by, a mundane world entirely, but not always visibly, permeated by the worlds of faerie or the supernatural. The protagonist of standard dark fantasy makes the discovery of the real, non-mundane nature of the world as an existential crisis; the protagonist of template dark fantasy has, typically, already made this discovery, or makes it in the first volume, and thereafter learns more in the course of solving puzzles, or acquiring refinements of technique for living in such worlds. Whether these protagonists are wizards, like Jim Butcher's Harry Dresden, or exorcists, like Mike Carey's Felix Castor, they are cousins to Chandler's Philip Marlowe and inhabit the same mean streets, even if they do so alongside vampires, ghouls and the more sinister denizens of faerie.

The same is often true of the heroines of paranormal romance to an extent that makes that subgenre a subset of template dark fantasy. Laurell Hamilton's Anita Blake (1993 onwards) – particularly in the earlier, better books – has always crimes and political quandaries to resolve, alongside her complicated amours with vampires and shape-shifters – crimes in which her skills as raiser of the dead was usually seen as a forensic technique and her legal right to execute supernatural transgressors a convenient plot device.

However, the driving force of the Anita Blake books is always, ultimately, Anita's relationships. What identifies a book as a paranormal romance has to be the extent to which its plot is determined by its erotic dimensions. Charlaine Harris publishes the Sookie Stackhouse novels as paranormal romance, which is right because the mundane world her telepath inhabits is one coping with the existence of vampires and others, and the plots of intrigue take much of their motive force from Sookie's relationships with supernatural beings. Harris's Harper Connelly books, on the other hand, are set in a completely mundane world, save for Harper's psychic power to find the bodies of murder victims and experience their last moments; Harper's emotional life is not defined by her power.

The importance of the erotic dimension is clear even in the special case of Stephenie Meyer's young adult Twilight novels (2005 onwards), which are, more or less explicitly, platforms for the author's strong religious views about sexual abstinence. The heroine's constant desire for the vampire Edward who courts her is the driving force of the books, along with the author's determination that it remain a tease until after Bella and Edward marry, at which point the emphasis shifts almost immediately to their off-spring and her odd relationship with Bella's former suitor, the werewolf Jacob. However, Meyer's use of the genre for her abstinence propaganda is itself an example of another aspect of dark fantasy in general and its more popular, commercialized forms in particular – these are books in which the supernatural is a free-floating signifier for race and sexuality in their various forms, in the way that superpowers are such a signifier in Marvel comics. The title sequence of *True Blood*, Alan Ball's television adaptation of the Sookie Stackhouse novels, shows a billboard with the slogan 'God Hates Fangs', punning on the anti-gay slogans of some American religious groups.

Most dark fantasy, and in particular most paranormal romance, is to some degree revisionist fantasy. Standard supernatural tropes are presented in ways that humanize them at the very least and in many cases domesticate them – one of the taproot texts for paranormal romance is Anne Rice's *Interview with the Vampire* and its sequels, which, if they did not invent the soulful misunderstood non-murderous vampire, certainly did a lot to popularize him. Those later treatments of vampires which return to the previous consensus and see them as essentially murderous – Barbara Hambly's *Those Who Hunt the Night* (1988), for example, or Joss Whedon's TV shows *Buffy the Vampire Slayer* and *Angel* – do so in the full knowledge of, and often with direct reference to, what Anne Rice had made a cliché.

In Whedon's work, most vampires are soulless bloodsuckers, but a few – Angel himself and his occasional ally Spike – are more complex, enabling Whedon to have his cake and eat it, so that the two vampires who are

Buffy's principal love objects retain the potential to turn on her in a moment if things go wrong. This is a strategy adopted by much template dark fantasy and paranormal romance: both Anita Blake and Sookie Stackhouse get caught up in vampire intrigues that have quite specifically to do with ethical debates about their relationship with humanity. Nor is this only a feature of template books, where there is a perpetual need to provide a context in which protagonists can be put in jeopardy, as the same trope occurs, directly concerned with vampires, in George R. R. Martin's *Fevre Dream* (1982), where the ethical debate among vampires is placed in a direct parallel to debates around slavery in the American period that culminated in the Civil War.

It can further be argued that dark fantasy is not only concerned with the effect of incursions of the other into the mundane, but with the ethical quandaries for both that this produces. Most dark fantasy is to some degree concerned with process as well as with consequences, which is why many key novels of the genre can be analysed in terms of a dialectical triad. Elizabeth Hand's *Waking the Moon*, for example, opposes the brutal legalisms of the male Benandanti to the murderous misandry of Angelica and her re-creation of a primordial matriarchy. Both abuse power, and both are trumped by the more humane feminism embodied in Oliver castrated by his lover Angelica, and reborn as a goddess to protect their child as a synthesis of what is good and just in both factions. In this dialectical respect, I would argue that Hope Mirrlees's *Lud-In-the-Mist* (1926) is a taproot text for dark fantasy in the way it presents both the dullness and class exploitation of the honest burghers, and the murderous wildness of faerie, and offers the rule of law, as presented by Nathanael at the climax, as the thing which will both rehabilitate both and allow them to live side by side.

Dark fantasy, like almost any other genre, has room within it to encompass its opposite. Some of the novels and tales of Angela Carter set up the possibility of an accommodation between the mundane and the other in order to dash our hope that this might be possible. Fortunato in *The Infernal Desire Machines of Doctor Hoffman* has the chance to achieve happiness and fulfilment with Hoffman's daughter, but chooses instead the path of duty and sterile boredom. In a particularly fine episode of *Buffy the Vampire Slayer*, 'Normal Again', Buffy has the chance to live an ordinary life with her parents at the price of destroying her supposed delusions by killing her friends and does not take it; though she is the victim of demonic poisoning, the episode allows for the possibility that the completely mundane place to which the poison takes her is an alternate world that actually exists – an interesting variant of the trope 'then I awoke and it had all been a dream'. Whereas Return, in a heroic fantasy (Sam Gamgee's 'I'm back', at the very end of *The Lord of the Rings* is the classic example) indicates the quiet chastened triumph of theodicy, in a dark fantasy, Return indicates failure and pathos.

There is, almost as a default, an overlap between the dark fantasy genre and fantasies of history in that all dark fantasy worlds have an implicit secret history. Tim Powers's *Deliver* offers an alternate view of Cold War espionage in which the crucial factor is less atomic secrets than contractual arrangement with djinns; M. John Harrison's *The Course of the Heart* involves a lost history of a European state; Elizabeth Hand's *Waking the Moon* involves a secret history of the relations between the sexes, a secret history all the more fascinating because of its allusion to the highly controversial theories of actual historians like Carlo Ginzburg and palaeoanthropologists like Marija Gimbutas.

In much dark fantasy, the protagonist is gradually initiated into a pre-existing body of lore and drawn into the wainscot society of those who already possess that lore, or into a conflict between such societies. The protagonists of the Jonathan Carroll sequence christened by John Clute the Answered Prayers novels (1987–93) inhabit what is recognizably the same world from novel to novel and share acquaintances – the reader is expected to retain information from one book to the next both as to these characters and to the mysteries they have uncovered. Some of Elizabeth Hand's fiction similarly shares concepts and characters – *Dark Light* (1999) is not so much a sequel to *Waking the Moon* as a pendant to it, sharing characters like Wernicke and the existence of the Benandanti.

Likewise, the central characters of template dark fantasy and paranormal romance series tend to accumulate knowledge and power from book to book. In Jim Butcher's Harry Dresden novels, for example, Dresden is caught up, simultaneously, in the internal struggles of the order of wizards to which he belongs, in the shifting balance of power between various kinds of vampire, the wars of the two rival courts of faerie, the affairs of those demonically possessed as a result of owning Judas's coins and so on, and, as the series wears on, he learns more of all of these worlds, and his learning curve is a significant part of the books' narrative drive. He also acquires more magical abilities, as does Anita Blake in the Laurell Hamilton series.

One of the stock differences between paranormal romances and other dark fantasies is that, as a default setting, they take place in universes in which that secret history is no longer secret. In the works of both Laurell Hamilton and Charlaine Harris, revelation of the existence of vampires and so forth has already happened, and the characters are all coping with that situation; this makes it possible for there to be a dimension of social acceptance to the obstacles the heroines' true love face.

In little more than a decade dark fantasy has become a definable genre with heavily commercial sub-categories and a number of definable genre rules. Like all genres, its existence is partly a matter of critical perception, partly a matter of the (not always rational) marketplace and partly a matter of the continued interest of writers and readers. It remains to be seen whether this process of generic evolution continues to develop the form or whether it will turn out to be a briefly fashionable subgenre like the locked room mystery or the Cold War spy story.

19

CATHERINE BUTLER

Modern children's fantasy

A survey of the last fifty years in children's fantasy, if it is to be more than a roll-call of those who have distinguished themselves in terms of popularity or critical acclaim, must step back from the fashions for individual books and authors to describe developments at a more general and, as it were, tectonic level. Such a description may be couched in literary terms, of plot, character and narration; or as reflecting changes in the world at large, especially the world as experienced by children; but ideally it should acknowledge and analyse the mutual influence of these factors. Social *mores* have changed greatly since 1960: can the same be said of children's fantasy fiction?

In British children's fantasy of the early 1960s, there was a distinct preference for real-world settings, usually rural or suburban, inner cities being generally the preserve of realist writers. Child protagonists would typically be white and middle-class, often holidaymakers or newcomers to an area. Indeed, a stock way to begin a book was with the train bringing the protagonist (alone, or with family) to the site of the adventure, as in Alan Garner's *The Weirdstone of Brisingamen* (1960) and Susan Cooper's *Over Sea, Under Stone* (1965). And an adventure it generally was, in the sense of being delimited in time, and bracketed by a life marked as recognizably ordinary. The adventure would be undertaken largely without the assistance of adults from the children's own circle and would revolve around, or be precipitated by, contact with a mysterious place, object or person. That contact frequently involved establishing some connection to the past (perhaps through ghosts, time slips, or the awakening of an ancient power), and such fantasies were usually conservative in the sense that they concerned an effort to maintain a rightful *status quo* by repelling some encroaching threat, or else to restore the *status quo ante* – perhaps by returning something lost or stolen. While character development might be complex and moral questions delicately poised, this complexity was ultimately underwritten by a set of universally agreed values. Much of the above description applies equally well to non-fantasy adventures such as Enid Blyton's

Famous Five series, and indeed some books (such as *Over Sea, Under Stone*) straddle the adventure/fantasy genre, with hints of the supernatural adding a numinous element to what might otherwise be a story set in consensus reality.

Fantasies fitting this description are still being published, but some of the factors that allowed them to flourish in the 1950s and 1960s are no longer so firmly in place. Normative assumptions about class, race and authority cannot be so lightly made in the more heterogeneous society of the twenty-first century; and opportunities for independent outdoor adventure are, for children up to a certain age (and especially those from middle-class backgrounds), considerably more limited than in the past. The nuclear families of classic children's fantasy can no longer be assumed, and the ubiquity of mobile phones and the internet has radically affected the ways in which young people organize and understand their social world. All this is well known, but it is worth noting the pressure exerted by such real-world considerations on the generic choices made by fantasy writers. Contemporary children's lack of independence militates in favour of fantasies set entirely in secondary worlds, or in which real-world protagonists are decisively removed from their familiar surroundings and transported to another time or reality, as in N. M. Browne's *Warriors of Alavna* (2000), Gillian Cross's *Lost* trilogy (2003–6) or Catherine Fisher's *Darkhenge* (2005). The fantasy quest may then become one of *self*-restoration or return. Alternatively, parents and other adults, no longer bastions of authority to the same extent as in previous generations, may be drawn into the adventure as more or less equal participants with the children. Several of Diana Wynne Jones's early books such as *The Ogre Downstairs* (1974) and *Eight Days of Luke* (1975) make this move, which has been continued more recently in Frances Hardinge's *Verdigris Deep* (2007). There has also been a growing interest in the possibilities offered by urban rather than rural landscapes as the setting of fantasy adventure, as seen in Michael de Larrabeiti's Borribles series (1976–86), Diana Wynne Jones's *Archer's Goon* (1984) and China Miéville's *Un Lun Dun* (2007).

It is now less common to find fantasies that are delimited in the sense that the end of the book and the resolution of the plot coincide with a return to non-fantastic 'normality'. Perhaps under the influence of realist young adult fiction, children's fantasies now usually ensure that encounters with the fantastic precipitate significant emotional growth, if not life-defining change, in their protagonists. Frequently they involve the acquisition of supernatural powers – a move with obvious potential for sequels and series, the proliferation of which has been one of the most striking developments in the field, particularly since the success of Harry Potter.

Fantasy is also sensitive to more general shifts in attitude, whether or not directly related to its traditional subject matter. Recent concern about ecological devastation, for example, has meant that pollution and global warming have displaced nuclear fallout as the environmental catastrophe of choice for dystopian fantasy; while Cold War-style totalitarianism is now less likely to feature than a world in which rampant capitalism, technology, political spin and pervasive marketing have reduced humans to oblivious engines of consumption, situations depicted in very different ways in Lois Lowry's *The Giver* (1993), Susan Cooper's *Green Boy* (2002), M. T. Anderson's *Feed* (2002) and Scott Westerfeld's Uglies quartet (2005–7). A different kind of example is provided by the representation of witches and witchcraft. With some exceptions, witches in early children's fantasy were unequivocally evil. However, perhaps influenced by the modern witchcraft movement, evil witches have come to share the stage with more positively conceived figures, such as those in Margaret Mahy's *The Changeover* (1984) and Monica Furlong's *Wise Child* (1987), for whom magic is a benign and natural talent. This, combined with the continuing tradition of comic witchcraft, such as that in Jill Murphy's Worst Witch books (1974–), means that 'witch' now signifies, not one familiar and identifiable type, but a broad field of semantic possibility that both writers and readers must learn to navigate.

Finally, the politicization of mythology has become an increasingly prominent feature during this period. Myth and folklore have long provided raw material for fantasy writers, with Celtic culture being an especially abundant source, both for writers from Britain and Ireland (Garner, Cooper, Fisher, Pat O'Shea, Jenny Nimmo) and for those who have imported such traditions into the New World, such as Lloyd Alexander, Madeleine L'Engle and, more recently, Holly Black. Nor have the the Greek and Norse gods been neglected, as Nancy Farmer's *The Sea of Trolls* (2004) and Rick Riordan's Percy Jackson series (2005–) demonstrate. While European mythologies have been treated as common property, however, American and Australian writers of European descent have become more reluctant to draw on the mythological traditions of their own lands. Patricia Wrightson's books *The Nargun and the Stars* (1973) and the Wirrun trilogy (1977–81) won numerous awards when first published, but her use of Aboriginal myth has since been criticized by those who see in it an appropriation of indigenous culture,[1] and recent Australian writers such as Garth Nix have found themselves warned off from using Aboriginal material.[2] Analogous sensitivities surround the use of Native American myth. It remains to be seen how the political implications of adapting (or appropriating) mythology will affect the genre in the future.

If, as I have suggested, children's fantasy was a generally conservative genre at the start of this period, the last five decades have seen a far more complex picture emerge. In the remainder of this chapter we shall consider the work of four influential writers within the genre, and ask how far it has proved possible to write radical children's fantasy – that is, fantasy that is self-critical, responsive to changes in the world beyond itself, and questioning of literary and political authority.

Alan Garner is an appropriate figure with which to begin our examination, since his work evinces a continuing fascination with the relationship between the shaping power of tradition (frequently understood in fantastic or magical terms) and the ability of individuals to determine their own destiny. This interest runs alongside a continual and ruthless process of formal and stylistic self-reinvention, and it is on Garner's own engagement with the power of literary tradition that we will concentrate here.

Garner's first book, *The Weirdstone of Brisingamen* (1960), was a startling debut, but its originality lay largely in its breathtaking revisioning of the countryside around Alderley Edge in mythic terms. In other respects it and its sequel were stories of the familiar type noted above, featuring middle-class protagonists who arrive in a new place only to find themselves inducted into its magical secrets and given a world saving quest. For Garner's decisive break with fantasy convention we must look to his third novel. *Elidor* (1965) is a strangely constructed novel that appears at first to be retreading Narnian territory. As in C. S. Lewis's *The Lion, the Witch and the Wardrobe* (1950) four siblings find themselves transported unexpectedly to a parallel world in need of redemption – a redemption to be achieved only by fulfilling the terms of an obscure prophecy. Garner reverses the proportions of Lewis's book, however, for only the early chapters are spent in the world of Elidor, and most of the novel concerns the children's attempt to keep hidden the treasures they bring back from that world for safekeeping. At home in Manchester, they find that the treasures take on an unprepossessing appearance, with a sacred spear, for example, becoming an iron railing. The transformation is a disguise, but one that has an ambiguous significance. Positively, it can imply the potential of nondescript objects to be revealed (when viewed rightly) as precious and powerful, like the wardrobe in Lewis's book. Negatively, the treasures' transformation suggests that even a magical realm may be reduced to dust at the touch of the mundane, and that a preoccupation with forlorn fairy lands may disable one from functioning in one's own world. For much of the book three of the four siblings are sceptical that the events in Elidor even took place, a pattern that simultaneously rehearses and subverts Lewis's example. Although *Elidor* ultimately validates the faith of the youngest child, Roland, it does so with some hesitation.

Elidor also introduces a note of moral ambivalence largely absent from Garner's earlier books, along with a new mistrust of authority. Garner was growing impatient with expository, Gandalf-style mentors and their habit of absenting themselves at times of danger – a habit to which Cadellin, the wizard in his first two books, had been particularly prone. In *Elidor* this scepticism centres on the figure of Malebron, a mysterious native of Elidor who sends the children into danger, first in his own world and later in theirs, but who provides them with no evidence that his cause is just, and then disappears from the book entirely. If Lewis's Pevensies were potential Kings and Queens of Narnia, the humbler Watsons are never more than foot soldiers in a war whose shape and purpose remain foggy to the last. Their brutal demobbing in the final pages of the book leaves them stranded 'alone with the broken windows of a slum',[3] with nothing tangible to show for their experience.

With *Elidor* Garner was beginning to deconstruct the unremarked ideological scaffolding of existing British fantasy: by blurring the sharp division implied by portal fantasies between the fantastic and the mundane; by picking away at good-versus-evil dualisms; by interrogating the assumption that child protagonists (and the implied reader) are middle-class and London-based; and by questioning the usual sources of expository authority, whether in the form of prophecies or of mentors such as Cadellin and Malebron. While none of these things is original to *Elidor*, in combining them Garner produced a fantasy that established new rules and boundaries for the genre, even as it evinced a distrust of rules and boundaries.

The fruit of these developments was *The Owl Service* (1967), Garner's most successful book for children. *The Owl Service* does without any obvious portal between the mundane and the fantastic: rather, the fantastic is shown to be immanent in the mundane world. An isolated North Welsh valley becomes a storehouse of mythic power associated with Lleu Llaw Gyffes, Blodeuwedd and Gronw Pebyr, whose tragic love story is related in *The Mabinogion*. This power is always present *in potentia* and is made manifest whenever it finds an appropriate conjunction of young, emotionally vulnerable people. *The Owl Service* offers a profound view of the relationship between mythological and linear time,[4] but its topos of repetition also suggests a view of myth as compulsive and obsessional, a force to be propitiated or resisted rather than unthinkingly revered. The book thus continues the trend begun in *Elidor* of approaching myth and prophecy with a hermeneutics of suspicion, rather than the faith conventional in earlier fantasies. In a decade that promoted individualism and questioned established structures of authority Garner was one of the first writers for children to expose and challenge the conservatism of high fantasy.

If Garner rewrote the tradition of primary-world children's fantasy, the revolutionary credentials of Ursula K. Le Guin as a writer of secondary-world fantasy are not so immediately apparent. In the first three books of her Earthsea series, beginning in 1968 with *A Wizard of Earthsea*, Le Guin uses many of the motifs given classic fantasy form by J. R. R. Tolkien in *The Hobbit* (1937) and *The Lord of the Rings* (1954–5). Like Middle-earth, Earthsea is a world (complete with endpaper map) in which medieval technology co-exists with wizardly magic, and humans with dragons. Like Tolkien's Frodo, Le Guin's protagonist, the mage Ged, is a figure born in a backwater but destined to determine his world's fate. And Le Guin's prose, supple and poetic as it is, shares with Tolkien's an archaic quality of cadence and word choice. Moreoever, in Earthsea wizardly power – which derives from an understanding of the language of creation, or True Speech – is understood as an arduous and learned *recuperation* of a magic originally indivisible from nature itself, and in this sense Le Guin's books share with Tolkien's an elegiac sense of being set in a world long decayed from its pristine glory.

Nevertheless, Le Guin's books also diverge significantly from Tolkien's model, particularly in the area of moral dualism. There is no Dark Lord in *A Wizard of Earthsea*: Ged's primary antagonist is an aspect of himself. Both Jungian psychology and Le Guin's commitment to Taoism inform a book in which wisdom and happiness are the products of an achieved balance between opposing impulses, rather than a reward for marching under the right banner. This has implications for the structure of her plots, which eschew battles, and in which quests are often inward- rather than outward-focused. In *A Wizard of Earthsea* Ged spends as much time fleeing from his shadow self as he does hunting it; while the quest for the ring of Erreth-Akbe in *The Tombs of Atuan* (1971) is told from the point of view not of the quester but of the treasure's guardian, the young priestess Tenar.

Even so, the three books of the original *Earthsea* trilogy culminate in what is a largely conventional form of closure. At the end of *The Farthest Shore* (1972) Ged has attained his own spiritual wholeness, restored the broken ring of Erreth-Akbe, and established the young king Lebannen on the throne, bringing peace to the Earthsea archipelago. These acts embody the achievement of balance between the realms of the spiritual and the political, the personal and the public. While Lebannen must come to terms with his new authority, Ged matches that acceptance with his own act of abnegation, sacrificing his magic in order to stabilize Earthsea's magical ecology. All this is fitting in the terms in which Le Guin had constructed her fantasy, and the Earthsea sequence seemed complete both to its author and to her readers. However, as Le Guin grew more committed to feminism in the 1970s the masculine bias of her trilogy became a source of increasing dissatisfaction. In Ged she had rejected the eurocentricity of high fantasy by creating a hero with red-brown skin, but she had been less vigilant with regard to gender. 'Weak as women's magic' and 'wicked as women's magic', dismissive formulae quoted in the first book,[5] were only confirmed by subsequent events. *The Tombs of Atuan*, in particular, with its portrayal of a death cult in the care of a female priesthood, tended to underwrite the humane superiority of the male-only wizard school at Roke. More fundamentally, Le Guin came to recognize that in the Western world 'heroism has been gendered' as male,[6] and that the kinds of heroic stories possible within that tradition excluded women as protagonists more or less by definition.

What turned out to be the fourth book in the Earthsea 'trilogy', *Tehanu*, was published in 1990. It centres on Tenar, the young woman – now a middle-aged widow – featured in *The Tombs of Atuan*. Ged himself, having foregone his magic, is present, but Le Guin places him somewhat to the side of the action. It becomes clear that he has not found it easy to establish a new role after a lifetime of magehood, and his sense of loss retrospectively complicates his sacrifice of power in *The Farthest Shore*. Instead, Le Guin describes a different kind of magic, learned not in the esoteric surroundings of a wizards' college but bound up with the practical tasks and skills of daily life, particularly the life of women. The lore-based magicians of Roke are represented as arrogantly contemptuous of Tenar, whom they dismiss both for her sex and for her social class. They are perhaps easy targets, but Le Guin was working very consciously against a tradition in which power is the surest path to success, and wished to forge an alternative heroism that did without 'quest, contest and conquest as the plot, sacrifice as the key, victory or destruction as the ending'.[7] In the book's conclusion the apparent passivity of women is re-evaluated as a subversive choice of freedom over power. This re-evaluation is personified in Tenar's foster-child Tehanu. Raped, half-blinded and dreadfully scarred by fire, Tehanu is also a dragon, with all a dragon's untamable ferocity, and a natural ability to speak the True Speech that wizards must painfully learn.

The Earthsea series has now been completed twice. *Tehanu* – 'the last book of Earthsea' – has itself been supplemented by two further books, *Tales from Earthsea* (2001) and *The Other Wind* (2001). Meanwhile, Le Guin, now in her eighty-third year, is three books into a new children's fantasy series, The Annals of the Western Shore, begun in 2004 with *Gifts*. There has been a great deal of secondary-world fantasy in the forty years since *A Wizard of Earthsea*; but few writers have tried more consciously than Le Guin to test the genre's flexibility and potential for reinvention.

Philip Pullman's major fantasy sequence, His Dark Materials, has an equally complex relationship with its literary and intellectual heritage. Pullman's immediate fantasy forerunners include C. S. Lewis and Joan Aiken; but he also places himself in a longer tradition of English radicalism going back to Milton and Blake. One way to think about His Dark Materials is as a reworking of *Paradise Lost* in Blakean terms, in which a cruel, Urizenic God is defeated by the promethean energy of youth. Blake famously wrote of Milton that he was of the Devil's party without knowing it: Pullman has commented that, by contrast, *he* is of the Devil's party and knows it perfectly well.[8]

His Dark Materials, consisting of *Northern Lights* (1995; *The Golden Compass* in the USA), *The Subtle Knife* (1997) and *The Amber Spyglass* (2000), tells the epic story of Lyra Belacqua, a girl who lives in the Oxford of a steampunk universe parallel to our own. Lyra's adventures – and, later, those of her friend and eventual lover Will Parry – take in several worlds and involve encounters with a range of beings including witches, armour-plated bears, harpies and angels. Particularly striking is Pullman's conceit of the daemon – a physical manifestation of a person's soul, that takes the form of an animal or bird. Daemons are shape-changers prior to puberty, but assume a fixed form thereafter.

This is not a work of alternative history in any strict sense, but Pullman hints that Lyra's is a world in which the Reformation never happened and an untrammelled Church has acquired hegemonic power. Organized religion is represented *à la* Blake as a force that represses people's true natures, and in *Northern Lights* this is symbolized in the horrific project to prevent children from gaining sexual maturity by surgically 'severing' them from their daemons. Lyra thwarts that plan, but her larger role within the sequence is to become a second Eve, one whose 'fall' into knowledge is a liberation rather than a curse, heralding the foundation of a Republic of Heaven.

With its narrative power and imaginative richness, His Dark Materials puts Pullman in the first rank of storytellers; but the work aspires to far more than entertainment. His polemical depiction of organized religion has been notably controversial, but Pullman has also been engaged in a *literary* rebellion against fantasy fiction itself. He has repeatedly stated that His Dark Materials is not in fact fantasy at all but rather 'stark realism' – a distinction he explains in terms of his intention to say something true about human psychology and the human condition. The implication that previous writers in the genre had failed to do this, relying instead on 'shoot-em-up games', speaks eloquently of Pullman's artistic loyalties and anxieties, although it is hard to acquit of a certain hubris.[9]

Another of Pullman's targets is more specific to children's literature. In *His Dark Materials* the Church's attempt to prevent sexual experience by severing children from their daemons is a barbaric act; but it is also a graphic example of the fetishization of innocence and the horror of 'growing up' that is one legacy of the Romantic idealization of childhood. Pullman finds C. S. Lewis to be a particularly grievous offender here, with the deaths of the Pevensie children at the conclusion of the Narnia sequence a definitive form of severance through which they are 'saved' from the temptations of teenage sexuality – a move that led Pullman to accuse Lewis of writing 'propaganda in the service of a life-hating ideology'.[10] Pullman's inversion of the values associated with the transition from childhood is thus an attack not only on the doctrine of original sin, but more generally on the construction of childhood in modern literature and culture.

Having overturned the Christian-Romantic model of human development, however, Pullman surprisingly preserves its structure intact. In *His Dark Materials*, as in the tradition it critiques, puberty is *the* life-defining event, the point at which the form of one's daemon becomes fixed for ever. Prior to the settling of one's daemon one cannot know 'the kind of person' one is, while afterwards significant change is not to be expected.[11] Coming from a writer whose project is one of liberation from ideological repression this is a highly restricted vision of the human potential for growth and self-determination. There are other indications, too, that Pullman's rebellion is not as wholesale as might first appear. In particular, the conclusion of his story is still in thrall to a moral and aesthetic vision that defines satisfying artistic closure in terms of self-sacrifice and self-denial – exemplified in the deaths of Lyra's parents and in Lyra's and Will's decision to part for ever. Whether or not Pullman is of C. S. Lewis's party without knowing it, he has not discarded his literary heritage quite as thoroughly as his own comments might suggest, and much of the power of his work comes from his ability to draw profoundly on a fantasy tradition to which he very much belongs.

J. K. Rowling has none of Pullman's iconoclasm, but in her own way she has done no less to reshape the nature of modern children's fantasy. Since the publication of *Harry Potter and the Philosopher's Stone* in 1997 Rowling has been by far the most widely read writer in the field. Her accessible style, humour, twisty but comprehensible plots and ability to people her world with vividly sketched characters have given her books unprecedented popularity. The Harry Potter series (1997–2007) ranges from social satire to plot-token quest fantasy, although its most pervasive generic debt is to boarding-school fiction, with its friendship groups, its emphasis on food and sport, its misunderstandings and out-of-bounds adventures.[12] Rowling's instinct as a writer is syncretistic rather than subversive, her main generic innovation lying in the marriage of two familiar types of fantasy structure. In the first of these the mundane landscape is secretly peopled with magical beings, who are carrying on the real business of the world under the noses of the general populace. Fantasies about magical elites always involve ideological questions, especially when the elite is a secret one. Such books must negotiate the insidious temptation to imagine oneself an 'insider', a feeling that can easily slide into scorn for those outside the secret. This is a recurrent issue within Rowling's series, where, although the contempt felt for non-magical people (Muggles) by some wizards is clearly meant to be deplored, even the sympathetic characters are characterized by attitudes ranging from casual prejudice to benevolent paternalism.

The second fantasy structure is that of the portal fantasy. In being taken to the wizarding school of Hogwarts, a place impenetrable to Muggles, Harry is effectively transported to another world, with its own customs and history. In the series' early books portal fantasy is the dominant mode, and the chapters set outside Hogwarts (generally dealing in Dahl-esque fashion with Harry's repressive foster-family) serve primarily as the school's unattractive foil. As the series progresses, Rowling emphasizes the ways in which magical and Muggle communities interpenetrate, and the exent to which events in one have important effects on the other.

The transition between these structures creates some problems of consistency. For example, it is entirely appropriate in a portal fantasy that a magical family such as the Weasleys should be ignorant of Muggle ways. Mr Weasley's fascination with non-magic users is comparable with that of C. S. Lewis's Mr Tumnus, whose Narnian bookshelf contains such volumes as *Is Man a Myth?*[13] However, the Weasleys live in modern Britain, where Muggle/wizard interaction and even intermarriage is commonplace, to the point where 'pure blood' wizards have become a rarity. Given this, and the fact that Mr Weasley is employed as an expert in Muggle technology, their lack of knowledge comes to seem quite implausible.

At Hogwarts Rowling shows us a wizarding world at once excitingly different from our own and reassuringly similar to it. She is exuberantly imaginative in combining fantasy ingredients, but does so by grounding the wizarding world in familiar literary models and in the mundane world itself, rather than by making it radically alien. Just as in mathematics a shape can be transformed by such operations as reflection and rotation, so Rowling applies a systematic set of transformations to the mundane in order to produce her brand of the fantastic. These include:

- *Realization*. The most common fantasy transformation, this involves taking things that in our world exist only as myth or folklore – magic wands, unicorns, dragons – and making them real.
- *Substitution*. Substitution occurs when something in the magical world exhibits a structural correspondence with something in the mundane world. *The Daily Prophet* is the equivalent of any real-world newspaper, while the wizarding examinations O. W. L. S. recall GCSEs. Much of Rowling's humour – like that of her comic predecessors, such as Jill Murphy – comes from using substitution in order to normalize the exotic.
- *Exaggeration* works by reproducing something from the mundane world in a more extreme form. Ordinary sweets come in many flavours; but Bertie Bott's come in *every* flavour. Some people keep dangerous pets; but Hagrid keeps *extremely* dangerous pets. In combination with substitution, exaggeration is Rowling's prime mechanism for satire – as in the regime of Dolores Umbridge at Hogwarts in *The Order of the Phoenix*, which caricatures the over-involvement of the government in regulating British state schools.
- *Animation* involves giving movement and/or sentience to inanimate objects. At Hogwarts the figures in portraits can move and speak; and angry letters shout at their recipients. In Rowling's hands, this technique is generally comic; elsewhere, as in Neil Gaiman's *Coraline* (2002), it can be an effective horror technique.
- Finally there is *antiquation*. Rowling's magical world is old-fashioned in many ways that have nothing to do with magic: the Hogwarts train runs on steam; the children write with quills; the Minister for Magic wears a bowler hat. All these belong to non-magical history, but are used here to distinguish the magical world from the mundane present.

Using these techniques Rowling is, as noted above, able to portray a world both exotic and cosily familiar – a combination that underlies much of her popular appeal. By contrast with Le Guin's Earthsea, which is a world with its own history, ecology and culture, Rowling's wizarding world is always recognizable as a version of the mundane – ironized, inverted, exaggerated or otherwise transformed as it may be.

Garner, Le Guin, Pullman and Rowling all approach fantasy with very varied intentions and expectations of what the genre can and should be. Their generic and stylistic diversity gives some impression of the range of modern children's fantasy. Our concentration on these four has necessarily involved neglecting other authors and aspects of children's fantasy, however. There has not been space to do more than allude to the healthy continuance of ghost and time-travel stories, to comic fantasy or to the anti-hero protagonists of such writers as Eoin Colfer and Jonathan Stroud. A more comprehensive study would also have considered the various texts in which fantasy borders realist, Gothic, horror and science fiction, which have all been influential in shaping what fantasy is and can be in the current age. What I hope to have shown is that, while not every fantasy writer is consciously engaged in iconoclasm and subversion, the redefinition of fantasy is a constant process, driven by the intelligent engagement of writers with the changing world around them. The next fifty years have already begun.

NOTES

1 Clare Bradford, *Reading Race: Aboriginality in Australian Children's Literature* (Carlton : Melbourne University Press, 2001), pp. 146–8.
2 Garth Nix, *Across the Wall: A Tale of the Abhorsen and Other Stories* (London: HarperCollins, 2006), pp. 167–8.
3 Alan Garner, *Elidor* (1965) (London: Fontana Lions, 1974), p. 160.
4 Charles Butler, *Four British Fantasists: Place and Culture in the Children's Fantasies of Penelope Lively, Alan Garner, Diana Wynne Jones, and Susan Cooper* (Lanham, MD, Toronto and Oxford: Children's Literature Association and Scarecrow Press, 2006), pp. 84–8.
5 Ursula K. Le Guin, *A Wizard of Earthsea* (1968) (Harmondsworth: Puffin, 1971), p. 15.
6 Ursula K. Le Guin, *Earthsea Revisioned* (Cambridge, MA: CLNE/Green Bay, 1993), p. 5.
7 *Ibid.*, p. 13.
8 Philip Pullman, 'I Am of the Devil's Party': Interview with Helena de Bertodano. *Daily Telegraph*, 29 January 2002, www.telegraph.co.uk/culture/donotmigrate/3572490/I-am-of-the-Devil's-party. html (accessed January 2009).
9 Philip Pullman, 'ACHUKA Interview', 1998, www.achuka.co.uk/archive/interviews/ppint.php (accessed January 2009).
10 Philip Pullman, 'The Dark Side of Narnia', *The Guardian*, 1 October 1998. Reproduced in *Cumberland River Lamppost*, www.crlamppost.org/darkside.htm (accessed January 2009).
11 Philip Pullman, *Northern Lights* (London: Scholastic, 1995), p. 167.
12 Pat Pinsent, 'The Education of a Wizard: Harry Potter and His Predecessors', in Lana A. Whited (ed.), *The Ivory Tower and Harry Potter: Perspectives on a Literary Phenomenon* (Columbia: Missouri University Press, 2002), pp. 27–50.
13 C. S. Lewis, *The Lion, the Witch and the Wardrobe* (London: Geoffrey Bles, 1950), p. 19.

20

VERONICA SCHANOES

Historical fantasy

What is the relationship between fantasy and history in historical fantasy novels? The historical fantasy is a hybrid of two seemingly opposed modes, fantasy, with its explicit rejection of consensus reality, and historical fiction, a genre grounded in realism and historically accurate events. Jana French, in her work *Fantastic Histories: A Dialogic Approach to a Narrative Hybrid*, argues repeatedly that the tension in historical fantasy comes from the opposition of two extremes, 'a clashing of two vastly different discursive mediations of the historical world'.[1] She writes that such a clash is generative of insights into the nature of historical writing precisely *because* such an extreme contrast 'radically destabilize[s] the normal contract between reader and text which tells us what kind of novel we are reading' (5). Thus French takes an extreme separation, or even opposition, between history and fantasy to be normative, and historical fantasies to be remarkable precisely because they put two radically dissimilar discourses into dialogue. But K. L. Maund in John Clute's *Encyclopedia of Fantasy* points out that 'Fantasy as a genre is almost inextricably bound up with history and ideas of history,'[2] relating fantasy to the historical swashbucklers of H. Rider Haggard and others, and noting that a number of fantasy authors such as Judith Tarr and fantasy scholars such as Farah Mendlesohn have been trained as historians. Writers of historical fiction and of fantasy must engage in world-building, in constructing and familiarizing their readers with a world foreign to their own and yet fully realized *as* a world complete unto itself with its own mores, customs and tensions. Thus in historical development, individuals and techniques, fantasy and historical fiction are not as polarized as French claims.

French herself concludes that historical fantasy highlights 'the common ground between realism and fantasy as narrative modes, foregrounding the conventions and ideological assumptions of the former in order to reveal its mediation of real world referents' (2). In other words, the literary texts she favours for study use historical fantasy to interrogate 'not only the traditional mimetic strategies of historical representation, but also the picture of "the real" that history presents' (10). French locates in these novels an epistemological tension between how we know what we claim to know about history and that which is left out of such discourse – this is precisely the role that Rosemary Jackson envisions for the genre of fantasy when she writes that 'fantasy characteristically attempts to compensate for a lack resulting from cultural constraints: it is a literature of desire, which seeks that which is experienced as absence and loss'.[3] In this case, fantasy represents the ways of knowing and making sense of the world that are excluded by the dominant discourse of history.

The frame scholar

Certain fantasy novels interweave stories of the present with stories of the past. Mary Gentle's *A Secret History: the Book of Ash #1* (1999) and Elizabeth Hand's *Mortal Love* (2004) both involve contemporary scholars seeking to understand the mysteries of women historical and mythical, demonstrating the gendered roles whereby men in this genre study and women are studied. We read the stories of their efforts as well as the stories they themselves seek to understand. These scholars' tasks are made more complicated and difficult by the magic that makes these novels historical fantasies. Thus the dynamic between history and fantasy is embodied in the troubled relationship between researcher and topic.

Mary Gentle's *A Secret History: the Book of Ash #1* (one of a four-book series originally published in the United Kingdom in 1997 as a one-volume novel) takes the form of a history of a fourteenth-century female warrior of Burgundy written by one Pierce Ratcliff and interspersed with communications between Ratcliff and his editor. Ratcliff begins by marking a sharp distinction between history and legend in relation to the legendary woman warrior Ash:

> Any historical personage inevitably acquires a baggage train of tales, anecdotes and romantic stories over and above their actually historical career. These are an entertaining part of the Ash materials, but not to be taken seriously as history. I have therefore footnoted such episodes in the Ash cycle as they occur: the serious reader is free to disregard them.[4]

Thus Ratcliff's initial appearance in the text (this quotation occurs on the second page of the novel) is one that not only demarcates historical truth from fantastic romance, but also establishes himself as a respectable scholarly arbiter of which is which via that standard-bearer of the scholarly text, the footnote, *as well as* implicating the reader in these distinctions. The 'serious reader', we are told, will wish to disregard fantastic episodes entirely – not even reading them for entertainment or for completion's sake.

Yet soon after making such firm distinctions about what belongs in the discourse of history and what is to be excluded, Ratcliff calls on the mutability of historical narratives, writing of his work that 'With the new material I have uncovered, I hope to bring to light, once again, those facts which do not accord with our idea of the past, but which, nonetheless, *are* factual' (5). Here Ratcliff acknowledges that scholarship actually makes and remakes our vision of the past, even when, or especially when, the fruits of such research conflict with previous historical paradigms. Ratcliff goes on to say that 'That this will then involve considerable reassessment of our views of Northern European history is inevitable, and the historians will just have to get used to it!' (5). He thus highlights that our understanding of history is a narrative construction, amenable to drastic change in the face of new evidence or theories; it is thus as much a discursive genre as fantasy itself.

Ratcliff acknowledges the constructedness of historical narrative when he writes of his own work – the same work he scrupulously demarcated as history above – that 'what it narrates is what these people genuinely *thought* to be happening to them. And, if you bear in mind the major alteration to our view of history that will take place when *Ash: The Lost History of Burgundy* is published, perhaps we would be wise not to dismiss anything too casually' (47). With this comment, Ratcliff calls into question the function of historical narrative: is it to reproduce a lost historical viewpoint so as to illuminate how 'these people' understood their world, or is it to explicate how we, looking back, understand what took place? And given our own cultural blinders and historical paradigms, how can we be sure that our viewpoint is less biased or more grounded in truth? Ratcliff then connects these questions with the malleability of historical narratives by relating 'what these people genuinely *thought* to be happening to them' to the paradigm-shift he expects his narrative to generate, connecting shifts in points of view today with shifts in points of view historically.

Yet, as skilfully as Ratcliff attempts to interweave fantastic legend and history, he is pushed to choose one category or the other by his editor, who is aghast to find 'GOLEMS???!!! In mediaeval Europe?!' 'What next?' she asks, 'zombies and the undead?!! This is fantasy!' (146–7). The editor is sent into a tizzy not by an incursion of fantasy into a scholarly history, but by the difficulties in marketing the resulting manuscript: 'I have no idea how I can explain to my editorial director, never mind sales and marketing, that the Visigoths are actually Turks and that this whole history is a farrago of lies!' (155). The text Ratcliff is trying to write partakes of both history and fantasy, but the resulting hybrid cannot be fit comfortably into existing market categories. Thus Ratcliff capitulates, writing to his editor that 'if too much emphasis on the "legendary" aspect of the texts is going to weaken the historical *evidence* . . . then let's by all means cut the golems out of the finished version!' (148). But such capitulation is of no help whatsoever when Ratcliff's historical fifteenth-century source materials are spontaneously reclassified from 'history' to 'fiction'. Library records maintain that these documents have always been classified as 'fiction', but Ratcliff knows differently and is helpless to explain what has happened. Surely this rather humorous meditation on the unreliability of historical sources is a gesture toward the delicacy of historical discourse itself, as it relies on materials that may or may not be accurate, and whose own genre may be up for dispute. Further, just at the moment when Ratcliff's entire project is thrown into question by the reclassification of his source documents, archaeologists find material evidence for the golems that had so alarmed his editor, redoubling the mystery around his textual sources: 'If these documents are so unreliable – why is the ARCHEOLOGICAL EVIDENCE backing them up?' (336). Thus we have a collision not only between genres, but between textual and physical evidence. What if, Ratcliff asks, these texts that are now called fictional are actually true? What would that do to our understanding of the relationship between history and legend? And if source materials are being spontaneously and untraceably reclassified, however will we be able to tell the difference between fantasy and history?

In Elizabeth Hand's *Mortal Love*, these questions are addressed by a journalist working on a history of the Tristan and Iseult mythos – a history of a fantasy, or so Daniel Rowlands believes. As he is drawn to a mysterious woman, Larkin Meade, he comes to realize that she is the eternal Iseult of myth, and that his research may in fact be about a truth, not a fiction. His tale is interwoven with a historical fantasy involving a nineteenth-century artist who finds himself working at a sanitarium housing a woman who we are led to believe is the same woman Rowlands falls for. Promising him studies of the Tristan and Iseult story completed by Edward Burne-Jones, Larkin leads Daniel to the Greater Outer London Folk-Lore Study Society, established in 1857. She explains to him that 'back then people believed there was a system for understanding everything – they just could never agree what the system *was*. These people thought it was folklore.'[5] Whereas Daniel is trying to use history to understand the truth about what he believes to be a myth, the folklorists of this society were trying to use myth to understand the truth about reality. And both Daniel and the Society's folklorists use similar methods. Daniel describes his project by saying 'I'm trying to trace all the versions of the story, not just the famous ones', whereas Larkin describes the Society's folklorists as 'scientific, in their own way – they had a sort of Darwinian approach, always looking for a single source for their stories' (52, 75). Both Daniel and the folklorists are trying to capture all permutations of a given story in order to understand its cultural importance.

Larkin herself is described as 'a primary source' reifying a gendered dynamic to the scholarship (men study, women are studied), and under another name she was kept in a sanitarium by Learmont, the president of the Folk-Lore Society. When Daniel allows his researcher's instincts to take over, he realizes that Larkin herself is the best possible source for the knowledge he seeks: 'His thoughts unspooled the way they did when he was researching a profile of a performer dead too soon or too late, with nothing to go on but the memory of bemused onlookers ... Secondary sources, not completely useless but unreliable, and never as good as – Of a sudden Juda Trent's words came back to him – *She is a primary source ...*' (306). Larkin's existence as a real figure changes the complexion of Daniel's research entirely; she becomes a living source, able to confound efforts at understanding and analysis just as Pierce Ratcliff's documentary sources confound his efforts at constructing a coherent historical narrative through their spontaneous recategorization. Larkin's effect on Daniel's researches is both destabilizing and inspiring, with the result that, by the end of the book, he has turned his efforts toward fiction, and is instead preparing to write a novel about the Tristan-Iseult mythos.

Both *Mortal Love* and *A Secret History* involve scholars trying to make sense of a complex and ever-changing historical record, of sources that don't stay put, of multiple points of view, of the power as well as the vulnerabilities of research. Each man struggles with the demands as well as the impossibilities of historical scholarship, and each is forced to reckon with the fantastic, that discourse which, as Jackson writes, is excluded from hegemonic narratives. The lines between history and fantasy blur in these novels, and they comment on the nature of historical fantasy itself, as they interrogate what we know of history with what we imagine.

The scholar as character

In the novels to be discussed in this section, scholars take active roles in the historical narratives themselves. Often, as in Barbara Hambly's *Those Who Hunt the Night* (1988) and Susanna Clarke's *Jonathan Strange & Mr Norrell* (2004), these novels examine the role of the scholar in a world of magic and the axis of knowledge that exists between the practical and the academic. *Jonathan Strange & Mr Norrell* and *The Alchemist's Door* (2002) by Lisa Goldstein equate scholarship with the use of magic itself, and in these two novels a pair of scholar-magicians bring about great changes in their respective histories.

Barbara Hambly's *Those Who Hunt the Night* (aka *Immortal Blood*) concerns a nineteenth-century Oxford don, a scholar who specializes in philology, etymology and comparative folklore, and a former spy, who is forced by the vampires of London to use his skills in finding out who is murdering them. While James Asher's skill at espionage is no doubt helpful in this task, we are told in no uncertain terms that he is at core a scholar. In his first encounter with a vampire, Asher is as much convinced of the truth of the vampire's story by his scholarly knowledge as by anything else: 'the tonal shift in a few of his [the vampire's] word endings was characteristic of those areas which had been linguistically isolated since the end of the sixteenth century,' Asher notices.[6] With his beloved wife unconscious and vulnerable, he castigates himself, '*Can't you stop thinking like a philologist even at a time like this . . . ?*' (9). The answer, of course, is no, and it turns out that it is Asher's scholarship and research skills that make him a formidable foe to the vampires as well as an ally.

When the fantastic intrudes on the real, previously useless knowledge becomes quite practical; *Those Who Hunt the Night* redefines the academic–practical axis of knowledge. In reviewing what he knows about vampires, Asher realizes that 'Around that central truth [the existence of vampires] . . . lay such a morass of legend at how to deal with vampires that he felt a momentary spasm of irritation at the scholars who had never troubled to codify such knowledge. He made a mental note to do so . . . ' (17). Here, Asher finds that knowledge that would normally be 'academic', in the sense of being of no immediate value, suddenly becomes quite urgently practical; when the fantastic becomes real, academic knowledge rapidly increases in practical value, and Asher finds himself at a loss in part because the academic knowledge wasn't thorough enough. Eventually, Asher sifts through his knowledge and realizes that 'silver was spoken of again and again as a guard against the Undead . . . He only hoped the folklore was right' (98). It is this 'academic' knowledge that saves Asher from becoming a feast for vampires on more than one occasion; the academic becomes practical even while the text calls knowledge that is useless or beside the point 'academic'. Towards the end of the novel, Asher loses his squeamishness about the vampires' means of living: 'Asher realized that the master vampire must have fed while he and Yisdro were waiting for him to finish with the police at Charing Cross; it had become, to him, a matter of almost academic note' (233). A page later, when he realizes what he must do to complete his quest,

'He was so tired his flesh ached, but he felt, as he often had in the midst of his work abroad or on a promising track in some research library in Vienna or Warsaw, an odd, fiery lightness that made such consideration academic' (234). Just as academic knowledge has become practical, so too have practical considerations – whether or not a vampire has recently drunk the blood of a fellow human being, whether or not one is too tired to continue – become academic. Further, the text implies that such slippage occurs whenever a scholar is in the throes of research: the feeling that fatigue is unimportant is familiar to Asher from his studies in libraries. Research itself becomes a kind of destabilizing fantasy that can reverse the relationship between academic and practical knowledge.

But Asher is not the only scholar in *Those Who Hunt the Night*. As a form of protection against the vampires, his wife Lydia uses the British Library to 'hunt through public records for evidence of where the vampires themselves might be living'; in agreeing to this plan, Asher says 'it's true I'll need a researcher who believes' (49). Lydia sets to archival work, examining deeds, wills and newspapers for evidence of unnaturally prolonged life-spans and properties that have not changed hands for generations. She also studies her medical journals (Lydia Asher is a research physician) for issues concerning vampirism. Indeed, it is these studies that allow her to arrive at the solution to the mystery well before her husband. Research and scholarship turn out to be the key to the identity of the vampire-killer, something Asher suspects early on in the novel: 'It was likelier that the killer, like himself, was a man of education, able to track by paper what he could not track in the flesh' (96–7). This indeed turns out to be the case. Human research threatens a race of superbeings. Vampires in this novel have powers over human mental states and are capable of much greater physical strength, but they are vulnerable because of a man's ability to track them through research. Scholarly skills are vitally important in this novel, for the hero, perhaps a figure for the writer of historical fantasy whose researches allow the novel to exist, and for the villain. The slippage between knowledge that is academic and knowledge that is practical suggests the slippage between that which is history and that which is fantasy in these hybrid novels.

The connection between fantasy and research is even clearer in novels in which scholars *are* magicians and magic is equated with research and scholarly knowledge. Susanna Clarke's *Jonathan Strange & Mr Norrell* posits exactly that. Taking place in an England of the Napoleonic wars that is somewhat different than the one we know (the north of the country has a proud history of being ruled by the Raven King, a long-lost magician), the novel concerns the lives of the two men who bring magic back into the world. Mr Norrell is initially portrayed as a 'practical' magician, in contrast to the scholars who have adopted that name since the loss of magic. The novel opens with the following sentence: 'Some years ago there was in the city of York a society of magicians. They met upon the third Wednesday of every month and read each other long, dull papers upon the history of English magic.'[7] These so-called magicians in fact perform no magic at all; they are purely scholars: 'They did not want to see magic done; they only wished to read about it in books.' Mr Norrell initially refers to himself as 'a tolerable practical magician', but then equates his success at practising magic with his studies: 'what is my reward for loving my art better than other men have done? – for studying harder to perfect it?' (19, 15, 20). Mr Norrell's practical skills are the direct result of more successful study. Indeed, Norrell is identified quite strongly *as* a scholar. His defeat of the York Society of Magicians is not a defeat of scholarship by practicality; it is the triumph of a superior and more obsessed scholar. Norrell is told by someone that he has 'the meditative air of a scholar', and he says of himself 'I have a scholar's love of silence and solitude' (48, 52). Indeed, Norrell's main obsession is with obtaining all books of and about magic in England; he hoards all such documents, keeping them from other would-be magicians. Despite such selfishness, Norrell insists that scholarship and research *are* magic: 'Books and papers are the basis of good scholarship and sound knowledge ... Magic is to be put in the same footing as the other disciplines' (120). Not only is magic based on research, but it is to be considered a scholarly discipline, such as classics.

But there is more than one approach to scholarship. Whereas Norrell is grasping, retiring, obsessed with order and research, his colleague Jonathan Strange adopts a far more intuitive, creative approach, saying, 'I have only the haziest notion of what I did. I dare say it is just the same with you, sir, one has a sensation like music playing at the back of one's head – one simply knows what the next note will be' (233). Strange's style of magic and his personality prove more pleasing to the London social scene; while Norrell emphasizes the importance of studying an overwhelming number of writings prior to beginning the most basic magic, Strange finds that 'the practice of magic makes the theory so much easier to understand' (280). This difference is at the root of their approaches to magic/scholarship. Strange begins with the practice and uses that practice to better understand theory, but he does not reject the notion of scholarship. Rather, he is eager to get at the hundreds of books that Norrell is selfishly keeping from him, and when he finds himself caught in a curse beyond his ability to break, he uses magic to penetrate the heart of Norrell's library in an attempt to find a solution.

Ultimately, Strange and Norrell are united. By the end of the novel, Norrell 'was forced to conclude that English magic could no longer tell the difference between himself and Strange', and both collaborate on a spell to summon the long-lost Raven King: '"It is as much your work as mine now," observed Strange. There was no trace of rivalry or resentment in his voice. "No, no," said Norrell. "All the fabric of it is yours. I have merely neatened the edges"' (745). The different approaches to scholarship/magic turn out not to be at odds at all; rather, both are required for the most powerful of spells. The novel ends with Strange and Norrell going off together to explore further reaches of magic, and as if to underline the rapprochement they have achieved, when Strange's wife asks how she should picture him when she thinks of him far away, he answers 'Picture me with my nose in a book!' (782).

Jonathan Strange & Mr Norrell uses avatars of different approaches to research as a way of considering how scholarship works and the relationship between theory and practice. As seen before in *Those Who Hunt the Night*, the presence of magic or fantasy disrupts the usual divisions between what is practical and what is theoretical/academic, but in Clarke's novel, the two positions are reconciled. The intersection between the two positions achieves a kind of equilibrium, a resolution to the rivalry, mistrust and differences that had characterized the magicians' relationship for several hundred pages, just as historical fantasy must seek balance between recognizable history and the fantastic.

Lisa Goldstein's *The Alchemist's Door* also concerns two scholar-magicians who must unite in the face of evil. Taking place in sixteenth-century Prague, it revolves around an imagined meeting between the Elizabethan astronomer-magician Doctor Dee and the Rabbi Loew, famed for protecting the Jews of Prague by creating a golem. These two kindred spirits are drawn together by a mutual need to save one of the fabled thirty-six good men who uphold the world and keep the forces of evil at bay. Despite their significant differences, it is their mutual love of scholarship that brings about their alliance: 'Dee leaned forward, his earlier uneasiness [at finding himself in the room with a Jew] forgotten. A moment later he was deep in a discussion of the transmutation of numbers and the attributes of God.'[8] Loew's discomfort with Dee is similarly leavened by the bond the two men share over scholarship: 'He's a Christian, of course, and he has all the peculiar ideas Christians have. But I think he's less hostile to us than others would be, and he's interested in learning' (114). Even when the two men are running for their lives, they stop to delve into the mysteries of the heavens: 'Dee and Loew looked at each other, shamefaced, two old scholars who would drop everything, who would even risk their lives, for a good disputation' (107). Scholarship becomes the defining feature of these two men, and is what allows them to work together for what turns out to be the common good.

As in *Jonathan Strange & Mr Norrell*, scholarship in this novel is synonymous with magic. Dee can create light; Loew can banish demons. Rabbi Loew achieves his greatest feat, the creation of a golem to protect the Jewish quarter, by finding direction in an old book. If we consider that reading and writing are evidence of scholarship – and in sixteenth-century Europe they were – then the golem itself is powered by learning, as it is brought to life and then extinguished by means of the word etched into its clay. In this novel, scholarship means drawing on ancient knowledge, and folklore is as important a source as any. In trying to determine why he is continually dogged by the number thirty-six, Loew turns to his books and finds that 'In all his studies he had come across only one meaning for the number thirty-six. And old Jewish tradition said that there were thirty-six righteous men who upheld the world' (34). The use of ancient sources confirms that the world around Dee and Loew has not changed significantly for many years.

In fact, Dee and Loew turn out to be the source of that change. In order to prevent the passage into the world of demonic forces, they must close the door between our world and all others permanently. In doing so, they make their own scholarship obsolete, for the alchemy and magic they have studied will no longer work. Such a radical break in history posits a different relationship between history and fantasy. Here is an explanation of sorts for why learned men once believed in magic and now no longer do; it is because the world once functioned in such a way as to make magic possible, and now it no longer does. The learning and scholarship to which Dee and Loew had devoted their lives is *no longer* accurate, but once it was. Such a view posits a very different understanding of history than, for example, *Mortal Love* or *Those Who Hunt the Night*. Whereas the latter novel suggests a secret fantastic component that exists throughout history, and *Mortal Love* posits that the fantastic has continued in more or less the same form throughout history (the story of Tristan and Iseult), this novel posits a history of radical breaks, a history that was *once* continuous with fantasy and is now vastly divergent. What, then, remains? At the end of the novel, Loew states 'Magic is gone from the world', and Dee replies that 'there is still learning' (276). Scholarship itself is the common thread between the fantastic world that once was and the historic world that Loew and Dee have created.

It is scholarship that draws fantasy and history together in this historical fantasy.

Conclusion

Rosemary Jackson posits that fantasy is a means of expressing 'that which lies outside the law, that which is outside dominant value systems'.[9] Historical fantasy is thus a subgenre that opens up alternative ways of understanding how history has worked, both in the sense of providing a 'secret' history (as made explicit in the title of Mary Gentle's novel) and in the sense that they call into question the distinction between history and fantasy that underlies the legitimacy of historical discourse. The books I have included in this study do so through the figure of the scholar. Not every historical fantasy involves a scholar, of course – Delia Sherman's magnificent *The Porcelain Dove* (1993) does not – but many do. Of interest to the reader may be Patricia Wrede's *Snow White and Rose Red* (1989), Marie Brennan's *Midnight Never Come* (2008) and Tim Powers's *The Anubis Gates* (1983); scholars are essential to all these novels. For reasons of space, I have chosen to discuss only a few.

These novels that do use scholars do so to address some of the questions brought up by the very existence of the subgenre. What gets to be counted as history, and how can we be sure that it is not fantasy after all? In these novels 'scholar' is often another term for 'magician', again blurring the boundaries for the modern reader between realism and history on the one hand, modes of discourse legitimized by the mainstream, and fantasy on the other. As a figure for the writer, who combines research with imagination in producing a historical fantasy, the scholar combines both sets of discourse in one person. Whether in the frame or as a character in the historical fantasy proper, the scholar allows the writer to destabilize assumptions about what counts as history, the meaning of academic knowledge, and how to negotiate such ground when it is constantly moving beneath our feet.

NOTES

1 Jana French, 'Fantastic Histories: A Dialogic Approach to a Narrative Hybrid' (unpublished dissertation, University of Wisconsin-Madison, 1996), p. 1.

2 K. L. Maund, 'History in Fantasy', in John Clute and John Grant (eds.), *The Encyclopedia of Fantasy* (London: Orbit, 1997), p. 468.

3 Rosemary Jackson, *Fantasy: The Literature of Subversion* (1981) (London: Routledge, 2003), p. 3.

4 Mary Gentle, *A Secret History: the Book of Ash, #1* (New York: Avon Books, 1999), p. 2.

5 Elizabeth Hand, *Mortal Love* (New York: HarperCollins, 2004), p. 75.
6 Barbara Hambly, *Those Who Hunt the Night* (New York: Del Rey, 1988), p. 10.
7 Susanna Clarke, *Jonathan Strange & Mr Norrell* (London: Bloomsbury, 2004), p. 3.
8 Lisa Goldstein, *The Alchemist's Door* (New York: Tor Books, 2002), p. 50.
9 Jackson, *Fantasy*, p. 4. Jackson's definition of fantasy is rather restrictive and excludes most of what the normal reader would place in that category. Nonetheless, I find her formulations on the functions of fantasy to be applicable even to those works she excludes.

21

GRAHAM SLEIGHT

Fantasies of history and religion

In his short story 'Novelty' (1983), John Crowley explores a counterfactual about religion and history. A writer who may be a self-portrait of Crowley sits in a New York bar and ponders the subject of his next work. He imagines an alternate story of Christianity, where Christ refused to take up his cross and instead lived on – making, in a sense, a fuller commitment to humanity that way. In doing so, he imagines another kind of religion from Christianity: at another point in the story, his editor mistakes this for pantheism. The writer responds:

> 'No. No. The opposite. In that kind of religion the trees and the sky and the weather stand for God or some kind of supernatural unity. In my religion, God and all the rituals and sacraments would stand for the real world. The religion would be a means of perceiving the real world in a sacramental way. A Gnostic ascension. A secret at the heart of it. And the secret is – everything. Common reality. The day outside the church window.'[1]

A religion of this kind – created from what we might call an aesthetic and moral critique of Christianity as it is – could perhaps never exist in the real world, or even in a sustained work of fiction. The work Crowley embarked on following 'Novelty', the four-book Ægypt sequence, is in part an embodiment of this idea of making the everyday sacramental, but Ægypt takes on so many other ideas that it is hard to see it as the sole motivation for the series. However, there are other works that have the same relationship to religion as that described in Crowley's story above. Let me, therefore, offer a definition: a fantasy of religion is a text that depicts or makes use of commonly understood religious tropes, but which recasts them in the context of additional fantastic narrative elements.

A clear example of this approach is the satire employed by James Morrow in his 1990 novel *Only Begotten Daughter*. Although it has a notionally science-fictional frame, being set a few years in the future and hypothesizing some near-future technologies, the overall affect of the book is clearly that of fantasy, as was recognized when it won the World Fantasy Award for its year. The book begins by following Murray Katz, a celibate lighthouse-keeper, who discovers that a sperm donation he has made has become a foetus: an immaculate conception. Overtaken by responsibility for his child-to-be, he brings home the 'ectogenesis machine' containing it, and ends up superintending the birth and childhood of the Daughter of God, Julie Katz.

The body of the book follows Julie's adulthood, as she arrives at her credo despite the best efforts of fundamentalist ministers and the Devil. At one point, rather than continue to wrestle with the stupidities of the world, she accepts the Devil's offer to take her to see Hell. There she meets her brother Jesus, who has been ministering to the damned since his own crucifixion. She discovers that almost every human has ended up in Hell, and Jesus feels that the best he can do is to dispense ladles of morphine, in a kind of soup-kitchen, to all the suffering. Julie joins him for fifteen years, all the time describing what has passed in the world since his crucifixion, especially the extraordinary intellectual structure of empiricism: as Julie says, 'That's the wonder of science. It welcomes new data. It's self-correcting.'[2] Jesus comes to share her enthusiasm for it, and Julie finally decides that she must return to the world. There, she preaches her new gospel, of reverence for the given and for science as the appropriate tool to investigate it. She is brought before a 'heresy trial' by one of the fundamentalists she has offended, is subjected to a televised crucifixion, and is offered an odd kind of resurrection fully in keeping with her belief system. The novel ends with her, now thoroughly mortal, re-entering the world for good, aged forty: 'Not too late to start a deferred but promising life' (312).

Of course, fantasies of religion need not be as overtly revisionist as Morrow's. Gene Wolfe is an author primarily known for science fiction rather than fantasy. His Catholicism is also a well-known part of his world-view; it is prominent in his most well-known work, The Book of the New Sun (4 vols, 1980–3). This occupies an unusual place between science fiction and fantasy. It is set on a far-future 'Urth', and many of the fantasy tropes that appear – wizards, magic and so on – can be understood from the text as, for instance, aliens or energy weapons. However, it cannot be denied that the experience of reading the Book has many similarities with that of fantasy. The protagonist, Severian, is an apprentice of the guild of torturers in Nessus, the pre-eminent city of one part of Urth. He is exiled from the guild for helping a prisoner to kill herself, and begins a series of picaresque adventures as he leaves the city. It becomes clear that Urth's sun is old and dying, and that many people await the arrival of a New Sun. It also becomes apparent – though more slowly and more obliquely – that Severian himself is a Christ figure sent and enabled to achieve this task. The many layers of imagery this invokes – Christ/Apollo, New Son/Sun, for instance – are left for the reader to understand. At the very least, though, Wolfe is creating a myth of a new Messiah. By casting Severian as a torturer, a member of the most despised profession in this world, he makes us rethink what a god would really think of the world, and how they would act. Severian narrates the story himself and is almost certainly lying at points; his chilly tone and implacable remove are very different from what might be expected. Notwithstanding his sins, some of which he admits, Severian is profoundly concerned with what constitutes right conduct. This is a common thread throughout Wolfe's work, including his most recent fantasy, *The Wizard Knight* (comprising *The Knight* (2004) and *The Wizard* (2004)). Although *The Wizard Knight* takes place in a fantasy secondary world governed by gods of a kind, its pantheon – based around the Norse mythos – is not radically remade. The advocacy in *The Wizard Knight* comes, more simply, from the young protagonist attempting to discover how he should behave in an unfriendly world.

Fantasies of religion often approach their subject obliquely or through misdirection. Nowhere is this more true than of G. K. Chesterton's *The Man Who Was Thursday* (1908). It begins in London with the recruitment of the poet Gabriel Syme by Scotland Yard to infiltrate a worldwide council of anarchists. When he does so, however, he discovers that each of the other members is also a spy with a similar mission. Each is codenamed for a day of the week – Syme is Thursday – and each takes their orders from the mysterious Sunday. The novel's action becomes increasingly surreal, as the six try to track down Sunday. Sunday himself is a figure increasingly mysterious the closer he is approached; his pronouncements imply that he is of more than earthly power. The book as a whole is shockingly brief, and astonishingly varied and funny. It can certainly be read as an allegory of the Christian work of the difficulty of understanding God; but it is a very unorthodox kind of allegory.

Both The Book of the New Sun and *The Man Who Was Thursday* were written by Catholics and may be read as providing paths (albeit unconventional ones) to a religious understanding. John Crowley's Ægypt quartet, as mentioned above, is neither as directly scathing as Morrow (though it also features savagely depicted Christian fundamentalists) nor as orthodox as Wolfe or Chesterton. It comprises *Ægypt* (1987; revised as *The Solitudes*, 2007), *Love & Sleep* (1994), *Dæmonomania* (2000) and *Endless Things* (2007). It tells several stories, each nested within the other, but the most recent – the one from which the others seems to subtend – is that of Pierce Moffet. His academic career in New York having failed, he goes like Smoky

Barnable in Crowley's *Little, Big* (1981) to an upstate rural retreat. There, in the village of Blackbury Jambs, he encounters again the work of the hsistorical novelist Fellowes Kraft, whose books he read as a child. Kraft lived near the town, and Pierce is asked by his descendants to see if he can complete the novel Kraft left unfinished at his death, a novel that bears a striking resemblance both to a book Pierce had conceived of writing and to the Ægypt that we have in our hands.

The historical sections of Ægypt, as seemingly taken from Kraft's manuscript, follow the lives of Renaissance thinkers such as John Dee and Giordano Bruno. Dee, Queen Elizabeth's court astrologer, is depicted as succeeding in his alchemical quest to transform base metals into gold. Meanwhile, Bruno formulates for the first time the idea that the universe is infinite, and that the stars are other worlds. For his pains, he is captured by the Catholic Church and burned in 1600. At the same time, in the present-day story, Pierce's lover Rose falls under the influence of a Christian cult called the Powerhouse, which also kidnaps a child. The analogue between the Powerhouse's corrosive certainties and those of the Renaissance Church is plain, but not overstated. The plot of Ægypt matters less than the density with which it's embedded with meditations of all kinds – some from fictional texts, some real – about history, religion, and how we make sense of things. The sequence in the end seems to be organized round the idea that at one time (say, when Bruno and Dee were alive) the universe operated by different laws to those it has now, and so their 'magic' really was possible. At some points, it suggests, the world shudders and passes through a 'passage-time' from one set of laws to the next. Pierce's present-day story seems to be taking place in just such a passage-time, flagged in particular by a great storm at the end of the second volume. The question of whether Crowley 'believes' in the story's premise is tempting, but unanswerable from the text and beside the point. What matters about Ægypt is the extent to which we as readers feel the poignancy and share the doubts of the characters as they impose their systems of belief – their stories – on the world. The final volume of the sequence embodies a Prospero-like renunciation of a magical way of thinking that had become increasingly prison-like for Bruno, Dee, and Pierce. The final turn of this fantasy is to give up fantasy and show us the world instead.

All the fantasies of religion I have described so far take Christianity as a starting-point, but the label can equally be applied to works which revise and critique other religions, including pantheistic ones. Prominent examples of the latter approach are Neil Gaiman's linked novels *American Gods* (2001) and *Anansi Boys* (2005). *American Gods* sets out to answer a relatively simple question: if the USA is made up of immigrant populations of all kinds, each bringing with them their own religious stories about the world, what happens when all those stories interbreed? The book begins by following a recently released convict named Shadow, who is recruited by a mysterious man named Wednesday to work for him. (Given Gaiman's deep immersion in the literature of the fantastic, one suspects that the allusion to Chesterton is deliberate.) Wednesday, it transpires, is the Norse God Odin, and he represents a group of similar deities, including Egyptian and Indian ones. They find themselves in opposition to more American gods, such as the deracination of culture and experience by consumerism. Though nothing is as it initially seems – no god is entirely to be trusted – *American Gods* does in the end bring home a sense of the costs of the New World.

Anansi Boys is different from *American Gods* in tone and, although it shares some of the same assumptions, cannot be considered a direct sequel. A Londoner, 'Fat Charlie' Nancy, is summoned to Florida for the funeral of the father whom he had always regarded with a kind of distant but embarrassed awe. His father, it transpires, was an incarnation of the African spider deity Anansi, but his powers were passed down to a brother whom Charlie had been unaware of, 'Spider'. The action of the book, much of it comic, follows the negotiation between Charlie and Spider for their father's legacy, but also embodies the tension between tricksterish fantasy and the mundane world from which Charlie originates. It also, far more explicitly than *American Gods*, engages with issues of race. Both books, though, have in common a sense that gods are stories we tell ourselves to make sense of things, and that they exist to the extent that we can vest belief in the stories.

Stories, though, are sometimes treasures to be concealed or uncovered. In the context of fantasies of religion, this often means that a deity's existence or power is guarded by a secret society of some kind. The American fantasist Elizabeth Hand has written several books featuring one such society, the Benandanti, of which the most well known is probably *Waking the Moon* (1994). The book concerns a return to the contemporary world of the Moon Goddess, whose existence has long been effaced from history by the patriarchal monotheisms. The Benandanti are described in the novel as a kind of puppet-master secret society, protecting the mundane world – and, indeed, shaping it – by holding back the moment of this return. Since the Moon Goddess demands worship in particularly bloody ways, both sides in this conflict have some degree of moral ambiguity to their actions. But the Benandanti do have their roots in real events – specifically, as a kind of anti-witchcraft force in Italy in the sixteenth and seventeenth centuries, as chronicled in Carlo Ginzburg's *The Night Battles* (1983). So Hand is able to use the given – the weight of the Benandanti's history – to amplify and enrich the debate at her story's heart.

It is worth saying, also, that there are a number of works of science fiction – far purer science fiction than Wolfe's Book of the New Sun – which partake of some of the characteristics of fantasies of religion that I have described. For instance, Dan Simmons's Hyperion/Endymion sequence, comprising *Hyperion* (1989), *The Fall of Hyperion* (1990), *Endymion* (1996) and *The Rise of Endymion* (1997), is explicitly about humanity overthrowing the old gods it has raised up, like the Keats poems it draws from. That these gods are ultimately rationalized in technological terms does not diminish the extent of Simmons's allusions to religion. The last two books in particular feature a Catholic Church whose excesses – including eventually crucifying the Messiah – are very close to those shown in *Only Begotten Daughter*. A later Simmons sequence, comprising *Ilium* (2003) and *Olympos* (2005), goes over some of the same ground, with the gods in this case being superhuman creatures drawn from Greek mythology and inhabiting Mons Olympus on a future Mars. Similarly, the sequence begun by David Zindell in *Neverness* (1988) sees its protagonist becoming a kind of god, though again one explicable in scientific (here, mathematical) terms. Perhaps one might say that the further science fiction approaches the far future, the closer it comes to the condition of fantasy.

Finally, it is worth considering a work in this vein not set in our own world, Terry Pratchett's *Small Gods* (1992). It is part of his well-known Discworld sequence though, unlike others, not part of any of the multibook arcs (the Watch books, the Witch books, and so on) for which it has become most famous. Its premise is that deities in the Discworld exist (like Tinkerbell) to the extent that people believe in them. The deity Om, now almost forgotten, is disappointed when he tries to manifest himself in the world: there is only enough belief to make him incarnate as a tortoise. He speaks to Brutha, a young but dim initiate in the church of Om, and the last remaining true believer in him: Pratchett's argument is that there is a distinction between a belief in the church (which is vastly bloated and punitively controlling) and a belief in its deities. Brutha is a holy innocent, like Severian in The Book of the New Sun, blessed with eidetic recall. Like Severian he too goes on a vast journey to and from a war-zone. Brutha and Om are accompanied in this by the church's Deacon Vorbis, a baleful figure whose suffocating certainties are clearly modelled on those of figures in the real world.

The body of *Small Gods* (as with many of the other books considered above) comprises Brutha's slow earning of wisdom – with which, at the end of the work, he becomes a just ruler of the kind his country has lacked for many years. Vorbis's totalitarian church believes that the world is round, whereas observable reality shows that it is flat, and carried on the back of a giant tortoise. Brutha, like Galileo, is condemned as a heretic for his assertion of the demonstrable truth and, at the climax of the novel, is to be burned alive for it by Vorbis. However, a passing eagle drops the Om-tortoise onto Vorbis, killing him – an almost literal *deus ex machina* moment. The most striking image from the book, though, is that of the small gods themselves, encountered by Brutha during his wanderings. These are the deities left entirely without believers but who may be associated with a specific place such as a crossroads. Hence, Pratchett imagines a Discworld in which gods are as plentiful as microbes are in our own world, and in which (as, once again, for the narrator on 'Novelty') everything is holy.

It will be apparent from the discussion above that any fantasy of religion based in our own world will also have a relationship to history in general terms. And so, there can also be works of fantasy that engage with history without a particular religious emphasis. A further definition suggests itself: a fantasy of history is a text that depicts or makes use of known historical facts, but which adds to them additional fantastic narrative elements. These fantastic elements may or may not contradict what is already known – it may, in other words, be possible to 'believe' that the fantasy of history could be true alongside our own. To be clear: fantasy of religion and fantasy of history are not mutually exclusive terms, and indeed there can be much overlap – as, for instance, with the Ægypt sequence. A fantasy of history is also distinct from the historically rooted fantasies of, say, Guy Gavriel Kay, who uses the real history of, say, Moorish Spain as the basis for a full secondary world.

As an example of books straddling the border between fantasies of history and religion, consider the work of Tim Powers, an American fantasy writer who first found prominence with *The Anubis Gates* (1983). The main thread of the book follows a semi-successful academic named Brendan Doyle. He is hired by an eccentric millionaire, J. Cochran Darrow, to give a lecture on Coleridge to a select group of a dozen or so interested people. Darrow reveals to Doyle that he has in fact discovered a means of time travel, and after Doyle's lecture he intends to take Doyle and the others – all paying customers – back from the 1980s to hear Coleridge give a lecture on Milton in 1810. The facts of Coleridge's life are all in accord with what is known, as is the period detail Doyle finds when he reaches the nineteenth century. However, Doyle is soon stranded in the nineteenth century, and as his adventures progress he discovers more about the seeming use of magic in this world. (The magic, among other things, rendered possible Darrow's time travel; this is not a book with a rigorous science-fictional underpinning.) He is also drawn closer to the life of William Ashbless, a minor contemporary of Coleridge's, on whose life Doyle had been hoping to do research. Indeed, after some body-switching loops of plot, Doyle finds himself inhabiting the body of William Ashbless. He realizes that he must live through the life whose biography he has memorized; he must write out the poems he knows by heart; he must, it seems, face the death Ashbless has ordained by history in 1846. Ashbless, of course, is a fictional construct. The Ashbless poems used in the text are by Powers, although he also manages to infer back from some Coleridge poems such as 'Limbo' and 'Ne Plus Ultra' his involvement with the supernatural forces at the climax the book. So *The Anubis Gates* gives an indication of how complex can be the interaction between a fantasy of history and its ground-bass of the known. Further examples can be found elsewhere in Powers's work; of particular note is *Declare* (2001), in which the real-life betrayal of the British intelligence services by Kim Philby serves as a starting point for an elaborate secret history in which the intelligence services have been wrestling with supernatural forces impinging on our world. The metaphors of a secret life clothed in clandestine falsehoods echo back and forth.

This is one obvious way of understanding the work of Thomas Pynchon, like both Hand and Powers an author persistently concerned with secret histories. His novels to date – *V.* (1963), *The Crying of Lot 49* (1966), *Gravity's Rainbow* (1973), *Vineland* (1990), *Mason & Dixon* (1997) and *Against the Day* (2006) – all take as their subject a particular historical and cultural moment, but riff on it in surreal and often fantastic ways. Of these books, *Gravity's Rainbow* is probably the most intense, its furious pointillism covering the end and aftermath of the Second World War in London and the rest of Europe. *Against the Day*, though, is surely the most encompassing and the most overtly fantastic. It begins at the Chicago World's Fair of 1893 and, over more than a thousand pages, reaches beyond the close of the First World War. Its story is told in various modes, often clearly non-mimetic, such as the thread concerning the Chums of Chance, teenage boys who fight crime from their zeppelin *Inconvenience*. This initially comic take on what John Clute has called the 'Pax Aeronautica' stories that proliferated at the time becomes darker as the book progresses. This is partly because of increasing uncertainty among the Chums about who is directing their missions and to what ends; and partly because their story looks more and more difficult to maintain as the world changes. The same can be said of all the other modes making up *Against the Day* – including the Western, the spy story, the detective story, the Lovecraftian horror tale, and so on. These stories are all piled up like a vast dam, trying to hold back the horror they all try to deny or propose alternatives to – the horror of the twentieth century as we have known it. Story and history argue against each other, with story advocating worlds we have failed to see.

So one pleasure of the fantasy of history – though a pleasure that can only be experienced within such a story – is the pleasure of the impossible counterfactual. An obvious name here is Howard Waldrop, a writer who has emerged from science fiction and whose output is almost exclusively short stories and novellas. (The best of these are collected in *Things Will Never Be the Same: Selected Short Fiction 1980–2005* (2007) and *Other Worlds, Better Lives: Selected Long Fiction 1989–2003* (2008); all the examples below are collected in these two volumes.) Waldrop's most honoured story to date is 'The Ugly Chickens' (1980), positing a means by which the dodo survived until the recent past in the American South. The intricate tracery of history leading to this is fascinating, but subordinated to melancholy for this outcome that never was. 'Fin de Cyclé' (1991) is set in an alternate-world France at the end of the nineteenth century, where a group of unlikely artists and malcontents – including Jarry, Méliès and a very young Picasso – collaborate on an unusual defence in the Dreyfus Case. 'Heart of Whitenesse' (1997) conflates three Marlowes: the Elizabethan playwright Christopher Marlowe takes on the role of Raymond Chandler's detective Philip Marlowe in a plot resembling that undergone by Joseph Conrad's Marlow in *Heart of Darkness* (1899). Reading Waldrop, one remembers a remark by the science fiction writer Theodore Sturgeon: that fiction is fact the way it ought to be. As Sturgeon admits, though, the slippery word there is 'ought'.[3]

The 'ought', in a sense, denotes whatever an individual writer brings to shape their material. In the case of the fantasy of religion, it may be an urge to critique or revise existing dogmas about larger epistemological questions. In the case of the fantasy of history, it may be that the writer feels certain ideas about our past and culture can only be made apparent by going beyond the facts and physics of the world we know. In general, fantasy is more story-shaped (and story-saturated) than mimesis, and the given world is its soil.

NOTES

1 John Crowley, 'Novelty' (1983), in Crowley, *Novelties and Souvenirs: Collected Short Fiction* (New York: Perennial, 2004), p. 46.
2 James Morrow, *Only Begotten Daughter* (New York: William Morrow, 1990), p. 187.
3 Theodore Sturgeon, *The Golden Helix* (Garden City, NJ: Doubleday, 1979), p. 331.

FURTHER READING

REFERENCE

Ashley, Mike, and Contento, William G. (eds.). *The Supernatural Index: A Listing of Fantasy, Supernatural, Occult, Weird, and Horror Anthologies* (Westport, CT: Greenwood, 1995).

Barron, Neil (ed.). *Fantasy and Horror: A Critical and Historical Guide to Literature, Illustration, Film, TV, Radio, and the Internet* (Lanham, MD: Scarecrow Press, 1999).

Bleiler, Edward F. *The Guide to Supernatural Fiction* (Kent, OH: Kent State University Press, 1983).

(ed.). *Supernatural Fiction Writers: Fantasy and Horror*, 2 vols. (New York: Scribner, 1985).

Burgess, Michael. *Reference Guide to Science Fiction, Fantasy, and Horror* (Englewood, CO: Libraries Unlimited, 1992).

Cawthorn, James, and Moorcock, Michael. *Fantasy: The 100 Best Books* (London: Xanadu, 1988).

Clute, John, and Grant, John (eds.). *The Encyclopedia of Fantasy* (London: Orbit, 1997).

Currey, L. W. *Science Fiction and Fantasy Authors: A Bibliography of First Printings of their Fiction and Selected Nonfiction* (New York: G. K. Hall, 1979).

Hall, Hal W. *Science Fiction and Fantasy Reference Index, 1878–1985: An International Author and Subject Index to History and Criticism*, 2 vols. (Detroit: Gale Research, 1987).

Magill, Frank N. (ed.). *Survey of Modern Fantasy Literature*, 5 vols. (Englewood Cliffs, NJ: Salem, 1983).

Pringle, David (ed.). *Fantasy: The Definitive Illustrated Guide* (London: Carlton, 2003).

(ed.). *Modern Fantasy: The Hundred Best Novels. An English-language Selection, 1946–1987* (London: Grafton, 1988).

(ed.). *The St James Guide to Fantasy Writers* (New York: St James Press, 1996).

(ed.). *The St James Guide to Horror, Ghost and Gothic Writers* (Detroit and London: St James Press, 1998).

Stableford, Brian. *Historical Dictionary of Fantasy Literature* (Lanham, MD: Scarecrow Press, 2005).

Tymn, Marshall B., and Ashley, Mike (eds.). *Science Fiction, Fantasy, and Weird Magazines* (Westport, CT: Greenwood, 1985).

Tymn, Marshall B., Zahorski, Kenneth J., and Boyer, Robert H. (eds.). *Fantasy Literature: A Core Collection and Reference Guide* (New York and London: Bowker, 1979).

Wolfe, Gary K. *Critical Terms for Science Fiction and Fantasy: A Glossary and Guide to Scholarship* (New York: Greenwood, 1986).

CRITICAL

Armitt, Lucie. *Fantasy Fiction: An Introduction* (London: Continuum, 2005).

Attebery, Brian. *The Fantasy Tradition in American Literature: From Irving to Le Guin* (Bloomington, IN: Indiana University Press, 1980).

  Strategies of Fantasy (Bloomington and Indianapolis, IN: Indiana University Press, 1992).

Baldick, Chris. *In Frankenstein's Shadow: Myth, Monstrosity and Nineteenth-Century Writing* (Oxford: Clarendon Press, 1987).

Barthes, Roland. *Mythologies: Selected and Translated from the French by Annette Lavers* (New York: Noonday Press, 1972).

Bettelheim, Bruno. *The Uses of Enchantment: The Meaning and Importance of Fairy Tales* (New York: Knopf/Random House, 1976).

Bloom, Harold. *How to Read and Why* (New York: Scribner, 2000).

Booth, Wayne C. *The Rhetoric of Fiction* (University of Chicago Press, 1983).

Botting, Fred. *Gothic* (London: Routledge, 1996).

Bould, Mark. 'The Dreadful Credibility of Absurd Things: A Tendency in Fantasy Theory', *Historical Materialism* 10.4 (2002), pp. 51–88.

Bowers, Maggie Ann. *Magic(al) Realism* (London: Routledge, 2004).

Bradford, Clare. *Reading Race: Aboriginality in Australian Children's Literature* (Carlton: Melbourne University Press, 2001).

Brooke-Rose, Christine. *A Rhetoric of the Unreal: Studies in Narrative and Structure, Especially of the Fantastic* (Cambridge University Press, 1981).

Butler, Charles. *Four British Fantasists: The Children's Fantasy Fiction of Penelope Lively, Alan Garner, Diana Wynne Jones, and Susan Cooper* (Lanham, MD; Toronto; Oxford: Children's Literature Association and Scarecrow Press, 2006).

Butler, Robert Olen. *From Where You Dream: The Process of Writing Fiction* (New York: Grove Press, 2005).

Campbell, Joseph. *The Hero With a Thousand Faces* (New York: Pantheon Books, 1949).

Cawelti, John. *Adventure, Mystery, and Romance: Formula Stories as Art and Popular Culture* (Chicago and London: University of Chicago Press, 1976).

Clute, John. *Look at the Evidence: Essays and Reviews* (Liverpool University Press, 1995).

  Scores: Reviews 1993–2003 (Harold Wood, Essex: Beccon Publications, 2003).

  Strokes: Essays and Reviews, 1966–1986 (Seattle: Serconia Press, 1988).

Creed, Barbara. *The Monstrous-Feminine: Film, Feminism, Psychoanalysis* (London: Routledge, 1993).

Crouch, Marcus. *The Nesbit Tradition: The Children's Novel in England, 1945–1970* (Tonbridge: Ernest Benn, 1972).

De Camp, L. Sprague. *Literary Swordsmen and Sorcerers: The Makers of Heroic Fantasy* (Sauk City, WI: Arkham House, 1976).

Delany, Samuel R. *About Writing: Seven Essays, Four Letters and Five Interviews* (Middletown, CT: Wesleyan University Press, 2005).

   Silent Interviews: On Language, Race, Sex, Science Fiction, and Some Comics (Hanover, CT: Wesleyan University Press, 1994).

Eco, Umberto. *Travels in HyperReality: Essays*, trans. William Weaver (San Diego: Harcourt Brace Jovanovich, 1986).

Faris, Wendy B. *Ordinary Enchantments: Magical Realism and the Remystification of Narrative* (Nashville: Vanderbilt University Press, 2004).

Fendler, Susanne, and Horstmann, Ulrike (eds.). *Images of Masculinity in Fantasy Fiction* (Lewiston, NY, and Lampeter: Edwin Mellen Press, 2003).

Filmer, Kath. *Scepticism and Hope in Twentieth Century Fantasy Literature* (Bowling Green, OH: Bowling Green State University Popular Press, 1992).

Fish, Stanley. *Is There a Text in This Class? The Authority of Interpretive Communities* (Cambridge, MA: Harvard University Press, 1980).

Forster, E. M. *Aspects of the Novel* (London: Arnold, 1927).

Frazer, Sir James George. *The Golden Bough: A Study in Comparative Religion* (London: Macmillan, 1890).

Frye, Northrop. *Anatomy of Criticism: Four Essays* (Princeton University Press, 1957).

   The Secular Scripture: A Study of the Structure of Romance (Cambridge MA: Harvard University Press, 1976).

Furst, Lilian R. *Romanticism in Perspective* (New York: Barnes and Noble, 1969).

Genette, Gérard. *Narrative Discourse: An Essay in Method*, trans. Jane E. Lewin (Ithaca, NY: Cornell University Press, 1980).

Hume, Kathryn. *Fantasy and Mimesis: Responses to Reality in Western Literature* (New York and London: Methuen, 1984).

Irwin, I. R. *The Game of the Impossible: A Rhetoric of Fantasy* (Urbana, IL: University of Illinois Press, 1976).

Jackson, Rosemary. *Fantasy: The Literature of Subversion* (London: Methuen, 1981).

James, Edward and Mendlesohn, Farah (eds.). *The Cambridge Companion to Science Fiction* (Cambridge University Press, 2003).

Jameson, Fredric. 'Postmodernism and Consumer Society', in Hal Foster (ed.), *Postmodern Culture* (London: Pluto, 1983), pp. 111–25.

   'Postmodernism, or the Cultural Logic of Late Capitalism', *New Left Review*, 1.146 (1984), pp. 53–92.

Jones, Diana Wynne. *The Tough Guide to Fantasyland* (London: Vista, 1996).

Joshi, S. T. *The Weird Tale: Arthur Machen, Algernon Blackwood, M. R. James, Ambrose Bierce, H. P. Lovecraft* (Austin, TX: University of Texas Press, 1990).

Kent, David A., and Ewen, D. R. *Romantic Parodies, 1797–1831* (Rutherford, NJ: Fairleigh Dickinson University Press, 1992).

Kristeva, Julia. *Powers of Horror: An Essay on Abjection*, trans. L. S. Roudiez (New York: Columbia University Press, 1982).

Kuznets, Lois R. *When Toys Come Alive: Narratives of Animation, Metamorphosis and Development* (New Haven, CT: Yale University Press, 1994).

Le Guin, Ursula K. *Dancing at the Edge of the World: Thoughts on Words, Women, Places* (New York: Grove Press, 1989).

  The Language of the Night: Essays on Fantasy and Science Fiction, ed. Susan Wood (New York: Putnam, 1979).

Leonard, E. *Into Darkness Peering: Race and Color in the Fantastic* (Westport, CT: Greenwood Press, 1997).

Lewis, C. S. *Of This and Other Worlds* (London: Collins, 1982).

Lovecraft, H. P. *Supernatural Horror in Fiction* (1927), ed. E. F. Bleiler (New York: Dover, 1973).

Makdisi, Saree, and Nussbaum, Felicity (eds.). *The Arabian Nights in Historical Context: Between East and West* (Oxford University Press, 2008).

Manlove, Colin. *Christian Fantasy: From 1200 to the Present* (Basingstoke: Macmillan, 1992).

  The Fantasy Literature of England (Basingstoke: Macmillan, 1999).

  The Impulse of Fantasy Literature (Basingstoke: Macmillan, 1983).

  Modern Fantasy: Five Studies (Cambridge University Press, 1975).

McCloud, Scott. *Understanding Comics: Invisible Art* (New York: HarperCollins, 1994).

McHale, Brian. *Postmodernist Fiction* (New York: Methuen, 1987).

Mehan, Uppinder, and Nalo Hopkinson (eds.). *So Long Been Dreaming: Postcolonial Science Fiction and Fantasy* (Vancouver: Arsenal Pulp, 2004).

Mendlesohn, Farah. *Diana Wynne Jones: Children's Literature and the Fantastic Tradition* (New York: Routledge, 2005).

  Rhetorics of Fantasy (Westport, CT: Wesleyan University Press, 2008).

Mendlesohn, Farah, and James, Edward. *A Short History of Fantasy* (London: Middlesex University Press, 2009).

Monleón, José B. *A Specter Is Haunting Europe: A Sociohistorical Approach to the Fantastic* (Princeton University Press, 1990).

Moorcock, Michael. *Wizardry and Wild Romance: A Study of Epic Fantasy* (London: Gollancz, 1987).

Nikolajeva, Maria. *The Magic Code: The Use of Magical Patterns in Fantasy for Children* (Stockholm: Almqvist and Wiksell International, 1988).

Olsen, Lance. *Ellipse of Uncertainty: An Introduction to Postmodern Fantasy* (Westport, CT: Greenwood, 1987).

Prickett, Stephen. *Victorian Fantasy* (Bloomington, IN: Indiana University Press, 1979).

Propp, Vladimir. *Morphology of the Folktale*, trans. Laurence Scott. 2nd edn (Austin, TX, and London: University of Texas Press, 1968).

Punter, David. *The Literature of Terror: A History of Gothic Fictions from 1765 to the Present Day* (New York: Longman, 1980).

Rabkin, Eric S. *The Fantastic in Literature* (Princeton University Press, 1976).

Rank, Otto. *The Myth of the Birth of the Hero: A Psychological Interpretation of Mythology* (New York: Journal of Nervous and Mental Disease Publishing Company, 1914).

Sale, Roger. *Fairy Tales and After: From Snow White to E. B. White* (Cambridge, MA: Harvard University Press, 1978).

Sandner, David. *Fantastic Literature: A Critical Reader* (London: Praeger, 2004).

Schlobin, Roger C. *The Aesthetics of Fantasy Literature and Art* (Notre Dame, IN: University of Notre Dame Press, 1982).

Scholes, Robert. *Structural Fabulation: An Essay on Fiction of the Future* (Notre Dame, IN: University of Notre Dame, 1975).

 Structuralism in Literature: An Introduction (New Haven and London: Yale University Press, 1974).

Senior, W. A. *Stephen R. Donaldson's Chronicles of Thomas Covenant: Variations on the Fantasy Tradition* (Kent, OH: Kent State University Press, 1995).

Shippey, Tom. *J. R. R. Tolkien: Author of the Century* (Boston: Houghton Mifflin, 2000).

 Roots and Branches. Selected Essays on Tolkien (Zollikofen, Switzerland: Walking Tree, 2007).

Thompson, Kristin. *The Frodo Franchise: The Lord of the Rings and Modern Hollywood* (Berkeley, CA: University of California Press, 2007).

Todorov, Tzvetan. *The Fantastic: A Structural Approach to a Literary Genre* (Cleveland and London: The Press of Case Western Reserve University, 1973).

Tolkien, J. R. R. '*Beowulf*: The Monsters and the Critics', *Proceedings of the British Academy* (1936), pp. 245–95; reprinted in Daniel Donoghue (ed.), *Beowulf: A Verse Translation*, Norton Critical Editions (New York: Norton, 2002), pp. 103–30.

 'On Fairy-Stories', in *Tree and Leaf* (London: Allen and Unwin, 1965), in Verlyn Flieger and Douglas A. Anderson (eds.), *Tolkien: On Fairy Stories* (London: HarperCollins, 2008). pp. 3–84.

Veldman, Meredith. *Fantasy, the Bomb and the Greening of Britain: Romantic Protest, 1945–1980* (Cambridge University Press, 1994).

Wall, Barbara. *The Narrator's Voice: The Dilemma of Children's Fiction* (Basingstoke: Macmillan, 1991).

Ward, Michael. *Planet Narnia: The Seven Heavens in the Imagination of C. S. Lewis* (New York: Oxford University Press, 2008).

Watson, Victor. *Reading Series Fiction: From Arthur Ransome to Gene Kemp* (London: Routledge, 2000).

Watt, James. *Contesting the Gothic: Fiction, Genre, and Cultural Conflict, 1764–1832* (Cambridge University Press, 1999).

Whited, Lana R. *The Ivory Tower and Harry Potter: Perspectives on a Literary Phenomenon* (Columbia: Missouri University Press, 2002).

Wolfe, Gary K. 'Contemporary Theories of the Fantastic', in Frank N. Magill (ed.), *Survey of Modern Fantasy Literature* (Englewood Cliffs, NJ: Salem Press, 1983), pp. 2220–34.

Zamora, Lois Parkinson, and Faris, Wendy B. (eds.). *Magical Realism: Theory, History, Community* (Durham, NC: Duke University Press, 1995).

Zipes, Jack. *When Dreams Came True. Classical Fairy Tales and Their Tradition* (New York and London: Routledge, 1999).

Cambridge Companions to . . .

AUTHORS

TOPICS

Printed in Poland
by Amazon Fulfillment
Poland Sp. z o.o., Wrocław